Taming *the* Wolf

Taming *the* Wolf

Peace through Faith

Greg Stone

Greg Stone is Founder and Managing Director of Taming the Wolf Institute, a non-profit dedicated to peacemaking.

TAMING THE WOLF: *Peace through Faith*

Taming the Wolf Institute
Westlake Village, CA

Scripture quotations taken from the *New American Bible Revised Edition*, © 2008, 1991, 1986, 1970 by Confraternity of Christian Doctrine.

Taming the Wolf Institute website: www.tamingthewolf.com

ISBN: 978-0-9848853-0-5

Cover art and design by Tracy Stone.

Printed in the United States of America.

TO
Saint Francis of Assisi,
who devoted his life to bringing Christ's peace to all people.
His prayers quiet our fears and call on us to treat one another as brothers and sisters.
The legacy of his love of all creation inspires us to wake each morning as he did and declare,
"Good morning good people."

Contents

EXPANDED CONTENTS

Illustrations

Figures

Tables

Taming *the* Wolf

St. Francis & the Wolf of Gubbio

THERE WAS IN ITALY the town of Gubbio, a prosperous village that had a great problem. A wolf was eating their livestock, and attacking the people. Nothing the townspeople did protected them from the wolf.

Never had they seen such a fierce predator. He killed a shepherd, then the shepherd's brother and father when they went out to deal with this menace. The next morning the town was abuzz with the story told by the shepherd's mother and sisters.

The mayor of Gubbio announced he would send three of his best guards to find and slay the wolf that very afternoon. At dusk the townspeople could hear shouts and clashing of metal from the woods. Then it was quiet. The guards had met the wolf.

Late in the night the only survivor of the encounter struggled into the anxious town and collapsed. After he was revived, he told his tale of their fight with the fierce and powerful wolf.

As the story rushed through town the wolf grew larger and more ferocious. Fear was in the eyes of everyone in Gubbio. Children were kept close by; weapons were at the ready and the defenses of the town were raised.

The mayor consulted with his advisors and decided to inquire if Francis of Assisi would help them. They had heard that he could talk to animals and that God talked to him.

Several brave messengers were sent to find Francis and ask for his help. They had the good fortune to find Francis in Assisi at the house of Bernardo di Quintavalle, his first follower.

They told him of the tragic attacks and explained how the frightened people were almost in a state of siege. They thought Francis was the only one who would be able to help them. They begged the simple Holy man to help and implored him to come with them right away.

Francis was moved by their plight and wanted to do what he could. He promised they would leave in the morning, but that night they should eat and rest with his Brothers. After dinner they prayed with Francis for a solution and slept with hope in their hearts.

Dawn found them walking down the hill from Assisi on their way to Gubbio. In time they arrived at the woods near the town. The messengers pointed to where the wolf had slain two guards not far from the road. They stayed in a tighter group as they hurried the rest of the way, watching for the wolf.

The gate to the town was opened as they arrived and was quickly closed behind them. The entire town followed Francis to the town square where the Mayor eagerly greeted them. They went into the town hall to eat and discuss what Francis would do with the wolf.

The mayor wondered what, if anything, Francis could do with such a challenge. The mayor hated that wolf. He knew the men who were killed and their families. One of the guards was his wife's cousin. If he were younger, he would have led the guards after the wolf.

Unable to contain his emotions, he said he wanted Francis to strike the wolf dead or send him to the town of Spoleto, their old enemy. Either would satisfy a need for revenge and stop the attacks.

Francis listened quietly as the mayor described what had happened to their peaceful town. He had much empathy for the families of the victims and wanted to meet the wolf and hear his story, too.

Francis announced that the next morning he would go the woods where the guards had been killed to see if he could find the wolf. That night he prayed for the wisdom to find a solution that would benefit everyone.

Early the next morning, refreshed and confident, Francis was accompanied by the townspeople to the gates of Gubbio. They wished him well and retreated to their homes, worried that Francis would share the fate of the shepherds and guards.

He walked on to the woods, ready to engage the wolf. As he neared the first stand of trees, the wolf appeared and began to stalk Francis. His slow, deliberate steps, the walk of a predator, announced his intention. He drew nearer and nearer, closing in a circle around the holy man from Assisi.

Seeing the wolf, Francis felt a connection. He made the sign of the cross and called the wolf to meet him in peace under the grace of the Lord. The wolf watched as Francis came closer. "Come Brother Wolf, I will not hurt you. Let us talk in peace." The wolf froze in mid step, struggling with doubt and uncertainty.

Finally, understanding that Francis meant him no harm, the wolf inched closer to Francis and then sat back on his haunches, ready to listen.

Francis told the wolf that he had come from Gubbio and described what the townspeople were experiencing because of the wolf's actions. He described the pain and resentment they felt.

"How did this come to happen?" Francis asked the wolf. "Why did you kill the livestock and people?"

The wolf told his story. He had been left behind by his pack because he was injured and couldn't keep up. He could only catch prey that didn't run fast, like sheep and goats. He preferred to eat deer and rabbits, but, with his injured leg, that was out of the question. He explained to Francis that all he wanted was to eat when he was hungry.

Francis implored him to further explain his actions. The wolf continued. The first shepherd he had killed was trying to protect his flock and the wolf had no choice but to fight back and kill him. That afternoon two more men came after him and instinct took over. He quickly killed them, leaving their bodies where they fell. The next day the three guards came hunting him. He was only defending himself when he fought them. Two were slain. As the third man was no longer a threat, he let him go.

Francis could see that the wolf was only acting to fill his needs. He had made unfortunate choices that affected people of whom he knew nothing. Through Francis the wolf was able to feel the pain of the people in Gubbio and he felt remorse. He was sorry for the pain he had caused, but he needed to eat. What could he do?

Hours passed as Francis prayed. The wolf watched closely, not fully understanding, but sensing that Francis believed he felt remorse at having caused such pain.

When Francis emerged from his contemplation, he quietly suggested an answer to the dilemma. It was a suggestion that could meet the needs of both the town and the wolf. He proposed to the wolf that the townspeople could feed him and, in return, the wolf would stop killing the people and their livestock.

The wolf thought this would work well for him, but worried the people would still want to kill him. Francis understood the wolf's concern and assured him he would present the idea to the townspeople in such a way that he would be forgiven and welcomed into the town. He knew they could let go of their fear and hate if they saw the wolf ask for forgiveness and accede to a peaceful relationship. Francis extended his hand. The wolf showed agreement by placing his paw in Francis' hand and Francis began to call him Brother Wolf.

Francis and Brother Wolf walked back to Gubbio.

As they neared the gate, the citizens could not believe their eyes. Francis and Brother Wolf continued to the town square, although the mayor and the entire town watched with hate and fear. Brother Wolf had to keep his eyes on Francis to still his fear.

Francis called out, "Come, the wolf will not hurt you. Let us talk in peace. I have spoken with Brother Wolf and he apologizes for his actions and wants to make amends."

Francis told them the wolf's story. "He has the same needs as you and only wants to eat and not go hungry. Can the people of Gubbio feed him if he promises to never again take the lives of the people and their animals? Remember, our Savior taught forgiveness. He taught us to love our enemies."

The citizens returned skeptical stares. Francis continued, "This will be your wolf. He can't be killed or passed off to Spoleto or Perugia. He will serve the town as a defender as long as he will live."

The citizens of Gubbio asked Francis to talk privately with them, to help them understand his suggestion. The Mayor guaranteed no one would hurt the wolf while they conferred.

The people of Gubbio talked with each other for hours. Relatives of the dead were the hardest to convince. They harbored a hard place in their hearts for the wolf.

Francis wept with them and touched them in a way that softened their hearts. Finally, after many tears, they found compassion for the wolf. At Francis' suggestion, they addressed him as Brother Wolf.

Francis asked the Mayor of Gubbio and Brother Wolf to declare a pact. The people would be safe from Brother Wolf. Brother Wolf would be safe from them. Everyone expressed joy that the shadow of fear had been lifted from their town.

The wife of the shepherd, the man who was the first to fall, brought out food to feed Brother Wolf. She was crying in relief to have the burden of hate lifted from her spirit. Brother Wolf was humbled when he found his apology accepted. More food was brought out and soon everyone was eating together.

Word spread to other towns. Soon the people of Gubbio were proclaiming proudly that they had a special wolf, Brother Wolf. He lived another two years like that until he died, cared for by the generous and forgiving town of Gubbio.[1]

INTRODUCTION

RESOLVING CONFLICT IS DEMANDING. The personal journey on the path to reconciliation with former enemies can be arduous, and the path is not always clearly marked. Travelers who engage in a pilgrimage to peace are often in need of a practical guide, a manual that charts a route through the stages of reconciliation, a manual that presents concepts, skills, techniques, analysis, ritual, and interpersonal tools that have been proven useful in resolving conflict. *Taming the Wolf* is such a handbook.

Though your path to peace will be unique, the principles and practices others have discovered that are presented in *Taming the Wolf* may prove valuable on your personal journey. The following introductory remarks address how you might best use the material in your quest to resolve conflict and reconcile relationships.

The Purpose

Unresolved conflict ruins lives. Our happiness depends on our ability to manage and resolve conflict. With this in mind, *Taming the Wolf* guides readers through the conflict resolution process, providing concepts and techniques that can be used to overcome the difficult challenges that impede resolution and reconciliation.

In addition, the companion *Taming the Wolf Journal Workbook* contains prompts designed to guide the reader through planning and preparation for mediation or other conflict resolution processes. The approach is practical, designed to provide real life solutions to trying situations that crush our happiness, impair our success, and turn life into a burden.

Taming the Wolf may also inspire readers to assist others in addressing unresolved conflict that is ruining their lives within the family or at work, or within a faith community. When we assist another and increase their happiness, prosperity, and contentment, we often experience greater joy in our own lives. After we experience success in resolving conflict in our own lives, we often recognize we have a duty to go beyond resolving immediate personal conflicts. Our responsibility extends to transforming the world – through our families, communities, organizations, businesses, and nations – into a more peaceful and prosperous place.

When we encounter unresolved conflict, we find the situation is usually a result of interpersonal opposition that has become locked into place over time. Individuals or groups battle one another and become stuck in the oppositional embrace of conflict. The conflict escalates from modest contest to a hostile impasse in which neither side will let go. We take and hold stances opposite each other with regard to intentions, actions, views, or desires. We wrestle desperately over our differences.

All too soon, conflict takes on the qualities of a runaway train: we feel like we are hurtling down the tracks toward disaster with Fate at the controls. We recognize that in order to avoid the ruinous consequences of unresolved conflict *something has to change*. We must undergo a transformation but we are left wondering how we might bring about such change. *Taming the Wolf* answers the question and guides the reader through a process of transformation that invigorates our move to resolution and reconciliation.

In addition to providing a practical road map for the journey, *Taming the Wolf* explores spiritual aspects of conflict resolution including the role faith plays in peacemaking and reconciliation. The mediation style presented, with its emphasis on the role of faith, might best be called *spiritually transformative*. A spiritually transformative style of mediation seeks to bring the resources of faith to bear on the conflict resolution process and at the same time recognizes that through conflict resolution we experience spiritual transformation. In the *Taming the Wolf* approach, reconciliation and spiritual transformation go hand in hand.

Who Should Read the Book

Conflict affects everyone. No one goes through life, or even a single day, without encountering differences with others that necessitate working through problems in order to maintain harmonious and rewarding relationships. The majority of differences are easily resolved. Most of us move through social interactions smoothly, applying social graces and manners intuitively.

A small percentage of the differences we encounter escalate into destructive unresolved conflict. While the differences that escalate into conflict affect a very small percentage of our interactions, they impact our happiness and success in disproportionate measure.

Taming the Wolf guides those motivated to make their life more productive, more enjoyable, and more harmonious through the resolution process. Valuable techniques and principles that can be applied are presented and explained. The manual will hold special value for readers who:

- face the adverse consequences of unresolved conflict;
- struggle with escalating conflict that is ruining their life;
- desire to help others resolve conflict;
- worry about the destruction conflict inflicts on our global neighborhood;
- dream of a more peaceful world where all can prosper;
- wish to deepen their faith through the practice of peacemaking;
- struggle to reconcile with others who adhere to a different faith tradition;
- seek more effective ways to resolve conflicts.

Taming the Wolf was not designed for use by one side to gain an advantage. When possible the greatest benefit can be achieved by both parties applying the material in a collaborative effort. Nonetheless, in situations where the opposing party refuses to engage with the material, an individual party can still significantly improve the conflict resolution process by applying the concepts themselves.

The Structure

Each chapter is divided into the following sections:

- Excerpts from the legend;
- Discussion of mediation principles;

- A Franciscan View;
- Passages from scripture.

Excerpts from the legend inspire us to contemplate how St. Francis approached conflict. Story and metaphor transport us beyond limited rules of logic to touch our intuitive core. As you read the excerpt allow yourself a moment of contemplation. Ask how you might have acted in Francis' position or how he might act in your position.

Discussion of mediation principles provides a foundation in the theory and practice of mediation, acquainting you with concepts and practices employed by mediators. Studying this material prepares you to take an active and informed role in the process. The discussion section introduces concepts and skills that increase your chances of success.

A Franciscan View introduces St. Francis and the views of contemporary Franciscans. As we seek the courage to change, the power to forgive, the humility to apologize, and the compassion to embrace others, it helps to have a guide – Francis of Assisi – who spent his life seeking to understand the teachings of The Prince of Peace. The reader may or may not be a Christian or a Catholic, nonetheless, Francis, the Universal Brother, speaks in a language we all understand, the language of brotherhood and compassion.

Passages from scripture direct our attention to the larger context of the spiritual life. After applying mediation principles in response to prompts, some readers may still experience impasse. They may find their hearts have been hardened by the conflict. In spite of their attempts to shift perspectives, they may be stuck. Reading sacred texts shifts our attention to a transcendent context from which flows new and unexpected insights.

The Journal Workbook

This companion publication contains self-analysis prompts that will assist you to engage the conflict resolution process at a personal level. The prompts raise issues you may not have considered previously and motivate a deeper level of conflict analysis. Although the prompts are more comprehensive or exhaustive than you might find elsewhere, they are the types of questions that typically come up in mediation. They are arranged to guide you through the stages of mediation, helping you gain deeper awareness of self and others. The prompts are not checklists to be completed but rather invitations to contemplative self-analysis. They provide you with a road map for the assessment and identification of factors driving a conflict.

How to Read the Book

Taming the Wolf helps you become a fully prepared participant in mediation, a participant able to make informed decisions and choices. You may wish to scan quickly, reading from cover to cover to locate techniques you can apply immediately to your particular conflict. Most readers, however, will want to approach *Taming the Wolf* in a step-by-step manner.

The book is designed to guide you through the mediation process from the pre-convening stage to reconciliation. The structure follows the actual process and prepares you to make decisions from among the available options.

You will want to analyze and assess the conflict, log your results, enter journal accounts that capture your feelings and insights, and note additional resources you may need to consult. You will also want to document brainstorming sessions and narratives related to the conflict in your *Taming the Wolf Journal Workbook* that will serve as a *confidential mediation journal.*[1]

The journal workbook serves a number of purposes: it allows you to create a record of the conflict, to which you may return later for clarity; it motivates you to analyze the conflict at a deeper level than otherwise might be the case; and it provides a narrative of change, a story of the spiritual transformation that takes place as reconciliation is achieved. The journal will become a record of your progress. Later, you can return to a chapter and revise your responses to the prompts, taking into account additional information you have procured or the results of deeper contemplation.

After logging responses a number of times as different conflicts arise you may find the prompts become second nature. You may begin to think in conflict resolution terms and your conflict resolution skills may become conflict *prevention* skills.

An Overview

Mediation is a transparent process. This means the mediator makes sure parties are fully informed regarding the process. There are no hidden tricks; there is no manipulation. The mediator approaches the process with open hands and an open heart. As much as possible, he explains specific steps and asks permission from the parties to proceed. In this way parties are consulted and their agreement is solicited.

Mediation honors choice, not only in terms of the outcome, but also in terms of procedure. For example, before meeting with parties in separate sessions, the mediator explains the value of separate sessions and clarifies the ground rules. After explaining the proposed guidelines, the mediator asks parties if they wish to adopt suggested procedures or not. This is just one example of *process transparency* and *party choice*.

Mediation honors choice. *Party self-determinism* is a foundational principle. In order to make good choices, in order to take a self-determined role, a party must be fully informed. *Taming the Wolf* was written to provide you with the information you will need to engage the process in such an informed manner.

Taming the Wolf encourages informed participation by introducing mediation from the participant's viewpoint. In keeping with the tradition of mediation transparency, *Taming the Wolf* describes the mediation process in detail, educating readers and inviting them to become active participants who shape events as they unfold.

My intention, my hope, and my prayer in writing *Taming the Wolf* was to contribute to your success in resolving the conflicts that keep you from experiencing the happiness, contentment, and joy that should be yours.

CHAPTER ONE

St. Francis Introduced

S AINT FRANCIS OF ASSISI will serve as our guide as we learn to tame the wolf that stalks us as we pursue peaceful, happy, and productive lives. Francis will become our mentor as we transform hearts and minds during the reconciliation process. We will come to know Francis during our conflict resolution journey but it is worth pausing at the beginning of the journey for a brief introduction.

As we anticipate meeting Francis we may ask, What does a peacemaker look like? What qualities allow a peacemaker to calm turbulent seas of conflict that threaten to capsize our lives? What temperament makes a reconciler able to inspire love where previously there was only hate? What skills allow Francis to facilitate reconciliation?

In *Taming the Wolf: Peace through Faith* I set out to answer these questions, starting with the legend that inspired this book.

History of the Legend

The legend appears in "*The Little Flowers of Saint Francis*, undoubtedly one of the most popular classics of Christian spirituality, [which] is an Italian translation of the Latin text of *The Deeds of Blessed Francis and His Brothers* by Ugolino Boniscambi of Montegriorio."[1] *The Little Flowers* "are a collection of beautiful stories about Francis which greatly emphasize the supernatural."[2]

The story of Francis taming the wolf appears as chapter 21 of *The Little Flowers* with different titles being used in different translations: "The Very Holy Miracle That Saint Francis Worked When He Converted The Very

Fierce Wolf of Gubbio," or "St. Francis Delivers Gubbio from a Fierce Wolf."[3] The paraphrased version of the legend presented in this work remains true to the original tale, with minor alterations intended to help convey the stages of conflict resolution.

The story, in the various forms in which it has been retold, focuses on a neutral third party coming to the aid of two parties in conflict. Jean François Godet-Calogeras describes the legend and its role in Franciscan life: "The story of the wolf of Gubbio is the story of a conflict between two parties in which Francis gets involved. Through the events and Francis's intervention, the author elaborates a whole theory of conflict resolution or peacemaking. As Franciscans are friends of peace, we are deeply interested in such theory to inspire our own action."[4]

Another Franciscan, Leonardo Boff, synopsizes the story in the following manner: "The conversion of the wolf of Gubbio is a metaphor for Saint Francis' stance toward an exploiter and toward a whole band of oppressors who were intimidating and stealing from the people of the city. His strategy is not a harsh attack on oppression, but a sweet and soft approach through dialogue, an appeal to the sensitivity that always exists in people, and the certainty that collaboration is more effective than competition."[5]

Franciscans return repeatedly to the legend for guidance when it comes to the core principles of peacemaking, thus *Taming the Wolf* is not the first handbook to present a vision of reconciliation in the tradition of Francis, nor will it be the last. *Taming the Wolf* will take its place alongside other works in the enduring peacemaking legacy of Saint Francis of Assisi.

Who Was Saint Francis?

A history of the events in Saint Francis' life and a history of the legacy of the saint can be found in numerous writings. The first and by all accounts most accurate history can be found in *The Life of Saint Francis* by Thomas of Celano (1228-1229), which appears in the definitive three volume series of early documents on Francis.[6]

The previously mentioned *The Little Flowers of St. Francis* can also be found in those volumes. Though *The Little Flowers* and its antecedent work

The Deeds of Blessed Francis and His Brothers were written approximately one hundred years after the death of Francis they provide valuable insight into his spiritual legacy.[7]

The Life of St.Francis by St. Bonaventure is another biography I found valuable in my quest to know Francis. The work is included in a collection of Bonaventure's writings translated by Ewert Cousins.[8] Bonaventure, a younger contemporary of St. Francis who went on to become minister general of the Franciscan Order, followed in the mystical footsteps of Francis by spending time in contemplation on Mount La Verna where Francis took refuge. Bonaventure's spiritual advancement endowed him with an ability to present the life of Francis with unique spiritual insight.

Another well-known biography, *The Road to Assisi*, by Paul Sabatier, who was not a Franciscan, has provided a popular introduction to Francis for readers around the world.[9] Our journey together will be enriched by the writings of Franciscan scholars and friars who have captured his life, teachings, and gospel way of life, especially in "The Franciscan View" sections.

The Francis you will meet in these pages, however, should not be mistaken for the definitive Francis, but rather Francis as he touched my heart, the Francis I discovered in the context of conflict resolution. *Taming the Wolf* is a reflection of the manner in which his life spoke to me and thus is colored by my personal prejudices and my unique relationship with Francis. You are encouraged to seek your own encounter with Francis as you journey on the path to peace. Perhaps you, too, will adopt Francis as your mentor in your efforts to resolve the conflicts ruining your life.

The Prayer of Saint Francis

The prayer known as *The Prayer of Peace* or *The Prayer of St. Francis* augments the legend and provides inspiration to which we can turn for encouragement as we move toward reconciliation. The prayer can help us refocus our intentions as we encounter obstacles and barriers.

This special prayer so perfectly captures the work of reconciliation that it might be considered a mediator's mission statement. A moment spent in contemplation with this prayer can be valuable to mediators and parties alike.

Historical records tell us the prayer commonly called *The Prayer of St. Francis* "…was not penned by the Francis of history but is from the spirituality of the Saint Francis of faith."[10] Leonardo Boff provides an attribution that rings true: "When prayers that are so inspired and universal emerge, it is a sign that their author is the Holy Spirit, who tends to act anonymously in the gentleness of hearts open to the divine."[11]

> *Lord, make me an instrument of your peace.*
> *Where there is hatred, let me sow love,*
> *where there is injury, pardon,*
> *where there is discord, union,*
> *where there is doubt, faith,*
> *where there is error, truth,*
> *where there is despair, hope,*
> *where there is sadness, joy,*
> *where there is darkness, light.*
> *O Divine Master,*
> *Grant that I may not so much seek to be consoled*
> *as to console;*
> *to be understood, as to understand;*
> *to be loved, as to love.*
> *for it is in giving that we receive,*
> *it is in pardoning that we are pardoned,*
> *and it is in dying that we are born to eternal life.*[12]

"The Prayer of Saint Francis seeks to make us instruments of peace, of that peace that emerges from the heart of God and that makes its way into the heart of all things."[13] The prayer foreshadows the style of mediation and conflict resolution presented in *Taming the Wolf*. I call it *spiritually transformative mediation* – a style of mediation that draws upon the resources of faith and seeks to bring about a transformation in our spiritual awareness. It is a style of mediation that conceives of all conflict having a spiritual basis.

"Those who want to be instruments of God's peace must be themselves peaceful persons, steeped in essential care and filled with the spirit of the beatitudes, which is what brings peace. From within themselves they must radiate a peace rooted in their deepest identity."[14] The preceding passage captures the change we seek in order to resolve conflict, a change that works simultaneously in two directions: horizontally as we reconcile with the other party and vertically as we reconcile with God.

You may wish to attach a copy of this prayer to the inside flap of your confidential mediation journal; it can serve as a constant reminder of the mission ahead. Or you may wish to print the prayer on a small card that can be consulted during the difficult conflict resolution process.

Canticle of the Creatures

The Franco Zeffirelli film *Brother Sun, Sister Moon*, a biography of St. Francis, took its title from the *Canticle of the Creatures*, which St. Francis wrote near the end of his life. The song allows us to glimpse how Francis saw the divine in all things and how he celebrated creation. This perspective will become important later when we begin to consider how we view the world in which we have become embroiled in conflict.

> *Most high, all-powerful, good Lord,*
> *Yours are the praises, the glory, and the honor, and all blessing,*
> *To You alone, Most High, do they belong.*
> *and no human is worthy to mention Your name.*
> *Praised be You, my Lord, with all Your creatures.*
> *especially Sir Brother Sun,*
> *Who is the day and through whom You give us light.*
> *And he is beautiful and radiant with great splendor;*
> *and bears a likeness of You, Most High One.*
> *Praised be You, my Lord, through Sister Moon and the stars,*
> *in heaven You formed them clear and precious and beautiful.*
> *Praised be You, my Lord, through Brother Wind,*
> *and through the air, cloudy and serene, and every kind of weather,*
> *through whom you give sustenance to Your creatures.*

Praised be You, my Lord, through Sister Water,
who is very useful and humble and precious and chaste.
Praised be You, my Lord, through Brother Fire,
through whom You light the night,
and he is beautiful and playful and robust and strong.
Praised be You, my Lord, through our Sister Mother Earth,
who sustains and governs us,
and who produces various fruit with colored flowers and herbs.

Praised be You, my Lord, through those who give pardon for Your love,
and bear infirmity and tribulation.
Blessed are those who endure in peace
for by You, Most High, shall they be crowned.

Praised be You, My Lord, through our Sister Bodily Death,
from whom no one living can escape.
Woe to those who die in mortal sin.

Blessed are those whom death will find in Your most holy will,
for the second death shall do them no harm.

Praise and bless my Lord and give Him thanks
and serve him with great humility. [15]

Franciscan Orders: A Brief Description

When I speak of Franciscans you may wonder who fits the description. The following is a brief introduction to the formal structure of the Franciscan world, but it should be noted that while there are official members of Orders or organizations, a Franciscan might include anyone who admires and follows St. Francis in his attempt to live a Gospel life as taught by Jesus Christ.

Formally, Franciscans are those who observe the Rule of St. Francis of Assisi and typically belong to one of three orders: the Friars Minor, the Poor Ladies or Clares, and the Brothers and Sisters of Penance.

The First Order dates from 1209 when St. Francis obtained from Innocent III official but unwritten approval of the simple rule he had composed for the guidance of his first companions. This Rule was subsequently rewritten by St. Francis and solemnly confirmed by Honorius III on November 29, 1223. The Second Rule is now observed throughout The First Order of St. Francis.

Today, The First Order comprises three distinct bodies. The Friars Minors were founded in 1209. The Friars Minor Conventuals and the Friars Minor Capuchins, which grew out of the parent stem, were constituted as independent orders in 1517 and 1619 respectively. All three orders profess the rule of the Friars Minor approved by Honorius III in 1223, but each one has its own particular constitutions and its own general minister.

The Second Order, the Poor Ladies, was founded in 1212. St. Francis did not draw up a formal rule for these Poor Ladies and no mention of such a document is found in any of the early authorities. In 1219, Cardinal Ugolino (who later became Gregory IX) imposed a Rule upon the Poor Ladies at San Damiano. St. Clare, toward the end of her life, recast the Rule and on August 9, 1253, Innocent IV approved this Rule, revised by Clare, which continues to exist today. The Poor Clares today include all the monasteries of cloistered nuns professing the Rule of St. Clare approved by Innocent IV in 1253.

The Third Order was founded in 1221. The foundation of the Brothers and Sisters of Penance came about not by a process of division but rather by addition. St Francis had in mind a confraternity of penance, a lay brotherhood that would be a middle step between the cloister and the world for those wishing to follow in the saint's footsteps and who were debarred by marriage or other ties from entering the First or Second Orders.

The Brothers and Sisters of Penance or Third Order of St. Francis now have two distinct bodies: one is Secular; the other is called Regular. St. Francis founded The Third Order Secular in about 1221. Men and women in the Third Order Secular do not take Vows of Chastity, Poverty and Obedience. With Vatican Council II the Third Franciscan Order (lay brothers and sisters) became a unified Secular Institute in its own right under the leadership of one General Minister for the entire Order. Vatican II strongly emphasized the layperson's vocation in the Church and also recognized the autonomous nature of the SFO as the Third Order of St. Francis is now called. According to a 2002 consensus the total number of members is over 431,000 in 49 constituted national fraternities and 31 emerging national fraternities.[16]

The Third Order Regular comprises some 500 independent Franciscan congregations of men and women. John Paul II officially approved a new Rule for the Third Order Regular Brothers and Sisters in vows in 1982. Members of the order authored "The Rule and Life of the Brothers and Sisters of the Third Order Regular of St. Francis."[17] It is an inspirational document that expresses Third Order spirituality and tradition and honors four fundamental values: Conversion, Poverty, Minority, and Contemplation – which are woven into the web of fraternity to be lived in simplicity and joy.

Note: *Regarding Faith Traditions*

St. Francis plays a vital role as our guide but it is not a prerequisite that you be Catholic or even Christian in order to apply the material. Men and women of all faiths have universally embraced the basic concepts, such as unconditional love and compassion, which comprise the spiritual foundations of peacemaking. The universal nature of these ideas, shared among men of all faiths, provides us with a common point of departure that leads to a shared vision of conflict resolution and reconciliation.

St. Francis, often called the Universal Brother, speaks to men of all faith traditions as well as to those who lack a tradition but who nonetheless come to the subject with an open heart and spiritual yearning. While most readers will be comfortable with the sacred texts quoted, other readers may wish to supplement this work with sacred texts from other traditions.

Taming the Wolf does not seek to restrict or dictate the tradition through which you search for peace and reconciliation. Importance is placed on the inner transformation you experience during the reconciliation process. In addition, there is no suggestion that you must be a person of faith before you can engage in reconciliation and peacemaking – all who seek peace are invited to explore these concepts and practices. The true measure of success of *Taming the Wolf* is the fruit it bears as you apply the contents to resolving conflict.

The shared task at hand is to resolve unwanted and unresolved conflicts and to assist others to resolve the conflicts ruining their lives. Outcomes are measured in terms of hearts healed and relationships reconciled regardless of the theology or religious practice the parties bring to the process. Success will be measured in the peace that descends upon your world like a sweet rain that washes away pain and suffering.

CHAPTER TWO

Preparing Your Story

—————————————

There was in Italy the town of Gubbio, a prosperous village that had a great problem.

A wolf was attacking and eating the people and their livestock.

Nothing the townspeople did protected them from the wolf. Never had they seen such a fierce predator.

He killed and ate first a shepherd, then the shepherd's brother and father when they went out to deal with this menace.

The next morning the town was abuzz with the story told by the shepherd's mother and sisters.

—————————————

Mediation Principles

THE LEGEND BEGINS with the story of what happened; we learn about events that have transpired, events that have left the town of Gubbio and the fierce wolf locked in conflict. This is the scene that awaits Francis, our model mediator. Before he can facilitate a resolution he will need to learn more about the events that have taken place; he will need to sit with the people of Gubbio and explore the history of the conflict.

Like the citizens of Gubbio we take our first step in resolving conflict by preparing to tell our story and name the conflict. Our initial task involves assessing the exact nature of the conflict that is ruining our life in order to sharpen our focus for the journey ahead. As we anticipate meeting with a mediator, we map the factors that have contributed to the contentious nature of the relationship and we prepare an accurate account of the events that led to conflict.

We cannot change that which we cannot name, so before we can resolve the conflict we have to identify the situation we face. This first step takes on a quality of discovery – in order to shape a better future, we must unravel and understand the troubled past. This discovery work is best accomplished through storytelling – in the process of explaining what happened we gain additional insight into events and our feelings about them.

There are parallels between how we tell the story of what happened and classic drama. In most dramas a hero (or heroine) passionately wants something but then faces an obstacle that cannot be overcome, causing him to change his approach to achieving his goal. When he changes, his opposition also changes and once again he must adjust. At the end of the play the hero overcomes all odds and achieves his goal – or in the case of a tragedy he fails but is wiser for having tried. The dramatic structure is based on how humans deal with conflict, thus most dramatic elements can also be found in our real life conflicts. When we relate the story of what happened to a mediator we are conveying our personal drama, often complete with the story elements of character, motive, setting, coveted objects, elixirs, and dramatic beats or incidents that move the story forward with suspense as we encounter the opposition of villains.

In this chapter the discussion will focus on fleshing out the story elements that will appear in your narrative account. The following descriptions are not meant to be an exhaustive catalogue of factors that precipitate conflict, as a comprehensive list would be too long for this book. Instead, I will present brief descriptions meant to inspire analysis, provoke introspection, and stimulate memories that will help you compile a textured account of the history of the conflict. As you read the discussion section you may want to respond to the prompts in chapter 2 of the *Taming the Wolf Journal Workbook*.

Where possible I will suggest fundamental conflict paradigms that undercut and explain all types of disputes. For example I will offer a conflict paradigm for analyzing the conflict in terms of our needs to be, to do, and to have. This approach helps identify factors common to all conflicts, which in turn allows us to construct a narrative that allows the other party to understand and appreciate our interests. The more clearly you present your story, the more likely mediation will end up satisfying your interests.

The Conflict Narrative: What Happened?

When you seek to resolve conflict, telling your story is vital. In disputes that reach the courts, attorneys spend considerable time describing the dispute in legal briefs and oral arguments. They want the judge or jury to know precisely the nature of the matter being contested.

Rules of evidence, trial procedure, and limited court time force attorneys to present a story that does not reflect all aspects of reality. Ironically, a legal case does not represent "the whole truth." In a trial litigants rarely feel they have been given a chance to truly tell their story. Legal arguments rarely provide a complete analysis of the factors that pit two opponents against one another.

On the other hand, one reason mediation is successful as an alternative to litigation is that mediation provides a forum for disputants to tell their story. Mediation produces increased party satisfaction by allowing parties to fully explain their point of view, by giving them a chance to present all their thoughts, emotions, and concerns. Thus, in order to take full advantage of mediation you will want to spend adequate time preparing to tell your story of what happened.

Consequences

Before we get to the table to share our story we may need added motivation. We may need a nudge. Our primary motivation for resolving conflict is the realization that unresolved conflict can be extremely destructive, exacting a tremendous financial, physical, emotional, psychological, and spiritual toll. Even seemingly benign conflict, left unresolved, can render us ill with its steady drumbeat of stress and uncertainty.

Most of us have experienced the sleepless nights, the loss of appetite (or compulsive eating), and the obsessive worry that accompany conflict. Our troubled mind drifts from important tasks to fantasies of making our nemesis disappear or making them suffer the pain we feel. Bad humor clouds our mood, leading to upsets with those with whom we have no quarrel. Our relationships across the board suffer. At times we sink into depression; our entire future appears compromised, threatened by the consequences we fear.

Missed opportunities skate by unnoticed as our attention narrows to the fight in which we are engaged. We lose faith in our fellow man and fail to notice uplifting expressions of kindness aimed in our direction. Our animosity toward "the other" turns inward; we suffer guilt and wonder if our flaws, our shortcomings, are the real cause of our troubles. We consider offering an apology, but our stomach churns at the thought of humbling ourselves; we are repulsed by the idea of being subjected to the will of the other, so we shore up our defenses and vow to fight to the end no matter how grim that end might be.

We daydream visions of the painful revenge we hope to exact. Our careers suffer or may be ruined. Our family suffers. Home is no longer a sanctuary, domestic tranquility is compromised when we lash out and vent conflict-driven frustrations. We become consumed with the struggle and dire nightmares take shape in the back of our mind: we imagine an adversary launching a violent, surprise attack with fatal consequences to our loved ones. These fearful imaginings spike our adrenalin and wrack our bodies with nervous energy.

Each of us has suffered at least some of these symptoms of unresolved conflict. Thus it is easy to visualize conflict as a fierce wolf stalking us, threatening our contentment, happiness, and survival. When we assess the situation, we consider the consequences – what does our wolf look like? If we continue on our current path, what outcome do we fear will result?

A prerequisite for our taking remedial action is an accurate recognition of the devastation and ruin that will take place if we do not change course. In the majority of instances, unless we truly understand the stakes and the adverse consequences we will reap we will fail to engage in the hard work needed to resolve the conflict. Thus our call to action is the recognition of how conflict ruins lives.

Conflict Presents Risk & Opportunity

Conflict can play a negative role in our lives, ruining our health, happiness, and prosperity, or it can result in growth that makes us wiser, happier, stronger, and more committed to our relationships. The difference rests at least partially on how we manage and resolve conflict.

If we assume we are the effect of external forces and have no choice or options we may sink into apathy and accept the script Fate has written for us. On the other hand, if we understand the damage we might suffer if we fail to resolve the conflict we may actively seek resolution and reconciliation.

We may decide to set aside the script Fate has prepared and seek to write our own script, though we know that, ultimately, others will also have a say in how the script unfolds. Yet another option is to view conflict as an opportunity to bring increased compassion and understanding to the characters in our personal story. We may conceive of reconciliation as a spiritual vocation, as a way of life.

When conflict is resolved the result can be a more collaborative relationship. The intense dialogue that occurs when we address differences can be therapeutic and uplifting; incorrect assumptions and prejudices fall away leaving us with a much brighter and more optimistic view of the world. When managed properly conflict generates growth experiences.

In the end the way we view our role in resolving conflict has a direct effect on the consequences we will experience. Therefore, it is worthwhile for us to spend time assessing our attitudes toward conflict and conflict resolution. Do we feel we can make a difference? Are we willing to take advantage of the opportunity to resolve conflict?

Conflict Can Be Understood

Often confusion surrounds conflict. In most cases we do not clearly understand what it was that landed us in our current dilemma. We experience uncertainty regarding the future; conflict is something that feels just out of reach of our comprehension and our control.

A common confusion lies in the difference between a *problem* and a *conflict*. They are similar but not identical. The task of moving a large rock up a hill may present a problem but not a conflict. Gravity works against us when we try to move the rock, but gravity does not *intend* to oppose us. Gravity is an existing natural force – a function of the position of the rock on the hill. A problem arises from our desire to move the rock higher but that is not conflict.

On the other hand, if a wolf attacks us every time we attempt to hoist the rock up the hill the situation begins to take on the color of conflict. The deciding variable is the degree of intentionality. If we ascribe intentions to the wolf we have a conflict; if we believe the wolf acts according to instinct and not intention then it is a problem we face.

If a hermit living on the top of the hill rains arrows down upon us when we try to move the rock we have a situation that rises to the level of conflict. His attack is intentional. The hermit can choose to ignore us and let us get on with our business but he decides to prevent us from achieving our goal. When we engage in a struggle with another person or another causative agent who consciously *intends* we call it conflict.

In some instances when we have a problem, such as a need to move a rock up the hill against the force of gravity, we convert the problem into a conflict by assigning blame to others for the conditions we face. We assume or imagine or fabricate an intentional agent as the source of our difficulty.

When we assess our conflict it is important we determine whether or not we have turned a simple problem into a conflict by incorrectly assigning oppositional intention to another person. Do we face someone who *intentionally* opposes our interests, needs, and goals – or do we face a problem in satisfying our needs, a problem for which we have incorrectly blamed others thereby causing conflict?

For example, we have a problem moving a rock up a hill but we become angry at a wolf we happened to see in the distance and we blame the wolf for our problem, arguing that having seen the wolf distracted us and made it difficult to move the rock. The wolf does not oppose our efforts and we have no conflict with him, we have simply turned a problem into an artificial conflict.

In a slightly different scenario, conflict may arise if we are moving the rock up the hill against the force of gravity and we ask another person for help and they refuse. Conflict is found in opposition to our intentions: "I want help" is opposed by "I will not help."

As we assess the conflict, it is important to discern the difference between being upset with a problem and being upset with an actual conflict. In the legend, it is written that the village had "a great problem." We can also say, more precisely, that the town of Gubbio and the wolf were engaged in a major conflict with fatal consequences.

Opposing Forces Create Conflict

If we return to the question *what is conflict?* we find that its basic property is a state of opposition. People become locked in conflict as a result of opposing goals, intentions, efforts, desires, interests, needs, values, beliefs, emotions, and identities. Individuals or groups become entangled in conflict with one another as a result of opposition and then find themselves unable to break the oppositional embrace.

They find themselves engaged in a conflict dance. They may engage in a tug-of-war in which they pull against one another, both claiming ownership of the same object, or they may push against one another, preventing each other from moving forward toward a goal.

We struggle when we cannot have something we *want*. We struggle when we are forced to accept something we *do not* want. We struggle to pull toward us those things we desire and we struggle to push away from us those things that repulse us. Whether the parties in conflict are pulling in opposite directions or pushing in opposite directions they can be found frozen in an oppositional embrace. When the conflict is unresolved they continue to wrestle and may eventually destroy one another.

There are many ways in which two or more individuals or groups can become locked in a battle of opposing goals, purposes, intentions, emotions, efforts, interests, needs, values, and identities. When you begin to assess your conflict you will want to identify the factors that stand in opposition to one another. For example, list goals that are opposed, interests that are opposed, and intentions that counter one another. Identify the push and pull in your conflict.

In your assessment look for *"if I win, you lose"* scenarios, as they are a common symptom of existing or looming conflict. As you construct your narrative of what happened, look to identify a conscious agent that has the power to oppose the outcome you desire or intend.

Conflict over Be, Do, & Have

In your assessment look for opposing intentions regarding: 1) who you want *to be*; 2) what you want *to do*; 3) what you want *to have*.

Be aware that being, doing, and having are interdependent. For example, in the legend the wolf must hunt (do) in order to procure food (have) in order to survive (be). The townspeople of Gubbio want to travel safely (do), own livestock (have), and survive (be) by avoiding the wolf.

The wolf's desire to eat in order *to be* opposes the townspeople's desire to not be eaten. A cursory glance at opposing interests tells us: a) the survival of the wolf appears to be contingent on the non-survival of the livestock and townspeople; b) the townspeople's survival appears to be contingent on the wolf not surviving. The survival of each appears to depend on the non-survival of the other. This is typically the case when parties are locked in the oppositional embrace of conflict; an either/or and win/lose situation exists.

In your assessment look for factors opposed to one another in an either/or dichotomy. Search for "if I win, you lose" scenarios. This is where you will no doubt find the core of the conflict. Assess the situation and name the players who oppose what you want to have, what you want to do, and who you want to be.

Conflicts over What We Want To Have

Conflicts commonly arise out of opposition regarding ownership and possession. When we have a need or desire to possess something and that need or desire is opposed we have conflict. When a person's needs and desires for material possessions are not met in peaceful or collaborative ways that person is often prepared to exert greater effort or apply greater force to fulfill their wishes. They are prepared to engage in conflict behavior.

Arguments surface over who has the right to possess disputed items and debate rages regarding which party deserves to have their needs met and which party deserves to go without. Relative power and willingness to use power become factors in the struggle to possess. The list of possessions over which we can fight is endless, so you will want to list the specific items you are seeking to possess or retain in your conflict.

WHAT WE WANT TO HAVE: MONEY. Conflicts over money are commonplace, thus deserving special mention. Money, which is used as a medium of exchange, translates into power to possess a broad range of goods we need or want. The subject can become tainted with negative emotions from previous bad experiences and these negative emotions can resurface during a conflict. Thus, when money becomes the focus of a dispute, negative emotions tied to past painful experiences almost always cloud the situation, forcing us to assess previous upsets that distort the present moment.

Money, an abstract symbol of value, derives its worth from people's willingness to exchange symbols of value (paper money, metal coins or other financial instruments) for actual goods. When the use of an abstract symbol for value becomes complex, esoteric or even deceptive, the likelihood of conflict increases significantly.

Sophisticated investment vehicles that can be understood only by tax accountants or computer geniuses result in confusion that leads to disputes. Conflict arises when mortgage contracts loaded with fine print are misunderstood. When consumers and investors baffled by government monetary policy fail to correctly predict the future, conflict over failed expectations arise. The list goes on and on. Thus, in preparation for mediation, carefully assess the role money or other vehicles of exchange play in your conflict, paying particular attention to any confusion that may be present.

WHAT WE WANT TO HAVE: SCARCITY. Conflict becomes almost certain when what we need or desire becomes scarce and we must compete to satisfy our needs. Scarcity acts as a conflict trigger. This is particularly true when people have enjoyed a high standard of living and subsequently goods become scarce. Historically it is not those who are consistently poor who foment revolution but rather those who lose the prosperity they once enjoyed.

Scarcity triggers conflict over which party will have their needs met and which party will go without. Scarce land is often a source of conflict, particularly when the land is considered unique (and thus limited) by virtue of historical or religious importance. For example, in the Middle East a long-standing dispute over the partitioning of Jerusalem continues to this day. A shortage of consumer goods can cause conflict as trivial as a department store shouting match or as significant as deadly riots. Scarcity, perceived or actual, becomes a major factor to be considered and the issue of how we remedy scarcity becomes paramount.

When we consider the ability *to have* from the viewpoint of social concerns, we find situations where hoarding and greed exist alongside poverty. In such instances, moral rights or obligations with regard to possessions come into play; the distribution of goods becomes the subject of debate and values concerning fairness and justice are contested.

Different political systems expound different norms and values with respect to what is fair and just when it comes to owning personal property. Conflict then arises over which social or political system provides the most fair and equitable personal property rights.

In any social or political system a perception that unfair manipulation has affected the availability of goods creates a conflict flashpoint. Among *those who do not have* jealousy emerges giving rise to an assumption that *those who have* used coercion, manipulation, and dominance to acquire possessions. Class warfare leads to conflict between *have* and *have-not* groups. This type of conflict is not limited to grand scales. These same dynamics can operate within a family, a business, an organization, or a community.

Many social justice clashes fall under the heading of conflicts regarding exchange in which we are faced with the need to analyze systems of exchange – systems of buying, selling, and trading goods – for fairness. A breakdown in perceived fairness of exchange can occur at the level of the individual or throughout the broader society.

As you assess your conflict determine the degree to which scarcity, real or perceived, has been a factor, either for you or for the other party.

WHAT WE WANT TO HAVE: EXPECTATIONS. Unmet expectations generate conflict. Though we may possess all that we need or deserve, if our expectations have been disappointed we are prone to conflict. Expectations – how we imagine the future – become important as our continued survival depends on our ability to accurately predict the possessions or resources we will have in the future. If we fail to predict accurately – if our expectations are not met – we may lack what we need to survive. Though most of the time the results of failed expectations are not life threatening in the majority of the conflicts I have mediated unmet expectations played at least a modest role.

Here's an example. There may have been an agreement that construction of a fence would result in the payment of $2000 to a builder, but the actual work involved and the resulting quality of the finished product may leave the builder feeling he exceeded the terms of the agreement. He may grow to have an *expectation* of additional compensation. When that expectation is unmet conflict may result.

The expectation of additional compensation in return for extra work may or may not have been expressed by the builder; nonetheless, when he delivers a job with additional value he may expect the homeowner will recognize his exemplary work and reward him accordingly. The homeowner may refuse to meet the builder's expectations, even though the job turned out to be more difficult than planned and the final work exceeded specifications. The homeowner bases his expectations strictly on the contract. While the homeowner may stand on firm legal ground (as a contract formalizes expectations) the builder's unmet expectations may lead to conflict.

In another example, we may not have a contractual right to a bonus from our employer, but if we believe we have delivered beyond the call of duty we may expect to be rewarded for our results. If that expectation is ignored we feel cheated and conflict ensues.

Expectations based solely on our subjective evaluation of a situation very easily turn into convictions regarding what we deserve. In many situations we silently assume we will receive what we deserve and that assumption grows into an unshakeable expectation. Such expectations, when disappointed, lead to conflict. We feel we have been intentionally wronged and we feel justified in our noisy protest. Thus, an important task in conflict resolution involves addressing expectations, stated or unstated, that have been disappointed.

Unstated expectations can be particularly troublesome as the actual cause behind the conflict is not made known. Rather, the expectation remains an unvoiced assumption in the mind of one party. In mediation we bring these hidden expectations to the surface and handle the upset they have caused. In your assessment determine if you or the other party have expectations that are implied but not overtly stated.

WHAT WE WANT TO HAVE: OWNING PEOPLE. Another example of conflict that arises over possessions is the misguided sense that we own another person, a sense of entitlement that sometimes surfaces in domestic cases. The assumption that one owns another person causes extreme levels of conflict. An example of the *need to own* gone terribly wrong is the jealous mate controlling their spouse as they would a possession. Efforts to own another person translate into efforts to dominate and control that person's body and affections, which often leads to deadly conflict.

While there are cultural differences regarding the rights of one spouse to dominate and control the other, conflict arises any time contentious issues relating to owning and being owned surface, even in cultures that accept certain forms of possession and control of a spouse. Slavery is not a stable condition that fosters peace and contentment; eventually, resentment and revolt are the response to being treated as a possession.

ASSESSING THE NEED TO HAVE. In assessing your conflict in your journal workbook, consider how factors related to having or not having specific possessions or property drive the conflict. What desire, need, or intention *to have* is opposed? What role does actual or perceived scarcity play? What values guide the exchange of money or goods? What property rights are assumed to exist? Have issues of fairness and justice with regard to property rights arisen? Is greed involved? Are your expectations or the expectations of the other party clearly stated and realistic? Is there an agreement? What unmet expectations fuel the conflict? Does a combination of unmet expectations and scarcity play a role in your situation? These and other questions help determine the precise nature of the conflict with regard to the *need to have.*

Freedom To Do

Conflicts arise over opposing views of what we are permitted *to do.* When our behavior is outlawed or restrained, particularly with force, considerable strife can result. When a person or group wishes to do something and another person or group opposes that desire or intention to act we have conflict. Conflict surfaces when one side has an intention to pursue a goal, while the other side is equally determined to prevent the realization of the goal.

In this category we find abuse of power, domination, and coercion. We consider freedom of speech, freedom of movement, freedom to protest, freedom to pursue happiness, or the freedom to worship as one chooses. Conflicts include family disputes over how much freedom children or teenagers are given – questions of autonomy are contested. Conflicts may involve the right to travel over private or public lands. They may concern disagreements over behavior allowed in the public square, such as erecting holiday displays or praying at school events.

Disputes may emerge over how we decide what is accepted behavior. A party may consider a certain behavior to be a matter of private choice while others consider the behavior has a negative impact on society, as might be the case with sexual behavior.

The question of what constitutes valid restraint of unwanted behavior may be hotly contested. An example would be disputes in which the freedom of public expression impinges on others' safety. Or when repressive governments sharply limit individual expression, such as the freedom to write or speak opinions, violent conflict or insurrection results.

Norms that regulate permissible behavior – what one may do – frequently cause conflict. Differences arise over values that determine what constitutes approved behavior ot sanctioned behavior. While one group may approve of a certain behavior another group or faction may outlaw the same behavior as it offends their values. Conflict emerges over who should be allowed to determine the accepted standard. Which group should dictate policy?

Differences in culture may affect how we judge actions as respectful or disrespectful. In cross-cultural settings our actions may inadvertently signal disrespect and we might not be aware we have given offense. The fact we are unaware of accepted norms in another culture may itself communicate disrespect, as we may be perceived as neglecting others' concerns.

In analyzing your particular conflict consider restraints on your behavior that cause you upset: what action does the other party want you to stop? Conversely, what behavior are you trying to prevent or restrain? Be specific.

In summary, conflict surfaces when others prevent us from doing what we wish to do. Conflict arises when we attempt to restrain others preventing them from doing what they wish.

The Need To Be & Identity Conflict

Conflict arises over who we are allowed *to be*. Identity-based conflict concerns outward expressions of *who we are*, such as our position or title, and it concerns inner expressions of core identity, such as our faith.

You may have heard, "If that's who you want to be, you're not welcome here." Or, "We do not permit your kind here." Or parties may hold different views over who is allowed to assign and impose identity – you may have heard the protest (frequently expressed by teenagers), "You don't get to tell me who I can be."

The following discussion touches briefly on a few sources of identity conflict; you will want to compile your own list.

Positions with status attached often become the subject of disputes. A conflict over the desire *to be* occurs when there is a contest over position and title, for example, when vice presidents vie for the position (the identity) of company president. Students may battle over who gets named "most likely to succeed" or "most popular." We may experience conflict over the selection of a leader to head a community group or parish project. In your assessment in evaluate the role played by your desire for position, status, or prestige.

In addition to issues regarding individual identity, the identity we assume as a member of a group can generate conflict. For example, in some tribal cultures being a member of one tribe automatically makes one the enemy of another tribe. Feuding ethnic communities engage in horrendous acts of violence, torture, maiming, and murder over identity issues. Inner-city gang members inflict injury and death on rival gang members; assuming the identity of one gang puts them in opposition to a rival gang identity. Such collective identity can lead to "us versus them" thinking that spawns conflict.

Class and status also erect identity boundaries that foment divisiveness. Those deemed inferior may be refused membership or admission to groups, clubs, or events, leading to hostility. Exclusion breeds discontent: opponents clash over the criteria used to determine who fits in. When we fail to conform to an identity approved by the majority, whether in the family, the business, the parish, or the community, we risk being rendered an outcast. In your assessment note conflicting values regarding the identity you must assume in order to be accepted by a group.

Historically, religious identity has fomented conflict: members of one religion target members of another. Such religious conflict does not usually concern spiritual matters, but rather results from religion being co-opted for other purposes such as political power. Such conflict often centers on religious group identity rather than on the state of spiritual being. Rarely are the concerns theological or spiritual; usually disputes concern external trappings of religion alloyed with issues of territory, power, and politics. Comingling religion and politics frequently results in religious identity becoming a flashpoint for violent conflict.

Conflict over religious identity is not confined to differences between faiths, but may arise within a single tradition. Factions that advocate for opposing social values can divide faith communities. For example, conservative factions may fight liberal factions, a phenomenon we have seen in recent years.

A more subtle conflict may arise between individual members of a faith tradition over what it means to be an immortal soul, what being immortal means for our choices in this life, and how those choices relate to our salvation. These and other issues regarding *who should be considered among the faithful* set up conflict.

While some aspects of our identity are interior and personal, other aspects are based on external characteristics or birth circumstances. Racial prejudice zeroes in on one physical aspect of identity, skin color; a person is granted less right *to be* as a result of such an isolated physical property. We can modify our desire for possessions and restrain our behavior but physical aspects of identity are less flexible. For this reason identity-based conflict can be particularly cruel. As a culture we recognize this fact – in response we draft legislation against hate crimes and decry genocide. We protect citizens against crimes motivated by physical aspects of identity.

Conflict also arises from inner qualities such as personality traits, beliefs, or preferences. While others may assign us an identity based on our external appearances, we create an inner identity based on our choices regarding who we wish to be. Our personal choices write the story of the unique character we seek to be in our life drama. When the personal freedom to express that unique identity is challenged conflict emerges.

Struggles concerning our chosen personality traits or beliefs may be subtle. For example, in a marriage one spouse who finds conservative traits laudable might clash with the other spouse who values more expressive and nonconformist traits. The conservative spouse may desire to be seen as a pillar of the community while the other strives to be seen as the life of the party. As long as they grant each other freedom to assume the individual identity they desire conflict is minimal. However, conflict ensues if the conservative partner insists they be seen together as pillars of the community or the more expressive spouse insists they be seen as bon vivants.

It should be noted that the perceived importance of exercising the right to maintain a distinct individual identity varies among cultures. Some cultures place great importance on individual expression of uniqueness or even eccentricity while other cultures mandate conformity. Nonetheless, in either type of culture, difficulty in managing differences regarding who we choose to be increases the likelihood of conflict.

As we prepare to narrate the story of our conflict we need to assess opposition to who we are or who we wish to be. Are we permitted to be who we choose to be? Does the other party seek to restrict our identity or persecute us? Do they seek to restrict our choices? Or are we attempting to limit the identity to the other party? Do we seek to restrict their choices regarding who they can be?

THE NEED TO BE: DISRESPECT. Insults to self-image and identity become conflict triggers. A simple display of disrespect signals disapproval of our identity. Disrespect communicates another's low evaluation of who we are. A show of disrespect challenges our right to be who we are without being dishonored or disparaged. Just as dashed expectations are a common cause of conflict, disrespect plays a role in almost all conflict.

THE NEED TO BE RIGHT. A subcategory of identity-based conflict emerges when our need *to be right* is not honored. The need to be right – a special case of the need *to be* – frequently becomes a critical factor in conflict. Being wrong becomes associated (mostly unconsciously) with a cessation of survival, while being right becomes equated with continued survival.

As an illustrative example, consider driving on a mountain road approaching a cliff. If you correctly anticipate the distance to the edge of the cliff, you brake in time to avoid catastrophe. If you miscalculate the distance, you catapult to your death. At an unconscious level the mind draws on such experience: it equates being right with survival and equates being wrong with death.

When someone makes you wrong it is common to experience a surprising overreaction to the criticism. We experience a vague but nagging sense that our survival is threatened. Our typical response is to argue persistently that we are right – as though our lives depend on it – even when the stakes are insignificant.

Thus, even when actual life-and-death outcomes are not at stake, we experience strong emotions when it comes to being right and being wrong. As a result of this latent psychological factor conflict takes on exaggerated importance. Our unconscious association of deadly consequences with being wrong leads to an altered sense of urgency. We cling passionately to our need to be right. Tell someone they are wrong, even with gentle tact, and you risk provoking a strong emotional response. The underlying dynamics of "I am right and you are wrong" are more intractable than we anticipate.

Thus it is important that we assess our need to be right and/or our need to not be wrong. An important mediator task is guiding parties away from statements that communicate "I am right, you are wrong."[1] In your self-analysis, evaluate the strength of your attachment to being right and the strength of your negative emotions when you are made wrong.

ASSESSING THE NEED TO BE. As you document your specific conflict in your journal workbook, consider obvious aspects of identity that play a role in the conflict – race, religion, nationality – then evaluate more subtle issues regarding your ability to be who you want to be.

Are you being prevented from assuming an identity you desire, such as becoming a member of a particular group or holding a position within a company? Do you feel your identity is under attack? What role does disrespect play? Has the other party disrespected you? Do they object to who you are? Has a lack of respect caused you to feel under attack? Has someone insisted you are wrong? Does the other party defend being right as though his or her life is on the line, though it is apparent he or she is in error?

Be, Do, Have *Are Interdependent*

We have considered issues of *being*, *doing*, and *having* individually but in actual conflicts they are interdependent. Typically, we act (*to do*) in order to own (*to have*) things that support our identity (*to be*). For example, we trade stocks in order to procure money that allows us to purchase a Ferrari that signals we are a powerful and capable person. In mapping your conflict assess how these factors are interrelated.

Here is an example. A hypothetical effort to resolve an employment dispute focuses on the disgruntled employee's salary but encounters an impasse. The company representative becomes frustrated. What more can he offer? However, the mediator discovers the employee's interest does not concern money but rather status and position: the company failed to promote him to vice president, and thus he was not granted the increased status he desired.

While the company assumes the employee desires the new position in search of higher pay, the employee's real interest concerns identity: the employee wants the added status of vice president. The company assumed the employee was concerned with a need *to have* but he was concerned with a need *to be*. The employee may well understand the company does not have sufficient earnings to increase his salary, nonetheless he would like his personal value acknowledged with increased status. He wants to be recognized as important and valuable.

In many cases it may be difficult for a party to communicate their identity needs, as to do so may appear self-centered and ego-motivated – traits often viewed negatively. Thus it is easier to talk about money. However, if money is not the real interest or both parties realize there can be no movement regarding money negotiation stalls. If a mediator fails to analyze the relative importance of be/do/have he may fail to foster party satisfaction.

Another common example comes from my experience with probate disputes. In contests over a will the conflict may appear to stem from a desire to receive money or control property but, to the heir, money and property may only be symbols of the worth attributed to them by the deceased parent. An heir may look at the inheritance as a symbolic means of gauging how well loved they were (compared to other siblings). Thus, when impasse occurs the real issue may be the heir's need to be loved by the deceased parent – they desire love and respect that acknowledges who they are.

It is important in all types of conflict to recognize or intuit subtle party concerns regarding self-image at the same time one explores what the party wants to have or do. In negotiation a successful approach is to combine and balance the factors of *be, do, have* to arrive at a solution that provides satisfaction. If the process hangs up it may signal too much importance has been given to one factor to the exclusion of the others.

The importance of accurately recognizing party interests in negotiation will be addressed in greater detail later in the book. The topic is mentioned at this early stage in the process in order to stress the importance of correctly assessing the drivers of conflict.

We dig beneath the surface to explore the needs to be/do/have individually and then we assess how they affect one another with questions such as: What do we need *to do* in order *to have* what we want? Or what do we need *to be* in order *to do* what we want? Or what must we *have* in order *to be* who we want to be? We make an effort to understand the links between our different needs and desires.

Feelings Are Important

The importance placed on analyzing and assessing conflict may inadvertently lead to the impression the process is restricted to quietly reasoned matters of logic. The task may seem to be solely an exercise of the intellect, but that is not the case.

Understanding our feelings is just as important or more important; all stories include an emotional arc. We need to allow our feelings to surface and take center stage as we prepare to tell the story of what happened. If we do not understand emotions that are integral to the conflict our progress will slow.

For example, when we are prevented from possessing something we want, we experience a visceral reaction – and that reaction becomes a vital part of our narrative. When it comes to issues of blunted having, we might experience jealousy, frustration, longing, or grief. When we have been stopped from acting or behaving as we wish we may feel enslaved, hurt, fearful, frustrated, or enraged. Emotions are part of experience.

Perhaps nowhere are feelings more important than in identity-based conflict. When we are denied possessions, we can give an account of the measure of our loss; when our freedom to act has been frustrated, we can address the specifics of being stopped or restrained or imprisoned. The narration in these cases has a partially objective component. However, when it comes to identity, to who we are, feelings provide the heart of our story.

In some identity conflicts there may be something tangible at stake, such as a job title, but in many cases we experience identity intimately with our emotions. How we feel ties in with who we are – for example, I *am* sad, I *am* angry. We name our state of being with an emotion or feeling. Thus, when it comes to issues of identity it is particularly important to assess the emotional component of events as we prepare to tell the story of what happened.

Personal Historical Wounds

Personality or psychological factors associated with past trauma or upset may drive conflict. This is a subcategory of identity-based concerns, as it relates to the manner in which we construct our identity or sense of self. Historical wounds (past trauma) become part of who we are. The manner in which we incorporate these wounds into our identity can determine how likely we are to be drawn into conflict.

For example, a person who has experienced repeated emotional trauma builds defensive walls to protect against future emotional intrusions. This defensive perimeter becomes part of how they see themselves. A violation of this protected emotional space, even if accidental and unintentional, may be perceived as a threat to survival.

In this type of situation, when memories of past events are triggered, conflict is ignited. Current events do not drive the conflict; the past is in the driver's seat. The accumulation of our past experience, conscious and unconscious, metamorphoses into our current identity. We develop a hair-trigger sensitivity to stimuli that tell us an enemy is present though the enemy exists only in the past. We are constantly fighting yesterday's battles.

It is not uncommon for conflicts to be ignited by mutual triggering of psychological defenses – the walls we build as a result of our past failures to maintain a safe and secure personal space. In the past others hurt us. This predisposes us to build emotional fortresses armed with early warning devices that trigger our defenses, which often cause us to initiate conflict prematurely. In other words, when current events trigger the (often unconscious) memory of past upsets we stand ready to defend and fight. The simplest provocation activates contentious tactics.

In these cases we are not fighting the person in front of us in the present moment but rather a person with whom we fought in the past who caused us to suffer loss. To others we appear overly sensitive and easy to offend, edgy and irritable, and perhaps a bit crazy. Thus, when we assess a conflict it pays for us to analyze our responses to the other party cautiously – are we responding to a present danger or have previous emotional upsets been triggered? Likewise we ask whether the other party is actually fighting us or fighting someone who hurt them long ago.

Though it is vital we recognize our early warning system may trigger and initiate conflict prematurely and without sufficient cause, we must also be careful to recognize actual coercion, abuse of power, and attempts to harm us. At times our defenses may actually be working *for us* rather than against us. The present time conflict may include *actual* efforts designed to destroy us physically, emotionally, and spiritually. That which we perceive as a danger may be an actual danger.

The challenge is to determine whether or not a real and present danger exists or whether the appearance of imminent danger has emerged solely from our emotional and psychological defenses (or from the other party's defenses). We may need a mediator's help to sort out these factors but this does not prevent us from beginning the task on our own. A well-prepared narrative of what happened will help the mediator determine the nature of the situation when the time comes.

It is worth mentioning there are rare but not unheard of situations in which one party's goal is the destruction of the other party for no purpose other than to render them non-existent. In these cases unbridled narcissism or evil intention may need to be identified. The question of evil may need to be considered carefully. (See chapter 18.)

However, it is extremely easy to mistakenly ascribe evil as the cause of conflict; we have a tendency to glibly demonize those with whom we disagree. The occasions when we overlook actual evil are rare. It is not that often that we try to resolve a conflict the other party fully intends to escalate. Honest assessment of the factors that led to conflict helps us avoid ascribing evil when it is *not* present, and makes sure we do not fail to recognize evil when it *is* present.

Procedural Flaws

In addition to the substantive sources of conflict mentioned above, disputes can arise out of procedural mishaps such as communication failures, poorly crafted contracts or agreements, accidents and unforeseen missteps that occur in the course of our normal affairs. You will want to inspect the history of a conflict and identify minor adverse events that went unnoticed and uncorrected, leading to needless escalation of conflict.

Problems with communication are pervasive. Omitted or confusing communications cause situations and events to appear other than they really are. Simple communication failures, fodder for Hollywood comedies, can be the source of conflict, however, the remedy – repairing past communications – can be relatively simple.

Ineffective procedures – for example, procedures that prevent employees or vendors from doing their jobs efficiently – cause frustration and result in outbreaks of conflict. When cumbersome or overly bureaucratic procedures are enforced, it may appear to those affected that someone is intentionally erecting roadblocks in their path. They imagine they are being stopped and prevented from doing their job when the impediments actually originate from poor planning, inefficient systems, and flawed organization. Those affected tend to blame other people rather than identify institutional flaws.

In your analysis consider the role such procedural factors play. When such institutional or organizational causes of conflict are discovered, conflict is usually resolved quickly and relationships are repaired. In other cases, awareness that procedural mishaps are creating problems may lead to subsequent improvement in the way activities are organized; conflict resolution thus leads to improved organizations.

Of course, there are exceptions. On occasion, bureaucratic and administrative roadblocks are the tools disgruntled or destructive employees use to covertly express upset and dissatisfaction. When they feel unable to overtly state their problems they turn to sabotage. Thus, when a procedural problem does not resolve but rather continues occurring, we suspect that what appears to be a simple procedural problem masks a more serious problem. A disgruntled party who finds it difficult to confront another party directly will often use such covert administrative errors and procedural barriers as smokescreens to disguise their opposition.

When you assess conflict determine whether contributing factors are minor procedural problems or problems with miscommunication that can be fixed easily, or more personnel counter intention. The process of mediation in which both parties tell their story will shed light on the actual situation.

Participants Vary

Conflict affects everyone. The potential cast of characters that will appear in our drama is varied. The number of participants also varies: one individual might oppose another individual; a business may fight another business; communities oppose other communities; faith groups compete with other faith groups. At times we even experience inner conflict, a self-versus-self conflict: our heart battles our mind, our values clash with our impulses, or our earthly existence clashes with our divine nature.

Notice the relationships of people involved. Who are the characters in your story? How many participants or stakeholders are involved? The steps you will take to resolve a conflict are determined by the nature of your opponent, so it pays to know exactly who opposes you.

Conflict Venues Vary

Native Americans ascribe great importance to place. In our conflict narrative we also acknowledge the conflict setting. For example, the workplace is a common setting perhaps second only to domestic settings. Hospitals, where life and death drama unfolds daily, are a common venue for conflict; conflict may flare up in the local community when neighbors clash or citizens battle officials; at the local parish conflict may erupt among parishioners or between clergy; schools are veritable conflict incubators. Conflict plays out daily in courts; divorce courts are often the scene of volatile conflict; in the public square civil rights conflict unfolds with each new generation; on the freeway varying skills and differing road manners pit motorist against motorist and on occasion culminate in a crash or freeway shooting.

We typically act in different ways depending on the setting in which we find ourselves: job site pressures might cause a foreman to act in a manner he would never consider at home; when we are forced by illness to spend time in a hospital we may act in a way that differs from how we behave in the workplace or at home; the relative anonymity that comes with being at the wheel of a car may foster hostility we would fear to express in face-to-face meetings with strangers.

We may also discover that specific settings act as emotional triggers, causing us to act out of character. Discovering the source of such triggers is invaluable and may lead to a rapid advancement of the resolution process. Setting thus becomes part of the conflict map we sketch in our assessment. As we assess the conflict we ask if we must alter a physical setting in order to resolve the disagreement.

Conflict Escalation Patterns

Conflicts tend to escalate in predictable patterns. In order to predict the future path of the conflict we identify the current stage of escalation. This allows us to plan future responses that will diminish the conflict rather than promote escalation. Knowing where we are in the life of a conflict allows us to take control of events.

A mediator will assess the degree to which the conflict has escalated. If it is not sufficiently ripe – if hostilities have not escalated to the stage where both parties recognize they will suffer adverse consequences if the fight continues – it may be difficult to convene mediation.

Unfortunately, most of us must be faced with dire consequences before we agree to engage in a conflict resolution process. The pain must be sufficient to motivate remedial action or we may fail to see why we should engage in conciliatory efforts. When we lack an appreciation of future consequences the current situation may appear tolerable; we may believe the conflict, if left alone, might simply disappear. If either party fails to appreciate the consequences of their current approach there may be little hope of convening a conflict resolution process.

In the legend Francis has been summoned to help resolve a conflict that *has* escalated: the wolf and the citizens of Gubbio have squared off in mortal combat. Lives are at stake. They have reached the stage of escalation where they are willing to destroy each other even if they will also be destroyed in the process. It is obvious they have need of a peacemaker such as Francis. But it is not necessary for us to wait until people have been seriously hurt before we engage in conflict resolution. Not if we understand the pattern of escalation.

We must understand the more the conflict escalates the more damage will be done to the relationship. The cost of resolving the conflict – financial, emotional, physical, and mental – may increase substantially. Parties who resolve conflicts in early stages of escalation tend to maintain stronger relationships and do not spend resources funding the fight rather than funding the fix.[2] In addition, it is often difficult (without assessing the stage of escalation) for a party to anticipate the moment when the other party might increase the stakes dramatically with a violent or damaging response.

The pattern of escalation typically involves predictable steps that take us from believing the conflict is hardly worth our attention to the stage where we are willing to lay down our life to defeat or punish our adversary. Friedrich Glasl described these steps as follows:[3]

- You have lost faith in resolving the matter through fair discussions.
- Talking is useless; it is time to act unilaterally. The other party also feels talking is useless.
- You have used deniable punishment. The other party has used deniable punishment.[4]
- Veiled attacks have been made.
- Your honor has been offended. You have offended the other party's honor.
- Actions have taken place that would cause another to lose face.
- Threats and ultimatums have been issued.
- It is time to stop the other side from controlling you.
- It is time to attack the other party and destroy their ability to operate.
- You no longer care if you survive; you wish to destroy the other party.

These steps can be reduced to the following descriptive stages:[5]

- Stage 1. Hardening
- Stage 2. Debate & Polemics
- Stage 3. Actions, Not Words
- Stage 4. Images & Coalitions
- Stage 5. Loss of Face
- Stage 6. Strategies of Threat
- Stage 7. Limited Destructive Blows
- Stage 8. Fragmentation of Enemy
- Stage 9. Together into the Abyss

When we identify the conflict escalation stage we can avoid actions that force the conflict to the next higher stage. Instead, we engage in actions that reduce conflict to a lower stage.

For example, if we are formulating Strategies of Threat, we anticipate our next action will likely include delivering Limited Destructive Blows. We also recognize we recently passed through a stage where there has been a loss of face. With this knowledge we can change direction. Rather than deliver limited destructive blows we engage in Face Saving and Face Restoring actions. We purposely de-escalate the conflict. The strategic attempt to reduce the level of conflict may be a form of concession that signals our good intentions and makes it easier for the other party to convene mediation.

Stage of escalation may be one of the most important variables to assess as you begin to name the conflict. The stage of the conflict indicates where we are in the progression of our story. The analysis answers the questions: Where do we exist in the life of this fight? Where might we be headed? What can be done to wind down this conflict?

The Wolf as Metaphor

The wolf in the legend can be seen as a metaphor representing the danger inherent in unresolved conflict. The wolf represents a threat to our happiness and survival, a threat to our contentment and equanimity, a threat to our freedom. The wolf represents forces that cause us pain and make us suffer. Yet, at the same time, the wolf has a natural beauty that draws us close. It can be a metaphor for the way in which we are attracted to things that cause us suffering – until we clarify their power over us and tame the wolf.

The wolf represents the stalking enemy who appears out of the distance advancing toward us with fangs bared. It also represents the hidden enemy growling in the shadows of our minds. Thus the wolf represents internal as well as external threats: it represents destructive emotions that lay waste to our peace of mind; it is a metaphor for loss of faith and hardening of the heart; it represents sins of greed, lust, pride, envy and hatred that strip our self-respect and sever our ability to listen to the divine within. The internal wolf represents the way we sow the seeds of our own discontent.

As you analyze the conflict ruining your life, pay attention to the "who, what, and where" of your narrative. Allow the metaphor of the wolf to stir your deeper intuition. How might you describe in an artistic, poetic, or dramatic manner the wolf that advances from outside the walls toward you? How might you describe the wolf that wanders the inner courtyards of your mind?

How might you visualize this creature with a dual nature, with an inner and outer presence? What does the wolf look like when he stalks you quietly and what does he look like when he attacks? What about the wolf is most threatening? What does the wolf want?

All Conflict Is Spiritual Conflict

As we assess our battles, we discover many factors precipitate conflict, some simple and some complex. Nonetheless, from the *Taming the Wolf* perspective, all conflict has its roots in the spiritual. Conflict, in this view, is a symptom of our estrangement from our divine nature. It is a symptom of our separation from our most basic identity, which is spiritual in nature. In this framework conflict might be considered an illness of the spirit.

All conflict is a failure, to a greater or lesser degree, to live a life of unconditional love. Conflict arises from a failure to infuse relationships with lovingkindness. When love is diminished, inhibited, blocked, or refused we tend to pull away and recede into ourselves. In the absence of a loving relationship we assume postures and positions that give rise to conflict. When there is a failure of compassion we break away into isolation and build a world susceptible to conflict.

We can hypothesize that if we are able to greet life with the face of a Franciscan, with the unconditional love of St. Francis who lived according to Christ's teachings, we will cease to encounter conflict related to our desires to be, do, and have. This is a hypothetical ideal and not something most of us can realize all of the time, not even Francis. Nonetheless, there is value in moving toward such an ideal, toward the model presented by Francis, when we are faced with the need to resolve conflict.

The belief that all conflict arises from spiritual foundations may not speak to your heart; it may be a new or foreign concept. Do not feel compelled to include this analysis in your assessment if it does not speak naturally to you. The theme will be revisited throughout the text with examples that shed further light on the hypothesis. Later, as you study the text and apply it to your life you will have time to assess the role the spiritual may play in your conflict.

The Importance of Assessment

The prompts in the *Taming the Wolf Journal Workbook* are designed to assist you to evaluate the factors driving the conflict. The prompts can be used to map the conflict and help you discover and flesh out the elements of your narrative account of what happened. Regardless of whether you use the prompts or not it is important to spend time assessing the conflict. Thoughtful analysis of the conflict prepares you to tell your story in a way that accurately conveys *what happened*. It helps you uncover the underlying factors that need to be addressed if conflict is to be resolved.

You are encouraged to assess the negative consequences of leaving the conflict unresolved and the consequences that emerge from your current response. In the past, in response to conflict you might have resigned yourself to the role of a victim in order to bring about peace. Or you may have become enraged and adopted a scorched earth policy that resulted in mental or physical violence. *Taming the Wolf* provides alternative approaches that eliminate the need to capitulate or resort to harsh measures.

Taming the Wolf will guide you past unworkable or untenable options and toward choices that preserve and enhance relationships. Conflict resolution is not a simple matter of making nice; resolving conflict is rarely a mundane matter of restoring politeness and good manners. If I were to suggest such a naïve view this book would be rendered unusable in many instances; for example, in instances when injustice drives conflict. Instead, we must prepare diligently and apply more substantial remedies. Conflict resolution is hard work. The rewards, however, are commensurate with effort expended.

The importance of self-analysis and assessment cannot be overstated. In many books you will read of others' experiences or become versed in mediation theory. While such scholarship has value, *Taming the Wolf* takes a different approach and guides you through the process of resolving your own conflicts. The value you take away will be determined in great measure by how diligent you are in completing the self-analysis and assessment steps.

As you assess what happened you will cobble together the basic elements of your conflict narrative, the story you will tell when asked, What happened? The self-analysis will help you bring added depth and texture to your story so the other party can better glean from your narrative how you see the world and what is important to you.

A Franciscan View

In the Franciscan tradition Saint Francis helped friars recognize the dangers posed by clinging to possessions, dominating and coercing others, and assuming an identity based on pride. Four factors presented a danger to peaceful relations: power, prestige, position, and privilege. The antidotes to these poisons provided by St. Francis are humility and poverty. In order to administer the antidotes we must understand them in the proper context.

The Franciscan concept of poverty is related to a desire for brotherly relations. "Francis was not really interested in the poverty of material possessions, rather he was concerned for the type of poverty that would lead to interdependence and the love of the brothers for one another."[6]

While clinging to earthly possessions has liabilities, Francis went beyond this concern, "The necessity of the other for Francis thrust him into radical poverty whereby everything that hindered his relation to the other was stripped away."[7] Poverty was not embraced for its own sake or for a show of piety but rather in the pursuit of relationship.

Francis recognized that scarcity, which gives birth to competition, leads to conflict. If we see the other person as a source of competition for valuable resources we fear them and our attention turns away from loving one another as Jesus taught. Ilia Delio, O S F helps us understand Franciscan poverty when she writes, "We are called to be dispossessed of earthly things so as to possess God. To possess means 'to cling to,' to hold on to something so tightly that other possibilities are 'squeezed out.' Each of us is called to be poor, to empty ourselves of all that we cling to so that we may receive the gift of the Holy Spirit."[8]

In other words, when we cling to impermanent and transient possessions we also let go of that which is most valuable, our relationship with the divine. Francis recognized how fear born out of perceived scarcity closes our hearts to the gifts of the Holy Spirit. Paradoxically, while we worry about possessions our most valuable possession disappears.

> Poverty, according to Francis, is the sister of humility. When we are dispossessed of things we are free to turn to the other in love. We no longer have to place ourselves over and above the other because to be humble is to know ourselves before God. Humility is related to poverty because when we can accept the truth of who we are and recognize that everything we have is gift, then we are free to give ourselves away in love.[9]

Thus we see how the concept of poverty leads to the companion concept of humility. In the Admonitions (guidelines for living in a fraternal manner) Francis provides a glimpse of his view on how to avoid problems regarding status and position. He instructed the friars on how to be true to one another: "Those who have been constituted in a position over others should only glory in that superiority in the same way as they would glory if they were deputed to assume the office of washing the feet of the brothers."[10]

In *The Little Flowers of St. Francis* we find the story of Francis guiding the gifted Brother Masseo in a lesson of humility.[11] Brother Masseo possessed "the grace to preach God's Word to the great benefit of people."[12] Yet Francis assigned him to the most menial tasks – as a doorkeeper, alms distributor, cook – and when the rest of the friars were taking a meal he was to eat outside so he could greet visitors and tend to their needs.

The other friars protested and asked for the tasks to be divided among them but Brother Masseo responded with humble patience, saying he was happy to continue with his assigned duties. Upon seeing "the love of the friars and the humility of Brother Masseo... Francis preached a wonderful sermon" in which he declared, "The greater God's gifts, the greater our humility must be, because God turns his back on virtues housed in pride."[13]

In keeping with the theme of humility when it came time to name the order Francis said, "I want this fraternity to be called the Order of Friars Minor."[14] In taking this name for the order Francis highlighted the importance of avoiding conflict that comes from a love of position, power, and prestige, a belief he emphasized throughout his life and teachings. "In the *Earlier Rule 1221* we find the first and most clear reference to the fact that no brother in the Order was to be called 'prior': 'Let no one be called 'prior,' but let everyone in general be called a friar minor. Let one wash the feet of the other.'"[15]

This theme, in which humility and poverty are linked to relationships, finds an echo in contemporary Franciscan life. For example, in a recent Capuchin position paper Brother Helmut Rakowski tells us that the theme of the Seventh Plenary Council of Assisi "never allows you to think for a moment that Franciscan *minoritas* can be described exclusively in terms of humility and submissiveness, or even as a kind of collective inferiority complex. Starting on the basis of the Trinity, minority unfolds as an active virtue, meant to build up relationships."[16]

From a Franciscan view, when we find power, prestige, privilege, and position destroying our relationships we consider how we might turn to humility and poverty as solutions. "Franciscan minority today demands courageous choices for a more fraternal world."[17] As we assess the conflict in which we find ourselves we should determine the extent to which the factors of power, prestige, position, and privilege play a role. We may wish to assess the degree to which Franciscan poverty and humility might foster better relationships.

Scripture

Therefore, we are not discouraged; rather, although our outer self is wasting away, our inner self is being renewed day by day. For this momentary light affliction is producing for us an eternal weight of glory beyond all comparison, as we look not to what is seen but to what is unseen; for what is seen as transitory, but what is unseen is eternal. (2 Cor 4:16-18)

There are different kinds of spiritual gifts but the same Spirit; there are different forms of service but the same Lord; there are different workings but the same God who produces all of them in everyone. To each individual the manifestation of the Spirit is given for some benefit. To one is given through the Spirit the expression of wisdom; to another the expression of knowledge according to the same Spirit; to another faith by the same Spirit; to another gifts of healing by the one Spirit; to another mighty deeds; to another prophecy; to another discernment of spirits; to another varieties of tongues; to another interpretation of tongues. But one and the same Spirit produces all of these, distributing them individually to each person as he wishes. (1 Cor 12:4-11)

He said to them, "Is a lamp brought in to be placed under a bushel basket or under a bed, and not to be placed on a lampstand? For there is nothing hidden except to be made visible; nothing is secret except to come to light. Anyone who has ears to hear ought to hear." (Mk 4:21-23)

Attend to yourself and to your teaching; persevere in both tasks, for by doing so you will save both yourself and those who listen to you. (1 Tm 4:16)

CHAPTER THREE

Responses to Conflict

The mayor of Gubbio announced that he would send three of his best guards to find and slay the wolf that very afternoon.

At dusk the townspeople could hear shouts and clashing of metal from the woods. Then it was quiet. The guards had met the wolf.

Late in the night the only survivor of the encounter struggled into the anxious town and collapsed.

After he was revived, he told his tale of their fight with the fierce and powerful wolf.

Mediation Principles

IN THE LEGEND, the Mayor of Gubbio, faced with an ongoing threat, decided to dispatch three guards to attack and slay his adversary, the wolf. He may have assumed his decision was logical, or his decision to attack may have been the only option to which he gave any thought. In either case it was a response that led to failure. Lives were lost; the conflict escalated. The example of the mayor's failure hopefully inspires us to pause and consider the ways in which we typically respond to conflict.

In many instances the manner in which we respond may be unique to the situation; we may respond in a manner appropriate to the circumstances. However, on occasion we may respond without giving our decision much thought. We may respond in a knee-jerk manner, without reason; we may develop a habitual manner of greeting conflict, responding in the same manner regardless of the situation and in spite of previous failures.

Conflict often presses our buttons and triggers rote, patterned responses that prevent us from operating in the present moment. Emotional baggage from previous conflicts blurs our reason. In response we close our eyes and go for a ride, allowing events to unfold randomly. Eventually we consider the manner in which events transpire to be the inevitable and natural consequence of conflict. We fail to recognize the role unreasoned, stock responses play in the outcome; we fail to recognize our contribution to adverse results.

If we hope to resolve and manage conflict in an effective manner we need to become aware of our routine responses. If we are not in control, if we do not measure our response to the unique situation we face, we will encounter difficulty. Success requires agility and situational appropriateness but when we respond in a habitual manner lacking in flexibility. Thus, as we prepare for mediation it pays to assess who we become when faced with the stress of unresolved conflict.

This introspective task – becoming aware of our conscious and unconscious reactions to opposition, challenge, adversity, and stress – is critical to success. The introspective work that helps us identify how we respond when faced with conflict can be invaluable.

Your Personal Approach to Conflict

Though we cannot live life free from conflict we can learn to manage conflict. In order to successfully manage a conflict and guide events toward resolution and reconciliation, we start by discovering the ways in which we habitually cede conscious control to automatic, patterned, pre-programmed responses. For example, faced with opposition we may seek to control, dominate, coerce, or manipulate. Faced with even the slightest opposition we may act on a primal urge to defeat and crush the other party, literally or metaphorically. We may marshal all the power at our disposal in achieving that competitive goal.

Or we may strive to restore harmony at any cost: we may become subservient and deferential, banishing outward signs of opposition in attempts to appease or accommodate the other party. We may sacrifice personal needs or abandon our point of view in order to reduce conflict. In addition to competition and deferential accommodation our responses may include compromise; we may seek to "divide the pie." Or we may respond with avoidance, seeking escape from the situation.

We may become compulsive in our use of one or two of these approaches. For example, part of the time we may respond in a compromising manner, compulsively seeking to "divide by two," while on other occasions we retreat to an isolated mountain cabin, avoiding conflict by ducking all human interaction.

While most of us can arrive at a fairly accurate inventory of our habitual responses through introspection and a period of heightened observation, profile instruments have been developed to aid our self-assessment. One test instrument, based on a model developed by Kenneth Thomas, graphs responses to conflict on a grid that charts the value assigned to "concern for one's own interests" versus the value assigned to "concern for others' interests" (see fig. 3.1).[1] The grid provides a visual display of how we behave when faced with conflict. Locating ourselves on this grid helps us to anticipate how we will tend to react.[2]

If we are primarily concerned with satisfying our own needs and have little regard for satisfying the needs of the other party we may respond competitively, perhaps in a dominating, coercive, or manipulative manner. In contrast, if we are willing to sacrifice our interests in the pursuit of peace we may accommodate the needs of a more aggressive party. Our focus may turn to satisfying the other party's needs to the exclusion of our own.

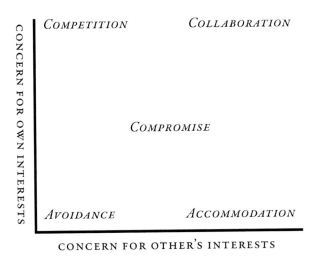

Fig. 3.1. Responses to Conflict

In the first case our test scores will fall high on the left side, signaling we greet conflict with an attitude of competition. In the second case our scores will fall to the bottom and far right portion of the scale, identifying accommodation as our common response.

In the daily drama of life we may "dance" with someone whose response pattern compliments our own. It is not uncommon to discover relationships that revolve around opposing tendencies. A competitive person who demands loyalty to the satisfaction of their needs might dance with an accommodating party who suppresses their own needs and focuses on satisfying other's needs. I mention this not to advocate such relationships but rather to point out how habitual dynamics can foster symbiotic relationships that may not be optimum for the individual.

Perhaps the most common response to conflict is avoidance. We abandon our needs *and* the needs of the other in an effort to circumvent a collision of interests. We decide it just isn't worth the fight.

At times this response is valid. There are times when the cost of conflict is perceived to be so extreme that the best solution appears to be avoiding the conflict and foregoing satisfaction of all interests. For example, two individuals may discover their views clash so intensely that they decide not to go into business together. While neither party will realize satisfaction of their business interests neither party will suffer from ongoing conflict.

Thus a party may choose to avoid conflict and forfeit their interests while also abandoning any effort to forward the satisfaction of the other party. There are times when avoidance is sane and consistent with the situation at hand.

Compromise is a middle path we choose when we are not prepared to abandon our interests *but* we are also not prepared to engage in the fight required to force the other party to abandon their interests. The solution involves each party abandoning a portion of their interests while also satisfying a portion. Each party accepts a limited defeat and enjoys a limited victory in order to avoid a struggle that will destroy all gains.

Though a party might optimistically consider a compromise to be half a win, more frequently we perceive a compromise to be a partial loss. We take half a loss rather than suffer a complete loss; we suffer but so does the other party. Compromise sits higher than avoidance on the scale measuring self-interest but compromise nonetheless retains the feel of avoidance. When we compromise we slide up the scale toward competition and we slide to the right on the scale toward accommodation. While we compete more than we avoid we also give up gain in order to avoid a full-tilt clash. Nonetheless, in many instances compromise is the best solution possible, particularly when dividing the pie makes sense.

As a rule, however, most mediators strive to surpass compromise and facilitate a collaborative process in which the interests of both parties are given maximum consideration. Collaboration takes us closer to satisfying our interests and closer to satisfying the interests of the other party by seeking creative solutions that provide maximal satisfaction to both parties.

The collaborative approach is not based on win-lose or divide-the-pie thinking but rather seeks to expand the pie through thorough analysis of interests and creative exploration of ways to satisfy those interests.[3] Parties who collaborate move to "the same side of the table" in problem-solving mode, seeking to find a solution that maximizes satisfaction.

We can use the Thomas grid to remind us of our choices. While collaboration may provide the greatest satisfaction in the majority of cases, each approach (avoidance, competition, accommodation, compromise, collaboration) is valid in specific situations. At times it may make sense to avoid a conflict: the situation may present great danger and little chance of satisfaction, which makes walking away a rational decision. Likewise, competition may be appropriate at times. For example, if the other party refuses invitations to collaborate, a competitive approach may be needed in order to educate them regarding the consequences of competition versus the advantages of collaboration.[4]

In a similar manner, there are instances when our interests are minor while the other party's potential satisfaction is so great that accommodation provides the greatest overall benefit. In such cases we benefit more from contributing to their considerable happiness than from satisfying our minor needs.

There are other times when we may sacrifice immediate interests to satisfy the demands of an ongoing relationship. We accommodate in the short term in order to maintain a long-term collaborative partnership. On other occasions we may not choose to collaborate because the process is time intensive and our needs are too minor to warrant such an expenditure of resources.

These examples highlight the fact that when another party opposes our interests a variety of appropriate responses are possible. Adhering to a single pattern in all situations is not optimum. Ideally we want to master the skill of employing a wide range of responses appropriately.

For example, if we compulsively avoid conflict our needs remain unmet but our relationships also suffer as we do not appear to care about the needs of the other party. Habitual competitiveness damages relationships and often motivates others to engage in reciprocal competitive behavior that results in conflict escalation. If we compulsively seek compromise we fail to discover creative approaches to maximizing satisfaction; not only do we leave potential benefit on the table, we force others to surrender benefit. A habitual pattern of compromise can lead to an uncomfortable feeling that our glass is perpetually half-empty. Accommodation, when habitual and unreasoned, may result in a loss of self-respect and a surfeit of unsatisfied interests. This may build unexpressed resentment that causes stress and illness or results in violence.

In the assessment section of this chapter you will be asked to note your habitual responses to conflict. One method to assess your habitual responses is filling out and scoring the aforementioned Thomas and Kilmann Conflict Mode Instrument. Once you have completed scoring the test, read the accompanying descriptions of responses to conflict provided by Thomas and Kilmann.[5] While this test will provide an excellent start to understanding how you handle conflict, paper-and-pencil instruments are limited so you will want to go further in your analysis using the *Taming the Wolf* prompts in the journal workbook.

Also, we behave with nuanced and changing styles within any one category (avoidance, competition, etc.). We compete, compromise, or avoid in different ways. At times we compete with charm while at other times we compete with brute force. We may have developed a smooth and affable manner of competing that makes it difficult to recognize how passionately and frequently we compete. It is not uncommon for us to have developed social graces that mask the intensity of competition. As we analyze our behavior and our feelings we may be surprised to discover just how devoted we are to winning.

Likewise, we may not have realized the extent to which our accommodation of others is not a function of being nice but an inability to honor our own needs. In studying our habitual responses to conflict we increase our self-awareness as well as our ability to respond effectively.

In your assessment, attempt to understand the nuanced ways you respond to conflict. Spend one week observing how you react to others who oppose your wishes or intentions. Take notes on your responses. Be mindful of responses that occur before you have had time to think. What are your habitual responses? Do you turn away in avoidance or nod with an accommodating manner? Do you bristle at a perceived challenge and quickly assume a competitive posture? Do you instinctively propose dividing the pie?

Pay close attention to stimuli that trigger particular responses. Certain settings may trigger habitual reactions or specific people (or types of people) may trigger reactions. For example, consider your typical responses to store clerks. While you may find your primary response is accommodation, you may respond to *younger* store clerks with a competitive demeanor. Or you may respond differently to women than men.

We all have unique sets of triggers that activate knee-jerk behavior. The task is to discover those habitual unreasoned responses. As you engage in this self-assessment you will greatly increase your ability to apply different styles of conflict management. This self-study will help you break habits and patterns that lead to failure.

Also spend a week observing how people around you respond to conflict. Observe a person who shrinks from conflict; observe someone who responds with belligerent competition; find a person who suggests a compromise at the slightest sign of a conflict; observe someone who draws others into collaboration. Note how your family, friends, and close associates respond when conflict arises. Does their approach trigger a particular response in you? Observe your common responses while observing how the other person responds: for example, observe how you react when the other person is competitive. Note thoughts that come to mind when you encounter someone who accommodates your needs: does accommodation provoke a desire to push your interests further or does it cause you to reciprocate?

When we assess motives, behaviors, and responses, we assess complex phenomena. Our purpose is not to reduce complex variables to simple answers or to reduce your life to the simplicity of a machine. The purpose of examining categories of responses is to provoke observation of the unique and complex stream of thoughts, behaviors, emotions, and feelings that make up your world during a conflict.

The Spiritual Response

An additional response to conflict not commonly mentioned in mediation literature is turning inward to summon the resources of the indwelling Spirit. In this response to conflict we retreat in contemplative prayer to consider the role played by the divine within.

We may contemplate establishing an "I and Thou" relationship with the other party.[6] The I-Thou collaborative dialogue is more profound than mundane collaboration as it calls on us to embrace the other with our eyes on the divine. It calls on us to bring a deeper and more authentic self to the table.

This response might be called *divine collaboration* as it calls on us to enter into a sacred relationship with "the other" who is created in the likeness of God.

This sacred endeavor is not contingent on the other's willingness to collaborate. Instead, in seeing the other as a brother or sister, whether or not the other considers they are a brother or sister, we become mindful of our interdependent nature. Ilia Delio, in *Franciscan Prayer*, captures the nature of this response: "contemplation is a penetrating gaze of the other and oneself – of the other, as the one in whom God is enfleshed, and of oneself, as one who is capable of union with God."[7]

When we greet the other in this manner our presence often creates a desire in the other to collaborate. When you recognize the divine in another they often recognize those same qualities in themselves. They find a spark of love or compassion, a stirring of empathy, a slight inclination to act in a brotherly or sisterly manner. In divine collaboration the concept of working on the same side of the table reaches new heights.

As you observe yourself in conflict situations become aware of your ability (or inability) to recognize the divine in the other. Pay special attention to moments when you observe a hardening of the heart—instants when your affinity for the other person plummets and you turn away, shutting them out.

When we harden our heart we objectify the other and fashion boundaries that establish separateness or otherness. We sever the spiritual connection that simultaneously transcends and penetrates material boundaries. This results in a precipitous drop in affinity and caring. The other becomes object. As the other person becomes solid, bounded, and wholly "out there" in our eyes, ironically, we feel ourselves becoming bounded and limited. These feelings of solidity, bondage, and limitation are symptoms of a hardening heart.

We also discover the opposite – times when we dissolve boundary and separateness, times when we pervade the space of the other with compassionate affinity that invites the immaterial embrace of the divine. Solidity gives way to lightness of being, our heart softens with love, we long to serve and uplift the other. Understanding arrives magically as our empathy and our understanding of the challenges the other party faces give birth to insights that defy words.

I am not speaking here of sympathy, the weighty emotion that can cause us to sink under the burden of shared adversity, but rather uplifting, compassionate empathy that acknowledges our divine nature and recognizes we will ultimately transcend all adversity. In such moments we embrace suffering and divinity simultaneously.

When we have mastered our response to conflict, when we become versed in greeting the other with the spirit of the divine, our ability to successfully manage conflict broadens. We become aware of "the difference between being passive peace lovers and being active peacemakers."[8] We embrace a sacred mission that calls on us to actively bring peace to the troubled. We find our reconciler's heart and follow the path to peace Francis walked.

As we become skilled at viewing our physiological, emotional, mental, and spiritual responses to conflict – such as hardening of the heart – we gain critical skill in managing our response to conflict.[9] This is a vital early step in our journey.

A Franciscan View

As we discuss the manner in which we greet conflict I am reminded of the phrase "the face of a Franciscan." In the face of Francis we find courage, devotion, honesty, and radical empathy. His contemplation of the suffering of Christ brought to his demeanor a vulnerability that was reflected in his gaze, a countenance that made it appear he was taking a long loving look at creation. When we follow Francis we aspire to greet others with the face of a Franciscan. We aspire to a presence that allows the other to see who they are as a divine creature.

We can surmise Francis did not attack conflict with abandon but rather would retreat to a hermitage cave for a period of solitude in which he would allow silence to become a foundation for peacemaking. I can imagine Francis preparing to assume the role of mediator by letting go and allowing silence to prepare him for a simple infusion of God's peace.

Thus, for Francis a retreat to the caves was not an avoidance of conflict but rather preparation for facilitating reconciliation. Francis did not remain long in hermitage but rather went out in the world as a mendicant friar to address the suffering of others. Silence served to remind him that he was a pilgrim in this world – and the most important aspect of his pilgrimage was relationship. Francis brought the contemplative world out of the retreat and into the everyday world. He applied the hard won fruits of solitude and contemplation to the realm of interpersonal relations. Thus it is that we find a contemplative heart shining through the face of a Franciscan.

When Francis advised friars to follow the Holy Spirit and his Holy manner of working he was instructing them to show the world the face of a Franciscan, to journey into the world as a pilgrim, in order to encourage, affirm, and revere individuals who were also on a pilgrimage in this world, their eyes turned toward the next.[10]

Scripture

Do you not know that the runners in the stadium all run in the race, but only one wins the prize? Run so as to win. Every athlete exercises discipline in every way. They do it to win a perishable crown, but we an imperishable one. Thus I do not run aimlessly; I do not fight as if I were shadow-boxing. No, I drive my body and train it, for fear that, after having preached to others, I myself should be disqualified. (1 Cor 9:24-27)

> *For I have said that they would gloat over me*
> *exult over me if I stumble.*
> *I am very near to falling;*
> *my wounds are with me always.*
> *I acknowledge my guilt*

and grieve over my sin.
My enemies live and grow strong,
those who hate me grow numerous fraudulently,
Repaying me evil for good,
accusing me for pursuing good. (Ps 38:17-21)

For godly sorrow produces a salutary repentance without regret, but worldly sorrow produces death. For behold what earnestness this godly sorrow has produced for you, as well as readiness for a defense, and indignation, and fear, and yearning, and zeal, and punishment. In every way you have shown yourselves to be innocent in the matter. (2 Cor 7:10-11)

There is no fear in love, but perfect love drives out fear because fear has to do with punishment, and so one who fears is not yet perfect in love. We love because he first loved us. If anyone says, "I love God," but hates his brother, he is a liar; for whoever does not love a brother whom he has seen cannot love God whom he has not seen. (1 Jn 4:18-20)

Wisdom is a better defense for the wise than ten princes in the city, yet there is no one on earth so just as to do good and never sin. Do not give your heart to every word that is spoken; you may hear your servant cursing you, for your heart knows that you have many times cursed others. (Eccl 7:19-22)

CHAPTER FOUR

Faulty Perceptions

Late in the night the only survivor of the encounter struggled into the anxious town and collapsed. After he was revived, he told his tale of their fight with the fierce and powerful wolf.

As the story rushed through town the wolf grew larger and more ferocious. Fear was in the eyes of everyone in Gubbio. Children were kept close by; weapons were at the ready and the defenses of the town were raised.

Mediation Principles

IN THE PREVIOUS CHAPTER we focused on assessing how we typically respond to conflict. We asked ourselves who we become when we are faced with challenges and opposition. In this chapter we explore our perception of the other person in the conflict, the antagonist in our drama.

As we prepare to deliver our narrative account of what happened we begin drafting a description of the villain who opposes us. While this character description may play well within our version of the story, if we wish to resolve the conflict we must verify the accuracy of our description. We must double-check our perceptions. We perform a reality check in which we unearth bias or error that taints our view of the other party.

Tainted Perceptions

In order to perceive reality clearly we must recognize the subjective or emotional factors that color and distort our perceptions. Otherwise, we run a real risk of remaining hopelessly locked in a conflict as a result of false assumptions or false perceptions.

Often, as we look back at prior conflicts we are haunted by regret. We recall the sickening feeling of knowing we have hurt another as a result of a rush to judgment that led us to act unwisely or unfairly. As much as we would like to avoid the truth we recognize our flawed perceptions led us to hurt another.

We may have assumed the other party harbored evil motives. We may have taken hostile action only to later discover our error. Sometimes we never discover the error but we live with uncertainty, unsure our aggressive actions were justified. If we are honest with ourselves we acknowledge those troubling incidents in our past. Reflecting on past errors, as unpleasant as that may be, helps us recognize how our perception of the other party may fuel conflict.

Perhaps for the first time since the conflict began we take time to assess the accuracy of our assumptions and perceptions. This requires not only an open-minded curiosity about the other's story but also a desire to assess the role our bias plays. It becomes clear that if our perceptions are heavily distorted we will not be able to listen accurately to the other party's story.

In the early stages of conflict resolution the mediator anticipates bias and poses questions that encourage a party to inspect their opinion of the opponent. Experience has taught the mediator an important lesson: if each party clings to radical misperceptions of the other party the process will come to a standstill. Thus, early in the process the mediator coaxes parties to explore and test their perceptions of their antagonist. The mediator guides parties through a reality check and listens closely to the narrative description of the adversary. Like a detective unraveling a mystery the mediator probes for supporting evidence.

If a mediator is not yet involved you will want to begin this reality check on your own. Though it is extremely difficult to overcome biased perception without assistance, you can begin the process of becoming more acutely aware of your perceptions.

During the actual mediation the mediator will attempt to remedy distortions that fuel conflict but at this early stage do not concentrate on changing your perceptions as much as correctly identifying them. Before we can change our views we first must identify those views. Like the author of a drama we must spend time polishing our description of the villain in our drama. The following sections address that task.

False Attributions

Attribution Theory argues that people interpret the behavior of others by making assumptions regarding their motives.[1] When we observe another's behavior we imagine the inner narrative unfolding in that person's mind. We craft a story that explains *why* they did what they did. Based on those assumptions we construct our master narrative – the story we draft to make sense of events in our life – and we include the motives and intentions we ascribe to our antagonist.

As though we are writing a novel or memoir we create an imagined stream of consciousness for the other person, an inner narrative explaining *their* behavior in a way that allows *our* story to hang together. From our point of view other people become characters in the drama that is our life.

Attribution Theory argues that when we assign causes we select from two categories: the first category contains *dispositional* causes such as character, attitudes, intentions; the second category consists of *situational* causes in which behavior is motivated by external circumstances.[2] We tend to attribute the behavior of others to dispositional factors such as their character or intentions, while we attribute our own behavior to situational factors. This brings about *false attribution error*,[3] a bias in which we end up incorrectly attributing motive or disposition to another.

For example, when a car swerves in front of us on the freeway forcing us to brake suddenly we likely assume the driver possesses a character flaw ("he is rude") and we assume his intention was to threaten our safety ("the fool was trying to kill us"). In our mind we were threatened by bad character and evil intention. On the other hand, when we swerve suddenly in front of another car we justify our behavior, assigning cause to situational factors such as lack of visibility, an imagined road hazard, or the poor handling qualities of our car. Or we simply admit we were distracted and claim it is human to err.

When parties assign blame they tend to excuse their behavior in the conflict as being forced on them by external circumstances beyond their control (situational causes) and they attribute the behavior of the other person to unworthy character or evil motives (dispositional causes). They grant themselves the benefit of a doubt based on an intimate knowledge of their subjective reality. They view their behavior in an understandable light, while seeing the behavior of the other party as arising out of evil motive or flawed character.

Stereotypes based on race, class, ethnicity, gender, age, and religion contribute to false attribution. The majority of people are not overtly prejudiced nor do they imagine they harbor prejudices, however, they often attribute the behavior of others to dispositional factors. When they script the other party's inner story – a story of disposition, character, and intention – stereotypes seep into the analysis. Partial truths bolster the imagined inner story we create.

For example, cultural stereotypes are frequently used for positive purposes when we prepare for important cross-cultural interactions, such as conducting business in another country. In such instances, we study the idiosyncrasies of the other culture in an effort to be conscientious and to understand what pleases a member of that culture. We attempt to understand the types of behavior they view as appropriate.

Such stereotypes have limited utility along with potential downside. Applied without caution and discernment they produce false attribution error in which a party, consciously or unconsciously, writes the other party's inner story using stereotypical assumptions.

The visiting executive assumes his counterpart from another culture will think or act in a certain fashion dictated by his culturally motivated character. While the assumptions may be correct in many situations, at other times they are wrong and possibly insulting because they neglect individual character and interests. In similar situations during conflict resolution we must consider the unique individual in front of us and use extraordinary caution when we construct an imagined inner story based on a *culturally appropriate* attribution of motives, intention, or character.

For example, a young woman may assume the older Caucasian male boss with whom she is in conflict clings blindly to extreme conservative values. She may assume he disapproves of the work she has done in organizing a generous contribution of company funds to a non-profit agency that provides aid to the poor in a third world country. When he calls her into his office to discuss her actions she fabricates a stream of consciousness narrative for the boss. In the story she imagines, he berates her for using company funds to assist those who show a lack of motivation in helping themselves.

Based on this anticipated story she steps forward with what she considers to be a heroic posture and launches into a tirade, attacking the boss and dismissing him as shallow, callous, and lacking in moral insight. The boss fires her on the spot. Only later does she discover the boss is a major contributor to an international agency that funds micro-loans for women starting businesses in developing countries. His complaint, which she never heard, was that she organized the contribution in a manner inconsistent with accepted accounting procedures.

As a result of false attribution she turned age, gender, and class stereotypes into a flawed inner narrative for the boss, a narrative that led to the termination of her employment. While this example assumes a significant lack of prior communication between the two adversaries it is not entirely unrealistic. Often there is poor communication in organizations and we operate largely on assumptions. We commit the same types of error, mostly in more subtle ways.

In most cases we do not recognize we are working on the basis of assumptions we have written into assumed inner narratives. We fail to be truly mindful of our internal storytelling. We assume our perception is aligned with reality "out there"; but often the reality we assume exists occurs only in our story. During conflict resolution we are forced to realize that reality also includes the other person's narrative. To the extent that we fail to leave the door open for the other party to enrich our version of reality we manufacture barriers to resolution.

False attributions can be difficult to detect and even tougher to correct as they tend to be on-the-fly assessments of the other party that settle into our consciousness. When a mediator first listens to a party's story of what happened she is wise to guard against uncritical acceptance of false attribution. I am constantly amazed at the degree to which the first account I hear leaves me convinced I have heard an incontrovertible truth. Then I listen to the second party who has an equally convincing and compelling account of events that contradicts the first account.

In both instances the party holds a rock-solid certainty regarding the facts of the case – from their point of view. These contrary accounts cannot both be factual, yet they are both true to the individual who experienced them. The mediator does not seek to adjudicate one reality over another but rather acknowledges the truth of both accounts, as seen from the perspective of each individual. The task the mediator faces is helping craft the narratives into an acceptable shared truth.

But rewriting is difficult. Once assigned, imagined character flaws and evil intentions become difficult to erase from our minds. We unconsciously search for evidence to verify the story we have created and we are usually able to cobble together sufficient supporting details to make our story work.

The challenge is to motivate parties to rewrite their narratives – to alter their narratives just enough to create a basis for the parties to co-author a new narrative of the future. In order to facilitate this delicate rewriting task a mediator may mimic Columbo, the disarming, beguilingly naïve, and deceptively inquisitive television detective played by Peter Falk. Playing the bumbling detective, the mediator poses slightly oblique but probing questions that inspire a party to view the opposing party as a mystery to be solved rather than as a cardboard character to be propped up.

Overcoming False Attributions

How do we check our assumptions regarding the other party's evil intentions? In some cases we falsely attribute evil intentions when such intentions do not exist. In other cases we assume evil intentions do not exist, when in fact they do. In the former case, we erect an arbitrary barrier. In the latter, we open a door to those who intend harm. It is possible to error in either direction.

As a result we run into a dichotomy between paranoia and self-destructive glibness, causing us to vacillate between unwarranted fear and hopeful naïveté. In the conflict resolution process we learn to discern between erroneously demonizing the other party and genuinely unmasking a demon. We approach the other party with healthy skepticism, as a mystery to be solved; we accept we might not know all there is to know about them. We enter the process with a healthy dose of curiosity, with a sense of discovery and openness to unexpected revelations.

In order to unravel the mystery of our antagonist we need a process that differentiates actual evil intentions from false attribution of evil. That process is mediation: a process in which parties revisit and re-examine events. A process of working through varying (and sometimes contradictory) accounts of what happened. A process of sharing explanations of why things happened the way they did – explanations that provide the missing inner story.

In mediation we overcome our inability to share views and concerns. We gather information about the other party and overcome the barrier of false attribution. A bridge is established that allows careful, gradual, and comprehensive exploration of each party's worldview. In response to our gentle probing, our antagonist fills in the blanks in our story. Then we share our story and fill in the blanks in their inner narrative.

When we listen to the other party's inner story we acquire the material needed to rewrite our master narrative, especially sections of the narrative we scripted about the other party. Likewise we take the opportunity to provide answers the other party will need in order to reconstruct their narrative account of our behavior from their perspective.

Initially we may be reticent to share our inner life, our motives, intentions, and feelings, but with experience we begin to understand the importance of co-authoring a new narrative with our antagonist. In some cases, even while we still doubt that we will achieve a positive resolution, we begin to take an interest in knowing all that we can about the other party, so that even in the face of an adverse outcome we can better understand what happened.

Emotional Subjectivity

Our subjective world is colored by emotions; we see the world through emotional lenses. Our moods and temperament orchestrate the drama that is our life. In recent times objective truth based on material facts has become honored as an ideal, often causing us to dismiss our subjective awareness and our feelings as unreliably emotional. For some, emotions have taken on a negative connotation. Emotions are considered an arbitrary variable that foils our best rational intentions.

The elevation of the objective to sanctified status, however, lacks merit. The assumption that the objective trumps subjective awareness creates distorted expectations, as *all* events are observed through the filter of consciousness. It is impossible for us to truly know the objective world, as our only window on the world is exclusively subjective. For all we know there is no objective world that stands separate from and independent of our conscious awareness.

At a fundamental level what we call reality turns out to be a function of our subjective awareness. We cannot divorce objective reality from our subjective perceptions as though objective reality stands as an absolute that can be known. Rather, that which we call objective is actually inter-subjective; what we call objective is that which we can observe (subjectively) in unison.

My conscious subjective observation and your conscious subjective observation come together to form an inter-subjective agreement. We reach subjective agreement regarding the nature of that which we view. When we seek the objective we actually come together to perform a subjective reality check. This lends validity to the dynamic process of bringing parties together to craft a common narrative, for that process is ultimately the way we manufacture reality.

Thus, conflict resolution does not call for us to banish subjectivity but rather to understand the subjective lenses through which we view life and to work to correct distortions. Rather than shun emotions and subjectivity we embrace them as elements of the collaborative process.

Mediators realize emotional subjectivity plays a central role in the conflict and that no conflict is devoid of emotional factors. They realize destructive emotions play a critical role in conflict. The authors of *Difficult Conversations* note, "Each side must have their feelings *acknowledged* ... Acknowledgment is a step that simply cannot be skipped."[4] We cannot proceed to the problem-solving stage of the process while feelings remain unacknowledged.

One reason acknowledgment is vital is that feelings are strongly tied to our view of reality. When we do not acknowledge our opponent's feelings we imply our opponent is not lined up with reality. In denying our opponent's feelings we refuse to ratify that which is real for them. In response they shut down and refuse to move ahead.

An acknowledgment does not necessarily mean we *agree* with their reality but it does say we *recognize* what constitutes reality *for them*. When we listen and inquire into their perspectives we send a signal that we are not out to undermine their sense of what is real. Instead, we signal that we sincerely want to know how they have come to see the world as they do. Later in the process we may collaboratively rewrite the shared narrative account of reality but first we must signal that we recognize the existing reality in which they live.

Destructive Emotions

As we unravel feelings related to the conflict we usually discover the primary destructive emotion at work is fear. We then face the daunting challenge of defining and describing our fear, an emotion that usually serves to protect us from experiencing adverse consequences. Our fear typically protects us from danger but now we are being asked to sit with our fear. This typically causes discomfort.

When it comes to handling fear a mediator often asks us to engage in moments of mindfulness, periods of self-awareness. Rather than dismiss or avoid fear and its discomfort we embrace fear as a window on the conflict. With the mediator facilitating the process we gaze through this emotional window and begin, perhaps for the first time, to understand the struggle in which we are engaged.

As we explore the nature of fear we find it usually reflects our desire to avoid adverse consequences. Following this logic we ask ourselves what adverse consequences cause us concern. Consequences might include failing to procure something we desire, losing something we value dearly, or being forced to endure pain. Adverse consequences often involve loss of physical possessions, loss of one's body, of Face, of freedom. The be/do/have model we used earlier highlights consequences over which we commonly worry. In our assessment we identify the fears and adverse consequences at work.

When we scrutinize our perceptions of our antagonist we identify fears regarding what they will do to us. What consequences will they inflict on us if we do not act as they wish or as they demand? What harm will they make us suffer? What things that we hold dear will they take from us? What abhorrent conditions will they force upon us?

As our view of the opposing party can be expressed in terms of adverse consequences, exploring the consequences we wish to avoid clarifies our vision of the person with whom we are in conflict. Our fears define our antagonist. He or she is the character in our drama who will render us bankrupt, remove us from our job, take custody of our children, or cause us to suffer physical pain.

Two additional primary destructive emotions are anger and rage. With fear we anticipate consequences we will suffer at the hands of another, with anger and rage we anticipate adverse consequences we intend to exact on another. Fear speaks to how we will be harmed; anger and rage speak to how we will deliver harm. Just as we assessed fear we now assess the conditions that trigger anger or rage. When we move behind the curtain of blinding emotion what do we find? What does the wolf look like?

In our earlier discussion we established the idea that conflict arises from two opposing forces hopelessly locked together. Conditions have arisen in which we cannot or will not turn away and the other party cannot or will not turn away. Neither party will cease their attempts to move in a direction that opposes the motion of the other party. When we find ourselves locked in this oppositional embrace from which we are unable to escape it appears there is nothing left for us to do but rid ourselves of the other person, using violent means if necessary. The oppositional embrace generates a need-to-destroy that manifests as anger and rage.

A common though perhaps trivial example is the young child who sets his sights on going outside to play despite his unfinished dinner. His mother blocks his path and the oppositional embrace takes shape. The child, in his own mind, is unable to retreat yet his path is blocked. As a result of two opposing intentions colliding (and releasing emotion) he explodes into a tantrum. The more he fights the more resolute his mother becomes in opposition.

From a distance we recognize both parties have options: there are other ways they can handle the situation and in most cases, as the child matures and the parent gains experience, they find other ways of meeting their needs. As an example, however, this scenario illustrates a mild instance in which parties become locked in an oppositional embrace. Feeling stopped generates negative emotion that turns to rage. In extreme cases destruction of the other party takes precedence over our own survival. When we describe how we perceive the other party we can uncover the factors that trigger our destructive instincts; we learn to identify the forces that lock us in opposition.

Negative Emotions Hamper Reconciliation

Fear motivates *wall building* – we build walls to protect ourselves. Anger and rage motivate us to build walls that keep us in; we build walls that restrain us from acting out our hostile intentions. As we review the history of destructive emotions that have arisen during a conflict we discover the walls we have built to protect ourselves from others and we discover the walls we have built to protect others from us. Previously, we may not have fully understood the ways we protect ourselves; our defenses may have been invisible to us.

While being without walls can be dangerous when a real threat exists an equal danger exists in building walls that trap us within. We build defenses to repel intruders but those defenses leave us secluded and disconnected. We build walls the other party must destroy in order to reach us, while the other party builds walls we must destroy in order to reach them. The walls become impediments to relationship and they close down emotional rapport; they enforce separation.

When we are locked in conflict and cut off from relationship frustration builds. A desire to knock down the other party's walls surfaces. We want them to be able to see us, to hear us, to know we exist, to know we have needs, to know we suffer. The other party's defenses, paradoxically, become an affront to us that provokes our attack – the exact outcome the wall was constructed to prevent. When our needs are frustrated we vow to tear down the wall with force. Our attack threatens the other party who responds by reinforcing their defenses.

In the continuing cycle of attack-and-defend that leads to ongoing construction of defensive walls, those walls keep us apart, prevent resolution, and result in conflict escalation. Careful analysis allows us to begin to grasp how our defenses provoke attacks by the other party, and how those attacks motivate us to construct additional defenses. A rational approach calls for balance: we build walls needed for safety and destroy walls that serve no purpose. As we enter into conflict resolution we find a dual need to assess required defenses while removing barricades that prevent establishment of relationship and communication. If we are to reconcile we must build bridges rather than walls.

The mediator, working with the parties, facilitates the transformation of walls into bridges, finding creative and unique ways to dismantle defenses. We do not tear down all protections and leave ourselves completely exposed. Rather, we collaborate with the other party in identifying and removing walls that block a resolution that would benefit both parties. A twofold operation takes place: mediation guidelines maintain safety while increased communication brings parties closer together. The parties take measured steps toward each other while their safety, physical and emotional, is insured by process guidelines.

Scarcity Creates Conflict

A special case of false attribution arises in situations of real or imagined scarcity. A fear that others will seize the scarce goods we need colors our perceptions, resulting in a zero sum game: another's win is seen as our loss. When we perceive or fear scarcity we see others as potential enemies. We become compulsively jealous and possessive. We cling and hoard. We engage in conflict behavior.

Social Darwinism, an insidious philosophy based on a view of scarcity that postulated a fierce struggle for "survival of the fittest," is a philosophical, political, and economic model that pits each individual against all others, promoting an extreme win-lose view of the world. The carnage of the last century provides evidence of the harm such a philosophy of scarcity unleashes. When we become more acutely aware of human interdependence we tend to seek more positive and compassionate views of life.

The pressing need for global civilization to find a better path through our collective desert of hate, envy, and war – a need St. Francis envisioned centuries ago – demands a more enlightened philosophy and wider recognition within society of conflict resolution principles.

When Ian Morgan Cron compared the age in which Francis lived with the age in which we live, he concluded one remedy for today's social ills is the promulgation of Franciscan theology that can guide us in our effort to live in compassionate relationship with one another.[5] In Francis we find a charismatic saint who refused to accept the idea that scarcity was an inevitable cause of irremediable strife. Instead he saw scarcity as a call to compassionate action.

At the same time he recognized and celebrated the bounty of Divine creation, Francis recognized and combated mankind's tendency toward clinging and attachment. He was acutely aware of the role that imagined and real scarcity played in conflict. It is no coincidence that he was known as a peacemaker and, at the same time, chose a life of poverty as a way to teach the pitfalls of clinging and attachment. For Francis the solution to conflict over scarcity was to always place relationship first; in concentrating on loving and compassionate relationships we find the solutions to scarcity, especially imagined or manufactured scarcity.

When the problem of scarcity arises within the conflict resolution process the mediator assists parties in their investigation of whether or not the perceived scarcity is real or apparent, authentic or manufactured. Parties often come to the table with a *fixed-pie* view of the world based on an apparent scarcity. With the help of a mediator they learn to expand the pie in a way that utilizes scarce resources to meet everyone's needs.[6]

In many conflicts there has been a lack of creativity in the utilization of resources; in other instances false scarcity must be unmasked. In some cases philosophies such as Social Darwinism promote views that fix attention on scarcity and create false anxiety that leads to conflict over imagined or manufactured scarcity. As we analyze conflict we need to assess our assumptions and perceptions regarding scarcity.

Catharsis

At the outset of mediation it is not uncommon to find parties locked up emotionally, hesitant to unleash negative emotions. They harbor a fear that the other party will express negative emotions that will cause them discomfort. As a result, an unnatural truce takes place in which the parties decline to engage honestly with one another. They tacitly agree to keep their feelings bottled up and proceed as though it were possible to skirt difficult emotions and move directly to rational problem solving.

The unexpressed emotions, however, typically slow or stall the process and alter perceptions. A party cannot view the other party accurately through a filter of unsettled emotion; distortion is the inevitable result. False attributions emerging from unacknowledged negative emotion prevent problem solving.

For this reason, mediators recognize it is vital to encourage a party to release pent-up emotions in a controlled manner. However, they may encounter continuing apprehension. Parties may worry the release of negative emotions will produce discomfort and ruin the relationship or even instigate violence. A double bind emerges. In the absence of emotional release the parties will not move forward, yet they resist emotional release as they fear the result will be unpleasant.

At this point we seek creative ways of purging the negative emotions of anger, rage, jealousy, and fear. We seek catharsis – the cleansing of troublesome emotion – without provoking overt hostility or violence. Mediation seeks to transform negative emotions from impediments into materials used to build bridges. The mediator attempts to turn lead into gold.

Often this undertaking is accomplished in private sessions during which the mediator serves as a safe and empathetic listener able to field negative emotions without responding reactively. In such settings the process of unearthing, purging, and transforming negative emotions is facilitated. In *Difficult Conversations* this aspect of conflict resolution is called the "feelings conversation."[7]

When we engage difficult emotions it is important to keep in mind that mediation is *not* therapy, yet it *is* therapeutic. On the other hand there is a tendency in our culture to sequester emotional discourse as though it were pathology to be addressed exclusively by a mental health professional. Emotions that come to view in conflict resolution, however, are not signs of pathology but rather a natural component of a healthy life. The authors of *Difficult Conversations* note, "The problem is that when feelings are at the heart of what's going on, they *are* the business at hand and ignoring them is nearly impossible."[8] When we come into conflict with another person destructive emotions will be present – it is part of the conflict landscape.

Perhaps one reason we find conflict resolution so difficult is that we find negative emotions difficult – we have become less adept at managing destructive emotions. Because of this failure to manage our emotions we tend to arrive at false perceptions of others and are prone to false attribution. The mediator guides parties through these emotional challenges; nonetheless, a party has an obligation to begin work on managing destructive emotions on their own *prior* to mediation.

The scope of emotional catharsis experienced upon release of destructive emotions increases significantly when the process includes spiritual transformation. When we approach conflict as an opportunity for spiritual transformation we address emotions and their origins at the deepest level. Our focus shifts to the very nature of emotions and our ability to feel not only our own distress and suffering but also the suffering of others. The manner in which emotions define relationships with others and a relationship with the divine rises to the foreground in our contemplation. Focus shifts from mere release of negative emotions to a deep understanding of their nature and origin and our vulnerability to their power.

Francis provided one model for such a transformation – his intense and devoted contemplation of Christ suffering on the cross transformed him into a saint revered for his loving embrace of others, even lepers who previously caused him revulsion and fear. His approach offers a glimpse at one possible solution to the dilemma.

When Francis contemplated the broken and suffering Christ he came to know in a profound manner the horrible consequences we can exact upon another. He may have found peace in knowing that although he was also subject to adverse consequences heaped on him by his fellow man, the Resurrection places those consequences in proper perspective. Francis ceased attachment to that which was transient and fleeting in order to embrace that which was everlasting and supreme – his relationship with the Divine.

Francis followed this contemplative path to inner peace and gained an ability to greet others with unconditional love. Along the way he lost his fear of being stripped of possessions; in fact, he greeted poverty with open arms. He lost his fear of losing status; he embraced humility. He embraced those who might hurt him rather than brandishing a curled fist. Letting go of fear, anger, rage, and self-pity, he opened doors to loving-kindness.

When he managed his emotions he came to see others in a more profoundly accurate light – he saw them as creatures endowed with a divine nature. His was not a naïve or trivial path: Franciscan brothers were martyred, facing mortal danger with the open arms of love. Francis' example may not be something we can achieve or even something to which we can aspire. However, understanding his life may help us modify our views.

His example may motivate us to release destructive emotions – fear, anger, rage, and self-pity. When we gain insight into our emotions as Francis did we begin to imagine what it would be like to love our enemies. The tendency to demonize the other party with false attributions gives way to empathy that inspires us to be open to understanding our opponent's inner narrative. We might even ask ourselves how the divine might speak to our heart through the other party's story.

At this stage in the conflict resolution process it is too early to call on a party to summon unconditional love, nonetheless, Christ's teaching is mentioned in order to foreshadow our destination once we have released our clinging to destructive emotions and cleared away obfuscations that alter our view of the other.

Confronting Evil

In order to approach conflict resolution with steady poise and a clear eye we must be certain of our ability to confront and transform evil. When we are called upon to confront evil we often experience an overwhelming desire to run, to escape through avoidance. Contemplative or spiritually transformative mediation provides the advantage of tapping into the resources of the indwelling Spirit and when spiritual resources – reflection, contemplation, and prayer – are brought to bear on conflict, they shore up our ability to confront evil. As we experience spiritual transformation we discover new strength and a newfound willingness to face adversity.

Frequently, however, we vacillate when it comes to the opposition: are they actually evil or is our fear of evil clouding our impressions? This uncertainty exacerbates conflict and delays resolution. We seem unable to cut through our antagonist's smokescreens, unable to hurdle their defenses, and at the same time we feel unable to plumb the depths of our own misperceptions. We stumble into shadowy terrain that defeats clarity and certainty.

While it makes sense to move closer to the wolf where we can make a more informed evaluation we do not consider the move worth the added danger. Attributing evil to the other person becomes a strategic (though often unconscious) decision. We settle on a "safe" solution: we attack the other party and protect ourselves. Fear of evil muddies our perception and the wolf grows ferocious in our mind's eye. It becomes "obvious" that we should not risk being hurt or defeated. Therefore, survival instincts trump caution – we decide it is better to actively protect against possible evil than risk lowering our guard.

While we may know mediation has been designed to overcome the challenge of fear-driven reactions, we might not possess the courage or clarity of mind to engage in mediation. Though conflict resolution tools exist we may fear using them. When we encounter this dilemma, spiritual resources can make a significant difference, giving us the courage to embrace the other person and confront evil (should that turn out to be the actual situation).

Paradoxically when we no longer doubt our ability to confront evil we frequently discover we have falsely attributed evil where none exists. We discover our fear of evil has morphed mere shadows into a threatening reality. Once we engage in mediation we slow the process down to take a closer look at our fears, gaining the reward of additional clarity that comes with integrating spiritual resources into the process.

The residents of Gubbio had good reason to be afraid: the wolf had killed family and friends. The destructive emotion of fear that arose out of their suffering prevented the townspeople from analyzing all options. Though fear was justified it generated a destructive response that failed to improve the situation. Though the wolf had killed, a closer investigation of the type Francis was about to undertake would reveal the citizens of Gubbio were not dealing with actual evil but rather they were dealing with fear and anger that prompted new attempts to kill the wolf.

It took a saint employing spiritual resources to change the dynamic. Francis' mediation between the wolf and Gubbio took place in the external world as do most of our conflicts but, at the same time, we can imagine a spiritual force at work mediating and transforming inner worlds, bringing about change. When conflict obscures awareness and perceptions and hardens hearts it is often the subtle inner changes, such as the movement of the Holy Spirit that moves us past the barrier of fear of evil.

Understanding Why We See the Other as We Do

What perceptions of the other person fuel fear, anger, jealousy, suspicion, and hatred? To break the cycle of escalation we need to be aware of factors that cause us to target the other as evil. Self-analysis prompts in the journal workbook explore why we see the other as we do and motivate us to check our perceptions for accuracy.

The spiritually transformative party places an emphasis on self-assessment, self-analysis, and contemplation as tools used to monitor perceptual distortion that prevents us from seeing the other party as they actually are. When we recognize we are hauling emotional and perceptual baggage we begin to appreciate the value of contemplative prayer or mindfulness as practices that provide the strength necessary to overcome fear, anger, rage, and other destructive emotions.

A Franciscan View

As we discuss perceptions colored or distorted by emotion we are reminded that Francis honored the divine essence of all creatures. In other people he perceived the potential for heaven to come to earth. When Francis looked at another person the power of the Holy Spirit inspired him to peer beneath the surface and penetrate the false images of mundane identity. He pierced through stereotypes to draw out the best in those he met.

Francis instructed his Brothers to follow the Holy Spirit and His holy manner of working. It is safe to assume he realized in his own heart that it was the Holy Spirit of Pentecost that enabled him to probe beneath the surface and behold the human heart, the home of God. In *Franciscan Prayer*, Ilia Delio references St. Bonaventure on this topic: "We cannot love the God we cannot see unless we love the God we see within ourselves and in others. The more we are able to find God within ourselves, the more we can find God outside ourselves."[9]

Francis knew well the sting of false attributions: he was accused of being a fanatic, of being deluded, of being a naïve man. From his point of view, however, he was not deluded or a fanatic but rather realized that he could not be free until he held nothing back from the fire of God's love. As a result he entered into the Abyss of Love in his experience on Mt. La Verna where he was granted the imprint of the sacred Wounds of Jesus.[10]

The qualities that others attributed to Francis differed greatly from the inner reality Francis experienced. These false attributions failed to capture the life he lived. We can imagine how difficult it would be for an outsider to write the inner narrative of a man like St. Francis. They would be forced to imagine an inner state with which they had little or no experience. Francis became acutely aware of this problem of bias and prejudice and as a result taught the Brothers to be tolerant and forgiving in all their relations with others.

When destructive emotions made an appearance Francis was there to instruct the friars. He would turn to Scripture and encourage the friars not to lose hope. Delio captures this dynamic, "... when we allow the Word to take root within us through prayer and the indwelling of the Spirit then we bring the Word to life. In Francis' view, nothing is to hinder us from this vocation nor should we desire anything else."[11] Francis knew firsthand that there was a way to be lifted up beyond the destructive weaknesses of the human heart and this made him an effective peacemaker.

We can imagine that when Francis looked upon the citizens of Gubbio he recognized their need for safety and protection. He felt their loss and grieved. But then he was energized to do the unthinkable – to pay a visit to the perpetrator. Perhaps he intuited that understanding the pain of our worst enemy allows us to embrace them. Francis' boldness could certainly be seen in his resolute decision to accept personal risk by seeking out the wolf. Francis went forth to meet the wolf believing The Holy Spirit possessed the power to transform fear into courage.

Scripture

Rid yourselves of all malice and all deceit, insincerity, envy, and all slander; like newborn infants, long for pure spiritual milk so that through it you may grow into salvation, for you have tasted that the Lord is good. (1 Pt 2:1-3)

He said to them, "Why are you terrified, O you of little faith?" Then he got up, rebuked the winds and the sea, and there was great calm. The men were amazed and said, "What sort of man is this, whom even the winds and the sea obey?" (Mt 8:26-27)

"Therefore do not be afraid of them. Nothing is concealed that will not be revealed, nor secret that will not be known. What I say to you in the darkness, speak in the light; what you hear whispered, proclaim on the housetops. And do

not be afraid of those who kill the body but cannot kill the soul; rather, be afraid of the one who can destroy both soul and body in Gehenna." (Mt 10:26-28)

"When they take you before synagogues and before rulers and authorities, do not worry about how or what your defense will be or about what you are to say. For the holy Spirit will teach you at that moment what you should say." (Lk 12:11-12)

Since you have purified yourselves by obedience to the truth for sincere mutual love, love one another intensely from a [pure] heart. You have been born anew, not from perishable but from imperishable seed, through the living and abiding word of God . . . (1 Pt 1:22-23)

> *Even though I walk through the valley of the shadow of death*
>   *I will fear no evil, for you are with me;*
>   *your rod and your staff comfort me.*
> *You set a table before me*
>   *in front of my enemies*
> *You anoint my head with oil;*
>   *my cup overflows.*
> *Indeed, goodness and mercy will pursue me*
>   *all the days of my life;*
> *I will dwell in the house of the* Lord
>   *for endless days.* (Ps 23:4-6)

CHAPTER FIVE

Conflict Resolution Options

The mayor consulted with his advisors and decided to inquire if Francis of Assisi could help them. They had heard that he could talk to animals and that God talked to him.

Mediation Principles

IN PREVIOUS CHAPTERS we began to assess the nature of the conflict. We examined our typical responses and detected patterns in our behavior that may need to change. We also considered emotional and perceptual factors that color our view of the other party with whom we are in conflict. The idea that we might need to call on the assistance of a mediator was mentioned but up to this point we handled preliminary tasks on our own.

In the legend we find the Mayor of Gubbio dispatching messengers to solicit the assistance of Francis of Assisi. In our personal situation we also may have begun to consider whether or not we might benefit from the help of an impartial intermediary. We might be asking if this is the appropriate time to seek assistance in reaching resolution and reconciliation. At the same time we might wonder if mediation is the correct approach for our unique conflict. In this chapter we address these questions by surveying dispute resolution processes that might be appropriate for our situation.

Conflict Resolution Approaches

Mediation is the primary approach considered in *Taming the Wolf* but it is only one option along a continuum (see fig. 5.1). You will want to remain aware of all the available options, as you may need to resort to other methods before mediation can be convened. Or, if mediation is unsuccessful, you may need to resort to an alternative.

The diagram below identifies the major conflict resolution approaches. It is worth noting you can combine approaches to create a hybrid. For example, you can blend mediation and arbitration to create "med-arb" in which a portion of the conflict is resolved through mediation while other issues are resolved using arbitration.

CONFLICT RESOLUTON APPROACHES

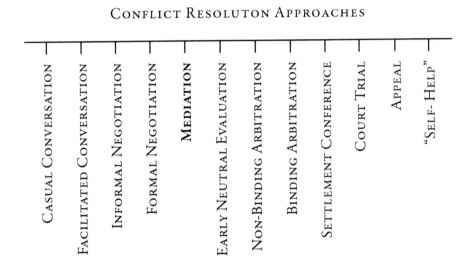

Fig. 5.1. Conflict Resolution Approaches

Mediation appears near the center of the continuum, while less formal approaches appear to the left and more formal approaches appear to the right. One reason mediation produces the highest level of party satisfaction is that it is the most flexible approach, blending informal and formal techniques.

While a party embroiled in conflict might move from left to right along the continuum, engaging more and more formal approaches as the conflict escalates, it is also common for a party to arrive at mediation after attempting processes on the right side of the continuum. For example, a party may file a lawsuit but before the trial commences a judge may suggest they attempt to resolve their dispute through mediation. You may move along the continuum in response to unfolding circumstances or you may plan resolution efforts according to your skills and preferences. The important concept to keep in mind is that the continuum offers flexibility.

Casual conversation is frequently employed to resolve disputes in their early stages, particularly by parties who enjoy a close relationship. Heart-to-heart discussion may take place over tea or coffee as two or more individuals address mutual problems and clear the air through give-and-take dialogue. The use of informal dialogue presupposes a low level of conflict escalation and the existence of a modestly good relationship.

This option also presupposes participants possess skill in discussing difficult topics, as not everyone possesses the aptitude required to carry on a dispute resolution conversation.[1] For people naturally skilled in conversation this approach may be so commonplace that they do not fully recognize they are engaged in conflict resolution.

However, when we lack the expertise required to converse in a non-threatening manner we become acutely aware of the difficulty of the task. We recognize there is a risk that we will escalate the conflict. For example, poorly worded or insensitive phrasing may inadvertently cause unintended insult, innocent comments may press buttons and threaten the other party. Thus, while some people enjoy an innate or a learned sense of managing conversations and easily demonstrate tact and empathy, others find that such conversations, almost without fail, make things worse.

Two solutions are possible: we can learn the skills needed or we can employ a third-party neutral to facilitate the conversation – which takes us to the second category: *facilitated conversation*. The facilitator may be a friend, relative, or trusted colleague, or may be a professional who assists individuals and groups to improve communication, guiding them over rough patches in interpersonal and business relationships.

Professional facilitators, for example, assist poorly functioning organizations in transforming the way they handle communications, the way they manage decision-making, and the way they achieve consensus. In the role of coach or trainer they assist members in improving relationship skills and encourage group members to become mindful of their personal responsibility for preventing escalation of conflict in the normal course of business.

When friends or relatives facilitate a conversation they may not bring professional skills to the intervention but by virtue of their close ties and common history they may augment the level of affinity, which sometimes can be all that is needed to resolve an emerging conflict. By increasing the caring and trust at the table they create ambient good will and optimism. This elevates the conversation to a more amicable tone than would be possible when the parties, who are disturbed or concerned over differences, try to facilitate their own conversation.

A special style of facilitated conversation is the *learning conversation*, which is typically used when factions of larger groups harbor divergent views on social or cultural issues. In the learning conversation a carefully designed process allows contentious coalitions to listen, perhaps for the first time, as their adversaries speak from a personal viewpoint. Each party expresses how they have come to their views and why those views are important to them. In the learning conversation formal presentations highlighting salient issues can accompany face-to-face conversation.

The goal of a learning conversation is not to alter the views and values of participants but rather to allow them to move beyond demonization of each other. The learning conversation fosters dialogue that may eventually result in identification of common interests or shared concerns, which become a point of departure for future discussion. While the substantive content of the conflict does play a role in the conversation, over time the focus shifts from debating positions toward a shared concern for the relationship.

In the learning conversation the facilitator gently directs the conversation away from abstract concepts and toward individual narratives and life stories that reveal how each party has come to their worldview. The result is increased acceptance of diversity and new appreciation for the core values of inclusivity and plurality. A shift from contentious debate to heartfelt empathy is the goal. One seeks to nurture the realization that peaceful coexistence is possible only when one has nurtured mutual respect and touched the heart of the other party.

The next option along the continuum, *informal negotiation*, is similar to conversation but involves an increased focus on problem solving. In conversation we express feelings and re-establish relationship. In negotiation we plan for the future: we agree on how we will address contentious issues when they arise in the future and/or we agree on a plan for making up for past damages.

Negotiations can take place face-to-face in an informal setting or can transition to *formal negotiation* in which a lawyer (or other professional negotiator) represents our interests. Formal negotiation is appropriate when the matter warrants careful consideration of existing law, for example, when it is necessary to negotiate a contract with detailed legal provisions. A mix of informal and formal negotiation may take place with the parties moving back and forth between the two approaches.

If negotiation breaks down parties move to the next step on the continuum, *mediation*. In this approach a trained third party facilitates negotiation, resolution, and reconciliation, assisting parties as they identify issues and interests and overcome impediments and barriers. Mediation is a flexible process that addresses issues related to relationship, identity, and psychological or emotional well being, as well as issues related to contractual agreements, civil rights, liability and damages, or other legal concerns.

When mediation takes place within the litigation context parties typically retain counsel and meet with the mediator accompanied by their attorneys. In such instances negotiation often begins with attorneys introducing the issues followed by an increase in party participation. As the process advances each party is encouraged to take a more active role while the attorney supports their efforts. The process often begins as a lawyer-to-lawyer negotiation and evolves into a party-to-party negotiation with each party becoming increasingly collaborative while attorneys provide legal expertise needed to formalize the resulting agreements.

In other instances parties may negotiate with one another with the help of the mediator and then turn to their lawyers when it is time to formalize and draft agreements. While negotiation of issues related to substance plays a central role in mediation, in my experience a re-negotiation of the relationship is just as important. In other words, the manner in which parties have treated one another comes to the fore as a central issue. All too often the real dispute is not about the substantive issue being negotiated but rather about the insult, slight, or disrespect that was perceived to have taken place.

Mediation is not confined to the litigation context though I will often refer to mediation in the litigation setting, as litigation is representative of adversarial processes in general. Mediation can be used in any conflict situation that requires a structured yet flexible approach to achieving resolution and reconciliation.

Mediators facilitate conflict resolution in a wide variety of venues from neighborhood justice centers to centers of world power where conflicts between nations are resolved. Large businesses or organizations, such as universities, employ mediators for the purpose of resolving in-house conflicts. Non-governmental organizations (NGO's) may retain staff to mediate conflicts within populations they serve. Religious leaders often play a role in peacemaking that takes place in mediation style interventions.

Thus I use the term mediator loosely to apply to all who mediate conflicts, realizing they may operate under different titles in different venues – titles such as conciliator, ombudsperson, reconciler, diplomat. *Mediation* and *mediator* are terms that encompass a broad range of activity best described as facilitating negotiation between opposing parties for the purpose of resolving a conflict and/or reconciling a relationship.

Mediation excels in combining informal and formal approaches for handling both substantive and psychological issues in a dynamic process that delves into the underlying causes of conflict at a deeper level than most other processes. For example, a court trial rarely allows for discussion of the interpersonal issues simmering beneath the surface. When issues regarding substance are merely a proxy for relationship problems a trial fails to bring about reconciliation. On the other hand, less formal processes often fail to offer the guidance required for the parties to negotiate complicated deal points. Mediation excels in addressing both relationship and substance. This flexibility allows mediation to significantly increase the opportunity for true reconciliation.

However, if mediation hits an impasse and parties are unable to achieve a collaborative agreement, they have the freedom to end the process without penalty and seek a third-party decision that resolves the conflict. In other words, they can relinquish self-determinism and rely on an outside ruling. In this transition – from a process that aims for a self-determined outcome to a process that relies on an outside decision – parties agree to place their future in the hands of an arbitrator, judge, elder, official, senior executive, or a jury. There is no significant downside in attempting to mediate: if mediation fails the parties can switch to a different process.

The first step in allowing a third party to adjudicate the outcome may be seeking preliminary information about the likely decision an outsider might render. This analysis of likely outcomes can be accomplished using *early neutral evaluation* (ENE) or *non-binding arbitration*.[2]

In ENE a lawyer or a retired judge listens to and/or reads a summary of the case and advises the parties on the most likely outcome if the case were to go to trial. Early neutral evaluators provide parties with reasoned opinions regarding the potential ruling of a judge or jury. The evaluator cannot promise his prognostication is infallible as trial outcomes are difficult if not impossible to predict. However, he can offer an educated guess based on extensive experience.

The ENE provides the party with a snapshot of how their case appears to an outside decision maker, it provides parties with a reality check. Even if a party does not agree with the evaluator's opinion, ENE still offers the advantage of jumpstarting the invaluable process of *litigation risk analysis*. Obtaining a realistic assessment of the risks involved in litigation allows the party to better determine their future course of action.

Non-binding arbitration is similar to ENE but more extensive. An individual arbitrator or a panel of arbitrators listens to arguments presented by both sides, makes a decision, and issues an award. Non-binding means the parties are not forced to accept the decision. Non-binding arbitration thus also serves as a reality check that allows parties to preview a likely outcome.

After the parties receive notice of the arbitration award they may reflect on the proceedings and conclude the decision is reasonable; they may accept the award and end the dispute. Or they may reject the decision and proceed to a binding process such as arbitration or a court trial. Often, however, the non-binding decision motivates parties to mediate. They are prepared to engage in facilitated negotiation, armed with additional knowledge regarding the likely trial outcome.

To understand how the award may anchor the subsequent negotiation, assume the non-binding award granted the plaintiff $500,000 in damages. In the following mediation the losing party (the defendant) argues that it will cost the plaintiff $100,000 to proceed to trial to achieve the predicted $500,000 verdict. Thus, the defendant argues, the plaintiff will actually net $400,000. So the defendant offers the plaintiff $400,000, the net amount they could reasonably expect to receive at trial.

In this way negotiation employs knowledge gained through a non-binding process to set the parameters of a settlement. (This is a simplistic example as rarely is the negotiation a "cut the pie" operation. A host of other concerns arise in an actual mediation.)

If either party rejects the non-binding award the parties may choose to engage in *binding arbitration*, a dispute resolution process designed to involve fewer procedural hurdles than a full-blown court trial and therefore to be speedier and less expensive. Arbitration became an option in 1925 when Congress enacted the Federal Arbitration Act in response to complaints from the business community seeking a faster and less expensive way to resolve disputes. Arbitration allows parties to enter into a formal agreement regarding how they will resolve future disputes using a flexible process that eliminates or shortens aspects of litigation.

For example, the discovery process can be abbreviated or eliminated entirely by agreement among the parties.[3] Time-consuming and expensive pre-trial motions can be eliminated. In arbitration, appeals are limited, shortening the process and lowering costs. Arbitration was thus designed to save time and money by allowing parties to design procedures to resolve disputes outside the courtroom.[4]

Arbitration is used extensively as an alternative dispute resolution (ADR) option; business and consumer contracts often contain clauses that mandate arbitration in the event of a dispute. You may have agreed to arbitration clauses in many transactions, for example, when you signed up for a credit card, when you visited the doctor, or when you opened a brokerage account.

Arbitrators are often retired judges or lawyers, though panels of arbitrators may include experts from specific disciplines or may include panel members who represent the interests of consumers. Recently, complaints have alleged that arbitration has become too much like litigation – time-consuming and expensive. Nonetheless, the original purpose of arbitration – to provide a streamlined process that saves time and money – is often achieved.

A *court trial* is a formal process with extensive rules regarding procedure. In both arbitration proceedings and trials procedural concerns play a significant role. For this reason a representative trained in the law is usually retained.[5] In a *bench trial* a judge renders the verdict. In a *jury trial* a panel of jurors renders a verdict. In either type of trial the outcome is placed in the hands of strangers who adjudicate the matter.

When a party feels the verdict is unjust *and* they have a compelling reason to argue that the law was not properly applied during the proceedings they may appeal to a higher court. The appeals process can add as much as two years before the higher court delivers a final verdict or orders a new trial which starts the process over again.

There are times when a party finds there is value in relying on a third-party decision. They may desire the emotional distance that comes from being able to say, "Twelve impartial jurors rendered a verdict. Don't blame me for their decision." In some situations distancing oneself from personal responsibility for the outcome proves valuable, particularly when one faces an adversary who refuses to put an end to a conflict.

In such cases the opposing party's identity may be so wrapped up in the conflict that they cannot let go of the fight – they are so committed to maintaining their opposition that they cannot end the dance and cannot allow you to end the dance. They cling to the oppositional embrace, forcing you to dance in spite of your desire to move on. In these circumstances you may find relief by pointing to a third party decision over which you have no control.

In relying on a third party decision you attempt to disengage from the conflict by substituting the court as a proxy opponent – in other words, you hope your opponent becomes convinced the court is their new antagonist. This does not always work. Sometimes the other party is antagonized by a loss in court and the conflict escalates yet again. Your opponent blames you for discrediting them in court and the oppositional dance continues.

Trial outcomes rarely satisfy the parties, as trial procedure dictates the manner in which their story may be told and the resulting narrative rarely matches either party's version of what happened. The account the jury hears is the story lawyers are trained to tell: it is the abbreviated account that procedural rules allow lawyers to present. Most of the time both parties leave the courtroom feeling they were not given an opportunity to make their concerns fully known. The appealing idea that you will have your day in court to explain your story to your peers most often turns out to be an unrealized dream.

For this reason litigation outcomes rarely meet party expectations even for those who win. Time spent and costs incurred add to the diminishment of satisfaction. The sometimes embarrassing public exposure of private matters and the emotional toll exacted by the fight, as well as stress and worry, render victory bittersweet. While parties may be able to live with the outcome the experience is rarely satisfying.

This situation has motivated courts to provide litigants ample opportunity to resolve their disputes through collaborative processes such as mediation. In one additional alternative provided by the court a trial judge refers the parties to a settlement judge who assists them in seeking resolution during a *settlement conference*. Settlement conferences take place in the month, week, or day before trial and can be similar to mediation, though some are more evaluative and less time is spent unearthing underlying factors. The focus often tends to be getting the deal done.

In the last thirty years there has been an ADR (alternative dispute resolution) revolution in the courts: over ninety-five percent of all cases filed no longer proceed to a trial. Court dockets have been reduced significantly, which enables the court to resolve disputes in a timely manner and to deliver improved party satisfaction. This improvement in the justice system is not fully appreciated by the general public unless they have personally experienced the changes.

In pointing out shortcomings of the legal system I do not mean to lessen the vital role the courts play in society. The prosperity of advanced societies can be attributed in large measure to the existence of a fair and independent judiciary. One has only to look at countries where these legal institutions are flawed or missing altogether to gain a rapid appreciation of their value. In addition it should be noted that processes such as mediation often work against a backdrop of a potential court appearance – the parties' willingness to work with one another, at least initially, may be partially fueled by the realization that the other option is an expensive and unpleasant trial.

Thus the previous comments extolling the benefits of ADR are not meant to disparage litigation but rather to reflect an appreciation for the creative manner in which the legal profession has sought more effective and more satisfying approaches to resolving conflict through ADR.

The preceding comments apply primarily to civil courts, though in the criminal courts advances are also in the works, especially in the area of restorative justice. The restorative justice approach calls on those who have harmed others to be accountable to their victims through reparations, rehabilitation, and reconciliation. A parallel effort on a larger scale can be found in Truth and Reconciliation Hearings, with perhaps the most notable example being the South African hearings that helped ease a society from its apartheid past into an integrated present with a minimum of violence and retribution.

Thus, judicial processes can provide vital conflict resolution services. Their role and their importance should not be forgotten or minimized while we concentrate on collaborative and spiritually transformative ways of achieving reconciliation.

In spite of the success of alternative dispute resolution and the many options available to parties in conflict there are a small percentage of people who either do not achieve satisfaction with the various approaches or who do not even attempt conciliatory methods before resorting to force. They move further and reach the extreme right end of the continuum where we find the ironic term *self-help* that means taking matters into one's own hands and using force or violence to dictate an outcome.

Self-help here refers to vigilante justice: to the disgruntled employee exacting revenge on co-workers and bosses; to extremists launching terrorist attacks; to the disillusioned spouse in a divorce case who becomes violent.

The extremely adverse consequences of self-help to all parties involved make it imperative that everything possible be done to first employ other conflict resolution methods. The phrase *self-help* applies not only to individuals but can also apply to groups as large as nation states that go to war over differences.

Violent or forceful action is frequently engaged as a result of a lack of knowledge of other options or a lack of skill in applying other options.[6] The person who resorts to violent self-help feels nothing else will work; there appears to be no other option except for direct and forceful action. For this reason, if we wish to diminish the use of force and violence around the globe, it becomes vital that we provide intensive training in alternative conflict resolution techniques.

Choosing an Approach

As you assess your personal conflict and decide which option along the continuum provides the best starting point the primary factors to be considered are choice and flexibility. We ask ourselves how important it is for us to assume control and determine the outcome. Are we comfortable with another person making decisions that dictate our future? We assess the degree of flexibility needed to resolve our specific conflict in a satisfactory manner. Will we need a process that focuses narrowly on issues regarding substance or will we need to focus on healing a relationship?

Mediators believe the best outcomes result when parties engage in flexible processes that allow them to first overcome relationship challenges. Once those challenges are met the parties are better prepared to enter into a collaborative effort to find a resolution that benefits all involved. In the majority of instances outcomes arrived at in a collaborative manner after the relationship is healed prove to be the most durable and satisfying.

When we keep in mind the entire continuum of options we maintain a flexible attitude that allows us to achieve reconciliation using multiple approaches if necessary. While we may understand that mediation offers the greatest advantages, the opposing party may need to experience other processes, for example an adversarial trial, in order to recognize the advantages of collaboration.

Initially, they may vow to never work with us or even speak with us but after suffering through the expense and delay at the beginning of the litigation process they may see the wisdom in selecting another approach. As they begin to hear themselves (or their attorney) relate their story in a public setting they may come to anticipate that a third party such as a jury will have little sympathy for their cause. They may recognize that they are better off negotiating directly with their adversary.

Keeping the continuum in mind we may be inspired to combine processes to create a hybrid approach that works best for our unique situation. For example, we may anticipate arriving at a collaborative solution for all but one issue, perhaps an issue that depends heavily for its resolution on a highly technical reading of the law. In such a situation we resolve the majority of issues through mediation and agree to submit the outstanding issue to an arbitrator knowledgeable in that area of the law.

As the dispute resolution profession has matured there has been increasing awareness of the need to draw upon a number of techniques and processes. The challenge is to avoid becoming rote and repetitive and to use skill in choosing the best approach for resolving a particular conflict. Success demands flexibility and creativity from mediators and parties alike, so as you assess your particular situation keep this big picture view in mind.

Cultural Differences

The continuum represents approaches available primarily within the context of the United States legal system, however, the concept of a continuum of dispute resolution options exists in all cultures and organizations. Many organizations employ a continuum of options that spans from informal, conciliatory, collaborative processes to formal adjudicatory processes in which individuals or committees render decisions. In all social groups, regardless of legal context, options range from casual processes that value self-determined outcomes to formal processes that rely on a third party decision. The third party may be a boss, a committee, or a person in charge of ethics or personnel matters.

The amount of emphasis placed on self-determinism versus top-down decisions varies from culture to culture, as does the weight given individual versus collectivist concerns. In some cultures individualism is an honored principle while in other cultures value is attributed to collective efforts and concerns. In the United States there is a tendency toward using the dispute resolution choices which honor the individual operating in a self-determined manner within a formal setting.

In China, a culture with a different emphasis, one tends to find a preference for the far left and far right ends of the scale. Options to the far left of the continuum play an important role in cultures that value harmony within a collectivist worldview. China, for example, has a venerable tradition of informal conciliation designed to maintain harmony in the community. Yet China's more authoritarian political and legal system utilizes choices on the far right of the continuum.

Such generalizations have limited utility but nonetheless demonstrate it is possible to analyze any culture, whether a nation, corporation or local community, for preferences in conflict resolution approaches. In some situations it will be necessary to understand these preferences in order to correctly anticipate choices your adversary will make. At the same time it is important to realize the individual may value options that differ from the preferences of the larger culture.

The qualifications of those who perform facilitation or adjudication roles may also differ: for example, an arbitrator may be a village elder, a respected senior family member, a respected senior government official, or a trained lawyer. In some cultures disputes may be mediated or adjudicated primarily by religious leaders. In the United States, where the legal system is well developed, mediators frequently have prior experience working in the legal profession. Thus, when it comes time to select a mediator a party needs to be aware of traditions that influence their adversary's comfort with the selection.

As we assess our options we need to assess the culture of conflict resolution that exists within the group or organization in which we operate. For example, within the business community some companies have been creative in addressing prevention and resolution of workplace conflict while others lag behind and use systems that rely heavily on top-down adjudication. We may live in communities with highly developed systems of conflict resolution or we may find there are few options short of filing a legal action or resorting to self-help.

In addition, we have to consider the combined effects of the variedlevels and types of culture in which we operate. In the pioneering days of mediation, neighborhood justice centers exported civil dispute resolution methods to troubled neighborhoods. The success of such initiatives depended at least in part on the larger culture in which the neighborhood was embedded. Justice centers fight an uphill battle when the larger culture promotes handling disputes through coercive means.

The reverse chain of causality can occur as well: if conflict resolution approaches become well known and widely accepted in a subculture those views may be exported to the larger culture. For example, school age children trained in the use of peer mediation to resolve conflict will eventually influence the dispute resolution culture within schools and that culture in turn will be exported to the family and the neighborhood. A change in one setting seeps into other settings. Ideally a concerted effort to promote nonviolent and non-coercive conflict resolution can be designed to spread throughout a culture and eventually throughout the world. That was the dream of St. Francis, a dream that may yet be realized.

Conflict Resolution in Faith Cultures

In *Taming the Wolf* emphasis is placed on a style of conflict resolution that recognizes the divine within each and every person. This style honors the divinity of the individual and recognizes the interdependent nature of God's creatures. Initially, this spiritually transformative approach will find acceptance in communities that already endorse and promote these principles.

In the future the spiritually transformative approach may gain wider acceptance within cultures and subcultures that traditionally do not celebrate the interdependence of all creatures and the presence of the indwelling Spirit. The use of spiritually transformative mediation may give rise to a universal culture that sees all men and women as interdependent brothers and sisters who share a created world. While the culture in which we live often determines our choice of a conflict resolution approach, it is also true that the manner in which we resolve conflict may also alter the culture.

Using a spiritually transformative model we may come to view prayer, through which divine providence operates, as another option along the continuum. For some people *self-help* will become *seek-divine-help*. Or we may come to view prayer and divine providence as a foundation that undergirds the entire continuum. In other words, as we participate in various approaches to conflict resolution we may call upon the indwelling Spirit to guide our actions and we may bring a compassionate heart to the table no matter which process we choose.

Mediation Team

On occasion we may need to assemble a team of advisers to assist us in mediation. For example, the mayor of Gubbio assembled trusted advisers. The team will likely begin with a lawyer who addresses legal and contractual issues; a pastoral counselor may be engaged to address emotional issues and help us make sound decisions from an ethical or moral viewpoint; an accountant may advise on financial and tax concerns; a specialist may clarify technical issues.

If the conflict takes place within a diplomatic setting specialists from various disciplines – science, public policy, economics, geography, culture, and international law – may be called into service. Each conflict will have its particular requirements; the key idea is to be open to creative input from a support team.

Typically the lawyer plays a lead role as he or she is a specialist in the prevention and handling of disputes. Lawyers work with clients to prevent or avoid conflict through proper negotiation and drafting of contracts; they help clients avoid conflict with governments by advising on rules, regulations, and statutes; they represent clients in court when a dispute has escalated; they defend clients who have allowed conflict to escalate into violence. They frequently represent clients in mediation. In many cases the lawyer, working with opposing counsel, chooses the mediator. (If you are involved in litigation, after reading this book you may choose to work more closely with your attorney on mediator selection, as you will have gained a sense of the style that will best address your concerns.)

Given the extensive and critical role lawyers play it is impossible in this limited space to cover the full range of concerns that might arise while working with an attorney in the mediation context. Nonetheless, it is worth highlighting a few critical concerns.

Lawyers vary in their experience with mediation and in the degree to which they understand the process. Even lawyers who have represented many clients in mediation may not thoroughly grasp the nuances of the process. Their misconceptions may have influenced previous mediations in which they participated. They may not have been aware of the bias they (inadvertently) entered into the process. Their experience with mediation may reflect how *they* approached the process, not the inherent nature of the process. The limits an attorney may have inadvertently imposed on the process may have shaped their past experience.

A lawyer may have insisted on hiring retired judges with evaluative styles or mediators accustomed to exerting a strong influence over the outcome rather than a transformative mediator skilled in repairing relationships. As a matter of preference (or bias) they may shy away from mediators with whom they are unfamiliar and they may avoid non-lawyer mediators.

In their choice of a retired judge with an evaluative style they may be imposing a legalistic bias on the process and may miss some of the more creative mediation styles that might better address their client's deeper needs. Given the predominance of legal minds in the room during such mediation the focus may lock in on legal issues that do not fully capture the underlying nature of the conflict. What began as a relationship problem may have only turned into a legal problem as a result of escalation. Addressing legal solutions may only postpone the day when the real issue surfaces.

If the mediation is not designed to plumb the depths of the conflict the resulting resolution may address only surface issues and may be a temporary fix for a long-term problem. While on occasion a legal decision is all a party may desire or need, at other times they seek a more profound result. Thus it is important that you share your concerns with your attorney so he or she can arrange for an approach that addresses your needs. In some cases you may understand factors driving the conflict are not what they appear to be on the surface. You may realize an outcome based primarily on the legal issues will not endure. You know the conflict will resurface if deeper issues are not addressed.

For example, your attorney may be prepared to enlist the services of a judicial-style mediator capable of applying pressure to get the deal done when you need a mediator with quiet sensitivity who can draw out your adversary and surface their real motivation. It is vital you determine whether or not the style your lawyer brings to the mediation meets your needs.

Another primary concern for parties working with lawyers is the dramatic shift in demeanor required when one transitions from trial preparation to settlement negotiations. Different mindsets and skills are required. An inherent tension exists between litigation – a process in which one seeks to destroy the other party's credibility and maximize the verdict in one's favor – and mediation – a process that values trust, collaboration, and cooperation in the pursuit of a mutually satisfactory outcome.

A conflict that has found its way to a court (or a court-like tribunal) typically starts down the litigation path with a lawsuit (complaint) that alleges bad behavior on the part of an adversary. This is followed by a response from the accused party that impugns the credibility and honesty of the party filing the original complaint.

During the subsequent *discovery process* lawyers attempt to access evidence that impeaches the credibility of the opposition, escalating the antagonism. After a grueling deposition in which the attorney for one side attempts to impugn the credibility of the opposing side by tripping them up, causing them to become flustered, or angering them, the likelihood the upset party will subsequently consider a collaborative process plummets.

In addition, in pre-trial motions attorneys seek rulings from the bench that limit the opposing side's ability to present their case. Such hearings raise the hostility level another notch. As litigation proceeds and the investment (financial and emotional) increases, a party becomes more and more devoted to defeating the other party. They become committed to victory. The fight intensifies as "hired gun" attorneys clash and stakes rise. As hostilities ratchet up it becomes increasingly unrealistic to ask a party to abruptly depart from the battle in order to embrace the other party in a same-side-of-the-table, trust-based collaboration.

The required shift in demeanor, attitude, and intention when transitioning from litigation to mediation is unsettling and difficult to execute. Performing this shift is analogous to driving at a hundred miles per hour on an icy road and slamming on the brakes. The result is a dramatic loss of control. The mediator, understanding the nature of the shift from litigation to mediation, proceeds slowly at the beginning. A skilled mediator guides the parties through this stage of shifting gears and takes them down the very different road of facilitated negotiation.

While the change may be difficult for the client it is also important to recognize how difficult it may be for the attorney.

At the beginning of litigation, attorneys frequently convince their clients that zealous advocacy is the only sure way to triumph. This is an argument the client is usually eager to accept. Gaining the unwavering support of an advocate who will take up the fight on your behalf after you have struggled as a lone warrior brings huge relief. Attorneys may tell clients what they wish to hear but at times they are justifying their approach to dispute resolution.

Later, however, faced with mediation and the possibility of a settlement, the lawyer must abandon the weapons of zealous advocacy and employ the more subtle tools of persuasion. At an earlier stage the party may have hired the attorney on the basis of his or her aggressive and intimidating demeanor – as they wanted the toughest advocate they could find in their corner. In mediation, however, the party is faced with the need to generate trust with the other party. The presence of a growling bulldog at your side does not signal you are prepared to work collaboratively. The legal ally who was once an asset becomes a liability.

In litigation the opposing side's concerns are targeted for destruction. In mediation the process fails to advance unless one gives serious consideration to the opposing side's concerns. Demonstrate, even unintentionally, that you intend to dismiss their concerns and mediation hits an impasse. The process shuts down until intentions and attitudes are modified and clarified. This shift from litigation (attack) to mediation (collaboration) does not happen easily. It requires a high degree of synchronicity between lawyer, client, and the mediator who orchestrates the change of direction.

A mediation I facilitated provides a good example of the type of animus that can build. One party, who was terribly upset by a deposition in which the opposing attorney harshly demeaned her and attacked her credibility, refused to communicate while opposing counsel was in the room.

The attorney who conducted the aggressive deposition, perhaps providing the zealous advocacy her client deserved, now stood as an obstacle to the settlement her client wished to achieve. As long as the despised attorney was in the room progress was impossible. The offending attorney's client – recognizing the rancor that had developed – took the lead position in the negotiation, allowing the attorney to quietly recede into the background.

The flexibility of mediation allows for such adjustments and encourages creative ways of solving problems, particularly problems that have surfaced as a result of insults or offenses given during adversarial litigation. A similar situation arose in another case. Bearing a grudge against the opposing party, a lawyer assumed an abusive demeanor. His offensive tactics threatened to derail the mediation process. Realizing no resolution was possible under such circumstances, I made sure the abusive lawyer and the opposing party were never in the same room at the same time. Litigation tactics inflamed the conflict, obstructing the path to resolution and reconciliation, but the flexibility of mediation allowed me to solve the problem.

On occasion litigation can foment such discord that parties, out of desperation, seek to change the tone of the proceedings by retreating to mediation. A party may extend an olive branch to the opposing party simply to avoid the adversarial demeanor of the opposing attorney. In such cases, "the bulldog in the corner" works indirectly to promote dialogue. The adversarial nature of the attorney creates a desire on the part of the opposing party to avoid further litigation (and further dealings with that attorney). But instances in which the actions of an aggressive attorney inadvertently promote conciliatory dialogue are uncommon. More often the aggressive demeanor convinces the other party they must fight to the bitter end. When zealous advocacy becomes too aggressive, parties may dig in and fight.

These examples are not meant to diminish the positive role attorneys play in conflict resolution, rather they are meant to highlight how important it is to consider the manner in which an adversarial attorney (retained for his ability to get tough with the other party) influences mediation, a process that requires different skills.

If your conflict has resulted in litigation (or other adversarial process), you and your attorney (or other representative) should discuss the degree to which the attorney will be required to shift gears as the nature of the process changes. Concerns should be aired in advance – before you find yourself in the middle of the process, when it becomes more difficult to change gears.

I also have seen clients struggle with the shift from litigation to mediation mode. I have watched attorneys recognize the need for a shift while their clients insist they not waver. The client expects the attorney to remain in fight mode and sends subtle messages that signal willingness to seek new representation if the attorney "goes soft" and promotes settlement.

In such cases, mediators assist the attorney by guiding the party to consider the possible adverse consequences of litigation – even when their attorney provides the best representation possible. The mediator's questions regarding litigation risk often provide a reality check that gives even the most aggressive clients pause.

When this situation arises, the mediator usually takes the lead and allows the lawyer to assume a lower profile until the client expresses willingness to consider alternatives. Once party expectations conform to reality the attorney gains the freedom to provide the best representation possible through a combination of aggressive and conciliatory moves. (Ironically, while most clients value their attorney for his or her adversarial skills, attorneys frequently demonstrate their best work during the resolution process.)

Though the scenario in which a client demands an overly aggressive approach is the more frequent situation, the reverse scenario, in which the client shifts to settlement mode while the attorney refuses to shift gears, is not uncommon. Attorneys sometimes cause clients to fear they might lose representation if they insist on backing off and play nice. In most cases the signals are subtle, nonetheless, the client who is dependent upon the attorney for representation understands the message.

When an attorney pushes for continued litigation and fails to engage in a robust attempt to negotiate a settlement, a mediator must use extreme caution in attributing motive. There are no doubt times when the push for litigation is driven by the attorney's desire to bill additional hours but there are also instances in which the attorney is providing the best representation possible and other factors, not disclosed to the mediator, dictate litigation is the best option.

Recent research, however, shows that continuing to litigate most often results in less favorable outcomes for the client.[7] The amount awarded at trial to the plaintiff who wins typically ends up being less than was offered in settlement talks. Amounts owed by defendants who lose end up being more than they would have paid in a settlement. The research supports advice mediators frequently give parties: you are more likely to satisfy your interests by collaborating than you are through a verdict. In the majority of cases the overly passionate litigant or litigants with overly litigious attorneys suffer a penalty for their aggression.

The topics of attorney-client relationship and varying styles of legal representation have been covered extensively in the literature. Some attorneys adopt an authoritarian or directive style, some prefer a client-centered approach, and yet others find a collaborative style preferable.[8] An emerging trend finds some attorneys limiting their practice to *collaborative law*.

In the collaborative law model, the attorney represents the client only in matters related to settlement negotiations. If efforts to settle are unsuccessful the client must retain a different attorney to handle litigation. In this model the collaborative attorney will not benefit from ensuing litigation. This gives a client confidence the attorney does not have an unstated interest in proceeding to trial (where additional billing will accrue). The potential conflict of interest is eliminated.

While I use the litigated case as an example, the same dynamics apply in other settings in which adversarial processes are employed. Hearings or other quasi-judicial processes that take place in other settings may be less formal but they suffer the same shortcoming: they promote or allow increased hostility. Adversarial approaches foster continued struggle rather than resolution and reconciliation. While the downside may be uniquely strong in the trial court setting, in general the adversarial approach has liabilities. Yet most of us gravitate toward a contest of wills played out in a setting in which we argue the merits of our position before a third party.

Preparation is Vital

The shift from litigation to mediation requires adequate preparation. While time spent on litigation preparation tends to be significant, it is rare to find an attorney and client who spend adequate time preparing for mediation. In litigation the attorney takes the lead and presents the case, so he or she must prepare extensively. In mediation the roles frequently shift: the client is expected to play a larger role, so the client, rather than the lawyer, needs to prepare more extensively.

In the courtroom, trial procedure limits the degree to which parties can speak their minds freely. In mediation, parties are encouraged to speak in depth, not only about the facts of the case but also about their feelings, motives, concerns, and interests. If this shift in focus – from attorney presentation to client participation – is not a part of the preparation confusion and miscues hamper success. Time may be wasted. A less-desirable outcome may result. One purpose of *Taming the Wolf* is to help parties remedy this failure to prepare adequately.

During the preparation stage the party and their attorney also have an opportunity to negotiate their relationship and arrive at a plan for working together smoothly during a negotiation. If the client and the attorney discover their goals or assumptions are not fully aligned there is time to discuss the differences. If the client harbors concern that the attorney leans unnecessarily toward pursuing litigation, out of habit or out of a desire to bill hours, the concern can be discussed before engaging with the opposing party.

Once you and your attorney agree on an approach you may wish to discuss the prompts in the *Taming the Wolf Journal Workbook.*[9]

The preceding comments apply equally to other advisers on the mediation team. For example, if you have an adviser, close friend, family member, or colleague assist with mediation instead of (or in addition to) an attorney you must check to make sure they do not hold biased or uninformed views that impede the process. Are they overly supportive in a way that prevents you from looking at your actual role in the conflict? Do their biases color your perspective of the other party, making it difficult to see them in a new light? When you involve allies there is a risk of adding bias that lessens your flexibility, humility, and creativity.

Perhaps the assembled team came together in an informal, impromptu manner – they are simply your closest confidants. You may not have given a lot of thought to selecting advisers. Thus there is a possibility you recruited an adviser who has a stake in keeping the conflict alive – perhaps you inadvertently recruited someone who benefits emotionally from your difficulty. It is worth asking if the friend or associate draws benefit from the increased importance that accompanies their role. For this reason, it makes sense to carefully vet those selected or those with whom you discuss the conflict.

As an example, one party was offered (and accepted) a very generous settlement from an insurance carrier. The recipient had good reason to be pleased with her ability to negotiate and satisfy her need to be compensated for damages she suffered. Yet, as she prepared to depart, I noticed she was noticeably forlorn.

When I inquired into her lack of satisfaction she revealed that her father, waiting at home, was expecting a jackpot, a legal bonanza. He had an unrealistic vision of a better life as a result of his daughter's minor but traumatic accident and subsequent settlement. The settlement she negotiated failed to meet her father's grandiose expectations and she was not looking forward to disappointing him. Fortunately she had not allowed her father's quixotic notions to scuttle the negotiation, as there was a reasonable probability that a jury would have awarded her much less. The pressure we might experience from those close to us, including those we have selected as our advisers, should be assessed and managed.

Many lawyers are excellent at listening to client concerns but often the cost is prohibitive when we require extended time to explore our thoughts and feelings. Frequently we seek a more in-depth dialogue designed to allow us to sort through conflicting thoughts and emotions. In such cases a pastoral counselor may become a valuable member of the team. Though they may not attend the actual mediation they can guide us through difficult stretches of introspection. Clergy trained in conflict resolution and reconciliation can be especially helpful.

In the legend the Mayor of Gubbio consulted with his advisers. The legend does not tell us who those advisers were but one can imagine a broad range of talents was brought to bear in resolving the conflict between the wolf and town.

A Franciscan View

In the journal *Spirit and Life* conversation is ascribed a significant role within the Franciscan life and "honest conversation" is noted as "the hallmark of Franciscan presence in the world."[10] Michael Blastic describes this conversation as being more than mere social nicety: "Conversation is more than the mere speaking of words. Conversation implies an exchange, a sharing of thought and feeling, a familiarity and close association with one another, and even a style of life as the medieval person might express it, a manner of life."[11]

This sentiment echoes our earlier discussion of the "Face of a Franciscan" in which we noted that a Franciscan greets strangers in the world while acknowledging their divine nature. As in all matters, Francis turned to Christ for instruction in this regard: "[Francis and Celano] described a spirituality of itinerancy modeled after a Christ who came to start a 'conversation' with us."[12]

Francis did not run from the mundane world but rather engaged the world in a divine conversation. "Francis did not seek to flee from the world nor did he want his brothers to do so. His spirituality was one of encounter with the world."[13] Yet we he did not resolve conflict by acquiescing to the norms of the world; rather, he met the world on his own terms, with a prayerful demeanor.

The Secular Franciscan Rule captures this mission: "Mindful that they are bearers of peace which must be built up unceasingly, they should seek out ways of unity and fraternal harmony through dialogue, trusting in the divine seed in everyone and in the transforming power of love and pardon."[14]

It is not difficult for us to imagine that Francis prepared by turning to prayer before going out to engage a conflict needing resolution – such as was the case with the wolf of Gubbio. Perhaps he retreated into contemplative prayer in order to call upon divine resources for aid in his mission. Delio captures his approach, "Prayer, therefore, leads us to know ourselves in God and God in ourselves, and in this relationship we are led in true humility by which we see clearly the humble presence of God all around us."[15]

As the role of a mediator can be challenging, we can safely hypothesize Francis was aware of the need to set his mind to the task in advance. When we set out to make peace we do not stumble into the world with indifferent intention, rather we must find the burning desire that will see us through the task. "Prayer is where we sort out our desires and are sorted out by our desires. Everything can lead us into relationship with God as long as we keep the flame of desire burning and let this flame enlighten the darkness of the heart."[16]

The preceding quote references an individual effort but Francis, in the role of peacemaker, would be in need of sufficient flame to shed light into the darkness filling the hearts of others. He would need to shine this light for as long as it took to illuminate their path to reconciliation.

We can speculate on the preparation he found necessary, preparation that took on the nature of a conversion, preparation that we may best understand with the help of the following passage: "[Francis] began to do penance and to acquire the spirit of compassionate love, and somehow a space opened up within him to embrace those he would otherwise reject. We might say that he came to embrace the leper by learning to embrace the leper within himself. Only when he came to a clearer knowledge of himself, his own weaknesses and smallness, could he see the greatness of God in the leper and those shunned by society."[17]

The prayer we engage as an approach to conflict or as a foundation for resolution and reconciliation is a profound, life-changing prayer. When we prepare with prayer, as a mediator or as a party, we go forward with a fresh vision, with a clear eye for "what is." This enhanced vision is vital if we are to succeed in unraveling the conflict narrative.

Contemplative prayer clears not only our mind but also prepares our heart. "Francis understood that contemplation begins with a pure heart.

Contemplation is not some type of intellectual union of the mind with God but ... is a deep penetrating vision of reality."[18]

The mediator or party who takes this Franciscan approach comes to the resolution process, whether in a conversation, a mediation, or a legal proceeding, with wisdom. Not the wisdom of the attorney or the judge, but rather "Wisdom [as] the vision of the heart whereby the heart sees the truth of things and thus knows in a way more deeply than the (intellectual) mind itself could ever grasp. It delights in God as good revealed in the interior of the soul."[19] The life of Francis thus provides clues to the importance of contemplative prayer in preparation for conflict resolution, no matter where on the continuum we engage peacemaking.

Scripture

"If your brother sins [against you], go and tell him his fault between you and him alone. If he listens to you, you have won over your brother. If he does not listen, take one or two others along with you, so that 'every fact may be established on the testimony of two or three witnesses.' If he refuses to listen to them, tell the church. If he refuses to listen even to the church, then treat him as you would a Gentile or a tax collector." (Mt 18:15-17)

There was a scholar of the law who stood up to test him and said, "Teacher, what must I do to inherit eternal life?" Jesus said to him, "What is written in the law? How do you read it?" He said in reply, "You shall love the Lord, your God, with all your heart, with all your being, with all your strength, and with all your mind, and your neighbor as yourself." (Lk 10:25-27)

"I answered them that it was not Roman practice to hand over an accused person before he has faced his accusers and had the opportunity to defend himself

against their charge. So when [they] came together here, I made no delay; the next day I took my seat on the tribunal and ordered the man to be brought in. His accusers stood around him, but did not charge him with any of the crimes I suspected. Instead they had some issues with him about their own religion and about a certain Jesus who had died but who Paul claimed was alive." (Acts 25:16-19)

CHAPTER SIX

Convening Challenges

Several brave messengers were sent to find Francis and ask for his help. They had the good fortune to find Francis in Assisi at the house of Bernardo di Quintavalle, his first follower.

They told him of the tragic attacks of the wolf and how the frightened people were almost in a state of siege. They thought Francis was the only one who would be able to help them. They begged the simple Holy man to help and implored him to come with them right away.

Francis was moved by their plight and wanted to do what he could. He promised they would leave in the morning, but that night they should eat and rest with his Brothers.

After dinner they prayed with Francis for a solution and slept that night with hope in their hearts.

Mediation Principles

THE PEOPLE OF GUBBIO recognized they needed help. Perhaps it was the local parish priest who suggested sending messengers in search of Francis. Or perhaps travelers passing through Gubbio told stories of the simple Holy man of Assisi who brought peace wherever he journeyed. In any event, the mayor and the citizens came to the humble conclusion that they needed outside help. They sent for Francis.

It can be difficult for most of us to accept the idea that we require outside assistance, particularly in a culture that prizes individualism and self-reliance. The very nature of conflict, however, often dictates that we draw upon third-party mediators. Calling upon a mediator does not represent a failure of individual enterprise or skill but rather reflects the difficult interpersonal dynamics that are innately at work in conflict.

As discussed in previous chapters, it can be nearly impossible for two individuals who have become locked in an oppositional embrace to disengage on their own. They are chained together and neither is in a position to release the chains. As much as they twist and contort, the lock that secures the chains remains out of reach.

This situation appears to be universal and slightly mysterious. The push-and-pull forces of affinity and repulsion trap us: when we try to escape from one another, we are bound together; but when we try to unite, we are pushed apart. In conflict this is especially true. We are unable to achieve unity but also unable to release that which binds us in opposition. We need a third person to help us get free.

The people of Gubbio recognized the wisdom of seeking assistance. This chapter takes up the topic of seeking outside assistance. We explore the convening stage – getting to the table.

Convening

Conflict escalates when two or more individuals or groups fail to find a way to get to the table to resolve their differences. Their relationship deteriorates drastically; the opportunity for a civil discussion disappears in a thicket of harsh feelings. It becomes clear that even when both parties desire resolution the convening step can be extremely difficult, often more difficult than the actual mediation.

At this stage parties identify internal and external barriers to convening. They need to ask themselves what stands in the way of getting to the table. They may have difficulty summoning the courage to reach out to the person with whom they are fighting. Convening seems futile. Upsetting emotions signal danger. Difficult questions surface. Who will take the first step? Will an offer to meet be mistaken for a sign of weakness? How do I know mediation will work? If I escalate the conflict, will I be able to defeat the other party?

As we assess the barriers to convening we become more certain we will need the assistance of a third-party neutral. Without outside help, there may be no way around impediments. For example, when both parties refuse to make the first move, fearing they will be perceived as weak, only a third party can break the stalemate.

In the legend the Mayor of Gubbio dispatched messengers to find Francis, a Holy man known to bring peace. We might mimic the mayor and seek a peacemaker, though most often we are not certain how to go about such a task. As a result, we back away from the idea of mediation.

If we find ourselves in court a judge may strongly recommend we meet with a court-affiliated mediator and make a good faith attempt to settle the dispute.[1] Lawyers also may recommend mediation and explain the potential upside. In other settings an influential elder or other authority figure may demand we seek resolution for the sake of harmony within the family or community. The task of locating a mediator who can help us convene the process thus begins in ways that are unique to the specific conflict and that uniquely reflect the temperament of the parties. But even with the assistance of a mediator or other third-party convener the question remains: How will we manage to get to the table?

Convening Challenges

Circumstances must be evaluated in order to chart a course to the negotiation table. Parties are encouraged to assess the consequences of continuing the fight. They should weigh pros and cons of continued conflict against pros and cons of mediation. What might they gain? What might they lose?

You will want to begin this evaluation on your own. Consult the journal workbook and list the pros and cons of escalation versus convening. Estimate the value the other party will assign to escalating or convening. A risk-and-reward picture will begin to take shape.

This preliminary evaluation may convince you mediation presents less risk than continuing the fight. On the other hand, if preliminary analysis shows you have more to lose by convening mediation than you have to gain, you will be unlikely to convene. (For example, if you are a battered wife you face risk that must be carefully evaluated.)

You need not consider mediation is the only choice. There are valid reasons to delay convening and valid reasons to seek an alternative approach. However, one advantage to convening that is often overlooked is the lack of a downside should mediation fail to result in a resolution. If mediation fails, parties can choose to resume the fight. The agreement to mediate is not an irrevocable commitment to resolution. It is a commitment to *work* on finding a resolution.

Often we make the mistake of postponing mediation without first conducting a preliminary evaluation of pros and cons. We react to unsettled emotions and delay convening out of a desire to avoid confrontation. But the longer a conflict persists the greater the risk irreparable damage will occur. Relationships may suffer; costs may skyrocket. A party can become so invested in the conflict they define themselves in that role. Hearts harden; accumulated hurts fester; desire for revenge grows; hope is lost; the party may sink into despair and apathy.

From a mediator viewpoint the earlier the parties convene the better. Nonetheless, one party or the other may not be emotionally prepared. The mediator must then decide which stage of escalation presents the best chance for convening in the future. He realizes a hesitant party may need to experience adverse consequences before seeing the wisdom of seeking resolution. The current situation and its consequences may not yet be sufficiently painful to motivate action, forcing the mediator to convene at a later date. Or he may offer to assist parties as they work through the barriers to convening.

The Barrier of Power Imbalance

Inaccurate perceptions of power may delay convening. One side may have an inflated sense of their power, which leads them to believe they have no need to meet with the other party. Or they may underestimate the advantages enjoyed by the other side and incorrectly figure there is no downside to ignoring the other party.

For example, though it may appear one side lacks power, interested third parties may be waiting in the wings to come to their aid. Outsiders may feel sympathy for the weaker party's cause and the new allies, using their power, might seek retribution on behalf of the weaker party in order to remedy perceived injustice. For example, a special interest group may believe the weaker party has been exploited and may contribute financial and legal power. The party that previously wielded power unwisely or arrogantly may suddenly find they are engaged in a struggle they failed to predict.

Or a party may overlook the adverse consequences of a moral lapse and fail to recognize the danger posed by unethical acts. They may not recognize their actions plant the seeds that lead to the bitter harvest they reap. While the cause and effect relationship between our moral acts and the conditions we suffer is not always obvious, the "what goes around comes around" dynamic is inexorable. Eventually we face consequences that arise from the causes we set in motion.

In other cases, for example in the non-violence movement led by Gandhi, the weaker party may withhold compliance and leave the more powerful party facing the unpleasant option of using coercive means that exact more harm than they can stomach. Or the weaker party, feeling desperate, may adopt a scorched earth policy of mutual destruction. They may set out to inflict as much damage as possible before they are defeated. The more powerful party may be caught off guard, overlooking the mutual destruction option because the other side's sacrifice of self appears irrational to them.

In pre-convening discussions the mediator raises the possibility of adverse consequences, motivating parties to reassess their reluctance to engage in conflict resolution. He helps the more powerful party, who may be less likely to convene, understand potential unintended consequences.

The weaker party faces a dilemma – if they suggest hypothetical adverse consequences will befall the more powerful party, the hypotheticals may be seen as a veiled threat. This will increase the more powerful party's use of coercive power. The mediator, however, can raise potential negative consequences without being seen as a threat. The mediator frames the hypothetical actions the weaker party might take as a response to the more powerful party's actions. He shifts the frame and asks, "What consequences might *your* actions bring about?"

The mediator thus positions the more powerful party as being in control. He frames their actions as the cause that will lead to the adverse consequences. He points out choices and notes those choices have consequences. He is able to float hypothetical scenarios without those scenarios being perceived as veiled threats.

The same dynamics apply when the weaker party misestimates the response their actions will garner. They may overestimate their power and underestimate the other party's willingness to use coercive means to cause considerable hardship. Unwarranted bravado may prevent an accurate assessment of the value that arises from humbly proceeding to the table. When the weaker party becomes conscious of how their actions may be self-defeating, they are more likely to choose a collaborative reconciliation process.

In the legend escalation prompts action. Men are sent to slay the wolf but they are killed, which motivates the mayor to seek outside help. Most conflicts are ripe long before such catastrophic and fatal events occur. However, the likelihood that parties will convene in a timely manner depends on their accurately assessing the consequences of delay. When they assess potential gains and losses they are more likely to convene the process and avoid further escalation.

Mediator Assistance with Convening

Typically a party is unaware that mediators possess experience overcoming barriers to convening. When a party attempts to convene on their own but encounters a wall of resistance, they may not realize a mediator is more likely to overcome that resistance. Parties may not seek help at an early stage because they cannot imagine a mediator having success where they have failed.

The party may not realize that simply because they are a party to the conflict their efforts to convene will be dismissed summarily by the other party. In contrast, a mediator who is neither an adversary nor a stakeholder may find a receptive audience. It is difficult for one party to sell the benefits of mediation to the other party, as their pitch will be seen as self-serving. An impartial third party, on the other hand, makes a convincing argument by appealing to the party's self-interest. The mediator is in a better position to discuss the party's unavoidable question, "What's in it for me?"

A mediator helps a party recognize advantages of mediation, while advising them of the minimal risk involved. Neither party is left feeling they will be forced to give up something of value. As the mediator has no stake in the conflict he can assume a slightly disinterested attitude, taking up possible benefits in a matter-of-fact manner. He speaks from a neutral posture that communicates: "It's your choice."

When the mediator encounters resistance he is able to query the reasons a party is hesitant without dismissing their interests. He poses questions that prompt assessment of pluses and minuses while maintaining a reasoned demeanor. He poses options and asks, "Does this make sense to you?" He helps each party conduct a rational evaluation of the plus-and-minus ledger.

In other instances, external circumstances force parties to the table before they make a conscious decision to convene. A trial judge may order the parties to mediation or settlement conference. Other powerful third parties may apply pressure and force parties to convene. For instance a family matriarch may insist on a resolution before the parties are allowed to attend family events. Or a business owner may insist employees mediate their differences or face termination.

Even when external pressure results in convening, the mediator must eventually achieve party "buy in." Parties may show up in the flesh but they may not bring their hearts and minds. While external circumstances may force the parties to convene, the mediator still faces the task of convening hearts and minds.

Convening can be a lengthy process that should not be skipped over lightly. The mediator constantly assesses the degree to which the parties are fully present and committed. If the parties are not present emotionally, mentally, and spiritually, the progress they appear to achieve will be a temporary mirage.

Parties often meet with the mediator to discuss what it might be like to take part in mediation before they agree to come to the table. Before making a commitment they want to explore imagined scenarios that allow them to experience (from the safety of their imagination) what it would feel like to participate. They want to visualize themselves at the table.

A mediator gradually introduces the process, never signaling that one party is more anxious to convene than the other and never signaling that one party fears coming to the table more than the other. The mediator creates the important perception that both parties are considering the idea of mediation while both retain legitimate concerns that give them pause.

He communicates to each party individually, letting them know there is a possibility the other party might agree to take part – if they can safely anticipate the decision to convene will be mutual. He might float the question, "If I can generate some interest on the part of the other party would you also express interest?" The possibility of reciprocal interest is floated as a trial balloon. Neither party is first to the table and neither must fear demonstrating apparent weakness. Neither need fear rejection. The mediator blurs time so it appears the decision to participate is simultaneous.

Parties commonly fear a commitment to convene is a commitment to settle on terms they may not fully accept. They may or may not express this fear, so the mediator stresses the voluntary nature of the process. He assures them he does not intend to force a resolution. Rather he will facilitate their efforts to reach a resolution *if* that turns out to be possible. Each party is reassured they will ultimately make their own decision regarding an outcome and, if the process is not working, they reserve the right to walk away without penalty.

Mediation is voluntary and risks are low, the mediator explains, reiterating that he does not possess the power to dictate a resolution. This last advisory is important. We are so accustomed to the model of third-party adjudication that parties will unconsciously assume the mediator will use power to extract a settlement.

In the early stages it is vital the mediator remind parties *they* will decide the outcome, even though the parties often try (usually unconsciously) to award such power to the mediator. I have observed parties attempt to convince the mediator he should just make the decision, but this is not a route to satisfaction. The mediator wisely shifts the power to make a decision back to the party, exploring and handling reasons they fear making decisions.

As you prepare to seek assistance note in your workbook the concerns that give you pause when it comes to convening. What issues will you need to take up with the mediator before you feel comfortable sitting down at the table to begin the reconciliation process?

Face Work

Face Work consists of helping parties Save Face, Restore Face, and Protect Face. Face refers to a person's need to be perceived in a positive manner. When we honor Face we recognize another's need to be admired, appreciated, and valued. When we tend to a person's esteem, we tend to their Face. When we ridicule, we Attack Face. When we suffer Face Loss, we suffer embarrassment and confusion, a sense of inferiority, and damage to our self-image. Face Loss happens as a result of put-downs, sarcasm, and snide remarks used to Attack Face. When we are harmed or overpowered we experience Face Loss.

We consider Other Face and Self Face. Variations of Face Work include Saving Face, Restoring Face, Protecting Face, and Honoring Face, as well as other ways we manage self-image.

When Face is threatened conflict is most often the result. We have a substantial need to maintain a favorable self-image that provides the inner contentment and exterior confidence required to sustain quality relationships. When we suffer Face Loss we lose confidence and contentment; we shut down our interaction with others, which exacerbates conflict.[2] Conflict resolution demands competent social interaction. Therefore, when we experience threats to Face our ability to resolve conflict plummets.

In most escalating conflicts we discover Face has been threatened or diminished, creating a minefield of sensitivities that must be navigated during convening. A party may strive to Save Face by entirely avoiding discussion of the conflict. They may not even admit a conflict exists.

For example, when a more aggressive party must admit a conflict exists that they cannot handle, they experience potential Face Loss as, in their mind, only ineffective, incompetent, or weak people are unable to resolve conflict. They perceive unresolved conflict as a sign they have lost control over conditions, a sign they lack the power to make things go their way. The opposite consideration – that being a combatant is unacceptable, as we should always be loving and caring and never engage in contentious behavior – causes Face Loss for those who believe unresolved conflict will cause them be seen as overly aggressive.

Admitting we are involved in unresolved conflict may imply we are flawed, which diminishes Face. As a result, our need to protect Face does not allow us to admit conflict exists and does not allow us to acknowledge our role in causing conflict. We would rather avoid the topic.

Stiff resistance to mediation therefore can signal a need to Save or Protect Face. To overcome this challenge during the convening stage the mediator endeavors to Restore Face while proposing process guidelines that Protect Face. This requires tact and skill. It requires finding appropriate language to frame conflict as a normal event in the course of human affairs. It requires a frame in which no stigma is attached to conflict and there is no cause for embarrassment.

Conflict resolution is advocated, not as a remedy for the party's flaws, but rather as a higher order social endeavor reserved for people advanced in awareness and social skills. The frame is positive rather than negative. We are not seeking to repair shortcomings but rather to engage our ability to create harmony and justice. The art of making peace is a spiritual endeavor.

Giving Advice

A mediator uses caution when it comes to offering advice. Receiving advice may threaten Face, especially if the party does not enjoy the freedom to reject the advice. When a mediator or other professional offers advice it places the party in the position of one who needs help. In a culture that values self-reliance and competence being seen as needing help produces Face Loss, as needing help is perceived as a sign of weakness.

The mediator thus avoids proffering advice and instead extols the virtues of self-determinism and choice. She frames mediation as a strategic exploration of interests and suggests, "Let's investigate possibilities that might have value to you." She does not represent herself as an expert with the answers but rather as a professional who facilitates a process that relies on the party's own efforts to find solutions to conflict. She presents herself as a resource the party may use in a self-determined and self-reliant quest to resolve conflict. The party can then find their own comfort level with the degree to which they depend on the mediator for advice and guidance.

Previous Face Loss

In most conflicts previous Face Loss looms large. One or both parties may express only a slight discomfort with the issues under contention, but they express certainty that the disrespect shown cannot be forgiven. They admit the substantive issues of the conflict might be amenable to resolution but insist Face Loss goes beyond that which is remediable. They express conviction that such insults have placed the matter out of reach of mediation. They can conceive of ways to work around the contract breach, the failure to pay, the disputed boundary, the broken treaty, the salary dispute, or the barking dog – but the insults and disrespect shown have made mediation impossible. "There is no way I will sit down with that kind of person," they protest. Face Loss is so painful that they cannot conceive of a way they might meet face-to-face.

The mediator advances cautiously. Any additional threat to Face ends the conversation. If a mediator suggests the party "toughen up" and confront the situation the dialogue ends. The convening conversation ends in failure if the mediator minimizes Face concerns by excusing insults suffered with the platitude, "We all say nasty things when we are upset."

Instead, the mediator creates hope that hints at the possibility of Restored Face. News that the other party may consider meeting to resolve the conflict might, by itself, begin to Restore Face. The fact that the other party considers them to be worthy of dialogue, that fact alone, may Restore Face and allow progress.

At other times the opposing party's expression of apology or regret (no matter how mild or tentative) may be necessary to motivate movement. The mediator might say (if true) that he has talked with the other party and they have expressed regret or sorrow over the current state of affairs. He explains they would like to explore ways to mend the relationship. This mild expression of a change of heart begins to Restore Face, as the mildly conciliatory expression does not overstate or over emphasize the previous Face Loss (which might inadvertently create additional Face Loss) but rather provides hope that one will be respected in the future.

It is easy to make the mistake of thinking a grave insult to Face requires an equally weighty preliminary expression of apology in order to jumpstart the process. My experience has taught me it is the change in direction – a move away from Face Threat toward Restoring Face – that makes the difference. This makes sense as an overly profuse apology at this stage appears unrealistic, unbelievable, and lacks credibility. The offended party can accept only a modest change or a modicum of remorse as a realistic expression of a desire to resolve the conflict. Anything beyond a turn in the right direction arouses suspicion. A dramatic overnight reversal of position requires substantial explanation in order to be believable.

Therefore the mediator proceeds cautiously. He must Restore Face without causing additional Face Loss – which may happen if he overtly points out previous Face Loss. If he says, "Boy, that must have been embarrassing," he inadvertently implies the party was vulnerable. He unintentionally threatens additional Face Loss by pointing out previous weakness. The party may reject this implication and walk away.

In the past they may have attempted to Save Face through denial. The mediator who now implies they were susceptible to being hurt by the other party poses a new threat to Face. At the same time the mediator knows reconciliation depends on Restoring Face. He knows the party's denial of previous Face Loss locks their negative appraisal of the other party in place. The tangle of Face issues cements the oppositional embrace. The challenge is to find a frame that correctly describes the conflict without causing additional Face Loss.

A party trying to convene on their own must also Restore Other Face while not openly acknowledging the other party's previous Face Loss. Most of us have had the experience of offering an apology only to have the other party deny our actions had any effect on them. "You embarrassed me? No way, I didn't even notice what you said. Forget about it. It's fine."

The offended party's inner dialogue, however, mixes unexpressed resentment over past events with unexpressed gratitude for the current apology. The offended party's impulse to make you grovel in apology is offset by their need to cover up the fact they were sufficiently vulnerable to suffer Face Loss in the first place.

"I Messages"

Face issues are the primary reason "I messages" work so well.[3] When you use "I" to frame the concern, you avoid Face threat. For example, "*I* feel *I* may have been rude and disrespectful. *I* have concern that *I* was unfair." Contrast this with, "I'm sorry *you* were hurt and embarrassed. I'm sorry *you* felt unwanted or insignificant." While the latter may be true, admitting that version of the truth invokes Face Loss.

The latter expression implies you have the power to make the offended party feel insecure and belittled. It drives home the reality that they were made to feel less. This is an uncomfortable truth. In order to Save Face the offended party denies they were made to feel bad. This slows the progress as we must now incorporate the lie that they were not hurt into the narrative. Shoving the hurt feelings into the closet, however, only assures that those feelings will make an appearance later in the process.

If the guilty party simply says "*I* was out of line" the offended party can accept the statement – as they can agree the guilty party acted badly, without having to admit they suffered harm. They can accept a frame that allows them to say, "While you acted badly I was not weak enough to suffer harm as a result of your actions." In this manner, the offended party Saves Face and the offending party Restores Other Face.

Later in the process, after trust has been restored, during a period of emotional healing, the offended party may express just how bad they felt. This situation in which a party voluntarily expresses their hurt feelings differs considerably from the situation in which the offending party points out (or implies) they had the power to cause the other party to suffer Face Loss.

If it seems I am presenting an overly fine-grained analysis I assure you nothing could be farther from the truth. When it comes to vital issues of Face one cannot be too discerning and one cannot respect the nuances enough. When it comes to Face Work in conflict resolution the mediator is an explosives expert disarming a bomb while sweat beads on his brow – it does matter which wire you disconnect.

Identity-Based Conflict & Face

The concept of Face Work proves valuable in discussing identity concerns. Face connects to a visceral understanding of threats to identity and it unearths memories of times when we were forced to turn away, our cheeks flushed with embarrassment. Face Loss triggers memories of times we observed another person lower their gaze in response to ridicule or the pain of inflicted humiliation.

While a dismissed employee might recover from the loss of a job when he finds new employment, the embarrassment of being locked out of his office and marched off the premises by security will not fade easily. A betrayed spouse may find happiness in a new marriage but will have a difficult time facing neighbors and relatives who witnessed her public humiliation as a result of her spouse's not-so-secret affair. The failing student may eventually overcome a learning disability and excel at his studies but will find it difficult to let go of the public humiliation a sadistic teacher inflicted. The service worker insulted by a wealthy patron may seek refuge in dreams of a better life but rancor may linger at having to Honor Other Face while suffering Face Loss. (While "the customer is always right" may be a useful motto, it presents difficulty when it comes to Face.)

Most of us can recall personal examples of Face Loss and we are aware of defenses we have erected to Protect Face. Sometimes we suffer Face Loss in the company of those who witness our humiliation, in other instances, our awareness of Face Loss may come in solitude. Face Loss hammers our sense of identity and sets us adrift in a sea of doubt regarding our worth. As you assess your conflict pay special attention to Face concerns. Allow yourself to surface feelings you may have set aside but which are nonetheless alive in your inner world. Assess situations in which you feel cautious or easily bruised. Also consider the possibility that you have caused the other party to suffer Face Loss, intentionally or unintentionally.

Unrecognized Threats to Face

It is not uncommon to find one party mystified by the intensity of the other party's response to a conflict. A party may understand the substantive issues fueling the conflict and yet not understand the heat generated by those issues – the other party expresses upset that seems out of proportion with the substance of the conflict. A mediator might mistakenly believe the parties simply hold different views regarding the importance of the substantive issues. After careful investigation, however, an unrecognized threat to Face will be discovered.

In such instances, the upset party has suffered Face Loss the other part failed to recognize – one party has unknowingly insulted the other, unwittingly fueling the intensity of the fight. The party who suffered Face Loss thereafter attempts to Save Face by hiding the hurt they feel. They Protect Face by assuming a hostile and adversarial stance. In many conflicts Face Loss remains unrecognized for some time, simmering below the surface.

During the convening stage the mediator is alert for signs of unrecognized Face Loss. It may be too early to address a party's wounded pride but we can explain how the process heals wounds caused by insults and disrespect. If the mediator pays close attention, he may detect a slight nod or a glance of relief but most likely the party will not express their full concerns at this stage.

The Mediator's Role & Face Needs

When we consider Face dynamics we begin to understand why a neutral third party is necessary for resolution of conflict. When the opposing party presents a Face Threat there is relatively little chance disputants will come together. While the threatened party may be wary of their adversary, they may find comfort in the mediator's presence. They may gain courage and hope when the mediator honors their Face in front of their adversary. Their inner dialogue says, "You may not respect me, but the mediator does. So you're wrong, I *do* have worth." A compassionate third party neutral alters the dynamics: where previously there was impasse, hope surfaces.

The mediator asks each party to express their concerns regarding procedure then asks them to anticipate the other party's concerns. They are asked to consider what it would take to bring the other party to the table. Questions include: "What would prevent the other party from coming to the table?" and "How can that barrier be overcome?" Initially, while emotional and psychological fears are paramount, risk is minimized by process guidelines that promote safety. These guidelines assuage fears by addressing concerns regarding procedure.

For example, one party may insist they not be called a particular insulting name. Or they may insist the other party not yell at them, or they may insist the other party's meddling spouse not be present in the first meeting. Agreements regarding joint sessions and private sessions are hammered out. For example, one party may express fear with regard to meeting jointly. This leads to an agreement to convene in separate sessions. A subtle negotiation shapes guidelines that often relate to Face concerns. As you assess your conflict ask questions that help you map a route to the table.

Choosing the Mediator

In the legend the mayor seeks out Francis because of his reputation as a holy man. Francis is reputed to talk to animals and the mayor's dispute is with the wolf. The mayor responds to the mediator's character – Francis is a holy man. And the mayor responds to a specific skill – Francis talks to animals.

In your selection of a mediator you will need to weigh character: is this someone you trust to be fair and honest? You will want to evaluate experience and credentials: is this someone with skills that relate to your specific problem? If the dispute concerns real estate is the mediator familiar with the profession? If the conflict revolves around ethical issues (as most conflicts do), does the mediator possess skill in plumbing the depths of the human soul?

My personal prejudice calls for assigning greater weight to an ability to touch the parties deeply and speak to their hearts rather than to specialized knowledge in law or business. In most cases a technical question is not central to the conflict. Questions regarding relationship, ethics, and communication usually are paramount. Ordinarily parties bring needed technical expertise to the table: they know their business. Besides, if a highly technical question within the context of a specific profession arises the mediator can help the parties engage an expert to clarify technical issues.

In most cases, however, if the issue in dispute is technical in nature the parties would have already consulted an expert themselves if their human relations problems had not prevented them from working together in the first place. If there were no relationship troubles they would have previously agreed on an expert to provide advice they both could accept.

Likewise, if the conflict revolves around legal issues the parties ordinarily retain legal representation. Lawyers spend time researching legal questions and arrive at an interpretation of the applicable law. One might argue that attorneys differ in their analysis of the law and its application; therefore, there may be a need for a neutral representative to render a decision. But a mediator is not a judge who decides matters of law.

In my experience, the last thing an attorney representing a client in mediation wants is for the mediator to comment on the way they practice law or on their legal conclusions. On more than one occasion I have witnessed mediators who are also attorneys offer an interpretation or analysis of the law, unwittingly instructing a party's attorney on the practice of law. This is not helpful and not well received.

If a party wants the mediator to analyze the strength of their case the mediator can assume the view of a potential juror. Rather than offer an opinion on how a juror will decide the matter, the mediator can pose hypothetical questions a juror might ask in an attempt to clarify the issues. These clarifying questions, posed from the point of view of a naïve juror, help the party and their attorney gain insight into how their story might be heard. Whereas previously they imagined their arguments were crystal clear and indisputable they now realize ambiguity creeps in when the story is filtered through the mind of a juror. They discover their story or argument can be viewed in ways they had not anticipated.

The mediator plays the role of the naïve juror who wants to understand the conflict. As one of my mentors, Judge Alexander Williams III, frequently pointed out to litigants, jurors ask basic questions such as, "Who is being reasonable and who is being unreasonable?"[4] These are inherently relationship questions: they are questions about respect and ethics and how parties treat each other. The effective mediator does not allow mediation to stall on issues of how the law will be interpreted by legal scholars. Rather he helps parties unearth relationship issues that are more important (for mediation).

If the discussion remains stuck on legal strategy the mediator asks the party and the attorney if they have completed a *litigation risk analysis* that identifies the strengths and weaknesses of their case and assigns probabilities of success to decisions a judge or jury will render with regard to the law or the facts of the case. The process involves assigning a probability of success at each branch of a decision tree that represents all major decisions that take place in litigation.

In my experience few attorneys or clients have been willing to undertake the hard work of a detailed litigation risk analysis but undertaking a precise analysis often turns out not to be a critical factor. For the purpose of mediation the task is to help the client understand litigation involves risk: the trial outcome is uncertain. (This is true of any adversarial process.)

Prior to being confronted with the need for a litigation risk analysis a party is often certain of victory. When difficult questions are posed and when probabilities are assigned to a decision tree, slam-dunk certainty fades. The shield of legal expertise they assumed would protect them suddenly appears less impregnable. For the first time, the party ponders the disturbing thought that they could lose, they could get hurt. Their attorney may be at the top of the profession but juries are unpredictable, results are not always just, and not always rational. Risk exists.

At this point the party's attention turns increasingly to solving problems and repairing relationships instead of standing firm on legal positions. (The above analysis is not restricted to litigation. The dynamics are the same in any adversarial setting in which a third party will decide the outcome.)

MEDIATOR SUBJECT MATTER EXPERTISE. The preceding discussion does not mean the mediator's experience in specific disciplines is not valuable. There are times when industry specific knowledge allows the mediator to quickly understand pertinent issues. Familiarity with nomenclature, customs, and protocols unique to an industry prove valuable. The construction business, for example, has industry specific practices and thus a mediator with construction experience is able to understand the issues more quickly than a mediator unfamiliar with the profession. Likewise there are unique aspects to healthcare, labor relations, civil rights, religion, and other fields where conflict may arise. Subject matter experience can be an asset.

The issue, however, is how much emphasis to place on such experience when choosing a mediator. While subject matter background is a plus it should not take priority over the mediator's ability to address relationships and facilitate personal interaction. If one is faced with an either/or situation it may be better to engage a mediator with relationship skills rather than a mediator with expertise on technical issues.

It is an error, in my viewpoint, to retain a technically proficient mediator in the hope that he will shift from the mediator role to a judicial role and decide which party's technical facts are most accurate. If one desires a quasi-judicial ruling on the merit of technical facts or the persuasiveness of a legal argument it is better to turn to *early neutral evaluation*. When it comes to mediator selection and the issue of subject matter familiarity the key factor to consider is the purpose and goal of mediation. Turning mediation into an adjudicatory process rather than a facilitative or transformative process reduces the odds of reaching an outcome that will endure.

In addition it pays to analyze the role technical issues have played in the history of the conflict. During mediation one may discover technical issues are a smoke screen hiding deeper personal issues. On numerous occasions I have listened for hours as parties debated the intricacies of proper protocol within an industry and the fine points of their rights under the law only to have a breakthrough take place when one of the parties finally reveals the *real* issue has to do with personal insult, loss of face, jealousy, or other common generators of conflict arising from human relations.

If you engage a mediator solely for his technical or legal expertise he may fail to uncover the actual source of the conflict. If one chooses a mediator based on technical or legal expertise and that expertise fails to satisfy both parties the process hits an impasse. When the mediator excels as a process facilitator and is able to guide the parties through difficult emotional, psychological, and spiritual terrain there is less chance of an impasse.

MEDIATOR CHARACTER. If you decide the mediator's character will be important, assessing that character is the next task. Questions you may wish to pose include: What values motivate the mediator? What satisfaction does he or she derive from performing the role of a neutral party? Is mediation a business or an occupation that developed when a previous legal practice closed? Is it a vocation or calling? Was the mediator drafted into service as an impartial intermediary as a result of a stellar reputation within a specific professional community?

Mediators come to the profession from many different paths and their varied experience lends itself to resolving different types of disputes. Currently the majority of mediators are lawyers-turned-mediators and retired judges. Trained non-lawyer mediators may have been social workers, therapists, business executives, pastoral counselors, or clergy.

Some approach mediation as a higher calling arising from a life-long interest in peacemaking, others have been drawn to the profession as the result of a life experience in which conflict played a major role. A mediator may have suffered frustration in achieving professional goals as a result of continuous conflict, and that frustration spawned awareness of the importance of conflict resolution. This new awareness motivates them to help others overcome the conflict that stands in their path.

A mediator may have been recruited by management or labor to represent them in labor negotiations and may have discovered they loved the process. Others may come to the vocation as a result of religious conviction. Franciscans passionate about carrying on the work of Francis see "taming the wolf" as a spiritual mission.

Those who mediate may not always hold the professional designation of mediator. Ombudspersons, clergy, peacemakers, diplomats, and others may mediate with professional skill and yet not change their title, or they may be called mediators temporarily during the period when they facilitate conflict resolution.

Preferred mediator qualities differ from culture to culture. Some cultures prefer a disinterested neutral third party; others prefer a village elder, a family head, or a religious leader. Within the business culture distinguished late career professionals may be preferred. In youth conflicts a peer mediator may be best suited to the task. Depending upon the nature of your conflict, the "expert from afar," the tribal elder, the distinguished professional, the peer mediator, the empathetic pastoral counselor, or the seasoned diplomat may be your best choice. Explore the balance of faith and intellect, creativity and resourcefulness, character and expertise you require. Generate a list of characteristics you will use to evaluate the selection.

Mediators also vary in terms of style.[5] Some are evaluative, which means they offer opinions on the matter at hand; they may suggest specific parameters for settlement. Retired judges, accustomed to rendering judicial decisions, frequently fall into the evaluative category. They may provide a focus on getting the deal done.

Other mediators adopt a facilitative style, which means they concentrate on guiding the process and assisting parties in reaching their own result. A facilitative approach leans toward increased empathetic listening. With this approach more time is spent exploring personal options for resolution than in an evaluative approach. The facilitative mediator focuses less on whether or not a deal is struck.

Yet other mediators employ a transformative style in which they focus on nurturing inner changes (transformations) that result in parties seeking a new relationship and a new reality. They tend to focus on personal growth and lasting change more than on completing a negotiation. They see settlement arising as a natural product of the profound inner changes taking place. Pastoral counselors tend toward a transformative style, placing emphasis on examining conscience and nurturing inner conversion.

Juxtaposed over such styles are directive and non-directive approaches. A mediator may be highly directive and guide the process toward possible outcomes with a strong hand. Or a mediator may be non-directive, allowing parties to find their own way through trial and error. There are also combinations of approaches. A facilitative mediator actively guides the process, in a directive manner, while encouraging parties to arrive at their own resolution, in a non-directive manner. He plays a strong role in guiding the process but not the outcome. Other mediators may be non-directive with respect to both process and outcome.

As far as I know the style advocated in this book has not previously been named. I call it *spiritually transformative* mediation. In this approach the mediator focuses on changes in spiritual awareness that result in changed relationships. He nurtures the view that relationship has a sacred component and provides a spiritual or religious context for future agreements. Matters of the heart and matters of the spirit play a significant role.

In the legend, St. Francis, who was capable of deep empathy and great compassion, was moved by the plight of Gubbio. In your situation will empathy on the part of the mediator be important? Will there be a need to heal wounds? I have found – even in what appear to be garden-variety business disputes – that inevitably human emotions and values play a significant role. The mediator specializing in helping parties hammer out deals may miss important "soft" variables and may reach outcomes that are not enduring, as factors below the surface are left unattended. Later these submerged factors surface and reignite the conflict.

As you anticipate mediation consider the importance of the style and depth of the process. Are you seeking lasting and significant changes or simply relief from an immediate problem?

Most mediators alter their style to meet the needs of the parties. In effective conflict resolution party needs determine the appropriate style. A party may want a mediator who guides them strongly toward a suggested outcome they can accept, an outcome that allows them to move on with their life. Others may find the conflict requires a gentle guide who fosters deep inner transformation and helps overcome significant barriers to happiness: they seek an outcome that allows them to embrace the other party in reconciliation. Some pragmatic parties seek immediate relief and a return to business as usual. Others seek a more enduring outcome in which long-term relationships are improved by sustainable inner changes.

While I prefer the spiritually transformative approach there are times when it is important to honor the exigencies of a particular situation and place priority on achieving peace, rather than focusing on a particular style of getting to peace. You may use the ideas in this book to work through your side of a conflict; you may dig deep into underlying factors. The other party, however, may not wish to put in the effort to engage in full reconciliation. Spiritual transformation may be foreign or objectionable to them. Rather than force the situation, use the skills and techniques from *Taming the Wolf* to bring about an expedited resolution that meets the other party's needs and allows them to move on. It is entirely possible they will return later and express interest in a more thorough process that leads to full reconciliation. They may recognize there is more to be achieved in the way of reconciliation.

The key idea is not to force another party to conform to a style for the sake of imposing your favored approach. With this in mind, realize that you can express your style preferences to a mediator while also allowing them to analyze and assess the best approach to the conflict.

After considering what you need from a mediator you will want to plan the initial interview to help you decide whether a particular mediator can meet your needs. You will want to choose the type of mediator who might best help you achieve resolution and reconciliation.

Your selection of a preferred mediator does not end the selection process, as both parties must agree on the selection. You might ask, how can two parties who agree on little else agree on the selection of a mediator? As the choice of mediator may itself become a barrier to convening you will want to consider how you will present your rationale for using a particular person. In many cases simply because *you* select a mediator the other party will reject him. How will you overcome this knee-jerk response?[6] Time spent considering these issues is time well spent.

Once the mediator has consulted with you and has established the steps necessary for convening he may become slightly aloof. A mediator realizes that, in many instances, the more time they spend with one party the more likely the other party will worry about their neutrality. A party does not usually want to hear that a prospective mediator has spent time getting to know the other party; they will be concerned that such familiarity creates bias they will be unable to overcome.

However, this is not always true. There are times when a party will consider the other party's prior relationship with a mediator to be an advantage. They may hope the relationship will allow the mediator to deliver bad news in a way the other party will accept – news they would not accept if delivered by a stranger or opposing party.

In most cases, however, a party is more likely to entertain the selection of a mediator if he has not met extensively with the other party and if both parties agree that preliminary pre-convening discussions be conducted on an equal and transparent basis. Ideally the mediator agrees to meet with both sides equally prior to formal convening.

The skilled mediator acts in a transparent and even-handed manner. If necessary, he asks both parties for permission to engage in separate pre-convening meetings to discuss their willingness to mediate. He explains he will need to become familiar with both sides of the conflict in order to assess whether or not mediation is the correct way to proceed. In some instances the mediator may retain staff to handle these preliminaries on his behalf.

The professional mediator understands parties may ultimately choose another mediator. He recognizes that he sells the process more than he sells himself and he is willing for the parties to choose another professional should they decide that is in their best interest.

Along the same lines, the mediator has an ethical obligation to reveal possible conflicts of interest. It may come to light that the mediator has a personal or business relationship with a close associate of one of the parties and the existence of the relationship raises doubt regarding the mediator's ability to remain impartial. In such cases the mediator refers the parties to another mediator. This is true even when there is no actual conflict of interest; the existence of an apparent conflict of interest is enough to raise doubt. Recusing oneself in cases of apparent conflict of interest is necessary to prevent accusations of unfairness should one party later regret their settlement decision.

FAITH AS A FACTOR IN MEDIATOR SELECTION. Typically, when we seek a mediator we do not consider the role the spiritual plays in the conflict. This may be an oversight. If all conflict, boiled down to its essential components has roots in the spiritual, then spiritual concerns should be taken into account in mediator selection.

In the litigation context the process takes place within a secular setting that may discourage us from entertaining faith concerns. This may also be the situation within a secular organization such as a corporation – the human resources department that handles conflict resolution may not be conversant with religion. In situations where it is not possible or desirable to choose a mediator with a particular religious or spiritual background the party may choose to enlist a pastoral counselor to provide outside consultation and guidance parallel to mediation.

Absent hope, parties rarely go forward. In the legend we find Gubbio gained encouragement from the fact that Francis was a holy man. The town understood Francis brought hope to those who suffered; his love of Christ imbued him with compassion that provided comfort, grace, and hope. These qualities endow a mediator with an ability to provide parties with the confidence needed to convene. Thus it is worth reflecting on how a mediator's spiritual formation affects his or her ability to facilitate and guide transformation.

Often a mediator's spiritual qualities or gifts enhance his or her ability to reconcile warring parties. Throughout history we find spiritual men and women engaged in peacemaking – Gandhi, Mandela, King, St. Francis, to name but a few. While lawyers dominate the mediation profession at this time I can imagine a future when clergy and gifted laity trained in reconciliation comprise a significant percentage of the pool of mediators available to the public.

Whether or not a background in spiritual formation is important is a matter of individual party choice. You will want to consult your own heart to determine the role spiritual qualities play in mediator selection. In the future it is possible that reconciliation centers staffed by mediators who bring the resources of faith to the process will spring up across the country. At present we can work to become more considerate of party concerns when it comes to the role of faith. During the convening stage a mediator might inquire if one or both parties view their mediation efforts within a divine context. If they do this may affect the process and the outcome.

A challenge arises, however, when one person holds a faith-based view and the other party holds a secular view or even feels antipathy toward religious or spiritual concerns. The mediator will want to assess the probability that common ground can be found: he or she may ask the parties how they wish to work with or around their differences.

When one party wishes to place spiritual concerns on the table while the other party finds the topic unacceptable the mediator will need to facilitate negotiation of process guidelines. This negotiation determines whether or not these differences will become a part of the mediation.

Parties may choose to avoid contentious issues related to their religious views while pursuing the resolution of other issues. At other times, differences in religious views may be part of the conflict and cannot be avoided. Guidelines for discussion may be designed to allow parties to handle the issues in a respectful manner. In some situations the mediator may find private sessions provide a setting in which parties can discuss closely held religious views, allowing the parties to work on framing their views in a manner that generates understanding.

One party may view any discussion of the other party's religious views as an attempt at proselytizing, which may provoke resentment. When the mediator assists with careful framing of the statements the resentment may diminish or vanish. Managed properly the discussion of differing views conducted in a respectful manner under well-conceived process guidelines may invigorate the relationship and heal past misunderstanding.

Faith may play a direct and central role in the conflict, such as conflicts within a church congregation or parish. The parties might ask themselves if the mediator should be a member of their faith or not. Should the mediator be an elder or deacon or member of the clergy? Will the mediator's involvement in the faith bring needed understanding or will it hamper the process? Will a neutral party with no stake in the outcome be better suited to the task?

As interfaith dialogue increases and values of inclusivity and plurality become increasingly accepted we may witness an increase in conflict that both requires and is uniquely amenable to reconciliation. In interfaith disputes it may be necessary to engage a team of co-mediators, with one mediator selected from each faith.

As faith groups increasingly share the public square it may be necessary to mediate peaceful co-existence on an ongoing basis, with creative use of learning conversations and conflict prevention protocols. Groups dedicated to mediating faith-based conflict may form and provide a valuable service to the community. Religious orders that already recognize the importance of interfaith dialogue, such the Franciscans, may specialize in designing programs tailored to mediating conflicts between faith traditions.[7]

Globalization, which has come upon us at breakneck speed, may be the impetus for religious groups to devote more time to designing and operating conflict resolution programs, programs that not only serve the public but which meet the sacred mission of each faith.

A Franciscan View

The importance of Face Work in the convening stage directs our attention once again to "the face of a Franciscan," which I first encountered in *The Threefold Way of St. Francis* by Friar Murray Bodo, OFM.[8] Greeting another with the face of a Franciscan is embracing another with a gaze that seeks the divine in all creatures. The concept provides a unique introduction to the potential ability of a Franciscan to convene reconciliation processes, especially those that require working with Face.

Friar Bodo captures the act of divine Face giving, "Everyone wants to know if she or he is good, beautiful, has something to give. The Franciscan gift to them is affirmation of the light, manifest or hidden, of their true face."[9] Franciscan Richard Rohr captures the manner in which love conveyed restores Face: "When someone else loves you, they give you not just themselves, but for some reason they give you back your own self, but now a truer and better self."[10]

Francis, in his holy manner of being, teaches mediators (and those who wish to resolve their own conflicts) the value that lies in our gaze upon the other, the value of nothing more than our humble presence. "The mystery of presence is *that encounter wherein the self-disclosure of one evokes a deeper life in the other*. There is nothing you need to 'think' or understand to be present; it is all about giving and receiving right now, and it is not done in the mind.

It is actually *a transference and sharing of Being*, and will be experienced as grace, gratuity and inner-goundedness."[11]

We can imagine the curative effect Francis' gaze had on those he encountered as he traveled the countryside. "The Franciscan charism is to reveal to the world its essentially good and holy face, so often masked with false faces that twist God's image into something unrecognizable except to the saints among us who remind us, as St. Francis does, that we are more good than bad. 'Buon giorno, buona gente,' *Good* morning, *good* people, St. Francis sang through the streets of the small mountain village of Poggio Bustone...."[12]

The preceding passage reminds us of the importance of presenting the face of Francis, which lifts up those besieged by conflict in a way that acknowledges them as good people, with a greeting that announces "good morning" no matter the time of day.

It is not a stretch to characterize the presence Francis brought to the task of taming the wolf as a prayerful presence. In the legend we learn that upon hearing of the conflict he turned immediately to prayer. He was not turning away from the conflict and doubting his ability, rather he was preparing for his encounter with the citizens of Gubbio and the wolf.

Friar Bodo helps us understand the approach Francis was taking: "This dynamic of focusing on the Other who draws me out and thereby frees me from my own limitations is the very center of what Franciscan prayer is. Spiritual exercises, silence, solitude – these are not for making me more self-conscious, but for making me aware of the one who made me, loves me, redeems me. This absorption in the Other purifies and motivates more than any self-analysis or penitential act."[13] Thus it was that Francis prepared, providing us with a model to emulate.

For parties about to engage the resolution process the following, written by Richard Rohr, provides valuable insight into the nature of prayer. "God fixes his gaze intently where I refuse and where I fear to look, on my shared, divine nature as his daughter or son (1 John 3:2). And one day my gaze matches God's gaze (frankly, that is what we mean by prayer)."[14] With these thoughts in mind we may approach prayer as preparation to meet the other party in the reconciliation process.

Friar Bodo, engaging in an experimental exercise of greeting the world (in this case travelers at Chicago's O'Hare airport) with the face of a Franciscan, provides a model exercise for mediators or parties anticipating the need to make themselves present for conflict resolution: "I tried to make eye contact, whispered to each face, 'I love you.' It made a difference to me, lifted my heart, and apparently did the same for some of those I passed, who halted briefly on their headlong rush and turned to look at me again as perhaps someone they knew, someone remembered. Some even smiled."[15]

When we practice giving the gift of the face of a Franciscan, we impart to Face Work a new meaning and vitality. We actively give the gift of a gaze turned toward the divine. We actively Give Divine Face to the other, which cannot help but transform the relationship.

"Awareness of the Other draws me out of self-preoccupation into the loving gaze of God whose countenance absorbs me, makes me forget my own problems or preoccupations, lost as I am in God's love. It is like the experience of falling in love, when we forget our own blemishes because someone loves us, someone makes us forget about ourselves. When you love me, I see only your love for me...."[16]

Scripture

Had I rejoiced at the destruction of my enemy
*   or exulted when evil came upon him*
Even though I had not allowed my mouth to sin
*   by invoking a curse against his life—*
*   ... then I should have remained*
silent, and not come out of doors! (Jb 31:29-30, 34)

The rich are wise in their own eyes,
*   but the poor who are intelligent see*
*   through them.*

When the just triumph, there is great
glory;
but when the wicked prevail,
people hide.
Those who conceal their sins do not
prosper,
but those who confess and forsake
them obtain mercy. (Prv 28:11-13)

And he was transfigured before them; his face shone like the sun and his clothes
became white as light. (Mt 17:2)

Bless those who persecute [you], bless and do not curse them. Rejoice with those
who rejoice, weep with those who weep. Have the same regard for one another;
do not be haughty but associate with the lowly; do not be wise in your own
estimation. Do not repay anyone evil for evil; be concerned for what is noble in
the sight of all. (Rom 12:14-17)

The high priest questioned Jesus about his disciples and about his doctrine. Jesus
answered him, "I have spoken publicly to the world. I have always taught in a
synagogue or in the temple area where all the Jews gather, and in secret I have
said nothing. Why ask me? Ask those who heard me what I said to them. They
know what I said." When he had said this, one of the temple guards standing
there struck Jesus and said, "Is this the way you answer the high priest?" Jesus
answered him, "If I have spoken wrongly, testify to the wrong; but if I have
spoken rightly, why do you strike me?" (Jn 18:19-23)

Let love be sincere; hate what is evil, hold on to what is good; love one another
with mutual affection ... (Rom 12:9-10)

CHAPTER SEVEN

Discovery & Deception

Dawn found them walking down the hill from Assisi on their way to Gubbio. In time they arrived at the woods near the town.

The messengers pointed to where the wolf had slain the two guards not far from the road. They stayed in a tighter group as they hurried the rest of the way, watching for the wolf.

The gate to the town was opened as they arrived and was quickly closed behind them. The entire town followed Francis to the town square where the Mayor eagerly greeted them. They went into the town hall to eat and discuss what Francis would do with the wolf.

Mediation Principles

IN PREVIOUS CHAPTERS the convening stage was introduced. We considered mediation as one option along a continuum of conflict resolution approaches, and we began exploring how to initiate the process, with an emphasis on Face Work. We also considered how to go about selecting a mediator.

In this chapter the legend of *St. Francis and the Wolf* finds the citizens of the town of Gubbio engaging in dialogue with the potential mediator, Francis of Assisi. In this preliminary exchange the citizens of Gubbio seek the counsel of Francis who listens carefully and tries to understand their plight as they explain how they have been harmed. In the following discussion we will take a parallel path and consider the topic of *discovery*. How will we know what happened? How will we deal with deception? Where might we find a safe place to meet and consider what happened?

Meeting with the Mediator

Francis meets alone with one party, the citizens of Gubbio, and seeks to discover the source of the conflict and determine what must be done to bring the parties to the table. During the preliminary stages a mediator may meet with one party and then the other in separate sessions in order to identify the exact conflict that must be resolved.

In the legend Francis launches the *opening stage* with the citizens of Gubbio who introduce him to the conflict through dialogue while sharing a meal.[1] In litigated cases parties introduce the conflict more formally by submitting mediation briefs.[2] In other judicial processes, for example, in labor grievance hearings, written documents may also be submitted. In other settings a letter, memo, or e-mail may serve to document the complaint. In yet other settings the petition for resolution of grievances may be informal and will not include the submission of written materials.

Parties or their attorneys may also speak with the mediator over the phone to plan the process. These discussions, along with written documents, provide the mediator with information regarding how to proceed. Parties are encouraged to disclose whether or not violence has occurred or threats have been exchanged, as convening a joint session under such conditions poses risk. If risk exists the mediator suggests starting with separate sessions.

When a mediator is not yet involved parties should consider these same concerns and seek creative ways of beginning the conciliation dialogue without putting themselves at risk.[3] If the potential of violence exists initial discussions should be conducted using shuttle diplomacy,[4] allowing parties to remain at a safe distance from one another.

Francis meets alone with the citizens of Gubbio first in order to gain an understanding of the conflict that will allow him to bring the wolf to the table, but Francis must be aware that the wolf may be watching and may assume he has become biased as a result of meeting behind the closed walls of Gubbio. Francis will need to raise this issue early in his discussion with the wolf and address concerns regarding neutrality, and demonstrates mediator transparency.

In mediation there are no inflexible rules, so the mediator cannot approach the task in a rote manner. Every conflict presents unique demands. He must remain alert and awake to possibilities. Thus, while it is not ideal for the mediator to meet at length with one party initially, it is not out of the question.

Discovery: Litigation versus Mediation

A preliminary task in mediation is the collection of information or evidence, a process known as *discovery*. In this step the mediator listens to parties and/ or reads documents and considers the following questions: What is this conflict really about? What happened? What are the facts of the case?

The informal discovery process common in mediation (which could be referred to simply as "finding out what happened") differs from the formal discovery process common in litigation (and other judicial processes). In order to provide a better understanding of the mediation approach I will contrast it with formal discovery used to prepare for trial. This brief review is not intended to provide a thorough education in the litigation discovery process, but rather to highlight important differences that will help you make informed choices regarding the conflict resolution path you will take.[5]

In litigation, discovery is a formal procedure guided by rules of evidence and by orders issued from the bench in response to pre-trial motions argued by attorneys. The rules of evidence and the judge's decisions determine what evidence will be admissible and in what form the evidence may be presented. (The same is true to some degree in all processes, such as hearings that rely on a judicial model.)

In this time-consuming and expensive stage of litigation attorneys interview their clients but more importantly they gather information (evidence) from the other side in order to assess the facts of the case they will use to construct arguments that support their client and defeat the opposition.

During the early stages of litigation a legal brief presented to the court explains the causes that motivated the party (the plaintiff or petitioner) to file a lawsuit. The brief explains the party's complaint and petitions the court for specific remedies; it explains the legal reasons the party is entitled to relief the court has the power to grant. The other party (the defendant or respondent) explains in their brief why the suit (the complaint) is inappropriate, invalid, or lacks merit.[6]

Briefs contain statements of fact that one side believes to be relevant and true, along with a discussion of the law that applies to that particular fact pattern. During the pre-trial phase motions regarding which facts or what evidence can be presented during the trial are argued before the bench.

Gathering underlying evidence is pursued in earnest and can be a grueling process as each side searches for facts that support their version of contested events and disprove the other side's version. For example, in the discovery phase attorneys often summon the other side for a period of face-to-face questioning called a deposition. Questions are posed and responses are recorded, frequently on videotape. Later, in the actual trial, written excerpts from depositions may be read or the video may be shown.

Attorneys also send lists of questions known as interrogatories to which the opposing party must respond. In this process (controlled by the rules of evidence and decisions from the bench), attorneys are allowed to compel the production of documents or other evidence they believe are relevant.

Discovery is expensive and time consuming. Hundreds of hours of depositions may be taken and thousands of pages of documents may be gathered. Depending on the lawyer's skill and tact or lack thereof, the discovery process may incite additional hostility between the parties, which further lessens their willingness to meet one another in good-faith negotiations. The discovery process in the litigation framework (or in other judicial processes) involves more than simply gathering cold, hard facts; it is the beginning of an adversarial contest in which each side attempts to discredit the other.

The trial lawyer's goal is to impeach the testimony of an opposing party or their witnesses in order to destroy their credibility. There is an underlying assumption that discovery will unmask a deceptive party and vindicate an honest and aggrieved party. While this may happen, litigation tends to push the parties far from the actual lived experience of the events driving the conflict. Litigation takes on a life of its own, moving beyond the conflict that prompted the parties to seek the court's ruling in the first place.

The discovery process may produce, in rare cases, a willingness to mediate, as the grueling experience may spur a party's desire to take an alternate path. When a party faces testifying under oath, when they face possible penalties for deception, when they realize they might be unmasked before a jury or judge, they may be willing to entertain conflict resolution efforts. In this way rigorous discovery may promote mediation.

In most cases the adversarial discovery process causes the opposite response – a party hardens their position. They resort to hair-splitting, half-truths commonly heard in the courtroom, even though they face trial lawyers who specialize in exposing half-truths and unmasking dissemblers. While a degree of truth may be uncovered most often it is a shallow truth that lacks the richness of a freely given exposition of what happened. Rather than move toward mediation most parties become angry and willing to risk being impeached.

This adversarial search for the truth creates harsh feelings that inhibit mediation, should it convene at a later date. The level of hostility may kill subsequent willingness to engage in a candid discussion. In litigation an attorney Attacks Other Face; the attorney's mission is to make sure only their client's version of events prevails in the jurors' minds. In non-coutroom settings where a party represents themselves in adversarial proceedings (hearings, community meetings, kitchen table quarrels), the party, on their own, often tries to impeach their adversary. They Attack Other Face.

If they are successful Other Face is seriously damaged. Relationships are also destroyed, as aggressive and accusatory questioning hardens positions so that even when a party might otherwise consider settlement negotiations they now refuse to consider a conciliatory process. I have witnessed mediation grind to a halt due to the emotional residue from an overly aggressive deposition in which the party's identity and integrity were stridently attacked.

On the other hand, attorneys might argue a deposition convinces a stubborn party their position is not as strong as they once thought. The deposition convinces them that under harsh cross-examination they will falter and fail to impress a jury. This realization may convince the party to consider the more amicable process of mediation rather than force a public courtroom contest. There is some merit to this view. When the opposing party has refused all invitations to mediate, there may be value to providing a reality check. This approach makes less sense when it turns a potentially willing party into a hostile party.

In other adjudicatory forms of dispute resolution, such as arbitration, discovery plays a lesser role, as rules often limit discovery in an effort to reduce time spent and costs incurred. Nonetheless, the discovery effort may still cause upset. In small claims court the process is greatly simplified; the discovery process usually consists of the judge ordering litigants to meet in the hall prior to trial to share documents they intend to present to the court. Anything they do not share is inadmissible.

You may feel the preceding discussion is irrelevant as you do not intend to end up in court. We typically do not sue fellow employees who make life at the office a tortured experience; we typically do not sue neighbors who make our life uncomfortable but do not break laws; we do not sue our teenaged children with whom conflict is a daily occurrence; we do not usually sue members of our parish, though we may often wish a court would hear our petition.

In spite of the small percentage of conflicts heard let alone resolved in a courtroom, it is worth contrasting litigation discovery with mediation discovery as inadvertently we tend to apply the adversarial litigation model to our day-to-day conflict interactions. We become defensive and accusative as though we were on trial. We advance arguments that support our version of the facts while tearing down the other party's facts.

On occasion we may appear at hearings before a panel of community officials or we may appear before an executive committee at work; we may plead our case with a boss or neighborhood council, or we may adjudicate conflicts within the family on an adversarial basis, employing ad hoc discovery processes aimed at ascertaining who is telling the truth.

Though we are not guided by the formalities of the courtroom in these other settings, we interrogate and we depose, we aggressively force each other to reveal evidence, and we defend our facts while impugning the facts the other party favors. We aggressively demonstrate that the other person's command of the evidence is flawed, while insisting we have a solid grasp of the facts that constitute reality. Thus, comparing the litigation (adversarial) approach with the mediation approach turns out to be relevant across a wide range of conflicts.

The tendency to adopt an adversarial discovery approach affects more than individuals. In clashes between cultures, evidence may be uncovered and presented by investigative journalists, spin doctors, or other sources of public relations propaganda. A heated battle over the validity of the facts ensues, with each faction firing off accusations of misrepresentation and deception. Such adversarial trial-by-public opinion can become an aggressive process in which specific versions of the facts are aired before the public who are treated as third-party decision makers. The final account of events on the record may not represent events as the parties lived and experienced them but rather represent events tailored to support polarized views.

In more private conflicts parties launch attacks and mount defenses designed to justify their position and curry the goodwill of recruited bystanders – impromptu juries of friends and associates – in an effort to garner opinion and solicit decisions that satisfy our previously mentioned need to be right.

Thus, the adversarial discovery process is not confined to the courtroom; the adversarial approach is common and ubiquitous. When we begin mediation a paradigm shift must take place.

Mediation changes the nature of the game. Our purpose for discovering and disclosing information changes: we seek to understand the other party rather than impugn their credibility. Parties no longer ask a disinterested third party to render a decision. Instead, the parties enter into a process in which they jointly determine the outcome. There is no reason to spin facts for the benefit of an outside decision maker, instead we have a reason to make facts clear so we can achieve understanding.

When we were caught up in the adversarial style of discovery we hurled argument and insult at the other party, but now we lean forward and listen closely. Parties seek candor and honesty, resulting in more give-and-take disclosure. Our language changes from "prove it" to "help me understand what you are saying."

Because we are no longer focused on reaching a verdict regarding who was wrong and who was right we solicit differing perspectives. The past becomes relevant only to the degree that it helps us negotiate a shared future – we turn our attention to the past only in an effort to find common ground that allows us to move forward in tandem, as the end result of mediation is not a verdict but rather an agreement regarding a shared future.

If past events require clarification (or apologies or amends) in order to assure a better future then those events are taken up and explored, but they are not explored with the motive of assigning blame and targeting punishment. Rather past events are taken up for the purpose of clarifying precipitating causes and ensuring harmful actions are not repeated in the future.

We may need to remedy existing imbalances, injustices, or inequities that left unaddressed will continue to generate conflict in the future. We do not ignore the past but rather we place a forward-looking frame around discussion of events that have transpired. We take up the past in light of how it affects the future. Mediation thus alters the focus and purpose of discovery. In mediation we change the manner in which we uncover what happened.

In mediation facts go beyond the facts sought in litigation. Evidence code provisions restrict evidence that can be presented at trial but there are no restrictions in mediation. During a trial complex and subtle emotional motivations are rendered irrelevant, whereas in mediation the quest to discover the genesis of conflict includes revealing such complex and subtle emotional factors.

In mediation we engage in a much finer-grained exploration of motivation and perspective. Mediation allows the parties to share facts or truths that they otherwise might wish to hide. In the respectful give-and-take of active listening parties reveal deeper thoughts, fears, and personal concerns, including heartfelt expressions of apology and regret that are out of place in the trial venue.

As the focus shifts, from impugning the other party's credibility to listening closely to their personal story, the stories become more authentic. The facts of the case are no longer abstract tools of rhetorical battle but rather the truths of living persons seated before you. The shift from litigation to mediation is analogous to the shift from a fuzzy black-and-white television picture to a pristine high- definition color presentation – in mediation the narrative of what happened becomes clear.

Facts come alive when they are shared in a mutually respectful and collaborative process. As firsthand stories are told the characters morph from cardboard stereotypes with base motives – characters conjured up by adversarial storytellers – to real-life, multi-dimensional players imbued with rich emotional lives and complex motives. In litigation, parties must defend false selves that are stage props in a courtroom drama. In mediation, parties are provided an opportunity to present themselves in a more honest light – flawed beings who hurt, suffer, care, love, hate, transgress, and fall short of who they dream of being.

We not only seek to discover facts but also to comprehend the complex living being in front of us who we now invite into our consciousness in order that we might understand them. In the trial process parties attempt to hide their shortcomings, as their flaws are the weapons the other side uses to destroy them. In mediation we share our shortcomings in order to reveal the truth of our flawed nature. Revealing our shortcomings we are able to better explain the harm we have caused and to better express our intention to make up for past damage. In court we defiantly deny our failures and seek to be exonerated or deemed victorious. In mediation we acknowledge our flawed past in an attempt to create a better future.

Trial lawyers who are focused on their (legitimate) role as zealous advocates may not fully recognize or consider the differences between litigation and mediation during the discovery process, especially when mediation is viewed as nothing more than a temporary detour on the path to trial rather than the primary destination. However, the person who desires resolution and reconciliation will want to consider the differences and select the approach that is best for them. (These comments apply to all adversarial approaches whether in the workplace, at home, at school, in the community, or at the local parish.)

When we shift from litigation discovery to mediation discovery the question becomes, what do we reveal and what remains private?[7] Confidentiality statutes make candid discussion possible in mediation, promoting in-depth exploration of what happened. Legislatures at the state and federal level enacted such confidentiality provisions knowing increased candidness promotes settlement, which in turn lessens the strain on court dockets and results in higher satisfaction for litigants.

If privacy is a major concern parties may consider negotiating additional confidentiality agreements. In non-litigated conflicts it is also wise to consider the role confidentiality should play. It is wise to consider how to structure agreements that protect privileged information. In some instances, forms of amnesty or immunity may be considered as methods of promoting full and honest disclosure.

The shift from a public forum – in which airing dirty laundry is often the goal – to a private process requires careful consideration of guidelines and procedures that promise confidentiality. In addition, parties may wish to agree in advance how the results of the mediation will be made known – sometimes a public statement is appropriate while at other times the matter should remain private to avoid unnecessary public shame.

With these thoughts in mind carefully assess what you hope to achieve in an adversarial discovery process and determine if those goals might be better achieved in mediation. This may affect the timing of your discovery efforts, as parties who have experienced a demanding litigation discovery phase often arrive at mediation unwilling to shift to the more introspective honesty that is required. It may make sense to begin with mediation and only if that is unsuccessful would you move to the contentious discovery phase of litigation or any other adversarial process.

Presenting "What Happened"

Francis converses with the mayor and his advisors over dinner. The mayor seeks to educate Francis regarding what happened (from his viewpoint). You may also relate your story in a casual conversation or, if mediation takes place within the context of a litigated case, your attorney may submit a formal mediation brief that provides a written explanation of the contested issues and possible settlement options. The mediator will read the brief before you meet but he or she may also ask for a verbal narrative of events.[8]

When it comes to long-term conflicts between regions, nations, or ethnic groups, there may be a need for a mediator to spend considerable time becoming conversant with an extensive conflict history. The task varies depending upon the scope and history of the conflict. In some conflicts a history of revenge must be untangled. Navigating through historically troubled waters, the process of exploring collective and personal histories, may take considerable time and effort. Many stories must be taken into account. Some will be accessible while others will be hidden from public view. Some may involve closely guarded secrets. One should not underestimate the amount of inquiry needed in order to sketch an accurate picture of the conflict history.

In *The Moral Imagination* John Paul Lederach uses the analogy of spiders and their webs to explain social connections to be mapped in peacemaking.[9] "A web … can never be thought of as permanent, fixed, or rigid. The spider's genius lies in its ability to adapt, reshape, and remake its web of connections within the realities presented in a given space."[10] This analogy calls on mediators to explore the complex social fabric surrounding a conflict; it is a fabric that is ever changing like a spider web.

In your assessment consider the following: What should you expect the other party to tell you? What do you expect you will be asked to disclose to the other party? What will you need to know in order to arrive at a decision about the future? What will the other party need to know in order to make a decision? Notice the questions do not ask for information needed to determine who is guilty but rather focus on what must be known in order to make valid decisions about the future.

When two or more parties narrate their story they may discover inaccurate or incomplete information has contributed to the conflict. It may turn out that each party possessed only partial information and the prior lack of information may have led to incorrect assumptions and false attributions.

In the world of dramatic comedy, acting on missing information leads to a comedy of errors but in real life the consequences are rarely humorous. The discovery that information has been missing or inaccurate allows the parties to remedy the situation by providing accurate information that clears up false assumptions and false attributions. Sometimes this step alone brings about resolution and reconciliation. Once all the needed information is in place there is increased clarity – the conflict often resolves as the parties discover and acknowledge they have been operating in the dark and have made mistakes as a result.

At other times the stories may simply bring to light differences to be addressed and reconciled. We assume we understand the motives of the other party but upon hearing their firsthand account we often discover they view events in an unexpected light. The other party may perceive us in a way that contradicts our self-image. What we see as virtuous they interpret as villainous. Discovering the difference in how the other views us and our self-image can be sobering. Recognition of the profound mismatch signals we must work to remedy distortions – distortions in how they see us and distortions in our self-image.

The differences in perspective will never be entirely erased due to the subjective nature of awareness. The mistaken assumption that facts exist independent of an observer leads to a false expectation that a fair outcome can be dictated by facts alone. This leads to the unrealistic view that if only the correct facts, cleansed of distortion, could be presented the conflict could be resolved on the basis of an objective standard.

Facts, however, always exist within a subjective context. Parties may find a degree of inter-subjective agreement – they may agree two cars collided – but then divergent subjective awareness comes into play. They will have experienced the crash from slightly different perspectives. The physical positions from which they viewed events will differ. The emotional positions from which they view will differ. The experiential filters that attach meaning and interpretation to experience will differ. Mediation embraces this malleable nature of facts: the process is designed to accommodate mutually exclusive reality claims.

The mediator is not dismayed upon hearing radically different accounts; she welcomes the reality that people view the world from different perspectives. The realization that there is no definitive objective reality based on indisputable facts out there allows the parties to creatively craft a common narrative for the future rather than crash to a halt over irreconcilable differences.

The move away from the premise of an objective reality frees the parties from the assumption that a judgment will be rendered based on an irrefutable set of objective facts.[11] Rather than being a barrier, the malleable, subjective nature of reality provides the freedom needed for us to structure new versions of reality that encompass the needs of multiple parties.

Parties go to trial under the illusion that they will get a chance to tell their story but few leave court (or other adversarial hearings) feeling they achieved that goal. The story told bears little resemblance to the story they wished to tell. Disappointment occurs in most processes in which a third party adjudicates the validity of our story. This happens because our narrative, already altered to meet procedural requirements, is filtered through the subjective reality of the judge or jury. It is impossible for them to know exactly what happened, yet they are called upon to write the definitive story of what happened in the form of a verdict. These final arbiters of accepted reality begin with a modified version of events and then arrive at a new reality in the form of a decision. This is a nearly impossible task but is the best possible outcome under the adversarial model. Luckily, we have a choice as to whether or not we wish to suffer through such adjudication.

Mediation encounters the same "multiple realities" dilemma but the process honors those multiple perspectives. Once I commented to participants, "You're in the same theater, but you're watching different movies." Subjective experience can differ so greatly we find it is impossible to arrive at a single account based on consensus. Once the mediator listens to the party narratives, he realizes there is no such thing as facts absent subjective interpretation. In mediation we allow the subjective interpretations to provide a richer version of the conflict, which in turn leads to more nuanced outcomes.

Here is how it works. The mediator informs participants that the goal is not to tell the best story (in order to convince a judge) but rather to tell the story that accurately reflects their personal experience. Participants do not tell their story to evoke a mediator decision but rather tell their story so the other party can fully appreciate their viewpoint.

Each party is asked to listen closely as the other tells their story. The mediator typically instructs the parties to direct their story to him ("tell me what happened") while the other party listens. This avoids the discomfort of addressing the opposing party early in the process. Nonetheless, while they tell the story to the mediator, the party listening gains insight into how their adversary views the situation.

Accounts of past events are heard within the context of the listener's experience. While one party relates what happened in their own words, the other party listens through the filter of *their* experience. Clarifying questions posed by the mediator refine the exchange. At the end of the narration one party has the benefit of having listened to their opponent's story from a detached observer's vantage point. Then the process is repeated with the other party relating their story to the mediator while the first party listens without comment.

While the opposing party's narrative may not match ours we begin to accept their version as accurate in terms of their experience of events. We reach the point where we say, "That's not the way I saw it happen. But I'll agree that is how you experienced it." We move away from attempts to establish rigid versions of reality.

This leads us to explore both the overlapping and differing portions of our narratives. We become genuinely curious as to why the other party sees events differently. We slowly accept the purpose is not to arrive at a definitive account of the past but rather to build a future together. Our attention shifts from adjudicating the reality of the past to figuring out how we will live together in the future.

The following example illustrates this dynamic. One party may absolutely refuse to accept responsibility for negligence – they deny they are to blame. Nonetheless they agree the other party suffered harmed and deserves help. They are willing to make things right but are not willing to admit negligence. At that point, the harmed party has an opportunity to accept amends or reparations but the opportunity is contingent on their willingness to forego placing blame. As long as the goal of the harmed party is to be made whole by receiving reparations for damages and as long as they refrain from forcing a statement of responsibility they can shape a satisfactory future.

At other times a harmed party may not care about reparations but may insist on an apology. The master narrative they wish to co-author includes the other party's apology. The narrative includes repentance and forgiveness. They must convince the other party to join them in writing that new narrative. Perhaps they forego reparations in return for an apology.

But I am getting ahead of myself. At this stage I simply want to convey the role a mediator plays in overseeing discovery and prompting the flow of information. The mediator exercises active listening, paraphrasing, summarizing, and prompting disclosure. She evokes narrative accounts rich in values, beliefs, emotions, reasons, memories, hurts, hopes, impressions and assumptions. This allows her to open windows into the hearts, minds, and souls of those trapped in conflict.

If she is like Francis she is attuned to Spirit; she taps into the divine within. Such a mediator gently and respectfully touches divine consciousness and promotes spiritual transformation.

Managing Deception

The preceding discussion may cause skepticism. You may say, "Hold on. Doesn't a trial determine the truth? Don't we need a process that identifies who is lying and who is telling the truth?" You might argue that litigation-based discovery assures no one will benefit from a lie. While this may be correct on occasion it is not universally true. Frequently the lie prevails in litigation.

There are instances when detection and punishment of deception are the primary goals and times when unmasking a lie is appropriate. In the majority of cases we are more concerned with satisfying our interests than with exposing lies. We prefer meeting long-term needs over enjoying the short-lived "gotcha" moment of exposing a lie in court. We come to realize that focusing on lie detection may actually diminish the degree to which we satisfy our interests. As you may find this counterintuitive the following discussion provides additional explanation.

When one focuses on exposing deception within a judicial setting one encounters the challenge of correctly identifying lies and truths. As noted previously, identifying and judging what constitutes a lie or a truth often leads to ambiguous results. Most of the time the lines are fuzzy. We live in a subjective reality.

While at times it may be clear that we are dealing with willful attempts to deceive, frequently we simply encounter different subjective truths. In the situation where deception is clear and unambiguous a verdict may correctly punish a party for their deception; however, more often valid subjective truths are inadvertently dismissed when we seek a verdict. In order to reach a verdict we may overlook more subtle truths.

The jury or judge or other decision-maker may end up rewarding the half-truth presented most convincingly through rhetorical storytelling. The pressure on the jury (or other decision-maker) to find in favor of one party over another can lead to the dismissal of a perfectly valid position, especially when partial truths exist on both sides of the argument. A jury does not face clear demarcations between fact and fiction; rather they face a blurry picture where truth and fabrication are interwoven in stories relating a complex stream of events.

Though only anecdotal evidence supports my argument I believe it is fairly common for frustrated juries to conclude both parties are being unreasonable and untruthful. Nonetheless they are required to deliver a verdict. Provided the opportunity to express their frank assessment the jury would probably tell both parties to get it together, consult their consciences, and work it out. Instead, juries often express dismay by granting one side a winning verdict while awarding that "winner" such low damages that in essence they lose. The jury sends a message: "You both lose. No one deserves a victory."

Even when a judge or jury or other decision maker correctly discerns outright deception the outcomes rarely have long-term value for shaping future relationships. A verdict that correctly punishes deception does little to contribute to honest relationships in the future; it simply punishes the wrong-doer for past behavior and ignores the possibility of shaping a better future.

In situations such as cases of criminal fraud where one party clearly is anti-social and uninterested in relationship, this outcome may be the best that can be expected. In most conflicts, however, relationship factors should be considered, and adjudicatory processes do not heal and transform the relationship. I am not suggesting a trial or other adjudicatory means of resolution can never be appropriate for detecting and punishing deception, rather I am pointing out that there are better ways to make sure we satisfy our interests. We must ask which dispute resolution option most effectively remedies unconscious or conscious deception.

Even if shortcomings of the adjudicatory approach are acknowledged, the question lingers: How does mediation, based on party self-determinism, collaboration, and willingness to engage in reconciliation efforts, handle deception? At first glance it appears that less formal and less rigorous discovery is vulnerable to manipulation by deception – the more amicable the process, the more easily a lie can be inserted. The mediator's lack of power to enforce decisions seems to further encourage deception. But these assumptions may be wrong. To better understand the advantages mediation offers we need to look closer at the nature of deception.

DECEPTION & THE USE OF NARRATIVE ACCOUNTS. For the moment we will set aside pathological lying and look at more common and subtle forms of fabrication: the accounts people use to reduce threats to identity and to avoid sanctions. Accounts are stories we use to excuse or lessen our transgressions, the stories we tell to make ourselves feel better.

We typically establish in our mind a self-image and a social identity (how others view us) that satisfies our desire to be regarded in a positive manner. We have a need to be liked; we have a need to be admired by intimate associates and those whose decisions affect our lives. When conflict threatens our self-image and our social identity our narrative account of events becomes skewed in an attempt to reduce the threat.

Typically we seek to behave and perform in a manner consistent with our image of self. Our actions, real or imagined, must be consistent with the identity we have created in order for us to maintain a viable self-image. Likewise, our actions must be consistent with the identity we want others to embrace; our failure to meet expectations threatens to diminish how others view us. Given we are not perfect, we all fail to meet our responsibilities from time to time and we fail to satisfy others' expectations – and thus we experience threats to self-image and social identity.

In an effort to be accountable we explain how we have fulfilled our obligations, performed duties, met expectations, and satisfied other tasks.[12] In situations that give rise to conflict, however, our actions often betray our positive self-image or social identity. We fail to meet obligations, fail to discharge duties, or fail to meet expectations.

We need to account for less-than-perfect behavior. "In predicaments, social actors use accounts to provide explanations of events that minimize undesired attributions for their behavior, thereby reducing unwanted implications for identity."[13] Seeking to offset failed expectations we create narratives that integrate failures and successes in a positive manner, allowing us to Protect Self Face. We minimize shortcomings or transgressions, and supply reasons for failures that bolster our self-image and social identity in the face of potential disgrace.

These accounts are most often not blatant attempts to deceive but rather attempts to accommodate identity needs. To protect our image we explain we are not responsible for the events that transpired or that we did not intend for our actions to create bad effects. Or we may insist the results of our actions are not as serious as they may appear.[14] We seek to diminish our culpability or reduce the assessment of damages we caused.

With an account of what happened we explain away discrepancies between our positive identity and the manner in which events transpired. Such accounts include: protestations of innocence; denial of involvement; denial of direct causality; excuses, justifications, and apologies; or a combination of the preceding. These narrative accounts are not objective truths but rather stories designed to protect self-image and social identity. While a party may try to avoid sanctions by presenting accounts that minimize their transgressions it would be an error to over emphasize such pragmatic concerns and overlook the equally important need to protect identity.

The party may be perfectly willing to suffer consequences as long as those consequences do not also involve a lessening of their image or identity. When someone says, "I paid the price for my mistake," the phrase can be translated, "I accepted the consequences, as I was not a bad or evil person. I made an error. Everyone makes mistakes." We can accept that we erred as long as it does not impact negatively on our positive core identity.

Our accounts are designed to weaken links between our behavior and prescriptions – laws, rules, traditions, commandments, duties, and responsibilities.[15] The power of prescriptions can be weakened through nuanced presentation of accountability. We explain how the rule or prescription did not apply in a particular setting in which we found ourselves, to a particular role we assumed, or under particular circumstances in which we were involved.

We take advantage of ambiguity in a prescription in specific circumstances. We argue that while we knew there was a rule or obligation, we did not know it applied to us at that time in that particular setting. You can probably recall examples of accounts you constructed to weaken the link between a duty or responsibility and your circumstances. You attempted to lessen the impact of your transgression.

Narrative accounts take advantage of weak or ambiguous prescriptions. We construct accounts that excuse our behavior by citing a lack of clarity regarding prohibitions. If we violated a prescription it was not our fault: the rule was unclear. We explain, "If the rule had been clear, I would have obeyed."

At other times we claim we had little or no control over events. We knew the results were unacceptable but we were not in a position to control events and/or it was not our intention to have events turn out the way they did. This link to prescriptions addresses intentionality, causality, blame, and sincerity.[16] We attempt to explain how we were not a knowing and willing cause of harm. "It was out of my hands."

Research confirms we tend to construct an account of events that stresses the weakest link between ourselves and the wrong we have done. We might stress the rules were ambiguous, or our duty was not spelled out clearly, or we could not be expected to control events from our position. The account the other party hears is colored by our focus on weak links we use to lessen our culpability.

Such an account may trigger an emotional response from the other party. ("They're lying!"). However, these accounts are not outright lies, they are creative storytelling designed to maintain positive identity. A frontal attack on the veracity of the narrative only results in stiffened resistance and increased defensiveness. Instead, we must enter into dialogue and explore links between prescriptions, identity, and behavior.

As a party we should consider the other party's narrative account to be a rough draft and not feel a need to judge its accuracy. The account is not an argument to be judged right or wrong – it is a presentation colored by aspirations. It is how the other party would like to be seen in the context of events that have transpired. It should be regarded as a conversation starter not a closing statement. It should be considered an invitation to investigate how the other party constructs his world, how he links his self-image and social identity with his behavior.

The flexibility of mediation allows the parties to redraft for clarity. Upon further inspection an account that appeared to be a fabrication may turn out to be a rich emotional response to adverse circumstances. When an account that appears to be a lie is explored in a non-threatening manner the originating party may feel safe enough to admit, "I didn't want you to think poorly of me. That's why I could not admit my role. I felt bad and didn't want to lose your friendship."

Upon hearing this, the other party, who previously thought the opposing party was being malicious, may respond, "You care what I think? I had no idea you cared." They realize the party dodging blame created an impression that was the opposite of what he felt – though he desired the relationship his seemingly self-serving actions telegraphed a lack of caring.

Apparent deception dissolves as the mediator facilitates deeper exploration of the thoughts, motivations, and emotions of the storytellers. Rather than arriving at a conclusion based on incomplete information the mediator works accounts like a Rubik's Cube, searching for a combination that brings clarity and collaboration.

Fortunately, research confirms the anecdotal observations of mediators: apology is the favored account for easing past a dilemma.[17] "By acknowledging personal responsibility and accepting at least partial blame, actors can attenuate the most severe sanctions by reinforcing the legitimacy and importance of an audience's expectations."[18] When we tell the other party they have a right to be upset and we admit we owe them an apology, we move from concern for Self Face to attention on Other Face. Though we have concerns regarding our self-image, we tend to the other party's identity.

People tend to group apologies with excuses and justifications they use to weaken other links; this allows them to simultaneously accept partial responsibility while lessening overall responsibility. Face Saving strategies are combined with admissions of responsibility and wrongdoing. We are willing to admit a mistake and accept the consequences if at the same time we can maintain our positive self-image and identity.

The partial apology may appear to the harmed party as a lie and an insult; however, when they recognize the apologizing party is Protecting or Saving Face it becomes easier to view the partial apology as a step toward dialogue and reconciliation. In mediation we spend time understanding such subtle motivations. We come to see deception less as an attack and more as a defensive move to fend off threat. In a process that relies on third-party judgments such as a trial, there is no room for a party to lower their defenses, whereas in mediation safety and hope allow a party to evaluate their previous efforts to Protect Face.

Narratives are presented, redrafted, presented again, and then further refined into a collaborative master narrative. When we treat accounts as a prelude to dialogue we encourage flexibility. We view accounts as expressions of emotional needs. As we promote flexibility and weave accounts into a shared narrative, problems with deception tend to fall away. Parties discover it is safe to be candid and honest with one another.

In contrast, judicial processes do not use strategic accounts to foster dialogue. Apologies are out of the question. Nuanced views of responsibility are rarely considered. Face Saving is of little or no concern. A trial or other hearing is designed as a contest in which one attempts to destroy the other's identity. If we destroy the other party's credibility we score a victory. The process induces continuing strategic fabrication. There is rarely a feeling that one has heard the actual truth. Juries realize this intuitively and shift from judging facts to judging people. They analyze who is being reasonable and who is being unreasonable, who is showing respect and who is showing disrespect.

We manage deception best by turning our attention to the future and away from punishment for the past. While there may still be a need for amends or reparation the process opens the door to apology and acceptance of responsibility within a Face Saving context that lessens the need for further deception. When threats to self-image are reduced candid narratives emerge.

MORE ON HANDLING DECEPTION. When a party refuses to let go of deception, when they are unable to make the transition to candid dialogue, the mediator employs other tools. He gently queries inconsistent narratives, contrary facts, omitted data, altered importance, missing time, and other artifacts that point to deception.

He does not level an accusation that the party is lying, but rather invites and coaxes them to consider how the other party or a jury will understand their story. He points out inconsistencies that will need to be addressed and asks for explanations he can present to the other party to explain matters that are not clear. For example, "At one point you said the light was yellow and at another time you said it was red. Help me understand how it could be yellow and red at the same time so I can get the other party to accept what you are saying."

In response, the party may begin to rewrite their narrative in a more truthful and consistent manner. "I hoped the light would stay yellow, but it turned red before I got there." The mediator then frames revised accounts as clarifications of earlier statements.

A trial lawyer does the opposite – he contrasts a party's prior statement recorded in deposition with testimony provided on the stand and points out the discrepancy: "In the deposition, you said A, now you say B. Therefore, you are lying and we cannot trust what you say." The attorney impeaches the testimony. The same dynamics occur in other adversarial approaches whether within the family, the workplace, or the community; we seek out inconsistencies in order to impeach the other party.

In mediation we encourage rather than discourage change. We note statements the party has made and ask for clarification, seeking revisions and updates. We encourage a party to move from deception toward honest and candid dialogue. The process moves forward if a mediator does not heap blame and shame on a party for their prior account but rather embraces change and flexibility.

As parties assemble a new master narrative there is give and take with regard to assumption of responsibility. Parties turn away from assigning blame and toward the future with renewed willingness to satisfy mutual expectations. They give up the need to assign blame and the need to shame the other party, since shame and blame are not rewarded in mediation. The parties give up the need to dominate each other and embrace a collaborative effort to create a better future.

As you assess your conflict and prepare for mediation take time to assess motivations behind your narrative account. Will you need to rewrite your narrative account to align with truths acceptable to the other party? Contemplate how comfortable you will be listening to accounts that do not conform to reality as you see it. What must you do to allow the other party the safety they need to revise or rewrite their account in collaboration with you?

DECEPTION BY NEGATIVE THIRD PARTY. There is one critical exception to the principle that deception can be lessened or eliminated in the give-and-take of shared narrative accounts. This exception arises when deceptive or false facts have been inserted into the conflict by a hidden destructive third party.[19] This troubling scenario occurs when a destructive third party has talked to one party and then to the other, providing each with false information regarding the other. Neither party is aware of this covert introduction of falsehoods into the conflict; both assume they are relying on factual data.

The astute mediator pays careful attention to falsehoods that create animus between parties when there is a common (albeit hidden) source of deception and lies. In later chapters I address uncovering the hidden negative influence.[20] However, it is worth noting this dynamic at this time as the influence of a destructive, hidden third party may first come to light in the discovery phase.

If you suspect a hidden and negative source of falsehoods plays a significant role, skip ahead (to chapters 11 and 18). The previously unrecognized falsehoods can sabotage shared narrative creation, so the mediator looks for the hidden influence at the first sign of impasse.

Importance of Place

Messengers take Francis to the site where fellow citizens died. Paying attention to location mirrors Native American traditions that treat place as an important aspect of individual and collective narratives.[21] Native Americans understand the manner in which our attention becomes trapped in the space and time of events.

Looking closely we discover the residual mental imprint of a traumatic incident includes the exact space and time in which events unfolded. If we focus attention on the exact place and time in these imprints or memories as we create our narrative, our emotions are released and our narrative is enhanced. When we travel in our minds to the location where events transpired, our memories, stored in the mind's warehouse, are released to view.

During the process of sharing narrative accounts a party may discover a need to address mental imprints that link place and time to conflict-related trauma. The physical setting can remain in the conscious or subconscious memory and haunt the individual or group psyche. In faith-based diplomacy, for example, it is understood that historical wounds must be addressed in order to bring about reconciliation and those historical wounds often involve specific sites where conflict erupted.[22]

While it is not common during mediation to revisit actual sites at which conflict has taken place, it is only time and expense that prevent such a visit. If possible it makes sense to stage a visit, but if we are unable to organize an actual visit we may accomplish similar goals through viewing pictures, video recordings, or other visuals.

The task of healing historical wounds may be accomplished in part through recognition of place, perhaps with the construction of a memorial or monument. Healing may begin when wounds of the past are honored through celebration of place. Memorials that acknowledge the wounded past often house items that document the history of the conflict and the trauma suffered. We remember the past so we do not repeat it. As these factors are explored the emotional upset often begins to fade, allowing the party to be more in the present moment.

When the location marks a place of divine intervention in conflict the locations become sacred places we visit on pilgrimage to rekindle in our hearts the Spirit that allows us to move forward on our life journey.

Stakeholders

St. Francis is greeted by the townspeople of Gubbio, including those who lost relatives or friends to the wolf. Though Francis breaks bread with the mayor he does not forget that all citizens of Gubbio are stakeholders. While a single representative may speak for a group, we need to include all stakeholders in the process or we risk a short-lived outcome.

The specifics of a particular conflict dictate how we choreograph stakeholder roles. Ordinarily the representative identifies stakeholders whose concerns must be honored. Some will have a direct stake in the outcome while others may be affected tangentially. With regard to your conflict determine in advance whose needs you will consider, whose needs you will represent, and how you will organize stakeholder participation.

It is important to assess who, if anyone, must approve an agreement. On occasion a mediator may believe she has facilitated a resolution only to discover critical decision-makers are not present to give final approval. This oversight may be inadvertent or may be a negotiating tactic. Using this tactic a party waits until late in the process and then gives notice that he requires approval from a distant boss to finalize the agreement. The authority figure may then insist the terms of the agreement be altered or he may add unanticipated conditions.

An experienced mediator anticipates this ploy and secures a commitment during convening that all decision makers will be present or available for approval. Adequate preplanning prevents the "missing authority" tactic. If the tactic surfaces the party who has been surprised wisely takes the negotiated deal off the table and announces all prior concessions are withdrawn. He happily signals his willingness to start over from the beginning. The party employing the tactic realizes they risk achieving less favorable terms in renegotiation, which often makes them reticent to continue the ploy.

If you previously addressed the need for all decision-makers to be present you are justified in demanding the process be restarted. During convening one might ask: If we come to an agreement is there anyone else who must give approval? If so, why are they not present? It is more difficult to hold a punitive stance that calls for restarting negotiations if at the outset you did not clearly insist all stakeholders be present.

Up to this point we have primarily considered personal conflicts, conflicts in which you make the decisions, but this will not always be the case. Like the Mayor of Gubbio you may find yourself negotiating on behalf of a business, a community, or a nation in conflict. You will want to determine if you have authority to negotiate a resolution. An honest appraisal is important. Make sure you have heard stakeholder concerns before negotiating on their behalf. If your authority depends on group consensus you will want to design effective consensus-building procedures.

Convening Rituals

Francis meets the mayor and begins the discussion over dinner. Sharing a meal may provide a needed ritual context. As an example of bringing ritual comfort to the process would be meeting around a kitchen table with coffee brewing and comfort food available. This setting may suggest the comfort of the family kitchen where difficulties may have been hashed out on a regular basis. Or the kitchen table may elicit recall of pleasant times when the family engaged in lively or warm conversation. Possible rituals that can enhance the process are numerous; it is worth assessing what might be appropriate or helpful in breaking the ice.

A Franciscan View

As we listen to the narratives, our own and those of the other party, we discover a tapestry of feelings and thoughts – if we are prepared to listen closely. At times we surprise ourselves with the insights that take shape in our own narratives as a result of our struggles. In his brief but illuminating text, *The Song of the Dawn*, Eloi LeClerc, OFM introduces the depth of meaning that emerges from *Canticle of the Sun*, Francis' praise of God incarnate that was written during a period of struggle.[23]

The story begins when Francis returns from his journey to the Middle East where he met the Sultan al-Malik al-Kamil and attempted unsuccessfully to bring peace to the region. He "returned weakened, sick, and almost blind."[24] As he mended under the loving care of Sister Clare, he struggled with dissension that had broken out among the Brothers.

"The vicars general to whom Francis had confided the governing of his order during his absence had allowed themselves to add new prescriptions to the friar's rule of life. These prescriptions, which tended to bring the brother's life into conformity with traditional monasticism, troubled the spirits of those who remained very attached to the primitive ideal of Francis."[25] Though there is no record of the actual conversations one can imagine the friars crafted accounts that challenged Franciscan prescriptions by weakening the links between those prescriptions and their behavior. As LeClerc notes, "Under such circumstances, everything could be questioned from day to day."[26]

There is nothing inherently wrong with rules designed to organize our actions and guide our relationships. Indeed, management of our collective efforts avoids anarchy. And there is nothing wrong with spirited debate regarding those guidelines, nonetheless, Francis experienced the friar's accounts, filled with justifications designed to marginalize his prescriptions, as dissonant and unpleasant. He retired to solitude and a period of darkness.

During this period he experienced a "very gentle light" that entered his soul and "made him see all things anew."[27] The result was "an immense surge of praise" that "lifted up Francis' soul," leading him to craft the *Canticle of the Sun*, celebrating the wedding of heaven and earth, a "song of man reconciled and saved."[28] In this song Francis provides us with an example of storytelling; with this example he mentors us as narrators and listeners.

The remarkable and illuminating aspect of Francis' response to discord is praise that went deeper than discussion or debate regarding the essence of "what is." He used the phrases "Brother Sun," "Sister Moon," "Brother Fire," and "Sister Water" and expressed a fraternity of all creation. "This was no simple, allegorical way of speaking on his part. He really felt in everyday life a brotherhood with the most material creatures."[29]

As LeClerc explains, this level of enthusiasm and creative lyricism does not spring from a mere idea but rather must arise from the lived moment. "Francis directly and intensely perceived the value of all life and all being as manifestations of creative love."[30] The narrative Francis authored tapped into deeper truths.

As we construct our narratives in a manner that penetrates the depth of our experience we may keep in mind Francis' example: "all the things Francis celebrated he knew in a very direct and realistic way."[31] He explored that which he knew with a wonder that came from his sensitivity as an artist and poet.[32] While we are not all blessed with the skill of artists and poets Francis can point us in the correct direction. When we bring depth of perception and artistry to conveying the essence of our experience we enhance the reconciliation process.

Speaking of *Canticle of the Sun*, LeClerc says, "these images, which establish a direct kinship between man and the world, are meant to express reality in its wholeness and in its unity. They erase all borders. They recover a plentitude of being that goes beyond every concept. These images constitute a move beyond any kind of split or rupture at the heart of being. They celebrate unity: the unity of man and nature, of spirit and life, of freedom and necessity. They sing of a return to the source of being, to the infancy of the world."[33]

While following in Francis' footsteps is a daunting challenge in which success might not be attainable, we can still learn to cast a deeper gaze upon the world as we prepare our story of what happened. We can learn to listen with a keener ear to the rhythms of the sacred within the story the other party tells. Even in hearing the *Canticle of the Sun*, we might find we have not listened closely enough; we "could easily be mistaken and miss the depth of the canticle, seeing only the expression of a candid and naïve vision of the world."[34]

When we listen again more closely we may hear "the profound experience of reconciliation" in which "the primal forces of desire, those great life and death forces, have lost their troubling and menacing side.... Francis no longer had anything to fear from these wild forces. He did not destroy them; he tamed them, as he tamed the wolf of Gubbio."[35] This is the terrain we seek to cover in our spiritual transformation as we learn to tame the wolf.

Scripture

So Jesus said to them, "My time is not yet here, but the time is always right for you. The world cannot hate you, but it hates me, because I testify to it that its works are evil." (Jn 7:6-7)

"Stop judging by appearances, but judge justly." (Jn 7:24)

Therefore, since we have this ministry through the mercy shown us, we are not discouraged. Rather, we have renounced shameful, hidden things; not acting deceitfully or falsifying the word of God, but by the open declaration of the truth we commend ourselves to everyone's conscience in the sight of God. (2 Cor 4:1-2)

For when you were slaves of sin, you were free from righteousness. But what profit did you get then from the things of which you are now ashamed? For the end of those things is death. (Rom 6:20-21)

 Do you see someone hasty in speech?
  There is more hope for a fool! (Prv 29:20)

For our struggle is not with flesh and blood but with the principalities, with the powers, with the world rulers of this present darkness, with the evil spirits in the heavens. Therefore put on the armor of God, that you may be able to resist on the evil day and, having done everything, to hold your ground. So stand fast with your loins girded in truth, clothed with righteousness as a breastplate, and your feet shod in readiness for the gospel of peace. (Eph 6:12-15)

CHAPTER EIGHT

Revenge

The mayor wondered what, if anything, Francis could do with such a challenge.

The mayor hated that wolf. He knew the men who were killed and their families. One of the guards was his wife's cousin. If he were younger, he would have led the guards after the wolf.

Unable to contain his emotions, he said he wanted Francis to strike the wolf dead or send him to the town of Spoleto, their old enemy. Either would satisfy a need for revenge and stop the attacks.

Mediation Principles

IN THIS CHAPTER we will focus on the desire to exact revenge. Even when a party has agreed to participate in conflict resolution they often candidly express a desire to get even. They want to make their opponent suffer. In violent conflicts the offended party may crave revenge that inflicts severe suffering on the offender, but even those of us involved in less violent conflict often desire to make the other side pay a price for their transgressions. While our overt and covert acts of retribution may not reach the level experienced in violent conflict they are acts of revenge.

The desire for revenge is not something we should push aside or ignore. If we are to achieve reconciliation we need to address our craving to make others feel the pain we felt. A desire for revenge may become part of our narrative, though addressing this desire makes us uncomfortable. At times we may find it difficult to admit we harbor dark thoughts of vengeance; at other times we bristle with hatred and find it hard to check our cries for revenge. In either case, we are well served by inspecting our emotions and thoughts in order to bring them under control.

The mayor candidly informs Francis he wants Francis to slay the wolf. We might expect the request would cause Francis to depart Gubbio, certain he had made a mistake in coming to help. Francis is unperturbed. He realizes the path to peace does not detour around hostile expressions; the transformation of hostility is integral to reconciliation. Just as Francis invites the mayor to articulate his dark feelings you will want to assess the role a desire for revenge plays in your conflict.

We will also consider briefly the relationship between revenge and justice. Is it justice or revenge we seek? The discussion will not present a comprehensive analysis of complex issues regarding the rule of law, justice systems, legal institutions, or the role of justice in society, nor will it be a philosophical essay on social justice, instead the focus will be on practical issues to be considered in resolving your conflict.

The focus will be on your desire for revenge but the discussion also applies when the other party seeks revenge on you. When you face vengeful opposition you will want to walk in their shoes so you can anticipate what to expect.

Desire for Revenge

In the conflict with the wolf the Mayor of Gubbio suffered the loss of close friends and citizens, which left deep emotional wounds. He asks Francis to strike the wolf dead. The mayor's request is not unexpected; the desire for revenge is not uncommon.

When we view the conflict in hindsight from a safe distance we notice the mayor does not ask Francis to find a way to assure that no more livestock will be eaten and no more men will be killed. He does not ask for a rational and peaceful solution or a safe future – he wants the wolf killed.

While killing the wolf may be one way to assure future safety it appears the mayor seeks more: his request includes a subtle plea for punishment. Though he does not express this desire overtly he hopes Francis will avenge the deaths of citizens. Implicit in his request is a bias the mayor may not recognize: a bias that says taking revenge is the only way to secure a safe future. Like the mayor our choices may be slanted by an unrecognized bias toward revenge.

Francis knew that in many cases the craving for revenge becomes lodged in our hearts, even though we may hide that desire out of fear that others will see us in a bad light. However, until we can satisfy or transform our desire for revenge it will shadow the proceedings. As you prepare for mediation inspect your vengeful feelings and note vengeful acts you may have already taken. When you respond to the prompts, you bring to the surface desire for revenge that has been unacknowledged. You prepare to explain your previous attempts to exact retribution.

Though you may have to suffer the embarrassment of admitting negative feelings, though you may have to humbly acknowledge you gave in to hostile urges, if you do not take this step the wolf will continue to roam in your consciousness.

Detecting & Assessing the Desire for Revenge

One reliable sign that a desire for revenge is inhibiting conflict resolution is unchecked escalation. When we trade harmful deeds in a tit-for-tat exchange we create a cycle of reciprocal revenge. If cycles of revenge continue, conflict escalates to the stage at which the parties are willing to destroy each other, even if they also will be destroyed. At this stage mutual deterrence is no longer a factor. A party may consider sacrifice of self is not too high a price to pay for the satisfaction that comes from inflicting deserved pain and suffering on the other party.

This dynamic – I will sacrifice myself to destroy you – is present in small measure at all stages of escalation but, as the conflict builds, sacrificing self in order to exact revenge becomes more overt. The logic of revenge – you should suffer as I have suffered so you will know my pain – becomes accepted wisdom.

Revenge is essentially an expression of our hurt. The most powerful expression of hurt we can muster is causing the other party to feel the pain they caused us. A party seeking revenge assumes the burden of his own future suffering in order to deliver a blow to the hated enemy, a blow that will ensure the enemy understands "this is how it felt to be hurt."

In extreme cases escalation creates a legacy of reciprocal revenge that is bequeathed to future generations taught to avenge real or imagined injuries suffered by past generations. Entire cultures cling to the desire for revenge and raise their children with an acute awareness of historical wounds – wounds the children have not suffered personally. This need to avenge historical wounds becomes imprinted in the collective psyche in the form of a group narrative of transgressions that must be avenged.

Motives Driving Revenge

WE NEED TO MAKE THEM UNDERSTAND OUR PAIN. Conflict escalates when one or both parties demonstrate they do not understand and/or care how their actions affect the other party. Revenge is an effort to make sure offenders "get it" and learn to care. We want the people who have hurt us to understand the full nature of what they have done – not intellectually but rather in a visceral manner. We seek to "educate" offenders by causing them the same pain they caused others.

This dynamic operates at its most basic level in the sandbox: children at play strike back at kids who hurt them with the admonition "See!" The desire to make the other understand our pain is fundamental, and we attribute great importance to delivering the lesson "this is how you hurt me." The desire is so strong we are willing to sacrifice our safety and tranquility for satisfaction.

Our (mostly unconscious) calculation is that when the offending party experiences pain commensurate with the pain they caused, they will learn firsthand what they have done and they will repent. When the offending party experiences the pain they caused others, they will be forced to care – as *they* now feel the hurt. In this light, revenge might be viewed as an attempt at enforced empathy – the party who takes revenge aims to make the offender understand fully and care deeply.

In those instances when the offending party appears not to heed our pain, when their attitude remains hostile, uncaring and insensitive, the desire for revenge intensifies. If the offending party cannot or will not empathize with our pain and suffering our only option is to deliver stronger retribution. We feel forced to increase their pain and suffering to the level at which they "get it." At a conscious or unconscious level we hope escalation will get their attention.

Unfortunately, pain and suffering do not bring increased understanding or heightened reason. Pain and suffering blot out reason, abort understanding, and preclude empathy. Our awareness is diminished, not expanded, by pain and suffering. When we hurt or suffer our focus draws inward and we become less perceptive. We become less able to learn. Thus revenge is not always a successful method of teaching the intended lesson. All too often revenge imparts a different lesson – that striking back is the appropriate and expected response. All too often, when we seek to teach a lesson, a spiral of reciprocal revenge ensues.

In this chapter we are not primarily concerned with whether or not revenge works; instead, we seek to understand the motivations behind our desire for revenge. Though revenge rarely educates and enlightens our enemies we still experience the need to make the offender understand how we felt when we were hurt.

WE NEED TO PROTECT OUR SELF-IMAGE AND IDENTITY. Many hurts for which we seek revenge are experienced as threats to our self-image and social identity. Pride – not trivial pride but rather deep existential pride – often takes on the role of our identity watchdog. *Watchdog pride* mandates that every transgression suffered must be avenged. Our ability to maintain pride in who we are depends on our ability to defend our identity from insult and injury. Unable to defend our identity we suffer humiliation and in the case of extreme attacks our actual survival is threatened.

Extreme transgressions that seek to completely destroy our identity, such as murder and mutilation, provide strong justification for revenge, strong enough to motivate us to take revenge on behalf of another who was maimed or killed. In such cases it is difficult though not impossible to move beyond revenge. Perhaps one of the most inspiring stories of moving beyond the need for revenge can be found in *Left to Tell* which recounts the story of Imaculée Ilibagiza, a survivor of the Rwandan Holocaust.[1] Given the opportunity to take revenge on the man who horrifically killed her loving family, she chose to turn away. Although her decision to forgive may be difficult to adopt as our own, Immaculée inspires hope that we, too, can journey from unimaginable horror to the peace of mind inspired by faith, a peace that allows us to forego revenge.

Most threats to our self-image and social identity are far less dramatic. They do not seek to end our entire existence. Nonetheless, lesser attacks also diminish who we are or who we can be – we die in small measure. Our survival as the person we want to be is threatened. The ridicule and humiliation we suffer at the hands of those who intend to make less of us diminishes our sense of self. Their attack renders us less than who we really are.

The slightest attacks on identity, even inadvertent slights, often evoke fierce responses, as they trigger unconscious fear that our survival is threatened. While the severity of attacks on our self-image is less than the severity of death threats, all attacks that seek to diminish our identity, who we want to be, appear to challenge our survival and motivate us to strike back. When we experience humiliation and feel threatened we rarely seek empathy – we seek to defend. Watchdog pride musters our defenses. We respond with increasingly forceful acts of revenge that demonstrate we have the power to survive and maintain our identity. We seek not only to serve notice to the offending party that we will strike back, we seek to reassure ourselves that we will continue to exist.

Revenge thus sends a message that we will defend our self-respect, our self-image, our social identity, and, yes, our existence against those who dare humiliate or harm us. Acts of revenge issue from our unconscious impulse to survive. When you assess the underlying needs revenge will satisfy consider ways in which your identity is threatened. Inspect your feelings and inner dialogue to make sure a trivial or mundane insult to your image or identity has not been inadvertently transformed into an unjustified life and death struggle that demands you deliver a blow to the transgressor.

WE NEED TO "BALANCE THE SCALES." Another revenge motive is the need to "balance the scales." We place transgressions committed against us on one side of the scale and adverse consequences we intend to levy in response on the other side. Motion pictures frequently feature characters whose self-respect has been crushed by their inability to make villains pay for their crimes. The self-respect of the hero is restored only when he makes the villain suffer the consequences of his misdeeds.

In such dramas, as in real life, it is not enough for Fate to deliver punishment. The hero must deliver the blow that restores equilibrium. Balance is restored by an act of revenge – an act that satisfies the audience's vicarious craving for punishment of misdeeds. During the period in which the hurtful deed goes unpunished the audience experiences discomfort, just as we experience discomfort when perceived wrongs go unpunished.

When villains (who have hurt us) remain unpunished we feel we do not live in a fair and just universe. The thought that a villain can cause harm without suffering consequences is abhorrent. It can literally make us ill. It is common to assume the only way to heal that illness is to restore balance with an act of revenge. Thus an additional motive for revenge is a need to balance the ledger between wrongs received and punishment delivered. This parity is sometimes called justice.

WE NEED TO DESTROY EVIL. Most of us are not involved in life-or-death clashes such as the conflict between Gubbio and the wolf. Our hurts and acts of revenge take place on a smaller stage. Nonetheless, when we consider whether revenge is valid we must take into account horrific acts of violence that appear to elevate revenge to an unassailable right. Some acts offend the conscience so profoundly it strains credulity to think there will be no revenge.

For example, in the brutal conflict that visited Rwanda feuding tribes inflicted death and crippling mutilation on men, women, and children. Other examples include the genocide in Bosnia and in Southeast Asia. The atrocities committed delivered wounds so horrific they stun the soul and wound the spirit. In the case of such extreme horror, we may consider revenge not only appropriate but a duty: evil must be destroyed. The motive for revenge becomes *to destroy evil*.

When we place our actions in the context of destroying evil we find revenge an obvious necessity. The horrors inflicted by thugs, terrorists, and tribal warriors must be avenged with annihilating blows. Only when evil agents are annihilated can we rest, satisfied revenge has worked its magic.

If we are honest we may find our inner narrative, even in less violent scenarios, includes this desire to strike a blow against evil. The office gossip, the vitriolic colleague who threatens our continued employment, is seen as evil deserving retribution. Later, in chapter 18, we will take up the issue of evil in more detail – for now we do not make a judgment regarding what is or is not evil but rather simply note that a desire to destroy evil becomes a common motive for revenge.

WE NEED TO DETER TRANSGRESSIONS. Revenge may be meant to deter future aggression. An example can be found in the seemingly intractable conflict between Israelis and Palestinians, which manifests in terror attacks and punitive military operations. The conflict produces outbreaks of reciprocal revenge with each side claiming their brutal acts are committed to assure their future safety. They claim revenge deters future aggression. The horror of the revenge each side inflicts is meant to stun the other into no longer engaging in violence. Each side believes that if the other side knows without a doubt that their aggressive actions will be met with brutal revenge they will cease being aggressors.

This same reasoning is found in the doctrine of mutual nuclear annihilation that played a macabre role in the Cold War. Governments developed and stockpiled weapons, promising to annihilate the first offender with a retaliatory strike. The promise to exact the revenge of mass extermination with a second strike nuclear attack enlists the promise of revenge in the cause of deterrence.

While the threat of revenge rarely works as a tool for peace over the long run, demonstrating a willingness to take revenge may deter aggression in the short term. The Cold War anticipation of widespread death and destruction set a standard for revenge as deterrence. Those who feared that another nation would engage in aggression rattled sabers and promised a second strike of devastating proportions.

This stance has recently been expanded to the preemptive strike doctrine that justifies delivering the second strike *before* a first strike takes place—based on the assumption that a first strike is in the offering. On a smaller scale we personally send threatening messages promising retaliation when someone appears to be contemplating threats that will cause us harm or oppose our wishes. In our assessment we should evaluate the ways we seek to deter transgressions with promises of revenge. How do we warn others that they should not seek to transgress against us?

WE NEED TO EXPRESS RAGE. The preceding discussion provided a short list of motives for revenge: to make the offender understand the pain he has caused; to defend identity; to balance transgressions and punishment; to defeat evil; to deter aggression. Revenge also erupts out of uncontrolled rage, the result of an outburst of violent emotion that overwhelms us during the period author Laura Blumenfeld calls "the boiling of the blood."[2]

Overwhelmed by uncontrolled rage we are driven to retaliation. We strike out with little or no thought. A button is pushed and we react. We rarely understand rage in the moment it occurs. Hasty destructive acts can only be understood in retrospect, when we look back and plumb the depths of primal forces that spur reactive behavior. In our assessment we will want to recall past incidents of revenge fueled by rage. With more than a tinge of regret or embarrassment we may recall knee-jerk responses to what we correctly or incorrectly perceived to be an injustice. The moments we were not fully conscious and not in control become difficult to explain – we do not look forward to confessing we acted without reason. We may conclude only a profound change in our character and our consciousness can prevent such bouts of uncontrolled rage.

Most of us pride ourselves on our composure and reason. Thus it is awkward to admit our behavior was not our own but rather surfaced from the depths of our psyche like a malevolent stranger. Typically we solve the dilemma by attributing the cause of our rash behavior to the other party – they triggered our rage. We transfer blame for our condition to their actions and dodge responsibility.

We say, "If only they had not pressed the buttons that set off my inner rage, they would not have suffered my wrath." There is a modicum of truth to the idea that a party who provokes another bears responsibility for the consequences, but this explanation does not offer blanket coverage for rage-induced violence. All too often we simply "go off." In the aftermath we are left searching for a way to take responsibility for the destructive part of our nature that we let off the leash.

In the end we may turn to spiritual transformation in our search for answers that explain the part of us that responds with rage.

Justice

"But I don't want revenge," you might protest. "I want justice." This raises a vital question: How do revenge and justice differ? When we speak of balancing the scales, getting even, punishing the crime, or retaliating against the evildoer, do we speak of justice or revenge?

When we argue we want justice we express a desire for a fair outcome, an outcome that balances harmful deeds committed with consequences levied. This does not differ entirely from revenge, which also seeks to levy consequences for harm done. Justice parallels revenge in the sense that offenders "get what is coming to them" – their punishment may include financial ruin, incarceration, physical deprivation, emotional torment, or even execution as payment for the harm they caused. In most conflicts the consequences are less dramatic, nonetheless we conceive there is a price to be paid. The punishment doled out (as justice) makes the offending party suffer adverse consequences.

One way to view the difference between justice and revenge is to consider how the measure of retribution is determined and how punishment is delivered. When we speak of justice we often mean we rely on formal judicial institutions to make determinations and deliver punishment. The matter is taken out of our hands and placed in the hands of a neutral third party. In this sense justice connotes a public adjudication of what constitutes a fair and just outcome, while revenge involves personal or non-judicial retribution.

"Justice" used in this way dictates we seek collective or public retribution. Our claims are put in the hands of institutions that administer and deliver justice for all members of society. (While this discussion will focus on legal institutions there are parallel systems of justice within most organizations, such as hearing boards that adjudicate disputes, or key personnel assigned the duty of administering justice to members of the group.) One can question whether or not such institutions are merely socially acceptable vehicles for exacting revenge. We might ask how justice delivered by formal institutions differs from revenge delivered by the individual.

One difference is the respect shown by institutionalized legal systems for proportionality. Punishment mandated by courts is measured to fit the crime. Legal codes shaped by society's moral codes dictate more or less predictable and principled outcomes. In a just outcome guilt or innocence is adjudicated against a formal set of standards (laws or regulations) and the force of the retributive blow is designed to be in proportion to the force of the transgression.

The Old Testament concept of an eye for an eye is an exhortation for "jurors" to moderate punishment to fit the crime. (The edict of an eye for an eye is often mistaken to mean one is granted approval to take revenge when the axiom was actually an attempt to moderate and reduce revenge. It was a call for proportionality.)

Rules of moral conduct codified into laws vary from culture to culture. Cultures disagree on the appropriate severity of punishment. Western society may find amputation of a thief's hand an outrageous and vengeful response, while other cultures see wisdom in incorporating such punishment in their criminal code. That which is considered just in one culture may be considered unprincipled revenge in another.

Attempts to create international standards of justice, with human rights serving as the foundational platform, seek to provide standards that differentiate justice from revenge across cultures. Perhaps the work of establishing a universal legal foundation for human rights is a process that seeks to define the difference between justice and revenge. Some might argue that revenge is a basic human right. This begs the question, is it a basic human right to take an eye for an eye? Or is this simply institutionalized revenge?

While one may argue convincingly that the use of formal legal institutions to administer fair and measured retribution establishes a shift from revenge to justice, it should be noted that there also exist codes of revenge that prescribe appropriate responses.[3] The Mafia, for example, developed its own code to guide acts of revenge.

Does minor retaliation necessarily fall into the category of revenge or can it be considered justice? Assume another party embarrassed us in front of friends. Out of a desire for revenge we start a whispering campaign that destroys their reputation. They become an outcast. Have we carried out justice or an act of revenge? These issues can be extremely subtle, the defining lines are blurry. In the chapter on forgiveness (chapter 17) we consider these issues in more detail.

In the final analysis the difference between justice and revenge may be subtle and open for debate. The cautious effort expended on determining with certainty the extent of the harm caused and the negligence or liability of the perpetrator, along with the effort spent codifying fact-finding procedures and valid outcomes, may recommend a formal justice system and the rule of law over personal revenge. Nonetheless, philosophically, the difference in many cases may be minor.

An important additional difference between justice and revenge concerns the agent that delivers punishment or retribution. In institutional justice systems prosecution and punishment of wrongdoers is taken out of victims' hands and entrusted to the state. In criminal cases in the United States parties (to a criminal complaint) are the United States (or an individual state) and the offender. The victim does not actively get even; the state doles out punishment and balances the scales on behalf of the victim and society.

This model of state as proxy victim has pluses and minuses. One plus, already mentioned, is the deliberative nature of the state's proceedings, which guarantees a just (balanced) response, a result which may not occur when an emotional victim allows passion to drive punishment. Revenge strikes from the wounded heart while justice results from reasoned deliberation.

Taking retribution out of the hands of the victim has other advantages. In the state as proxy victim model those who have been harmed are relieved from bearing the additional emotional burdens that accrue from personally carrying out acts of revenge. When the state carries out a sentence the punitive act becomes impersonal. Retribution is an act of justice taken by an abstract entity larger than the individual victim.

This may help curtail the cycle of revenge, as those who might seek to avenge the punishment delivered may look at the state as their opponent, not the individual. However, those who are punished for their transgressions may ignore such subtleties and hold their victim responsible for enlisting the court's help in punishing them. A cycle of revenge may ensue as punished offenders attempt to deliver payback to those who sought justice.

A possible drawback of state-administered punishment occurs when the victim feels distant and removed. Their need for parity remains unsatisfied. They are deprived of the certainty that a transgressor felt the same pain they felt. Knowledge that the other has felt one's pain is more direct in the personal administration of justice (revenge). An inability to deliver personal retribution may result in the desire for revenge being frustrated but not eliminated.

Dissatisfaction may fester and lead to a heightened desire to deliver a blow to the offending party. In *Revenge* Laura Blumenfeld tells the story of Albanians who rely extensively on a code of revenge and do not consider that state-administered justice balances the scales. The Albanians simply wait for the offender to be released from prison and then take revenge.[4]

On the other hand, the formal justice system does satisfy a need personal revenge may fail to fulfill – the need to receive public acknowledgment that one has suffered unjust wrongs. The additional message – that the offender was found to have violated society's norms – is an important validation of the victim's rights and rightness.

The public acknowledgment that the harm done was an evil deserving of punishment restores the victim's dignity. Damage done to the victim's identity is healed through the public pronouncement that the acts committed were wrong and worthy of punishment.

If a victim takes revenge the public expression or acknowledgment of the victim's rightness and the victim's return to dignity may not occur. Personally administered revenge lacks the broad public support that so often brings vindication and restoration of dignity. Personal revenge may instead invite public censure and loss of public standing. The unsanctioned avenger is likely to be denied public validation that his avenging acts were valid and thus may suffer guilt and/or punishment.

It is possible for state-administered justice to break down, as formal institutions sometimes fail to do their job. Government personnel may be incompetent or may suffer from individual or collective bias. When the state fails to administer justice fairly citizens take matters into their own hands. They drift away from the state justice apparatus and seek personal revenge.

In most regions or nations where one finds rampant personal revenge one also finds a lack of a functioning justice system perceived as fair and just. A prime example is the Italian Mafia. When the occupying governments of foreign nations failed to administer justice the locals were forced to turn to a private system of revenge. When an offense took place citizens had no recourse: no authorities were in place to maintain order, and no courts were available to administer justice. So the local population took matters into their own hands. Mafia "justice" thus morphed out of vigilante justice that arose when the formal justice system failed. In *Revenge* we find fascinating accounts of codes of revenge that emerged in places like Italy and Albania when the central government failed to provide reliable justice.[5]

Once it is in place a culture of revenge becomes difficult to dismantle. Whereas revenge once served the people, in the long term extra-judicial revenge serves only the powerful and corrupt. The solution becomes the problem, further worsening conditions. Attempts to rein in the powerful and corrupt through additional acts of revenge only result in further empowering those who are powerful and corrupt. Ad hoc systems of revenge cannot provide the formality and independence characteristic of an institutionalized justice system vital in delivering true justice.

Perhaps the most compelling argument in favor of formal state-run systems is there ability to address power imbalances. In a system of collective justice the state has the means to remedy situations in which the offender wields more power than the victim. When one party in a conflict possesses a surfeit of power, they are shielded from just outcomes unless independent institutions vested with power level the playing field.

The challenge lies in establishing a judiciary independent of special interests. When unethical power cabals usurp the justice system covert acts of revenge become the only option for those lacking power. When powerful special interests usurp the justice system, the courts, failing in their duties, create conditions that give rise to a desire for revenge.

While many of these concerns take on a serious nature within criminal courts the same dynamics are at work in civil courts designed to help the public resolve business, commercial, and personal disputes. The same dynamics appear in other organizations attempting to maintain order by delivering justice on behalf of its members. Within a company or other organization the absence of an independent authority delivering fair and just outcomes creates an environment in which cliques take power and assert their will, which includes dominating others.

If a cabal grabs the reins of justice within an organization, they can enforce bias and even corruption on the entire organization. Criminal organizations such as mobs rely on subverting the justice mechanisms of groups on which they prey. In such situations, where neutrality and ethics are lacking, a system of justice quickly becomes a system of revenge.

Within any organization, whether a family or a business or a church, recognized and honored methods of administering justice must be present if we hope to curtail revenge. The individual must feel he can rely on collective power to maintain fairness or he will set out to balance the scales through revenge.

Unresolved Conflict Promotes Revenge

When conflict goes unresolved – even small-scale conflict – the situation gnaws at our good nature, leaving us in a constant state of irritation or riding swells of anger. We may act out our anger with overt attempts to hurt the other but more often we respond with covert attempts to annoy, humiliate, frustrate, or sabotage the other party.

Frequently we take no action but we obsessively entertain thoughts of revenge. Our imagination gives us little rest as it conjures images of the suffering or demise of our antagonist. In the absence of a conflict resolution process the minor indignities we visit upon the other party out of revenge escalate to more serious attempts to punish the perceived wrongdoer. The clash may have started out as a minor difference of opinion, a response to an inadvertent slight, or a response to another's annoying efforts to dominate, coerce, or ridicule. The conflict increases in severity until the situation can no longer be ignored. From small seeds of disrespect conflict escalates to the point where it ruins our life, steals our happiness, and leaves us seething with malevolent thoughts.

In an earlier chapter, we considered the continuum of conflict resolution approaches. Revenge is a "self-help" choice at the extreme end of the scale. We don't always take a careful and considered journey through the continuum to arrive at this extreme. Instead, the self-help of revenge may be the first thought that comes to mind.

Taming the Wolf proposes a different approach: the first step is a facilitated conversation. Mediation follows if the conversation does not lead quickly to reconciliation. As we engage in mediation we do not take other options off the table. When we mediate we investigate and evaluate other options so that we gain a certainty that – at least for the present moment – mediation is our best option.

In this way we do not stash the option of revenge in the dark corners of our mind but rather we evaluate this "self-help" option that forces itself uninvited into our consciousness. We assess our thoughts and feelings concerning revenge. We analyze the extent to which our thinking, our perceptions, and our choices are driven by a need for revenge. We may begin to recognize revenge has very high costs. This motivates us to set revenge aside, at least for the moment, knowing we can reevaluate those costs if other options fail.

At this stage of assessment we identify our angry impulses. We bring them into the open in an attempt to avoid rage-filled, knee-jerk reactions. If we engage in mediation but our underlying thoughts and intentions stall in revenge mode the process suffers. Thus we must inspect our impulse to take revenge so we can clear it from our mind.

Rather than suppressing thoughts of revenge and pretending they do not exist we bring them into the light and transform them into expressions of needs and interests. We do not unearth our urge for revenge in order to cement it into our conflict resolution plan; rather we inspect the hostility in our heart so as to transform it.

When we allow destructive impulses to lurk in the shadows, we do not shine a light on those impulses because we are wary of how we will appear. We allow those impulses to live for another day. Left untended those impulses may cause us to strike out during a moment when our blood is boiling. In working diligently with the prompts we prepare to face the wrongs we have suffered with a calm mind and peaceful heart.

Beyond Justice-as-Revenge

In order to find true reconciliation we may need to move beyond revenge and common justice to apology, forgiveness, and spiritual transformation. When justice gives way to righteousness – not the judgmental righteousness of the sword but the transcendent righteousness of compassion – we find a way to touch the divine in the other and move beyond destructive urges.

Noting the importance of forgiveness in the reconciliation process, The Reverend Canon Brian Cox, a leading practitioner of faith-based diplomacy, has argued that if we cannot consider forgiveness it is not justice but revenge we desire.[6] At an early stage in the process we are justified in asking: Is it always possible for us to forgive? Do wrongs exist that cannot be forgiven? There are no easy answers but such uncertainty may be healthy. When we freely admit we might face limits that constrain our ability to move beyond revenge, we are free to *try* to move beyond.

When we acknowledge our flaws and shortcomings, when we accept we may fail, we are released from fear of failure and our heart is allowed to find its own way. In order to move beyond a desire for revenge we must recognize and acknowledge where we stand at the present moment – we may not be a forgiving person. The primary task at this stage is discovering where we stand instead of greeting the world with a false face.

With the preceding thoughts in mind, we briefly consider the value of taking time to unearth that which is unpleasant. Should we not avoid the unpleasant? Should we not avoid digging up pain or hatred or other distasteful emotion? After all, our purpose is to restore happiness and contentment not to prolong the despair of conflict. Avoidance, however, rarely bears fruit. Metaphorically, we are trapped in a cave with a large boulder blocking the exit. The boulder represents all that is unpleasant, all that we do not wish to confront. It prevents our departure from the cave. Until we clear the boulder in our path we are not free to exit.

Contemplation of Suffering

St. Francis' contemplation of Christ suffering on the cross played a significant role in his life. This focus on the unpleasant might seem maudlin, a focus that might fuel desire for revenge. Often the more we consider a wound we have suffered (or witnessed) the more we increase the urge to avenge that wound.

For Francis the opposite transpired. His contemplation of the crucified Christ opened doors to a life lived in unconditional love, a life lived in celebration of brotherhood, peacemaking and reconciliation. The story of Francis of Assisi may seem counterintuitive but, paradoxically, historical wounds produce an ongoing cycle of revenge with no end in sight or they produce a transcendent perspective from which transgressions are forgiven, resulting in peace and brotherhood. Francis discovered how to transform conflict into transcendent compassion, earning the right to be our mentor as we seek to transform conflict into brotherhood.

At this stage we are justified in maintaining healthy skepticism. We might ask if it is possible for us to find our own path to peace by understanding Francis' contemplation of the suffering of Christ. For Francis the wounds Christ suffered became portals to salvation. Can our wounds function in this manner or is the challenge we face beyond the reach of faith?

At first we briefly turn our gaze from faith and inspect our natural capacity as humans – do our natural instincts allow us to move beyond revenge or retributive justice or do natural instincts restrict us to violent responses in a battle for survival? Is an "eye for an eye" based on a natural law that erects the boundaries within which we operate? Is it our nature to engage in an endless spiral of revenge? Have we discovered our true nature in the violent conflict that plagues our planet? Are we foolish or unrealistic for desiring to go beyond such boundaries?

Or must we look beyond the mundane for solutions? Is the human condition so inherently flawed that the only remedy is recognition of our divine nature? If we are confined within the boundaries of our nature as flawed human beings, are we trapped in conditions that will never allow us to move beyond cycles of revenge? Or does the answer we seek involve transcending our limited human condition through a profound recognition of our divine essence? Will the boundaries of our flawed human nature collapse when we become aware of our true divine nature?

These questions surface as we wrestle with setting revenge aside. As we face craving for revenge we may find the only way to escape its lure is through a door that leads to spiritual transformation. The original premise of *Taming the Wolf* – that all conflict is spiritual conflict – re-emerges for consideration. The question is whether or not spiritual transformation sustained by deep contemplation of suffering, injustice, and hatred provides true hope for lasting change, for resolution of conflict, and for reconciliation. There is no blanket answer. The search is an individual matter.

Our Need for Revenge

A party to a conflict faces a conundrum. Walking away without exacting revenge leaves one feeling hurt and empty. Exacting revenge leaves one suffering the burdens of guilt, remorse, and ostracism. The solution to the dilemma lies in skillful conflict management that transcends the dichotomy between a desire for revenge and acceptance of injustice. In a later chapter the steps of apology, forgiveness, and reconciliation will be suggested as a potential path out of the dilemma.[7] At this point the reader's task is to become aware of his need for revenge, however small or large.

A Franciscan View

As a young man Francis experienced situations that might have left him bitter and vengeful. His captivity during the war between Perugia and Assisi is one example: "Perugia, Assisi's neighbor to the west, was at this time at the apogee of its power, having already made many efforts to reduce Assisi to submission. It declared war on Assisi in 1202.... Assisi was defeated, and Francis, who was in the ranks, was made prisoner."[8]

Francis' captivity lasted an entire year. "He greatly astonished his companions by his lightness of heart. Very often they thought him almost crazy. Instead of passing his time in wailing and cursing he made plans for the future, about which he was glad to talk to anyone who came along."[9]

In spite of enduring confinement with good cheer and refusing to succumb to the temptation to harbor vengeful urges, he struggled when it came to conforming his future to the divine passion taking seed in his heart. "His knight's heart sought to defend his town, his family, his honor through blood and warfare. Imprisonment in a subterranean dungeon changed him. Some might go through such an ordeal and harden, but Francis was driven into himself and into the depth of self-doubt. Driven to the hills of Mount Subasio that tower over Assisi and to the plains of Umbria he searched for something, a truth, one thing that was true, because up to that point, up to the wars, everything he had learned about security through wealth and power, had disappointed his expectations."[10]

After returning from his incarceration at Perugia Francis was swept up by another call to arms, but his heart was not invested in going to war. Before the campaign began he abandoned his plans and returned to Assisi.

While his dramatic conversion at San Damiano was yet to come, his devotion was beginning to stir. His life was changing as his faith strengthened and he was led to assess his conduct against his growing devotion to a Gospel life. "So many acts of unkindness and uncharitable behavior would never be done if we – as did Francis – lived in the present moment of being one with Christ, to the point where we saw Christ right there, right here, every moment of every day, in every situation.... Who among us would kill anything if Christ were standing next to us, or Christ was the one we were killing?"[11]

After returning to Assisi Francis took to wandering the fields in a reverie and took an interest in the poor that was not fitting for a young man of his status. His father, Pietro di Bernardone, was outraged with the image Francis presented to the community. "Bernardone's self-love had received from his son's embarrassment such a wound as with common people is never healed.

He might provide, without counting it, money to be swallowed up in dissipation so that his son might stand on an equal footing with the young nobles. But he could never resign himself to see [Francis] giving with lavish hands to every beggar in the streets."[12]

Pietro imprisoned Francis in a dark closet, and resolved to break his will. In Pietro's absence Francis' mother Pica set him free and Francis made his way back to the church at San Damiano, a church in disrepair, a church Francis would eventually rebuild after hearing the voice of God speak to him as he knelt before the cross. "At San Damiano, St. Francis's piety took on its outward appearance and its originality. From that time his way was plain before him."[13]

Pietro was enraged. "Bernardone, on his return, went so far as to strike Pica in punishment for her weakness. Then, unable to tolerate the thought of seeing his son the jest of the whole city, he tried to procure his expulsion from the territory of Assisi. Going to San Damiano he summoned him to leave the country.... Boldly presenting himself, [Francis] declared that not only would nothing induce him to abandon his resolutions, but moreover, having become the servant of Christ, he had no longer to receive orders from his father."[14] In the unloving actions of Pietro, Francis experienced the rage and desire for revenge that consumed his father.

Most likely we can recall similar times when we let rage take center stage in our lives, although we may not have given free rein to such outbursts. Catholic moral theologian Bernard Häring, writing about the virtue of patience, offers the following observation: "I know people who think that from time to time they have to treat themselves to a regular explosion of impatience with themselves or with others. Any person who employs this tactic should just watch as this impatient explosion occurs. He or she will not be able to deny that these episodes of letting off steam only become more frequent and more intense.... A much better solution is to collect oneself for a few moments, breathe deeply, breathe in the love and kindness of God and, in all simplicity, pray to God for patience."[15]

Francis went further. He devoted his life to living and breathing the love of Christ. The patience he gained through his devotion did not go unnoticed. History tells us that even one of the richest men in Assisi was impressed with Francis: "[Lord Bernard] thought about how Francis turned his back totally on the world, how Francis exhibited such patience under insult, how Francis handled two years of scorn – he always appeared peaceful and even-tempered."[16]

The attainment of a peaceful and even-tempered nature is not a task to be taken lightly. Most of us find ourselves closer to the following unflattering description: "It is far indeed from hatred of evil to love of good. They are more numerous than we think who, after some severe experience, have renounced what the ancient liturgies call 'the world,' with its pomps and lusts. But the greater number of those who have renounced the world have not at the bottom of their hearts the smallest grain of pure love. In vulgar souls disillusion leaves only a frightful egoism."[17]

This directs our attention to the manner in which we turn inward or turn away, allowing embers of revenge to smolder within our hearts, rather than extinguishing those burning coals as we kneel at the foot of the cross. The following passage from *The Little Flowers* exemplifies the latter:

> God called St. Francis and his friends
>   to bear Christ's cross
>   in their hearts,
>   in their acts,
>   in their language.
>   They experienced crucifixion
>   in their deeds,
>   in their disciplined living.
>   They liked this and wanted
>   more dishonor,
>   more affronts,
>   because they loved Christ.
>   They liked this much better than
>   worldly reputation,
>   worldly honors,
>   human esteem. [18]

When we bear the weight of that which taxes us with internal and external challenges we forge the patience and good nature that allowed Francis and the Brothers to endure persecution with good nature. Eventually, once we have gained control, we are able to help others who are suffering from conflict and we are able to bring peace.

> *The Spirit's best gift,*
> *His highest grace,*
>   *Christ gives to His friends:*
>   *To conquer self*
>   *for Jesus' sake;*
>   *this makes us willing to go through*
>   *sufferings,*
>   *hurts,*
>   *rejections,*
>   *troubles of all sorts.* [19]

"Our job is to look and listen. In these gestures we are to show grace, humility, and littleness. The act of listening is the beginning of an avenue of transformation."[20] When we assess our need for revenge we may think of Francis, then we listen carefully to detect the roar, the rumbling, or the murmur of our desire for revenge so that we might expose dark desire to light. When we are drawn by the urge for revenge it is time to seek the virtue of patience, which allows us to listen closely so that we might hear the sweet sound of the indwelling Holy Spirit moving within.

Scripture

The tongue is also a fire. It exists among our members as a world of malice, defiling the whole body and setting the entire course of our lives on fire, itself set on fire by Gehenna. For every kind of beast and bird, of reptile and sea creature, can be tamed by the human species, but no human being can tame the tongue. It is a restless evil, full of deadly poison. With it we bless the Lord and Father, and with it we curse human beings who are made in the likeness of God. (Jas 3:6-9)

Do not repay anyone evil for evil; be concerned for what is noble in the sight of all. If possible, on your part, live at peace with all. Beloved, do not look for revenge but leave room for the wrath; for it is written, "Vengeance is mine, I will repay, says the Lord." Rather, "if your enemy is hungry, feed him; if he is thirsty, give him something to drink; for by so doing you will heap burning coals upon his head. Do not be conquered by evil but conquer evil with good. (Rom 12:17-21)

Blessed are the peacemakers,
  for they will be called children of God. (Mt 5:9)

CHAPTER NINE

The Mediator Role

Francis listened quietly as the mayor described what had happened to their peaceful town.

He had much empathy for the families of the victims and wanted to meet the wolf and hear his story, too. Francis announced that the next morning he would go to the woods where the guards had been killed to see if he could find the wolf.

That night he prayed for the wisdom to find a solution that would benefit everyone.

Mediation Principles

IN THE PREVIOUS CHAPTER we explored revenge, a topic that can be uncomfortable to consider and difficult to discuss. Experiencing once again the helplessness and powerlessness that pushed us to consider violent and desperate acts can be unpleasant. Discussing acts of revenge we have committed can elicit regret. Emotions surface that cause us to doubt our ability to go forward. We may consider abandoning the conflict resolution process or we may be troubled by fantasies of a last-ditch attack that "gets it over with."

You may be convinced you should avoid the matter entirely. You may entertain moving to another state, changing jobs, or getting a divorce. Surfacing unpleasant feelings tempts us to retreat into old patterns of dealing with conflict, which would be a mistake. Instead, we can rely on a mediator or other facilitator to help us move past destructive emotions that surface during conflict resolution.

The Mediator's Role

Conflict resolution is not easy. We come face to face with situations that demand the assistance of an impartial third party. This outside help becomes vital when parties encounter barriers that prevent reconciliation. Without outside help the conflict resolution conversation takes place between two or more parties whose stances consist of opposing forces, emotions, intentions, or goals that shape the barriers that make it difficult, if not impossible, for communication to flow. As free flow of communication is crucial to the reconciliation process hope is diminished.

For instance, if we do not understand why our opponent assumed a hostile attitude in response to our actions, we might ask a clarifying question: "What happened to make you think *that*?" The attempt to clarify the situation, however, will most likely be seen by the other party as an attack on their integrity. The question will be met with a defensive posture. Their response will be evasive or defensive – "I don't have to justify myself to you. I can think any way I like." We take their rejection to heart and become equally defensive. We no longer want to reach out.

The impaired communication leaves us unable to clarify events. We know something has gone wrong but we cannot locate exactly what it might be. The communication jams simply because parties assume an oppositional stance and the natural dynamics of conflict impede resolution.

In a similar fashion, if we suggest a solution, our suggestion is seen as a strategic move intended to benefit only us. The other party harbors suspicions that the suggestion covers hidden motives. While our suggested solution may be perfectly valid it is rejected simply because *we* originated the solution. The other party devalues our ideas and responds negatively simply and solely as a result of our being their adversary.

Thus, when parties attempt to resolve a conflict on their own these natural dynamics of conflict create impasse. The problem lies with the dynamics of the situation: once conflict emerges parties are trapped in patterns they cannot change without the assistance of an impartial third party.

The same dynamics are at work when a party considers sharing candid feelings. They crash headlong into a wall of anxiety. Exposing our inner self in front of an opponent – who may be out to crush us – not only feels unsafe, it may *be* unsafe. The last thing a party embroiled in a conflict wants to do is expose his vulnerable inner self.

Our instinct to protect our identity and defend the essence of who we are is fundamental. Physical and emotional reactions triggered by the potential threat stop us in our tracks. Anxiety and stress shut the body down, sending a physiological message: "You are not going to expose yourself, you are not going to become vulnerable."

The parties face a dilemma – they want to share their honest feelings but the need to avoid emotional injury dictates a defensive posture. One party's defensive posture triggers the other party's defensive posture. They become trapped in a dichotomy: "I must express myself – but I can't express myself."

In addition, when difficult emotions are stirred we find our perceptions blur. We may begin to secretly wonder if our view of the situation is accurate. "Am I seeing things as they really are or am I losing it here?" In order to fend off uncertainty we toss doubt aside and become passionately wedded to our view, refusing to consider any other. We slip into the frame of mind that says, "there is only one reality – mine."

When doubt and uncertainty swell we experience the uncomfortable feeling of being scattered and confused, but if we hold rigidly to our views we experience tunnel vision. Either way we are unable to enter into a relaxed dialogue with the other party in order to explore multiple viewpoints.

When a mediator (or other facilitator) joins the conversation the dynamics change dramatically. The mediator does not stand in opposition to either party and does not play the role of an authority figure whom the parties must please. The mediator has no stake in the outcome and nothing to gain. Good mediators do not even focus on whether or not their efforts will result in a settlement; they do not become invested in a record of success, as that would inadvertently put pressure on parties to settle. The mediator knows that if she shows concern over reaching a settlement the party's desire to please her may push them beyond their comfort zone and beyond the bounds of a wise solution.

With a mediator present we have a triangle rather than opposing poles and thus each party has a safe person to whom they can express vulnerable feelings. As the mediator listens with empathy and guides the conversation, the parties discover that what they need most is someone who can listen – really listen.

Humility Rather than Judgment

Communication flows through many channels: spoken and written words; body language, including eye contact; actions that convey meaning, heart messages, and intuition. When combined these communication modes convey complex states of mind.

During difficult moments we treasure the mediator who listens to all channels on which we broadcast. We treasure a mediator who listens with her heart and grasps our meaning. We cherish empathy extended during the stressful task of unburdening thoughts and emotions that expose our weaknesses and insecurities. We seek a safe listener to whom we can express our passions and we seek someone who can feel as we feel, someone who can understand our inner life. We want to know we have been heard, not only with the intellect but also with the heart.

The last thing we want is judgment. Paradoxically we also do not desire coddling sympathy. Instead we seek empathy – understanding without judgment. Empathy eschews the type of sympathy designed solely to make us feel good no matter the nature of our transgressions.

We seek someone who can hear the good and the bad, the honorable and the shameful – someone who feels our pain, but does not overlook our sins. We want a listener who will not judge, but we also want a listener who has firsthand experience of the guilt that accompanies shameful acts.

We do not want a righteous judge who lives a perfect life. We want someone who has also committed transgressions and thus is prepared to help us address reprehensible episodes in our history. We want a mediator who separates our actions from who we are and allows us to hope we can remedy the past and create a better future.

The sympathetic aunt who prattles on, assuring us we can do no wrong, is unable to really listen and thus is not able to help. While everyone loves an uncritical ally in their corner, they also want someone who can walk with them in the dark places of the soul and assist with the journey back into the light. We want someone who can reflect the truth of who we are in our many colors and hues.

The quality that allows a mediator or other facilitator to listen without judgment and yet understand actions and thoughts of which we are not proud may be best summed up as humility. Francis possessed such humility. He considered himself to be the least of men before God. Through his prayerful acknowledgment of his own failings he became sufficiently humble to embrace flaws in those he met.

A mediator who has confronted her own shortcomings understands shortcomings in another and does not compulsively render judgment. While a mediator does not judge she also does not sweep transgressions under the carpet, realizing there are violations that call upon us to repent in order to heal. A mediator who has stumbled and then suffered through repentance, a mediator who has had to sit with the darkness of his or her own transgressions, has begun the preparation that allows her to sit with another as they face their demons.

In my experience it has been a rare mediation that did not include the parties' desire to walk away feeling better about who they are – even if they previously committed acts for which they were not proud. An informal confession frequently allows the party to move forward. If a mediator listens closely, he will often hear a party express a desire to tell it like it is – even if this means confessing non-praiseworthy acts. The frequency with which this happens leads me to believe that parties know intuitively that they must purge the blackness from their hearts in order to move from a troubled past to a future that delivers resolution, reconciliation, and peace.

We will explore confession and unburdening in greater detail in a later chapter. In this chapter we simply point to the need to trust the mediator and to the need for the mediator to listen with her heart. If a party feels the mediator cannot comfortably acknowledge their transgressions, they may wish to recruit a pastoral counselor as a member of their personal support team. (Though I use the term *mediator* throughout, in many cases a pastoral counselor or other conciliator whose charism is reconciliation will guide parties through conflict resolution.)

The above discussion is not meant to imply that a mediator is a therapist. As stated previously, a mediator is not a therapist though mediation may be therapeutic. One of the primary differences between a mediator and a therapist concerns the use of evaluation and judgment. A therapist is trained to evaluate, schooled to make judgments; they often label a person or diagnosis a condition, if not overtly then covertly. In contrast, the mediator's job is not to evaluate or judge. A mediator has no need for labels or diagnoses.

For this reason, a mediator can assist a party through troubling times related to conflict while escaping pitfalls associated with the labels therapists affix. The mediator does not seek out symptoms and does not seek to label the party's mental state. Instead, the mediator facilitates the party's self-chosen journey toward reconciliation, demonstrating empathy for the challenges the party faces, recognizing in the party the same human condition to which the mediator is subject.

The mediator strips himself of the power to make judgments and walks alongside the party. The mediator shares his heart, his intellect, his experience, and his training with the goal of helping the party resolve their conflict. A label or a diagnosis only places distance between a mediator and those he serves, which defeats his purpose. Francis and the mediators or pastoral counselors who follow his example close the distance between themselves and the parties they serve through humility. They establish working relationships based on compassion and love.

Active Listening

Empathetic listening may also be called *active listening*. The mediator remains engaged and responds, moment by moment, by asking clarifying questions, always working to more perfectly understand. The mediator puts himself in the party's shoes. He wants to know: When contentious events transpired how did you feel? What thoughts came to mind? What concerns gave you pause?

At times the mediator will paraphrase the party's story and then ask if he has understood correctly. The mediator starts with open-ended questions such as, what happened? This allows the party to tell their story in the manner they prefer. After the party describes the events from their point of view, the mediator asks questions that further clarify the narrative. These clarifying questions do not challenge the party nor do they cast doubt on the veracity of their story, but rather are questions intended to make sure the mediator truly understands what happened.

When we are caught up in a conflict questions may automatically appear to be covert challenges expressing doubt or impugning our honesty. For this reason the mediator is very careful to explain that his goal is to perfectly understand what occurred.

The mediator works in sequence from the big picture narrative to details. After he has heard the story and asked clarifying questions, he poses questions intended to verify factual details. The mediator uses a *funneling* approach – going from broad open-ended questions to narrow close-ended questions.[1] He pursues a detailed understanding of what happened.

As the mediator has no stake in the outcome parties are typically not threatened by his examination of their narrative. He usually does not elicit the defensive posture that colors responses one party would give to the other party. And he does not elicit the guarded presentation a party makes before a judge. The inclusion of an impartial third party (the mediator) thus changes the dynamics and makes an exploration of the conflict possible.

The mediator may work with the party to expand their perceptions regarding what happened. He may ask them to revisit the narrative from different points of view; this might include asking them to recount the events with selective focus on different senses. He may ask them to provide an account of what they were seeing and then an account of what they heard. He might ask them to speculate on how the events may have appeared from the other party's vantage point. The mediator attempts to loosen up perceptions and expand the points of view the party is willing to comfortably entertain.

The mediator makes sharing views between parties palatable by framing the narratives exchanged. He uses neutral language to place one side's views in a context that does not directly threaten the other side. As much as possible, he avoids activating emotional triggers and defensive posturing.

As the mediator does not have an upset with events that have transpired, he is not subject to destructive emotions – he does not add his own negative emotions when he frames narratives. He paraphrases the account to insure he has correctly understood the narrative. Such paraphrasing provides the parties an opportunity to hear their own stories without the color of destructive emotions. For the first time they may be able to view events in a less upsetting manner. This does not mean the mediator ignores the emotional content but rather that his paraphrase allows parties to gain a more neutral perspective.

Likewise, when the mediator facilitates the brainstorming stage he is able to advance suggestions in a neutral manner, reducing the tendency of parties to devalue suggestions coming from each other. The mediator creates a new dynamic that circumvents natural barriers that emerge when parties face off.

Francis no doubt spent hours with the mayor – at first he listened to the story the mayor chose to tell in his own words with his own emphasis. Francis then may have pursued questions that helped him understand the decisions that led the guards to attempt to slay the wolf.

He may have asked the mayor to explain how he felt when the bodies of slain citizens were returned to Gubbio. He may have asked, "When the bodies were carried through the gate, what went through your mind?" He may have asked for details regarding the first livestock taken by the wolf – his questions may have elicited the mayor's opinion regarding whether the wolf was on a wanton killing spree or was hungry and trying to survive.

The mayor may have found himself revealing more than expected. As he recounted the story, his troubled emotions may have settled slightly, allowing his perceptions to improve. He may have discovered feelings he had covered up or hidden from himself. By the time Francis completed his interview, Francis probably understood the mayor's situation almost as well as the mayor himself.

This process of listening to the party's narrative allows the party and the mediator to better assess the nature of the conflict to be resolved.

Listening to Self

While it is important for the mediator to listen closely, it is also important for you to listen to the signals your words and emotions are sending. While you are telling your story, engage in deep listening. Listen to your heart – there may be more to the story than was apparent at the outset.

This task of uncovering the deeper aspects of conflict may require additional techniques such as meditation or contemplative prayer. It may require spending time in a quiet place or taking long walks that encourage reflection. There is a difference between the crushing worry that loops endlessly in our minds and the practice of sitting with our thoughts (in meditation or contemplation). In the former instance we tend to unconsciously push thoughts away or follow them down dead end paths; thoughts spin around and around, chased by our worry.

On the other hand, when we sit with a conflict we observe our thoughts and emotions from a distance. We listen to self by becoming a still observer who views thoughts from the point of view of a stranger. We allow ourselves to be surprised and entertained by the manner in which our mind wrestles with the dilemma. We seek to see events from a divine perspective.

An analogy would be sitting on the banks of a flowing mountain creek, watching the water race past. Rather than trying to stop the rushing water or divert its course, we admire the way it races past us, swirling around boulders, slowing in calm pools but always moving downstream and out of sight. If we watch our thoughts and emotions in this same manner, allowing them to flow past as we observe from our detached and unmoving perch on the banks of our stream of consciousness, we grow peaceful and perceptive. Perhaps for the first time we actually hear the message of our heart.

Divine Listening

When St. Francis prays for wisdom to find a solution he enters into a new level of listening. He becomes attuned to the Spirit working within. As an outsider we might wonder why Francis prays for a solution. Can contemplative prayer play a role in conflict resolution? Does the process include a role for the divine within? While in prayer do we tap into resources we may have previously ignored?

The answers to these questions must come from within. They are not answers another can provide for us but rather answers that arise from our experience. In *Taming the Wolf* we raise these questions anticipating you will seek your own discovery. We analyze Francis' actions to see what we might learn for our own journey.

When Francis listened to the mayor call for revenge he showed empathy and was able to transform that desire into the mayor's commitment to participate in conflict resolution. Francis not only took an impartial perspective, he took a divine perspective. His view, which was the result of his deep spiritual devotion, was that all parties were brothers in the eyes of God. While he could empathize with the suffering of one side – for example, the suffering the mayor experienced – his deeper understanding prevented him from taking sides and joining one party against the other.

In accounts of the life of St. Francis the picture that emerges is of a man who listened deeply and became aware of the Spirit at work in the world. This makes him a model for mediators charged with the task of encouraging parties to find creative solutions – even divinely inspired solutions – that break the cycle of conflict escalation, end the cycle of revenge, and bring peace where there has been violence. This is the life Francis lived, a life dedicated to brotherhood.

When one listens to the Spirit within one unveils an awareness of self as soul – the listening draws us to know our essence as an immortal spiritual being. The act of embracing a transcendent perspective radically alters our idea of who we are and motivates us to approach reconciliation with fresh eyes. In Francis' relentless efforts to imitate Christ he underwent a transformation that imbued him with a transcendent point of view from which he recognized a profound and fundamental brotherhood of all creatures. From this perspective he was able to draw upon the faith that would sustain and support him as an agent of peace. The evening he was summoned by the messengers from Gubbio he renewed this perspective through prayer as he made plans to depart the next morning to seek out the wolf.

We find prayer playing a similar role in contemporary peacemaking. In faith-based diplomacy, as well as in mediation sessions convened to address conflict within a faith group, it is common for the mediator to enlist a team to pray throughout the entire proceeding, recognizing the role Divine Providence plays. In these cases listening to the divine is more than an afterthought, it becomes a formal part of the process. We may ask whether or not this is an approach we should engage in our unique attempts to resolve conflict.

Listening through prayer for the Holy Spirit moving within may bring us to consider the question: What does this fight look like to God? What would a solution inspired by the Holy Spirit look like? What features might a divinely inspired solution possess?

Safe Place, Sacred Place

Reconciliation requires we find a safe place or refuge from which to view the conflict as it is. In preparation for mediation you may wish to locate a safe place where you can find periods of silence and contemplation. You may wish to structure a retreat to provide yourself with time and space needed to allow the Spirit to work through the process.

For mediation you will want to identify a setting in which both parties feel comfortable. Though many mediations, especially those taking place within the context of a litigated case, are set in the courthouse, in a lawyer's office, or in a mediator's office this is not a given. The parties working with the mediator can explore options in the search for a safe location that will enhance the process.

When the conflict involves nations the diplomatic context may require the use of a neutral third-party government's facilities that provide adequate security and privacy. Divorce mediators often work out of quaint houses with comfortable, traditional settings where disputants can work around a kitchen table. St. Francis might consider a safe place is also a sacred place. Assisi has become known as a sacred site, a setting where a spirit of peace descends upon visitors. When we convene in a safe place that is also a sacred space, we invite an awareness of the divine to permeate the proceedings.

Safe places need not be confined to physical dwellings. With contemplative prayer one creates a safe place within the heart. Even when the external setting for mediation is not optimal we can create a safe space in our heart and carry that peaceful space wherever we convene. Ideally we come to mediation in a safe place with a safe space in our heart.

Even the seemingly benign task of reading this book may require a safe place within the heart where one can retreat to listen to the messages the Holy Spirit delivers. As one reads about conflict thoughts and emotions attached to previous conflicts begin to swirl; emotional distress tied to old unresolved conflicts may stir.

As a result, we experience diminished perceptions that make it difficult to understand the material in *Taming the Wolf.* When we bring to mind old upsets our vision may cloud with unsettled emotion, making it difficult to stay with the lessons. You may find it advantageous to calm your mind and heart with prayer or meditation before responding to the prompts in the journal workbook or before implementing suggestions. You may wish to read the excerpts from scripture to prepare for the tasks ahead.

In any event you will want to find a ritual that calms the mind before reading *Taming the Wolf* so the material may speak to your heart as well as your intellect. If you discover you have stirred up uncomfortable emotions during your study it may be a sign you need to take a break for contemplative prayer or for a quiet walk that allows insights to bubble up through your unsettled mind.

Another approach to preparing for significant conflict resolution is to embark on a pilgrimage to a sacred site such as Assisi with the goal of allowing the journey and the sacred space to enhance your preparation. The pilgrimage might be designed to focus on conflict and its resolution and might parallel the chapters in this book. If time and cost places a pilgrimage out of reach, in lieu of an actual pilgrimage you may wish to take a virtual pilgrimage through photos or video that transport you temporarily to another space.

A Franciscan View

In the preceding discussion we explored the need to prepare for reconciliation with *divine listening* in the form of contemplative prayer. In our attempt to understand this vital subject we turn to *Franciscan Prayer* by Ilia Delio, OSF.[2] Her definition of prayer parallels the preparation required for reconciliation, particularly if we wish to arrive at the process with a posture of divinely inspired transparency: "Prayer is that love of God that clears away the dross that covers the image of God in which I am created. It uncovers something that is precious and glorious within me.... It is the discovery of the new being within me."[3]

St. Bonaventure expressed a similar sentiment centuries earlier: "The mirror presented by the external world is of little or no value unless the mirror of our soul has been cleaned and polished."[4] Bonaventure might have coached us to tend to the work of cleaning and polishing the mirror of the soul before we step into the mediation room.

In this cleaning and polishing step divine listening is a focal point, as Susan Saint Sing reminds us: "Our job, as was Francis' eight centuries ago, is to look and to listen. In these gestures are grace, humility, and littleness. The act of listening is the beginning of an avenue of transformation."[5]

Francis was acutely aware of the need to listen to the Holy Spirit in solitude and often sought hermitage in the hills above Assisi: "Caves up and down central Italy were his hermitages. La Verna was a special place of mystical experiences for Francis."[6] For the early Franciscans, these moments of solitude, silence, and listening took precedence over the demands of daily life. "[Francis] often reminded the brothers never to let work interfere with the spirit of prayer and devotion."[7]

As we prepare for reconciliation we turn once again to Francis, who provides a model worth our careful attention. "He had learned in prayer that the presence of the Holy Spirit for which he longed was granted more intimately to those who invoke him, the more the Holy Spirit found them withdrawn from the noise of worldly affairs. Therefore seeking out lonely places, he used to go to deserted areas and abandoned churches to pray at night."[8]

Though the pace of our lives may be hectic and our obligations may press impatiently on our minds it is wise for us to seek "lonely places," quiet churches, or perhaps a remote retreat center at which we can engage in polishing and cleaning the mirrors of our soul while we engage in divine listening.

Too often we fail to properly value the importance of this preparation. The words of Delio serve to remind us: "Prayer that leads to the beauty of the image within is difficult for it requires honesty and humility. It requires freedom from expectations, projections, false hopes and self-centeredness. It means to be able to say, I am who I am with my strengths and weaknesses, gifts and failings."[9]

Francis no doubt spent many hours and many days deep in prayer at San Damiano – the small church in disrepair a short distance outside Assisi – before his divine listening was rewarded with the words that launched his conversion. "I am certain that on the day Francis followed the visual cues of the cross [of San Damiano] to their endpoint, the tumblers of the universe clicked, the portal opened inside Francis and grace flowed. By making himself available, *he was there to hear*. Portals open and close around us each day, each moment, and we must grasp them, seize them, for they are the message of our lives."[10]

So, too, we need to seek solitude and in prayer we make ourselves available as we listen closely, waiting for the portals to open as we seek to understand the conflict in which we are entangled.

Scripture

With that their eyes were opened and they recognized him, but he vanished from their sight. Then they said to each other, "Were not our hearts burning [within us] while he spoke to us on the way and opened the scriptures to us?" (Lk 24:31-32)

"I am baptizing you with water, for repentance, but the one who is coming after me is mightier than I. I am not worthy to carry his sandals. He will baptize you with the holy Spirit and fire." (Mt 3:11)

Then he sat down, called the Twelve, and said to them, "If anyone wishes to be first, he shall be the last of all and the servant of all." Taking a child he placed it in their midst, and putting his arms around it he said to them, "Whoever receives one child such as this in my name, receives me; and whoever receives me, receives not me but the One who sent me." (Mk 9:35-37)

"God is Spirit, and those who worship him must worship in Spirit and truth." (Jn 4:24)

Why do you not understand what I am saying? Because you cannot bear to hear my word. (Jn 8:43)

CHAPTER TEN

The Hostile Party

Early the next morning, refreshed and confident, Francis was accompanied by the townspeople to the gates of Gubbio. They wished him well and retreated to their homes, worried that Francis would share the fate of the shepherds and guards.

He walked on to the woods, ready to engage the wolf. As he neared the first stand of trees, the wolf appeared and began to stalk Francis. His slow, deliberate steps, the walk of a predator, announced his intention. He drew nearer and nearer, closing in a circle around the holy man from Assisi.

Seeing the wolf, Francis felt a connection. He made the sign of the cross and called the wolf to meet him in peace under the grace of the Lord. The wolf watched as Francis came closer. "Come Brother Wolf, I will not hurt you. Let us talk in peace."

Mediation Principles

IN THIS CHAPTER, the focus shifts to the party less willing to consider a move toward reconciliation. In the legend this party is the wolf. Not only is the wolf unwilling to consider reconciliation, he perceives Francis' approach as a threat and he stalks him, lips curled, teeth bared.

We may face an adversary who resembles the wolf, a party committed to continuing the fight, a party committed to our demise. We may be entangled in a conflict with someone who is hurt, angry, and eager to attack. This portends increased difficulty when it comes to convening – trying to convene reconciliation with a hostile opponent on your own is nearly impossible. If the mayor sent one of his men to greet the wolf the emissary most likely would be killed.

The situation calls for a mediator or other impartial third party. When Francis engages the wolf we have an example that provides hope that reconciliation might be possible, even in difficult circumstances. The following discussion takes up how an impartial third party invites the unwilling or hostile party to consider mediation.

Convening with an Unwilling or Hostile Party

Convening mediation with an unwilling or hostile party requires extensive experience addressing destructive emotions. The mediator who is uncomfortable with harsh or hostile emotions will experience difficulty. When a wolf begins to stalk an uneasy mediator – and growls a warning – the uneasy mediator will bolt.

In contrast, the experienced mediator is calm under fire and anticipates hostile emotion aimed in their direction; they do not end the conversation at the first expression of upset. Like a lightning rod, they attract the pent-up hostility built up over the life of the conflict. When Francis noticed the wolf stalking him, he knew the wolf was in no mood to resolve the conflict – but he did not scurry out of the woods and return to Gubbio with bad news. He knew his first step was to acknowledge the upset the wolf was expressing.

In addition, the mediator recognizes that a skeptical or unwilling party most likely will test him. If the mediator appears uncomfortable in the face of harsh emotions, the unwilling party will assume that particular mediator will be of little use in resolving the conflict. The hostile party will wonder how the mediator could possibly be of help if, at the first sign of unpleasantness, he shies away.

The mediator thus faces the demanding task of appearing tough enough to face unpleasant aspects of the conflict while remaining considerate, empathetic, and patient enough to listen to disturbing yet heartfelt concerns. The task requires not only empathy but also a finely honed ability to respond to rapidly changing and often conflicting emotional demands.

The mayor solicited the help of Francis and asked him to slay the wolf. The wolf expressed with his body language his intention to slay anyone reporting to the mayor. The wolf's response is more overtly hostile but nonetheless parallels the mayor's intention to make nothing of the opposing party. Perhaps the only difference was the intensity of hostile emotions and the degree to which the party was invested in violent solutions. The mediator's goal is to bleed off the destructive emotion that makes it impossible to move to the next stage.

If we assume the point of view of the hostile party we may be able to comprehend the dilemma they face when a mediator solicits their participation. We can safely assume that in the past too many well-meaning friends have told the hostile party, "Peace and love, brother. Just give it up." There has been an implicit suggestion by others that peace can be achieved in the absence of a fair hearing that takes the hostile party's needs into account.

When the wolf was a young cub he may have been ordered to make up with a sibling (or else!), while at the same time his mother failed to address the sibling's harmful acts that started the dispute. A previous lack of fairness in resolving disputes and a failure to address his real interests left the wolf holding a negative view toward "peace and love." Based on past experience he knows peace and love do not work. He knows he is being asked to compromise his interests – and this time he is not willing to give up the fight.

The last thing a reticent party wants to hear from a peacemaker knocking on his door is a suggestion that he give up his position and jettison his anger simply because "it is the right thing to do." The disgruntled party is not going to buy that argument; instead, he will take his chances by continuing the fight. The hostile party's frustration, built up over a lifetime of poorly resolved conflicts, is unleashed at the mediator.

A mediator must move quickly past this wall of resistance. The first step involves establishing good communication. In these first moments, the mediator telegraphs her intentions clearly, sending clear signals that promise she is not going to engage in judgment or coercion. This is not as easy as it might seem. In our daily affairs most of us carry ourselves with a posture of certainty, rightness, and self-confidence. These attitudes, however appropriate in other situations, send signals that can be misread. A hostile party may interpret the mediator's strong posture to mean he is willing to judge the hostile party and coerce him to take actions the mediator deems righteous.

In contrast, a successful mediator advances with a posture of *humility*. She realizes she cannot force a result. All she can do is humbly offer to facilitate a reconciliation process. The mediator approaches with an attitude of "use my help if you believe it might benefit you." She avoids the confident demeanor of one who has come to save you. She does not become defensive in the face of hostility and skepticism, but rather understands that even hostile actions such as the wolf stalking Francis provide a connection that opens dialogue.

Francis displays the sign of the cross, communicating that he bears a spiritual message and does not intend to cause harm. In a like manner a mediator must be aware of messages he sends through his demeanor, his body language, and his words. He will want to convey a humble and calm determination, without adopting a crusading persona that telegraphs he endorses peace at any cost.

He will want to avoid the attitude and demeanor of a peacemaker, as that posture implies the hostile party is the cause of the conflict that must be remedied. Such an attitude may imply the mediator will try to change the hostile party or heal him or constrain him. The mediator avoids the appearance of an "expert from afar" sent to straighten out the unwilling party. Instead, he communicates that he is a trained professional whom the party may choose to use in his own efforts to make peace.

Rather than being a peacemaker the mediator becomes a resource the hostile party may utilize in the process of becoming a peacemaker himself. Humility and inner peace are difficult to counterfeit, which is why the best mediators are typically elders who have encountered struggles and who have been humbled by experience. If the mediator is believable and his signs are clear, if his stated intentions are trustworthy and transparent, if he brings goodwill, then he will be transformed in the eyes of the wolf from a target of hostility into a symbol of hope.

When parties have been betrayed previously, however, all promises of reconciliation take on a false ring. The hostile or unwilling party will resort to subtle tests that challenge the mediator to prove his good intentions. The mediator should be willing to be stalked and tested; willing to have his sincerity and commitment to neutrality challenged; willing to have his promise of delivering a non-judgmental and non-coercive process assessed. Reputation is not the deciding factor; the party will want to evaluate firsthand whether or not to extend trust. These tests can be exasperating and confrontational but are necessary.

For these reasons, Francis allowed the wolf to stalk him. It was necessary for him to approach in a defenseless posture; it was important he demonstrate his only strength was the Holy Spirit and his only power was love and compassion. Mediators frequently experience being placed in the position of going out to meet the wolf. They have no power to render a decision; they do not deliver a verdict and they have no power to force a settlement. Compared to a judge, mediators are powerless. They must rely on skill, training, experience, and natural ability as a facilitator. Their ability to facilitate the transformation of conflict into reconciliation is the only power on which they can rely.

At this critical moment in the convening stage the mediator sets out to demonstrate that his promises and intentions are grounded in reality. The hostile party is skeptical of any claim that resolution is possible; his experience tells him such claims are invalid. The mediator understands this and candidly confesses he cannot make any guarantees regarding outcomes: mediation involves uncertainty and risk and does not always result in resolution and reconciliation. Rather than trying to overwhelm and defeat the hostile party's objections, he reverses direction and agrees with the party – the process *is* fraught with risk and uncertainty.

He assures the party there are no absolute promises to be made, no magic wands to be waved, and no potent potions to be administered. He agrees that many attempts at resolution and reconciliation are ill advised. But he continues to explain he is trained in processes that *have* worked for many other people. Yes, it is true, not all parties enjoy success, but a sufficient number – well over half of those who attempt mediation – find success, and those odds make proceeding down a difficult path worth the modest risk.

Having acknowledged that success is not assured and there is a possibility they will not be able to resolve the conflict, the mediator questions the party's alternatives: What is the likelihood other options will work? If they fail to resolve the conflict what are the consequences? The mediator transitions from an emotional assessment to a rational assessment based on risks and rewards. The mediator models the process by honoring the party's ability to assess the situation and make a rational decision.

The mediator continues to withdraw and makes it clear the party must evaluate risks and possible rewards. Ultimately the party must make the decision to proceed. Only when the hostile party considers the possible rewards outweigh the possible risks will they decide to mediate. The mediator offers to assist with a risk and reward analysis, but does not push his help.

He may express doubts and suggest mediation may be unsuitable for this particular situation. He may argue that he will need to evaluate whether or not it makes sense for him to spend his time resolving the dispute. He explains it is customary for him to ask preliminary questions to determine if mediation is the right process for a particular conflict. The mediator thus reverses roles and becomes the skeptic. Rather than the party evaluating *him*, he evaluates the party to see if the party qualifies for mediation.

Throughout this convening dialogue the mediator uses a non-coercive approach to promote a non-coercive process. The party will read the mediator's convening style as a clue to how events will unfold in the future. A coercive convening approach raises the suspicion that the process will be coercive. To avoid this perception the mediator stresses that nothing will occur without the party's involvement and agreement.

The party will not readily accept this promise; the adversarial and judicial models are too strongly imprinted on our psyches. A party assumes that no matter what the mediator promises, in the end, they will judge him. The promise of a non-coercive process that honors party self-determinism will need to be repeated many times.

Self-determination becomes the primary persuasive lever used to move hostile parties toward conflict resolution. This fundamental concept dictates that parties will determine their own outcome as a result of facilitated negotiation, an outcome that may or may not include resolution. The hostile party is informed that he will be given an opportunity to address the conflict in a creative manner. If he reaches an arrangement with the other party that has value for both they may resolve the dispute; if they overcome the wounds of the past, they may reconcile. If the results do not satisfy their needs, they can walk away. *They* determine the outcome; no one makes the decision for them.

This idea of self-determinism is so unique that it often takes considerable work to achieve "buy in" with a reticent or hostile party. The idea that a party possesses the ability to determine their own outcome is foreign and at times threatening. On the other hand, the promise that they will *not* be coerced into a resolution often provides sufficient comfort for them to give mediation a try. A party is much more willing to explore the process if they are not forced to commit in advance to the idea that their efforts *must* result in a pre-determined outcome.

A hostile party's willingness to come to the table often rests on a discussion of the hostile party's interests. There is no reason for the hostile party to take part if there is no hope their interests will be satisfied. When a mediator is genuinely interested he engages in exploratory conversation, "How might resolution of this conflict benefit you? If we are able to resolve this conflict, what interests of yours will be satisfied?"

Rather than advance general and vague notions regarding the advantages of making peace, the mediator focuses on party self-interest. He knows the unwilling party, the wolf, has his attention on how mediation will benefit him. Once the unwilling party begins to explore benefits it becomes easier to carry on a dialogue, as the focus of the conversation focus turns in his direction. Previously, during the conflict, it is likely no one has genuinely asked him what he wants.

Nonetheless, even though a wolf may enter into dialogue, typically he does not believe the mediator can make much of a difference. If it were that easy the conflict would have been resolved long ago. It is at this point the mediator introduces mediation as a process designed to overcome barriers to resolution, explaining that he will bring his experience and expertise to bear in guiding the process. He stresses they will work together to tailor procedural guidelines culled from similar guidelines that have worked in other conflicts. He conveys safety and hope based on his gentle but firm control of a process that has worked for others.

The Hostile Party Tells Their Story

Above all else, the mediator must be genuinely interested in what drives the hostile party in the conflict. A mediator must possess a sincere desire to hear the hostile party's unique story – for no other reason than the mediator has a genuine need to satisfy her curiosity. If her listening is perceived by the hostile party to be a tactic, the conversation fails to get off the ground.

It is difficult for a party to resist telling their story to someone who is genuinely interested. The mediator often prefaces her request to hear what happened with the following disclaimer: "Whether or not you enter into mediation, my curiosity has been piqued. I must know what happened to you." If a mediator is a passionate student of human nature and considers that her job includes constantly enriching her knowledge of human affairs, her genuine interest will be apparent.

The unwilling or hostile party slowly transitions from refusing to convene – resisting with force, anger, and threats – to telling his story. This movement provides a firsthand experience that confirms at a non-verbal level that change is possible. It is a subtle transformation that nonetheless brings about significant movement. This change in momentum is not usually overtly acknowledged by the mediator but it signals a new stage in the process.

Compassion Drives the Mediator

At the same time the mediator informs the hostile party he has no stake in whether or not the dispute is resolved, he communicates compassion for their welfare. He explains that while he cares about their needs he is unwilling to impose a solution. His passion is not unbridled enthusiasm that demands a result at any cost but rather concern for their welfare, which may or may not include reaching a settlement at this time. He understands and is able to embrace their pain, frustration, and hostility with empathy – he invites the hostile party into dialogue with his heart.

A mediator thus walks a fine line between showing loving compassion and showing the tough practical demeanor needed to tackle seemingly intractable problems. Francis, in his very presence, conveyed a loving peacefulness that induced a willingness to trust and seek reconciliation, but he did not accomplish this task from a position of weakness.

Before Francis engaged the wolf he had suffered imprisonment, he had lived through unforgiving conflict with his father, he had been the subject of abusive ridicule in his home town, he had traveled through a bloody war zone to spread the Gospel to an enemy leader, he had endured extreme deprivation and poverty, and he had tended to lepers who suffered social ostracism as well as physical malady. His devotional contemplation of the wounds of Christ had transformed those wounds into portals through which he traveled to understand divine mysteries. He arrived before the wolf armed with a wealth of experience, extensive insight, and deep devotion.

Francis was seasoned; he was not a naïve flower child. When he faced the wolf and made the sign of the cross this was not a weak gesture but rather a gesture that arose out of his exposure to suffering that had transformed his heart. The wolf no doubt felt his compassion. It may not be possible for most of us to greet another with the profound presence with which Francis greeted the wolf but we can gain inspiration from his story and aspire to model his approach.

Face Concerns Revisited

Having made preliminary progress in the convening discussion, the mediator often recognizes a need for Face Saving actions or words that allow the party to come to the table. It is not uncommon to find both parties sincerely harbor a desire to end the conflict but neither can take the first step. As discussed in earlier chapters, barriers to taking the first step often arise from a fear of Face Loss.

The reticent or hostile party may have announced to their adversary, to friends, family, to the community, or to the press, that they will never, under any circumstance, enter into dealings with the other party. They may have vowed loudly and publicly that they would make the other party pay for their misdeeds.

In these situations, in which the hostility has taken on a public face, an effort to reconcile entails apparent capitulation: the hostile party will be forced to break his vow to continue the separation and disrespect. Such vows create pressure on the hostile party to remain firm in their stance. They are unwilling to convene, as to recant is to suffer Face Loss.

In order to circumvent the impasse the mediator engineers a Face Saving path that allows the party to tell a new story, a rewritten narrative that is both believable and acceptable to those whose opinions they value. How this is accomplished varies in each unique situation but the foundational principles remain the same. Through conversation the mediator assesses the hostile party's previous positions, pronouncements, alliances, or promises that will be adversely affected if he agrees to enter into conflict resolution.

A mediator guides an exploration of new narratives that can explain and justify the hostile party's radical change of position. The mediator and the hostile party brainstorm hypothetical narratives. The mediator, in publicly recognizing the party's needs, Restores Face, demonstrating acceptance of their potential change in position.

As noted previously negative emotions impede convening. This is especially true with the hostile party. While the mediator may have tamped down the flames of emotion at the beginning of the convening conversation they flare anew as the conversation reaches new levels of frankness. Initially, the mediator encounters symptoms of underlying unpleasant emotions and then, when the potential of convening begins to seem real, those emotions reappear.

Thus, as obstacles to convening are gradually overcome and mediation becomes likely, emotions race to the surface. Painful memories connected to events that occurred during the conflict make it difficult to imagine being in the same room with the other party. The hostile party cannot come to grips with the thought of speaking to their opponent. The adverse physical reaction may be so overwhelming a face-to-face meeting once again seems impossible. This is the type of situation a mediator encounters when he goes out to meet the wolf.

Emotional Barriers Revisited

As noted in previous chapters convening requires moving past emotional defenses. During convening the mediator has limited time to discover the causes giving rise to the destructive emotions. While a mediator might develop a finely honed intuition for discerning barriers that prevent a party from coming to the table she must not only identify the correct cause of hostility but she must also work to defuse negative emotions that have been triggered.

Conflict arms a minefield of emotional triggers. With the hostile party, it is too late to avoid triggering destructive emotions; they are already in play. The focus turns to finding ways for the hostile party to *manage* emotions. If the hostile party perceives the mediator is willing to engage difficult emotions hostility often dissipates and the party listens to an explanation of how mediation honors feelings with a respectful hearing.

The hostile party typically regains control and explains how they feel when the conflict comes up for discussion. In this manner, destructive emotions are transformed into an agenda that helps the mediator plan the process. The mediator can suggest an agenda in which less-threatening issues are addressed first, followed by more threatening issues once trust between the parties has been partially restored. Or the hostile party may insist their greatest upset be handled first.

The mediator learns to recognize the difference between hostility leveled at him and hostility directed at the opposing party. When hostility is actually directed at the opposing party and not the mediator, venting those emotions releases pent-up frustration. Subsequently, the hostile party often executes an about face and embraces mediation enthusiastically.

When parties are provided with the opportunity to discuss their situation with an impartial third party who cares enough to listen the wall of negative emotion dissipates. The mediator becomes a bridge to the opposing party. He becomes a conduit of communication.

The key trait of a mediator is openness to genuine dialogue. In addition to the skill required to handle negative emotions the mediator's communication skills may substitute for the party's lack of communication skills. When the mediator approaches the reticent or hostile party he may find the hostility is actually an expression of exasperation with tangled communications. In the past a tangle of incomplete or misunderstood communications became hopelessly snarled. It appears there is no hope, as every time they try to resolve issues communications become even more snarled.

The mediator, by modeling a process of sorting out and correcting miscommunications, provides hope that such techniques can be used to unsnarl the situation. Previously, seemingly minor miscommunications escalated into unwillingness and hostility. When miscommunications are sorted out conflict de-escalates.

Beyond the Mediator

The above analysis focuses on the mediator's role, but we need to be mindful of our individual responsibility as a party. There are two possible scenarios: we are the hostile party reticent to convene or we are the party asking the mediator to engage with the hostile party.

In the latter case we may wish to assess the ways in which we can assist. If we are thorough and humble in our analysis of the conflict, we can probably provide the mediator with information that helps him understand the likely response of the hostile party. We can provide insight into how we have triggered the other party's negative emotions. We can provide minor concessions that signal to the hostile party a change is possible. We can provide an account of events that angered the other party, enabling the mediator to extend empathy. The mediator may say to the wolf, "I can see why you became upset when that happened. That would have upset me as well."

If we have not engaged a mediator or other facilitator yet we wish to reconcile with a hostile party, we need a creative approach that allows us to remain at a distance while we send signals that we desire to reconcile. For example, we might compose a letter in which we attempt to accomplish many of the same targets a mediator might accomplish. In the letter:

- we assume a humble posture and ask to be given a chance to make things right;
- we express a minor concession, perhaps an apology for a wrong we have committed;
- we tell the hostile party we understand they are upset;
- we acknowledge their desire to admonish us with harsh words and strong emotion;
- we acknowledge their skepticism regarding the possibility of re-solving differences;
- we acknowledge the need for guidelines for the process;
- we express concern that failing to resolve the conflict will result in a failure for all involved to satisfy their needs;
- we note a resolution of differences might provide an opportunity for mutual gain;
- we acknowledge our inability to anticipate the other party's con-cerns in their entirety;
- we express willingness to listen to concerns;
- we acknowledge we have no power to force a reconciliation;
- we agree that if anyone feels forced the process will not work.

Finally, we might send a copy of *Taming the Wolf* with a note that explains we discovered helpful ideas in the book that may allow us to move together beyond a troubled past toward a new future.

If you are the party that is hostile toward reconciliation you may wish to assess how you would react to a mediator's invitation to participate. How might you respond to the approach outlined in this chapter? What aspects of your opposition might you analyze on your own? Will your demands or conditions need to be met before you participate? Are your demands or con-ditions realistic, or are they ways of saying, no?

Perhaps, most importantly, if you are reticent to attempt to resolve the conflict and you are hostile toward the idea of reconciliation, or if you are simply too emotionally on fire to consider conflict resolution, ask yourself if your upset and hostility are truly your own – or whether other individuals are keeping the conflict alive. Do others have a stake in promoting the conflict and is their "advice" (gossip, rumor mongering, or character assassination) fueling your antipathy?

In later chapters we will take up the important topic of this negative hidden influence in more detail.[1] At this time it is worth simply noting the influences that affect your willingness to seek conflict resolution.

Role of the Divine

St. Francis sought to imitate Christ who taught in the Beatitudes a morality that issues from the heart rather than from commandments. If we follow this approach we consult our compassionate heart's moral compass, a guide far superior to any we will find sorting through volumes of rules. When we measure parties using rules and commandments as our yardstick we do so as a judge rather than as a humble mediator.

Mediation takes us beyond rules transgressed to matters of the heart. When we accept the lesson that we *should not* judge and we *should* resist the temptation to throw the first stone, we are provided with a foundation for the non-judgmental process of mediation. Francis followed these teachings with passionate devotion, which is perhaps the reason he became known as the quintessential peacemaker.

What might we learn from Francis when it comes to establishing brotherly and sisterly relationships with all whom we meet? Francis saw the divine within all people. Faced with conflict he sought the image of God in the other party. When he went out to meet the wolf he did not go forth to meet a stranger; he set out to seek the God with whom he was reconciled in the form of the wolf.

When we are able to see the likeness of God in the other party we begin to view reconciliation in its divine context. The most important characteristic of a mediator who engages in a spiritually transformative style of mediation may be the ability to see past transgressions to the divine essence of the person with whom they are working.

When we see the divine within the Other our perception has a profound effect on how they see themselves. The inviting demeanor of a mediator who refuses to judge may be the tipping point that enlists willingness to attempt reconciliation on the part of those who were previously reticent or hostile. When someone views the wolf in a manner that acknowledges his divine essence it may be the first time the wolf feels sufficiently respected to consider he is capable of healing wounds, resolving conflict, and reconciling with another.

The ability to see the divine in the other person does not come easy, and most often is fleeting. Nonetheless, even momentary clarity of vision provides a basis for respect and empathy that might otherwise elude us. In coming to view the other person in this way we may feel the Spirit move within and we may create a bridge to a meaningful I-Thou relationship.[2]

Engaging another with divine consciousness (or consciousness of the divine) may cause the person standing before us to undergo a transformation and unfold as a new person in our eyes, as well as in their own eyes. When we touch that which is sacred in the other they are lifted up and their divine essence is manifested.

We might find the other person struggles when it comes to finding the Spirit within but when we acknowledge the presence of that Spirit with a gesture issuing from our compassionate heart, the presence of Spirit within rises into view. The party is empowered to engage in the process with a new-found awareness of the divine within; they discover that which unites us as brothers and sisters.

When we experience conflict, we experience the pain of separation; we experience a distance that must be closed through reconciliation. The separation we experience echoes the separation from the divine that runs as a theme throughout our lives. In the act of moving away from one another we move away from that which is divine within us. When we close the distance between self and other through reconciliation, we also reconcile with the divine. This suggests that while we are trying to reconcile with one another we should pay special attention to reconciling with the divine – one effort reinforces the other.

Francis' life was testimony to this dual dynamic: the vertical relationship he enjoyed with God reinforced the horizontal relationship he experienced with all creatures. Francis discovered the divine in the wolf – this was the key to his ability to greet the wolf with unconditional love and compassion. When he went out into the woods outside Gubbio he did not go out to greet a monster with fangs that dripped with blood, rather he went forth to greet the divine consciousness that lurked, mostly hidden, behind those fangs.

You might question whether or not it is necessary to reconcile with the divine before reconciling with another person. Is it not possible to manage earthly affairs while paying no attention to divine affairs? Perhaps it does not make sense to advance a definitive answer to this question. The answer is best left as a matter for discovery and personal investigation.

However, my personal experience, which may echo yours, has convinced me that the reconciliation process is simultaneously vertical and horizontal – no matter which direction one tends to first, the mundane or the divine, both are affected. Some facilitators take this further and believe the Holy Spirit works through them. They humbly believe they do not personally hold the keys to reconciliation. In their view they are merely present to allow the Holy Spirit to work through them to open doors.

In most instances we probably do not engage in analysis of this nature. Mediators simply perform their role as best as possible. While Francis knew these dynamics intimately as a result of his strong faith, in contrast we may be faced with a need to learn how to look up as we look across the table. In the face of Francis we find a gaze that promises reconciliation precisely because he was reconciled with all of creation. In his eyes we find the promise of a departure from the ways of conflict and a movement toward love. In the face of Francis we glimpse the peacemaker inspired by the divine within. Often it is only this momentary and fleeting glimpse of the divine that convinces an unwilling and hostile party – the wolf – to engage the mediation process.

A Franciscan View

Francis faced the dissenting, the angry, and the disgruntled, among strangers and among friends. His father, who displayed such anger toward him, is an example of a hostile party struggling to overcome destructive emotions. "His bitterest trial however was his father's anger, which remained as violent as ever. Although he had renounced Francis, Bernardone's pride suffered none the less at seeing his mode of life, and whenever he met his son he overwhelmed him with reproaches."[3]

None of us are strangers to the difficult moments that arise when we are confronted by those who suffer with hostility. Like Francis, we feel the bite of their words, the sting of their rejection. Paul Sabatier quotes Francis' instructions for such moments: "You will find people full of faith, gentleness, and goodness who will receive you and your words with joy, but you will also find others, and in greater numbers – faithless, proud, blasphemers – who will speak evil of you, resisting you and your words. Be resolute to endure everything with patience and humility."[4]

Francis crafted Admonition 27 to guide the Brothers through such difficult situations. It reads: "Where there is love and wisdom, there is neither fear nor ignorance. Where there is patience and humility, there is neither anger nor disturbance. Where there is poverty with joy, there is neither cupidity nor avarice. Where there is inner quiet and meditation, there is neither care nor unsettledness. Where the Lord's fear guards *his courtyard* (Luke 11:21), there the enemy has no chance to enter. Where there is mercy and discernment of God's will, there is neither excessive demands nor hardness of the heart."[5]

Admonition 27 provides insight into Francis' state of mind as he approached the wolf and made the sign of the cross. His words help us understand the direction in which Francis must take the wolf in order to dissipate his fierce anger.

On one occasion the Mayor of Assisi and the Bishop of Assisi fell into a conflict as a result of the intermingling of politics and religion.[6] Escalation led the Bishop to excommunicate the Mayor and the Mayor to forbade businessmen to deal with the Bishop.[7] Francis enjoyed a friendship with both men so he was saddened to hear of their clash, which had all of Assisi on edge. He could not allow these two friends to continue their personal vendetta against one another, so he sent brothers to deliver the latest verses from his *Canticle of the Creatures*.

The last verse of the *Canticle* reads, "Blessed are those who endure in peace, for by You, Most high, they shall be crowned."[8] Upon hearing Francis' words expressing the power of his concerns the Mayor and the Bishop understood and "in words of forgiveness, they embrace[d] each other in peace."[9] As happened with the fierce wolf of Gubbio Francis' holy presence altered the dynamics.

Catch Me a Rainbow inspires us to learn from Francis in our attempts to become peacemakers: "Peace ministry moves us to be messengers of joy. So long as the elements of darkness exist in our world, people do not experience joy. We know better than to think joy will magically happen if we talk about it. Rather, we must address the problems we see around us. We create a different atmosphere for life. God's persistent love is the basis of our belief. It is God's nature to love. That is the source of our joy. As we deal with the darkness, the light of joy has a chance to enter."[10]

Keeping this in mind, we are not discouraged when we encounter the hostile party who is reticent to engage in a reconciliation process; we know the lack of joy can be overcome with a persistent but gentle presence. This presence, which Francis brought to conflict situations, speaks to a desire that is often hidden but remains alive in our hearts.

"The greater number of people pass through life with souls asleep. Yet the instinct for love and for the divine is only slumbering. The human heart so naturally yearns to offer itself up, that we have only to meet along our pathway someone who, doubting neither himself nor us, demands it without reserve, and we yield it to him at once."[11] Francis was such a person whose very presence called to men to yield that part of their heart that knows the divine within. Francis met the other person with his divine heart, regardless of their anger, and breeched the wall of hostility that defeated others who tried to intervene.

Too often, when we are tied up with expectations for an outcome we attempt to meet the reticent party's resistance with a demand for obedience. Moral theologian Bernard Häring cautions against this approach: "In an ethic with a lopsided stress on blind obedience, all the talk about virtue makes the very subject a source of irritation and contempt.... Virtue has nothing to do with going to obedience school."[12] Attempts to lecture or cajole the hostile party generate the contempt and irritation of which Häring speaks. In contrast, with Francis as our mentor we can learn to approach conflict in a Holy manner.

Scripture

"I myself once thought that I had to do many things against the name of Jesus the Nazorean, and I did so in Jerusalem. I imprisoned many of the holy ones with the authorization I received from the chief priests, and when they were put to death I cast my vote against them. Many times, in synagogue after synagogue, I punished them in an attempt to force them to blaspheme; I was so enraged against them that I pursued them even to foreign cities." (Acts 26:9-11)

For he is our peace, he who made both one and broke down the dividing wall of enmity, through his flesh, abolishing the law with its commandments and legal claims, that he might create in himself one new person in place of the two, thus establishing peace, and might reconcile both with God, in one body, through the cross, putting that enmity to death by it. (Eph 2:14-16)

When he left, the scribes and Pharisees began to act with hostility toward him and to interrogate him about many things, for they were plotting to catch him at something he might say. (Lk 11:53-54)

As they approached Jesus, they caught sight of the man who had been possessed by Legion, sitting there clothed and in his right mind. And they were seized with fear. (Mk 5:15)

Not only that, but we even boast of our afflictions, knowing that affliction produces endurance, and endurance, proven character, and proven character, hope, and hope does not disappoint, because the love of God has been poured out into our hearts through the holy Spirit that has been given to us. (Rom 5:3-5)

CHAPTER ELEVEN

Your Story

The wolf froze in mid step, struggling with doubt and uncertainty. Finally, understanding that Francis meant him no harm, the wolf inched closer to Francis and then sat back on his haunches, ready to listen.

Francis told the wolf that he had come from Gubbio and then described what the townspeople were experiencing because of the wolf's actions. He described the pain and resentment they held toward the wolf.

"How did this come to happen?" Francis asked the wolf. "Why did you kill the livestock and people?"

Mediation Principles

FRANCIS MAKES CONTACT with the wolf and asks, "How did this come to happen?" The other side – the wolf in this case – has a chance to tell his story. In previous chapters we covered the importance of narratives and allowing parties to search for a shared solution to their conflict. In this chapter we will briefly review material presented previously that bears repeating and we will take up new concepts that apply to the party who has been less willing to convene.

Creative Use of Narrative

Asking the open-ended question, what happened? invites a party to provide a narrative description of events – the story told from their point of view. The question is non-evaluative in nature; the mediator becomes an interested listener rather than a judge. Such open-ended questions do not guide a party toward specific details but rather allow the party to disclose the conflict history as they choose, selectively placing importance on events from their perspective.

This approach elicits a heartfelt and personal view of what occurred. While it may not be considered important in a court of law, it is very important in mediation. When a mediator fails to allow a party to present his or her story in the manner in which they choose he risks entering bias into the process. His questions, if too narrow, steer the conversation in particular directions altering focus and content. Francis avoids steering the conversation with the wolf in a preconceived direction: he sits quietly, listens with empathy, and takes in the story *as it is told*.

In most cultures we use storytelling to convey complex information within the context of our emotional stream of consciousness. As noted previously, rules of evidence in a court limit the personal narrative in an attempt to get at facts stripped of emotion. In an adjudicative process in which a judge, jury, or arbitrator must make a decision within a limited time period stripped down facts are often useful.

If you are involved in a dispute that has reached the courts your attorney or representative will limit your narrative. Their questions will focus on preparing for trial with pertinent facts; they will seek to meet strategic legal or rhetorical goals. Once their focus takes over the story you tell is designed to meet the strategic needs of the adversarial process. This shift may be so subtle you do not detect the change at first; you simply answer questions put forth by your attorney and assist him in building a case.

More than a few times I have encountered the situation in which, once I hear the unedited narrative of what happened, I realize the conflict differs from the conflict presented by the attorney in opening remarks. While the attorney believed the conflict revolved around Issue A (for which he prepared a legal argument), the real conflict had to do with Issue B, revealed only in mediation. Attorneys' bewilderment upon finding out for the first time what the conflict was *really* about has been mildly amusing for me. This misstep occurs when insufficient time has been spent allowing the party to relate the story of what happened in their own words with their own focus.

As you prepare for conflict resolution you can avoid this dilemma by using the *Taming the Wolf* prompts to prepare for mediation; they call forth a richer tapestry of emotions, perspectives, and meaning. This will allow you to take advantage of the opportunity to tell your story in a manner you prefer.

When we create our spoken or written narratives we typically see ourselves as heroes on an epic journey. We are the hero of our own story – perhaps a beleaguered hero, but a hero nonetheless. How we conceive our heroic character shapes our story. When we tell our story in our own words we enter a special world rich with meaning and significance.

It is here in the first-person perspective that decisions regarding resolution and reconciliation must be fashioned. If a decision does not make sense within the context of our inner narrative we will not achieve a durable resolution. We must be able to integrate a potential outcome into our personal inner story before we can accept it. If we do not see how our character plays a role in the future drama, if the new story proposed for the future does not make sense or does not appeal to us, we reject it.

If I perceive myself as a virtuous character who took action in an attempt to remedy a dangerous situation I will not accept an outcome in which I am pictured as a villain who wantonly caused harm. A resolution will not occur in the face of a story that contradicts the heroic character I see myself to be. On the other hand, I can accept a new narrative in which I am a well-intentioned character who received bad information and acted on that faulty information and as a result accidentally caused harm for which I now apologize (as I am well-intentioned). Thus the story that evolves must be consistent with our overall inner narrative and must be acceptable to our larger audience of stakeholders viewing our moment on stage.

Rarely will the story one party narrates match the story the other party tells. The challenge is to help parties write overlapping narratives regarding the future. In many cases the most a mediator can hope for with regards to the past narrative is that parties accept that they each viewed events from different perspectives. To achieve resolution they accept the idea that the difference in narratives of the past is irrelevant to the future.

The process calls for a ceasefire when it comes to arguing over which narrative of the past shall prevail as the official truth. A skilled mediator inspires parties to take a genuine interest in the other party's story and helps them see that that story, although not their story, is valid for the other person. When a party understands that listening to the other party's story will help them achieve resolution they listen more closely, searching for clues that reveal the other person. They come to know the character starring in the other person's drama.

In most conflicts one or both parties do not really know the person with whom they have become entangled. The parties may be relatives or spouses but they do not truly know the other person *as they exist in their inner drama*. They have never had the opportunity to listen closely to the inner narrative. When they come to realize their only hope for progress lies in understanding the motivations and interests of the other person (so that they can satisfy those interests) they listen at a deeper level to that which is not obvious, that which rarely comes into the light. It helps if they consider the other's story to be a mystery from which they must extract vital clues that lead to the dramatic ending – reconciliation.

Mythmaking plays a central role in this narrative process. This idea might arouse skepticism as in the midst of a conflict we seek simple truths; a myth would seem to be the last thing we desire. However, we all live within a myth of our own creation: we see ourselves as a heroic character on a life journey. We conceive ourselves to be struggling with trials and tribulations that test our character as we travel on our life journey.

Most of the time we remain unaware of the subtle mythmaking that colors our lived experience. Only when we summon this script from our unconscious and explore our personal heroic journey does its influence come into focus.[1] Then we discover that we constantly compose myths that inform the central stories of our lives.[2] We begin to ask what role does conflict play in these stories? How do the heroes in our stories address conflict?

While the mediator may help the parties rewrite the narrative surrounding the conflict, a party must be mindful that this singular conflict episode takes place within a larger narrative myth that guides them through their life journey. As you work with the prompts, place the specific conflict you are trying to resolve within the context of your mythic life journey.

In the dramatic script the question of how one overcomes opposition to arrive at a new equilibrium is the central spring or energy driving the drama. In conflict resolution a similar dynamic is at work: the central question we face is how we will overcome our opposition and resolve the conflict in order to establish a new state of equilibrium in our life.

Unfortunately, though we can learn from the parallels in drama, too many film dramas provide unreasoned approaches to resolving conflict: they present violent and coercive solutions. A challenge for peacemakers is overcoming the popular culture influence on conflict resolution behavior. The challenge the individual party faces is becoming aware of cultural influences that provide less-than-optimum choices.

Our culture is inundated with role models who resolve conflicts with violent force. These solutions make for exciting action films with magnificent effects, but they fail to represent options that will bring about a culture of peace. Too often these cultural influences seep into our consciousness. Those who lack experience with reasoned choice and peaceful resolution – often the younger members of society – may harbor the view that violent means are required to resolve conflict. In contrast the mediator helps parties create new myths, new roles, new heroic characters, and new narratives that produce optimum non-violent outcomes.

Once open-ended questions prompt a narrative the mediator employs clarifying questions to insure he has an accurate picture of what occurred. He gathers important details that help him flesh out the story. Using clarifying questions, he explores portions of the narrative that may not have been clear in the first telling.

When I introduce mediation to new clients I alert them at the outset that I may ask questions to clarify information I did not understand fully. I explain they should not consider the questions to be a challenge or a cross-examination but rather an inquiry that comes from a desire to understand. Without this warning they may unconsciously consider my questions to be a challenge and they become defensive. Judge Alexander Williams III, with whom I participated in settlement conferences, often said to parties, "You're the experts. I will never understand your case as well as you do."[3] He characterized clarifying questions as inquiry posed to the experts on the dispute – the parties themselves.

After clarifying major points that were previously unclear the mediator narrows the inquiry to close-ended questions often answered with yes or no responses or with specific factual information. As noted previously, the mediator's questions can be graphed as a funnel: they begin with broad open-ended questions then narrow as the mediator attempts to understand details. Your challenge as a party is to be as transparent as possible during this process, allowing the mediator to walk in your shoes and see the conflict through your eyes.

As the mediator listens he comes to understand the perceptions on which you rely. You may rely primarily on sight, hearing, or feeling. Knowing how you tend to perceive helps him understand how you might best engage with the process of recalling events. Some people rely on visuals, describing events in terms of how it *looked* to them. They might use language that says, "This is how it looks to me." Others rely on auditory cues describing what was said or how it *sounded*, "This is how it sounds to me." Or they may describe events in terms of how they *felt*, "This is how I felt about it."

Some describe events in linear, chronological narratives, while others move freely between the past and the present, ordering events according to variables other than time. Typically we are not aware that we perceive the world in unique ways and that we approach time differently. We assume we experience like everyone else. When we discover others perceive events in ways we may not have considered we open new doors of perception.

Impressions

In Gubbio Francis asked the mayor questions regarding how the townspeople viewed the wolf. In such preliminary meetings the mediator pays close attention to how parties perceive one another. These impressions are colored by emotions, values, biases, history, and prejudices, so while the mediator needs the information in order to understand the conflict she must also resist forming opinions and instead remain outside the conflict in a neutral or impartial posture.

When I first began mediating, I learned how profoundly the first party's account can lead one to prematurely misjudge the second party. I might hear a very convincing, cogent, and reasonable narrative from the first party. They would paint a detailed (and unflattering) picture of the opposing party. On my way to meet with the other party I knew what to expect: I had met people like *this* before.

I would inevitably be startled upon meeting the other party. They were not what I expected. Preconceptions spawned by the first party's narrative would take a beating. The second party painted a different, but equally cogent, picture of events. The experience drove home the lesson that we all see the world from a very personal, subjective viewpoint.

This does not mean we do not listen and it does not mean each party's view lacks veracity. There is always a modicum of truth in what has been said. The perception each party has of the other is real: it is how they see the other person and we must not disregard that vision. It is where we start. But we do not get locked into a static or fixed view – particularly one informed by our first impressions.

When you begin mediation, as a party, it is worthwhile to note how rigid your view of the other party may have become. And how rigid the other party's view of you has become. It is worth noting you will need to discover and deliver a more nuanced view of the characters on the stage in this drama. During mediation you will have an opportunity to test your perception of the other party. The other party will have an opportunity to test their perception of you. Each party plays a reciprocal role in the drama. Discovering the nature of the character you play in the other party's movie allows you to renegotiate the role you play. You can help them rewrite their script. As they redraft and polish, inevitably change occurs.

When a party discovers how their counterpart sees them it can be startling – the character they play in the other's drama is not who they know themselves to be. The mediator helps them understand that just as they have been misperceived they have miscast the other party. The dance of identity negotiation begins in earnest.

This does not mean you end up perceiving the other party exactly as they perceive themselves. A perfect match may be impossible. Nonetheless each party ends up realizing the other party is "not as bad as I originally thought." Parties renegotiate their relationship and recast their roles in the common drama. As each party shares their inner narrative – the why behind what they did – perceptions adjust. When we hear the other person describe the why behind their actions we see how what they did made sense from *their* viewpoint. We realize they were not operating within our frame of reference.

Francis tells the wolf how the townspeople of Gubbio have experienced his actions and he describes how the wolf is seen by those trying to kill him. Francis lays the groundwork for the wolf to come to the table, hoping that when the wolf realizes he is perceived as a cold-blooded killing machine he will want to correct the misperception.

Thus, a need to remedy misperceptions can motivate a party to engage in mediation. Learning that who they are is misrepresented and misunderstood prompts a desire to tell their story; they engage the process with the intention of setting the record straight.

In their effort to correct misperceptions questions arise: How did I come to see the other party as I do? What happened to make the other party think of me as they do? We pull the string on events that contributed to less-than-accurate views; we search for ways to eliminate errors and recalibrate perceptions to more closely align with all the information.

The Hidden Influence

It is common to find that each party's perception of the other has been colored by hidden, negative third party influences. We often hear one party talk about the other in the following terms: "Mrs. X warned me about them. I should have listened. She said they were shifty and up to no good." Too often we accept gossip, innuendo, and character assassination that taint our views. Most of the time we are not aware of this pernicious hidden influence. Innuendo and slanderous whispers settle into the lower reaches of our consciousness where they simmer and lead us to feel hostility against the other party that extends beyond reasonable bounds.

The influence of the negative third party sets in motion a self-fulfilling prophecy: after we hear bad things about a person we distrust them, which causes them to distrust us. The other party mirrors our distrust and becomes wary; we mistranslate their wariness as a sign of shiftiness. Their shifty behavior causes us to constantly question their motives, which in turn leads them to dislike us even more. Eventually they turn away from us and refuse to meet their obligations.

The end result fulfills the prophecy of the negative third party: it appears the one about whom they gossiped really was up to no good. We fail to realize the entire chain of events was set in motion by the subtle slander of a destructive third party acting as a hidden influence in the conflict. The hostility generated by this scenario tends to be significant and rarely dissipates until we review the history of the conflict and discover the source of animosity and misperception that have taken root in our consciousness.

This situation is common as all too often we accept the word of another without taking the time to check facts. We are particularly susceptible to words whispered in confidence during the destructive third party's counterfeit efforts "to protect us." Rarely do we bother to investigate in depth. Subject to this negative influence our view of the other becomes tainted.

As we gain experience and wisdom we come to recognize that the destructive, negative third party who operates as a hidden influence is *the* primary cause of conflict. We slowly learn to keep our own counsel and avoid thinking poorly or suspiciously of others. As you become experienced in resolving conflicts ruining your life you will learn to automatically look to see if this factor is at work. As you respond to the prompts make an effort to trace the chain of events and the influences that led to your current perceptions (and misperceptions) of the other and note any outside influences, no matter how subtle, that may have contributed to your misperception.

This factor plays a considerable role in failed attempts at conflict resolution, so I will take up the subject in greater detail in Chapter 18 when I address failed reconciliation. If you suspect this factor is stalling your forward progress at this stage read ahead and become more familiar with the influence of the hidden destructive third party.

Framing

The mediator guides early discussions modeling *framing*. Framing involves presenting information in words and in a style acceptable to the other party. There are many ways we can convey our concerns. Some approaches increase understanding and willingness to collaborate; other approaches trigger negative emotions and destroy willingness to communicate.

The mediator coaches the parties to avoid triggering unwanted emotions. A party learns to tell the same story with a different frame by watching the mediator paraphrase in ways the other party is willing to hear. One way to reframe a narrative is to use *I messages* that tell the story in first person terms, explaining how events made you feel rather than expressing "this is what you did to me."

In reframing the mediator does not misrepresent a party's concerns but rather finds a delivery that avoids negative reactions. Avoiding all negative reactions is impossible. The effort is to sufficiently minimize negative emotional reactions so the process builds momentum. At certain tipping points negative emotions may abort the process so we attempt to avoid the problem with skillful framing.

The mediator is transparent in his use of framing, modeling styles of communication parties may eventually adopt. The parties learn there are a number of ways to express their concerns, some more successful than others.[4] The mediator helps parties transform language meant to incite, wound, and offend into language conducive to resolution and reconciliation. Language is used to draw parties together rather than push them apart. Parties become aware of the manner in which their choice of language and their delivery style affects the process. They discover the connection between their approach and the results.

Avoid Blaming

Framing helps avoid "I am right and you are wrong" dichotomies. As previously discussed most humans have a strong need to be right. Being wrong equates at an unconscious level with non-survival while being right equates with survival. Most people fight to satisfy their need to be right, even when the consequences of carrying on the fight are dire. Thus the mediator looks for ways to help a party frame their statements and expressions without attributing blame.

Parties learn that while they may have a need to be right, being right does not necessarily translate into making the other person wrong. We may assume the two go hand in hand – if I make myself right the other party must wrong. A mediator demonstrates this is not necessarily the case. Parties learn to narrate events without adding commentary that assigns blame. They learn stories can be nuanced and multiple perspectives can co-exist without contradiction. An abstract model of the conflict playing field begins to look a lot more like a network of views rather than two poles in stark opposition to one another.

If a party becomes aware that in-depth discussion of what happened is going to take place they have less need to rush to judgments that attribute cause at the outset. A narrative delivered in a matter-of-fact manner avoids the blame, anger, and unproductive positioning that emerges in response to a style peppered with "you did this to me."

This does not mean you must avoid all discussion of how the other party's actions affected you. Rather you let your hurt be known in a frame that focuses on your hurt – not on fixing blame. When blaming takes place parties become reticent to convene and hostile toward the conflict resolution process. They may be willing to attempt to reconcile but they are not about to submit to being blamed at the outset. One path around this dilemma is to concentrate on *I messages*.

Using "I Messages"

In order to avoid challenging and blaming you use the *I message* technique to frame statements regarding personal wounds you suffered. An *I message* changes the focus from "you hurt me" to "I was hurt when …" Events are described in terms of how they affected the person speaking, leaving the attribution of cause open for discussion.

A party speaks from her inner narrative regarding, "how it seemed to me" rather than issuing evaluative statements that claim, "your actions caused me harm." *I messages* frame the narrative in terms of "this is how I felt when that happened." You speak from the heart regarding how you experienced events.

At first glance you might object and argue that such an approach is simple avoidance. Why not call a spade a spade and just tell the truth? "They hurt me. That is what happened." While this view has merit it lacks pragmatic value. When you accuse someone of hurting you, you risk ending the conversation. Few people tolerate being made wrong; most shut down and walk away. In most instances the conflict escalated partially as a result of blaming; continuing that pattern will not bring change. Blaming and shaming lead to cessation of communication and escalation of conflict. If one wishes to affix blame and elicit shame, one must expect continued escalation of conflict.

If you narrate the events that caused you harm you are being honest and accurate. It is difficult for another to challenge the fact that you felt harmed, for that is what you experienced; only you would know how you truly felt. The other party may respond that they would not have felt the same way but that does not speak to how you felt, which is the issue.

When you go forward in this manner using *I messages* to speak of your hurt the door is left open for the other party to enter into the narrative, as they are not automatically triggered into a defensive posture. They may even express empathy for the pain you experienced and they may acknowledge they caused your injury, while stating their intention was not to cause you pain. They may apologize for the unintended consequences of their acts. Or they may accept full responsibility and, without being backed into a corner, accept they intended and caused harm for which they now feel remorse.

Contrast these possible outcomes with the most likely response to blame, which is self-defense. We typically experience blame as an attack on our identity and when threatened we defend or retreat. We can recall our own history and realize how much more likely we were to offer an apology and make amends when we were not under direct attack.

Turning to the legend we realize that if the very first meeting with the wolf had taken place with the people of Gubbio and not Francis, the citizens would have levied blame at the wolf and perhaps the wolf would have blamed the townspeople. The emotions on both sides were too raw for a joint session to have turned out otherwise.

For this reason Francis went alone to encounter the wolf. When he first spoke with the wolf he may have told him of the town's pain and suffering and might even have mentioned the manner in which they blamed him but Francis would not have leveled blame at the wolf.

With an attitude that conveyed his understanding of how the wolf also may have experienced negative emotions and misgivings Francis might have asked if it was possible for the wolf to understand the feelings of the towns-people. He may have asked, "How do you feel about the town regarding you in such a negative and hostile manner?"

He might have provided the wolf with a context and a frame that would allow the wolf to look at the situation with fresh eyes. He may have left the door open to expressions of remorse and desire to make up for the damage caused.

The approach Francis takes with the wolf opens new doors. Francis meets the wolf with compassion and opens doors to the wolf's heart by providing the wolf with an opportunity to relate his inner narrative. The wolf under Francis' guidance begins to experience a modicum of hope that there might be ways the town of Gubbio could be approached with a plan for reconciliation.

Hope & Willingness

While many of the approaches discussed in this chapter have been repeated from earlier chapters, they bear repeating as the mediator or the party working on their own must apply these skills when it comes to the reticent and hostile party. Whereas previously one might have been able to stumble through the process, at this point the concepts must be second nature. The mediator must work quickly and advance with surefootedness. Missteps result in a failure to bring about the hope and willingness needed for the reticent and hostile party to agree to convene a process that might result in reconciliation. As a mediator or party it pays to review the concepts presented until they become a natural part of how one approaches conflict.

A Franciscan View

Francis was no stranger to working with those who had become angry, hostile, and destructive. His insights into peacemaking arose from dealing with the same types of struggles we encounter in our lives. There are times when we will face unpleasant emotions expressed by the other party such as anger or hostility. If we are to be successful in resolving conflict the manner in which we approach a disgruntled party makes a difference.

In another version of the *Taming the Wolf* legend, "St. Francis talked to the wolf: 'Brother Wolf, you've harmed and hurt people without God's permission. You've killed animals; you've killed people, made in God's image. Well! You deserve to go to the gallows, thieving, murdering criminal that you are. All these people are your enemies, wanting the worst to happen to you. But, Brother Wolf, I want to make peace between you and them, put a stop to your bad behavior, watch them forgive you of everything—'"[5]

At first glance Francis appears judgmental and righteous. Reading the words alone we imagine he is berating the wolf with a scolding tone. But when we step back and take into account all that we know of Francis it seems more likely that Francis spoke softly with a matter-of-fact tone.

He did not avoid an honest appraisal of the negative events that had transpired nor did he avoid speaking of the likely consequences that would accrue as a result of such actions. He was candid in his assessment of the retribution the wolf's enemies wished to exact upon him. Yet he was not blaming and punishing for he expresses his desire to bring about peace and to seek the forgiveness of those the wolf harmed.

Another story in *The Little Flowers of St. Francis* supports our speculation that Francis did not deliver his notice to the wolf in an accusatory or righteous manner. In "Three Thieves Become Friars" Brother Angelo harshly scolds and berates three thieves who show up at the friary door. As a result, "The robbers left with troubled minds and full of bitterness."[6]

Francis rebukes Brother Angelo, telling him, "Kindness brings sinners to God far better than harsh words."[7] He sends Brother Angelo after the robbers carrying an offer to meet all their needs if they stop their wicked ways.

Francis prayed for God to soften the robber's hearts as Brother Angelo pursued and caught up with the villains.

In response to Brother Angelo's humble offer the robbers were heard to say, "We rob, beat and hurt people, even murder. Though we do terrible things, we have no remorse, no bad conscience, no fear of God. But this good friar came to us; More! He apologized for his harsh words justly spoken. He confessed his fault with humility. He even brought bread and wine, and a remarkably generous promise from Father Francis."[8]

As a result of the kindness shown and the offer of forgiveness extended the robbers experienced a desire to seek repentance and a new path. They agreed on a plan: "Let us go to Francis; let's see if he offers any hope at all for God to forgive our sins. We will do whatever he says, for we may succeed in avoiding hell's pains."[9] Eventually the robbers became friars and followed Francis.

This story confirms our suspicions that Francis understood the need to approach the wolf with a non-judgmental demeanor and yet not ignore or avoid discussing transgressions committed. In his talk with the wolf Francis would have been gentle and loving yet firm in his commitment to address events that had taken place.

Francis was also fully aware of the toxic role unaddressed anger plays in conflict, as we discover in the story of "St. Francis and the Angry Friar." "One day at prayer in the friary at Portiuncula, St. Francis saw (by divine revelation) the friary surrounded and attacked by an army of devils. Not one devil could enter; the friars lived holy lives, and the devils therefore found no place to enter. Yet they persisted. One friar got angry at another, and privately thought about accusing him to take revenge. This opened the door and a devil came into the friary to cling to the angry brother."[10]

This story assures us that Francis knew that the destructive emotion of anger, when allowed to persist, was an open invitation to evil influences. Thus we can assume with confidence that he understood the importance of seeking out and eradicating negative emotions in the process of resolving conflict. The subtle nature of the anger portrayed in the story also alerts us to the fact that such invitations to evil influences need not involve anger that explodes with a burst of loud, dramatic action, but can also draw upon anger simmering below the surface. It can draw from the shallow pool of our resentment.

Negative and hidden third party influences, which have been invited into our lives inadvertently, often lie behind our anger or our destructive actions. Brother Ruffino almost lost his way due to an insidious destructive third party and as a result was on the verge of destroying the Franciscan Order. The tale of these events is found in "The Devil and Brother Ruffino."[11] In this "little flower" the devil, disguised as "the Crucified," appeared to Brother Ruffino and planted jealousy and sorrow in his mind by informing the brother that he was not "one of the elect." This destructive third party then nurtured the brother's doubt and depression when he said, "No one who follows Francis can enter [heaven]."[12]

As a result Brother Ruffino "lost every bit of trust and respect for Francis and could not disclose a thing."[13] This is the classic destructive third party at work behind the scenes, planting negative information the party does not feel free to share. Francis, with the help of the Holy Spirit, perceived the trouble taking root in Brother Ruffino's heart. He sent Brother Masseo to Brother Ruffino to help Ruffino recognize he had been deceived by false appearances intended to destroy him and the Order.

The fear and depression Brother Ruffino suffered and the damage done to his relationship with Francis were the result of falsehoods intended to cause harm. In a teaching moment Francis subsequently provided Brother Ruffino with a litmus test for future use: "the devil means to harden your heart against everything good; but Christ never hardens the hearts of His faithful ones...."[14] Using this test we can consult the heart of the party beset by anger and skepticism and assess for influences that have hardened their heart. At the same time we introduce compassionate influences that soften their heart.

In the Admonitions we discover negative third party influence was not something Francis took lightly. He considered the subject important enough to be included in his guidance to the brothers. In Admonition 25 Francis instructs the brothers, "Blessed is the servant who would love and respect his brother as much when he is far away from him as when he is with him, and would not say anything behind his back that he would not charitably say in his presence."[15] In this admonition Francis warns the brothers to avoid engaging in such harmful behavior. We should also be warned to not let such harmful behavior on the part of another push us into conflict.

He takes up the same theme in other instructions: "As in Admonition 25,

Chapter 11 of Francis's First Rule encourages the brothers to love one another and to avoid behavior that would tear down the brotherhood."[16] Francis anticipated the destructive effect of gossip on the Order. The amount of focus he gives to this problem is a good indication of experience he gained while sorting out conflicts. He wrote, "And all the brothers should guard themselves lest they calumniate [bad mouth; put down; slam; slander; malign] or contend with words. Rather let them strive to maintain silence, whenever God grants this grace to them."[17]

We have all felt the sting of put-downs and ridicule. We are aware of the role bullying plays in conflict. At the same time we should not overlook the slander we do not hear – the slander whispered into the ear of another – which cuts us silently and invisibly. The metaphorical knife plunged into our back when we are not looking sends us into pain-induced rage that may make us look mad to the naïve observer.

Francis was not naïve: he spoke out against these deadly practices. "And let them slander no one. Let them not murmur, nor speak detraction against others, because it is written: *'Gossips and detractors are hateful to God.'*"[18]

The excerpt from the Rule continues, "Let them not judge. Let them not condemn. And as the Lord says, let them not pay attention to the minute sins of others."[19] Here we have valuable instructions to guide us as we unearth the hidden influence driving hostility, anger, and rage from its invisible perch just outside our line of sight. We learn to expand our perceptions, broaden our view, and dig below the surface to locate these hidden sources of conflict.

The following prophetic statement guides not only our future efforts to maintain peace, but also provides us with clues that turn our attention to past events that gave birth to conflict. The statement sorts out causes that must be located in order to defuse animosity: "The loose lips of gossip, slander, and detraction have sunk many a fraternity. And isn't it so self-righteously pleasant to talk about our deep fraternal love for all when the cantankerous brother who drives us up a wall is on vacation or away on an extended assignment?"[20]

Scripture

For I fear that when I come I may find you not such as I wish, and that you may find me not as you wish; that there may be rivalry, jealousy, fury, selfishness, slander, gossip, conceit, and disorder. (2 Cor 12:20)

Do not speak evil of one another, brothers. Whoever speaks evil of a brother or judges his brother speaks evil of the law and judges the law. If you judge the law, you are not a doer of the law but a judge. There is one lawgiver and judge who is able to save or destroy. Who then are you to judge your neighbor? (Jas 4:11-12)

Then Simon Peter, who had a sword, drew it, struck the high priest's slave, and cut off his right ear. The slave's name was Malchus. Jesus said to Peter, "Put your sword into its scabbard. Shall I not drink the cup that the Father gave me?" (Jn 18:10-11)

Consider how he endured such opposition from sinners, in order that you may not grow weary and lose heart. (Heb 12:3)

CHAPTER TWELVE

Mining for Interests

The wolf told Francis his story.

He had been left behind by his pack because he was injured and couldn't keep up. He could only catch prey that didn't run fast, like sheep and goats. He really preferred to eat deer and rabbits, but, with his injured leg, that was out of the question.

He explained to Francis that all he wanted was to eat when he was hungry.

Mediation Principles

FRANCIS LISTENS to the narratives that reveal the nature of the conflict between the wolf and the people of Gubbio and becomes familiar with the positions and accounts of the parties, and with the rationale behind their actions. He guides the focus deeper to uncover the interests and needs the wolf must satisfy if there is to be resolution and reconciliation.

In the following pages we begin the task of mining for interests: identifying underlying interests and needs that must be satisfied in order to reconcile.

If we fail to identify our true interests or if we fail to recognize the true interests of the other party negotiations hit an impasse. If an understanding of the interests in play is absent, frustration rises and conflict persists.

Positions versus Interests

Parties tend to focus on positions they hold with respect to contested issues. They focus on "where I stand." Positions or stances, usually diametrically opposed, become rigid; parties remain locked in the oppositional embrace and engage in positional bargaining. When they address only positions there is little hope of a successful resolution.

It appears that the more the parties address their respective positions the more inflexible those positions become. Attempts to convince the other party to abandon their position usually prove futile. At the very moment a flexible and creative approach is most needed – at the beginning of the negotiation stage – the position-versus-position nature of conflict gives rise to inflexibility and lack of creativity. Disputants stagger like wrestlers clinging to one another seeking an advantage, not daring to move their feet (their stance) too quickly, as the slightest imbalance brings a risk of being toppled by their opponent.

To an outside observer the parties appear frozen like statues locked in rigid poses. Friends, family, or colleagues may suggest they lighten up and let go, but such advice rarely works as it overlooks the fundamental nature of the oppositional embrace – the parties *can't* let go! A mediator, recognizing the oppositional embrace, redirects the negotiation from a focus on positions to a focus on deeply held interests.[1]

As a visual metaphor imagine a solid horizontal line drawn across a page. Above that line, we have positions; below the line, we have interests. Positions reflect our public face, the outward posture or stance we maintain with regard to the issues. This is where we stand. Interests operate below the surface, motivating our positions. They explain *why* we assume a position or posture.

When we go below the line we seek to understand root motivations driving the conflict: we seek the reasons for positions. The mediator takes note of a position and asks, "What interests of yours does this position reflect?" Or,

"What needs are you trying to satisfy by holding this position?" She seeks to identify the true *why* behind a party's actions. She mines for a deeper understanding of factors driving the conflict.

In order to illustrate *above-the-line* and *below-the-line* dynamics take a moment to list the positions you hold in your journal workbook. In the legend the wolf's position might be, *I have a right to kill and eat livestock* and, if necessary, to *kill anyone who stands in my way*. Positions commonly involve demands you make on the other party. The wolf may say, I demand the right to devour livestock. The conflict assessment you began in earlier chapters will help you identify the positions you hold.

Next, assess interests that motivate your positions. With respect to your position what are you trying to be, do, or have? What needs are you trying to meet? What interests are you trying to satisfy? Seek to understand why you hold your positions. You may ask, what am I trying to accomplish?

When we inspect positions we realize they lead to labels. The townspeople label the wolf a *predator*. The wolf might agree that *predator* accurately describes his identity and reflects the position he holds or he may define his position-based identity as a *noble beast trying to survive difficult times*. Gubbio holds the position, we have *a right to hunt and kill the wolf because of the harm he has done and the danger he poses*. Their identity label might read *avenging posse*.

In your personal assessment, note identity labels you apply to yourself and labels others apply to you. The labels provide clues to understanding the identity that accompanies the position you hold. When it comes to assessing the other party's positions and interests initially we are limited to assumptions, but when the process goes forward we discover their interests by going below the line in discussions. We listen closely and discover their real interests. Until they share that information, we jot down our assumptions in our journal workbook: we list their positions and our assumptions about the interests or needs that motivate them.

We find positions and identity labels, for example *predator* or *avenging posse*, encompass behavior expectations: predators engage in certain types of behavior and avenging posses engage in certain types of behavior. Each party holds a position that relates to identity that in turn prescribes behavior.

When these factors remain in place, the drama, with its related suffering, unfolds. The wolf stalks livestock, swoops in for the kill, and feasts on his prey. When confronted he engages in mortal combat with guards dispatched to stop him. The townspeople who make up the avenging posse track and ambush the wolf in a quest to put an end to his life.

The wolf (*predator*) takes the position that he has a right to kill and devour livestock while the townspeople (*avenging posse*) claim a right to track and kill predators. Their positions stand in direct opposition; each party claims asserts their right to kill the other. The script is written. Predators do what predators do and avenging posses do what avenging posses do. As you assess your conflict, spend time analyzing the nature of the drama in which you are involved and the roles the characters have assumed.

Francis, in his role as peacemaker, does not accept the positions and labels presented. He goes *below the line* to assess the wolf's motives. He asks the wolf what need he is trying to satisfy. The wolf communicates his need for easy-to-kill prey (because he is injured) in order to satisfy his hunger and insure his survival. His position and position-related identity arise from his interest in survival: he needs to eat in order to survive. Francis thus discovers *why* the wolf considers he must hold on to the position of predator.

Most cases are not this simple. While there may be occasions when we are fully aware of our needs and interests and we can see clearly how the positions we have adopted are a strategic attempt to satisfy those interests, in many cases we may not even be aware of all the interests we are trying to satisfy. We may not be aware of the many levels of needs that actually motivate our actions.

Often we have not clarified the relative importance of our needs or the manner in which they drive our behavior. We have not stepped back and evaluated whether or not our position truly reflects our interests. Quite often we have not inspected closely the identity we have assumed and the rights we assert. We simply follow life's script and forge ahead based on minimally inspected assumptions. We are drawn into conflicts on the basis of appearances.

As a party explores *below the line* they arrive at a deeper understanding of their motives. Interests and needs they assumed were vital turn out to be less important. They may realize the position they have taken and the identity they have assumed will not lead to satisfaction of their true interests. They become aware, for the first time, of the need to decouple positions from interests in order to explore alternative methods of satisfying their interests.

Once a party shifts from a fixed position to exploring interests they become more flexibile and realize they can satisfy their interests in any number of ways. They realize there are a number of different positions that satisfy a particular interest.

Most positions, on the other hand, offer only one possible route to satisfaction. They have a win-lose and all-or-nothing quality that lowers the probability interests will be satisfied. When we hold a position we narrow our focus and stand our ground. Our position becomes a rigid "who we are" that leads to "what we must to do" to allow us to "have what we want." When another party opposes our position we freeze in a defensive posture.

Conflict causes us to narrow our perceptions, dig in our heels, and disregard our inner creativity. The fact that we stand in opposition to another – that fact alone – tends to lock us into a position. When the other party insists we *can't* have X – we want X even more. If the other party insists we *must* have X – we become certain we do not want X under any circumstance. We find ourselves opposing whatever the other party insists on. We stand in opposition.

When we are embroiled in a conflict we lose the flexibility needed to consider our true interests may be met in a number of ways. We lose sight of the fact that we hold fiercely to a fixed position simply because the other party has challenged that position. Intuitively we hate to give up our stance; we hate to be thrown off our position. Our inner sense tells us that if another person can move us off our position we have lost.

Thus we need to become aware of the degree to which our position has been dictated by our reaction to the other party's position. When we gain this awareness we turn away from positions to consider interests, which are more fluid and flexible and more conducive to creative collaboration.

The wolf, though injured, might be able to find another way to feed and sustain himself, but he assumes the only way to meet his needs is to present a fierce and terrible face to the townspeople as he snatches their livestock. The idea that he might gain the friendship of the townspeople by assuming the role of a guardian that protects against other predators does not occur to him. The idea that he might meet the citizens' need for an unusual and striking mascot does not occur to him.

In summary, above an imaginary line we find our positions, while below the line we find the interests and needs that motivate our positions. Our interests or needs are essential; they must be satisfied if we are to resolve our conflict and restore our happiness. Positions are secondary; they arise, consciously or unconsciously, from underlying needs and interests.

We move from a focus on positions to working with below-the-line interests. This allows us to discover what we must do to achieve satisfaction. As we let go of our hardened positions, relax our stance, and soften our posture our perceptions and creativity improve dramatically. We become flexible in our thinking, feeling, and communication. We may even cross over to sit with our opponent "on the same side of the table" to collaborate on shaping a solution.

Interest-Based Negotiation

The change in focus from positions to interests is a central theme in one of the early classics of mediation, *Getting to Yes*.[2] There are a number of terms mediators use to speak of this general type of negotiation but *interest-based negotiation* best reminds us that our focus is on satisfying our interests and the other party's interests.

As discussed, this model incorporates the visual of going *below the line*. Another term is *integrative bargaining* in which we try to integrate all factors, including interests and needs, in the negotiation process in order to achieve a truly comprehensive and satisfying solution. Integrative bargaining is often contrasted with *distributive bargaining* which focuses on dividing up available resources and distributing them to the parties. Distributive bargaining has been likened to *dividing a fixed pie*, while integrative bargaining has been likened to the idea of *expanding the pie*.

In *Getting to Yes* Fisher and Ury propose parties turn from positional bargaining to "principled negotiation or negotiation on the merits," which involves following four suggested principles: "1) People: Separate the people from the problem. 2) Interests: Focus on interests, not positions. 3) Options: Generate a variety of possibilities before deciding what to do. 4) Criteria: Insist that the result be based on some objective standard."[3]

They champion a problem-solving approach to negotiation in which we seek to sit on the same side of the table and collaborate in the process of finding or creating solutions to a common problem. Interests become pieces in a puzzle we must solve. Issues become a problem on which parties jointly focus their attention. They take their eyes off their opponent's throat.

These terms and phrases provide different ways of visualizing our negotiation efforts. We make the transition from wrestling with the other party in an oppositional embrace to a flexible, creative, problem-solving endeavor. We seek solutions. We are transformed from wrestlers into dancers. These abstract models and images help us conceive ways of breaking the grip we have on one another as we turn in tandem to examine and solve a shared problem.

Two additional books also inspired by the Harvard Project on Negotiation complement *Getting to Yes*. Author William Ury describes the series in the following fashion: "Where the focus of *Getting to Yes* is on both sides reaching an agreement, and the focus of *Getting Past No* is on the *other* side, overcoming their objections and resistance to cooperation, the focus of *The Power of a Positive No* is on *your* side, on learning how to assert and defend your interests."[4] This trilogy is recommended reading for those who wish to acquire a solid foundation in negotiation, a vital skill when it comes to resolving conflict.

For many of us a lack of negotiating skills may have been the factor that originally precipitated the conflict or blocked our path to resolution. When we feel uncertain about our negotiation skills we tend to put off working on the problem or we make clumsy demands. Therefore it is in our best interest to study negotiation.

Most parties, once they have been introduced to the concept of interest-based negotiation, significantly refocus their efforts in preparation for conflict resolution. In this chapter we will explore special issues that surface in our journey *below the line* to mine our interests. Throughout the discussion examples will be provided which are intended to help you begin the process of unearthing your underlying needs and interests.

Distributive versus Integrative Bargaining

As you consider the relationship between your positions and interests it is worth noting that the negotiation style will be determined by how you approach positions and interests. Bargaining over issues on which you have taken a position commonly leads to a negotiation in which a fixed pie is divided and distributed.

Distributive (fixed pie) bargaining is appropriate in many conflicts, but going *below the line* to integrate interests usually produces more satisfactory and durable outcomes. In negotiating an integrative solution we expand the pie, which means we expand the range of benefits available to each party. We look for creative solutions that meet the interests of both. We search for ways to add value that take us beyond the dimensions of the fixed pie.

Common scenarios in which we are able to expand the pie include instances when both parties want the same resources but for different uses. Creative solutions often involve each party utilizing a different portion of the available resources. As a hypothetical example imagine two groups each want to own the same island known for its rare coconut palms. Their positions appear mutually exclusive: they each seek sole possession of the island and its trees.

If a mediator asks them *why* they want to own the rare palms, one group might tell a story about needing the coconut shells and palm fronds to construct dwellings to protect them from the elements. They have developed a unique way to use these materials to create eco-friendly dwellings. They tell a story of survival needs. The other group might express a desire to harvest coconut milk for use in luxury baked goods sold and consumed in upscale metropolitan areas. Their needs relate to profits, pleasure, and ego.

If the two groups discuss their interests they might find a collaborative solution in which they work together to maintain the trees and harvest the portions they need, respectively. They might discover they can help each other satisfy their respective interests better than if they worked alone. Revenue from sales made to the luxury market may underwrite planting considerably more coconut palms, which would increase the amount of housing available for the local group. Through collaboration they may find additional ways to mutually enhance the well being of each other.

If they take a distributive bargaining approach they will divide the island in half with each taking their portion of the fixed resources. The total amount of shells and fronds available to the local group for shelter would be reduced, as they possess half as many trees. The export group, working with half as many trees, might be unable to serve their market due to a reduced scale of operations that increases per-unit costs. The effort becomes unprofitable. Meanwhile, both groups discard portions of the coconut they do not use, resulting in waste.

While they might divide the pie (partition the island) the results will not ultimately satisfy either party. Later on it is likely that a renewed struggle would emerge in which they use power to try to take over the entire island. In this scenario the resolution sets up conditions that lead to subsequent conflict.

If they seek an integrative or interest-based solution they will collaborate. They would negotiate mutual access to all the trees to harvest the portions they use to satisfy their respective interests. The amount of materials available for shelter would be increased, contributing to the welfare of the local group. The export group would gain the ability to supply luxury bakery goods in sufficient quantity to become profitable. The export group might leave all harvesting activities to the local group, providing them with an additional source of income.

In the literature this type of result is referred to as a *win-win outcome*. The fictional example illustrates how we might alter our thinking from a fixed pie model to a integrative model in which we increase the size of the pie – by changing focus from position – I want to own the island with the trees – to a focus on motivation.

Rarely are interests so singular and clearly defined. More often there are a number of tangible and intangible variables in play. In the collaborative effort postulated above the parties might be forced to learn to accommodate each other's values. One side might see the relationship with the island as spiritual in nature, with the palms being members of the Creator's family. The other side may arrive with a purely economic view of the world: the palms are assets to be exploited. The two cultures will need to negotiate how they interface with the environment in order to honor values. In this way they are careful not to show disrespect that will destroy the collaboration.

A multi-layered overlapping matrix of interests typically comes into focus during integrative bargaining. If the negotiation is respectful and principled a long-term relationship benefits both parties. The example of the island is simplistic yet conveys the principles at work. Your situation will probably require more creativity as you look for ways to expand the pie and increase the total benefits available. These opportunities may not be obvious and may come into view only after considerable problem-solving work. As you assess your conflict and the upcoming negotiation consider what might comprise the fixed pie and consider the ways in which the pie might be expanded.

Choosing a Style of Negotiation

The integrative, interest-based, or principled approach (whichever label you prefer) typically produces greater satisfaction. Fixed-pie solutions often promote a win-lose frame of mind that can make peaceful resolution difficult. Nonetheless there are times when simple division of assets comes close to satisfying party interests. In these instances it may be unnecessary to engage in the more time-intensive work of exploring underlying motives. Likewise, though exploring interests strengthens relationships there are times when one does not expect to maintain a future relationship – in such cases a quicker process may be preferred.

It is unwise to adopt rigid procedural tenets such as always engage in integrative bargaining or always seek to expand the pie. It is far better to tailor the process to meet the specific needs of the parties in the unique conflict being resolved.

On occasion one might mix distributive and integrative bargaining. Consider a hypothetical probate case in which an inheritance is to be divided between two siblings. In this example both brothers desire the same vacation property bequeathed to them (jointly) in their mother's will.

The terms of the will create conflict as the brothers do not enjoy each other's company and they reject the idea of vacationing together. Their mother was aware of this potential conflict but hoped that by leaving the property to them jointly she would force them to just get along. She cherished fond memories of camping with one son and fond memories of fishing with the other. She refused to honor one memory over the other by deciding who would receive the property.

The brothers refuse to vacation simultaneously and their schedules do not allow them to predict when they will vacation so they both demand unfettered access. Like their mother they harbor fond memories: one recalls days spent hanging out at the cabin and camping in the nearby woods, while the other recalls peaceful afternoons spent fishing on the lake. While they each want unrestricted access in order to satisfy their needs they are not concerned about satisfying the other's needs. Each one sees the other as the problem.

When it comes to the other assets in the estate neither has strong emotional attachments. They are willing to liquidate other assets to raise the cash needed to divide the total pie evenly in spite of negative tax consequences. Distributive bargaining works for the bulk of the estate; however, distributive bargaining will not resolve the issue of the vacation property. Though selling assets would provide each brother with enough cash to buy their own vacation property elsewhere, they are not interested. Too many emotional needs are tied to the property to allow for the property to be sold or to allow either brother to buy out the other.

During integrative bargaining they consult their interests and determine one brother is interested in owning the property so he can build a dock from which he can launch his boat for fishing excursions. He hopes to enjoy quiet seclusion on the lake while fishing, an activity that allowed him to escape the frequent family turmoil that took place when he was young. He hopes to escape the pressures of his current business and marriage in the same manner. In his view, owning the property and building the dock is a perfect solution.

The second brother's interest lies in using the rustic cabin as a retreat where he and his young children can camp at night while spending days hiking in the nearby woods. The brother hopes to duplicate the enjoyable moments he experienced with his parents. As he and his wife experience frequent periods of stress in their relationship, it is important for him to be able to avail himself of this retreat opportunity on the spur of the moment. This will allow him to protect the kids from his marital stress and instead experience enjoyable times in a pleasant setting.

Each assumes he can satisfy his interests only through sole possession of the vacation property. If they share the property they risk encountering each other, which will remind them of the tensions that spoiled their childhood family life, memories they are trying to avoid. On the surface each brother appears passionate about avoiding the other. It appears one brother will be forced to suffer disappointment while the other brother realizes his dream or they both will have to give up the property and suffer mutual disappointment.

The mediator guides the negotiation, exhorting them to exercise creativity and place a number of possible solutions on the table. After long hours of negotiation, they realize they can use money from the sale of other assets to subdivide the vacation property in a way that allows one brother exclusive waterfront access, complete with a private entrance to the property, while the other brother will have a separate entrance with exclusive access to the cabin and woods. Using creative landscaping they can plant trees that will serve as a visual border between the two sections of the property, allowing mutual privacy.

The mediator analyzes the exchange. She realizes the brother who loved to fish could easily find another site appropriate for a dock while the second brother could easily purchase another cabin as they are plentiful in the area. While she recognizes memories endow the dock site and the cabin with intangible value, if she is perceptive she uncovers even deeper emotional needs.

She may probe deeper in private sessions and discover that each brother has an undisclosed and unvoiced need for reconciliation. Throughout the process they both protest they want to be separate, but they also have a (mostly unconscious) desire to maintain proximity on the remote chance that one day they will overcome past emotional wounds and reconcile. In retaining the property and occasional proximity to one another they covertly address an unvoiced need.

After discovering this hidden need the mediator suggests they include in their agreement an annual meeting at a popular local inn for the purpose of conducting business related to the vacation property – a meeting to discuss permits, taxes, and improvements. She recognizes it is too early to facilitate reconciliation, but she also recognizes that by creating an opportunity for reconciliation to take place at a future annual meeting the agreement provides hope. The brothers will not express a hope for future reconciliation but their agreement to attend the annual meeting signals underlying hope.

Satisfaction of material needs (a place to vacation) may provide cover for more important emotional needs (a need to reconcile). In divorce mediation we frequently find layering of material and emotional needs of which a mediator must be acutely and intuitively aware. When parties become aware of the layers of interests their negotiated agreement improves. The result is heightened satisfaction.

As this example illustrates we can combine integrative and distributive bargaining. The mediator helps the parties determine when to use different negotiating styles. In preparation for negotiation to resolve your conflict give careful thought to how you will set priorities and how that will determine the bargaining style.

Mining Interests

To increase negotiating success it is important to arrive with a clear understanding of your interests and how those interests might be met in a creative manner. At times the approach will be straightforward, the interests clear. Frequently, however, we move through life without taking time to inspect the layers of interests and needs whose satisfaction contributes to our happiness. We fail to carefully assess our true interests – once we are embroiled in a conflict we need to remedy this failure.

In the *Taming the Wolf* approach we rely primarily on introspection and contemplative prayer to unearth the messages our heart sends. This prayerful and introspective path guides our journey below the line to mine interests. The assessment will be unique to each individual, thus no rote formulas will be offered. However, you may find value in surveying broad categories of needs to prompt recognition of overlooked factors. The following discussion, while at times philosophical, is meant to provoke a broader inquiry into your interests.

Human Needs / Spiritual Needs

One place to start with an inventory is with a hierarchy of basic human needs, "[for] the most powerful interests are basic human needs."[5] As Fisher and Ury note, "Negotiations are not likely to make much progress as long as one side believes that the fulfillment of their basic human needs is being threatened by the other."[6]

The First Pyramid

While most social science research is too abstract to offer assistance in this practical task, the pyramid of human needs developed by Abraham Maslow can serve as a template to prompt below-the-line inventory of unmet needs.[7] Most mediators are familiar with Maslow's heuristic pyramid (see fig. 12.1).

The labeled segments on the pyramid prompt our personal assessment. As you read the labels consider needs that fall in that category. You might find that while you assumed you were trying to satisfy one interest your true interest lies at another level. For a more in-depth description of each level represented, see the previously cited works of Maslow.

We can also consult the hierarchy for our assessment of the other party's interests. For example, while we might assume a financial settlement meets a party's need for safety and security, during negotiation we might suspect a level higher on the pyramid, the need for esteem, is more important to the party.

While a security need might be satisfied by a monetary settlement the need for esteem may require a public apology. If we fail to recognize the need for esteem an impasse results when we offer only a monetary settlement. We might puzzle over their rejection of a payment we assume satisfies their interest in security. We might conclude, incorrectly, that they are being difficult and do not really want to resolve the conflict.

We can use the pyramid to jog our memory and help us uncover the motives beneath our positions. In negotiation we might find we have not adequately explained our interests, leaving the other party scratching their head and just not getting it. We might use the pyramid to find ways of explaining what we really need.

Unfortunately, Maslow's model is plagued by anomalies. The original concept argued that a person would seek to satisfy a need lower on the pyramid before satisfying a need higher up, but the progression from lower to higher is often violated. People often pursue higher needs at the expense of lower needs.

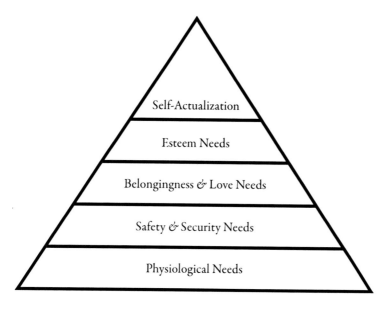

Fig. 12.1. Maslow's Hierarchy of Human Needs

Peak experiences (a secular term for a quasi-religious experience) associated with self-actualization, for example, are experienced by those whose needs lower on the pyramid remain unfulfilled. The anomalies raise an important question: Does the model provide an accurate and comprehensive picture of human motivation? Or is something missing?

The Second Pyramid

After some consideration it became apparent to me that a second pyramid, representing spiritual or transcendental needs, was required to accurately map the subterranean landscape of needs and motivations. The second pyramid is inverted; its broad base is at the top (see fig. 12.2). We can imagine the pyramids overlap, with the largest need category in the first pyramid (physiological needs) intersecting the smallest segment of the spiritual pyramid (see fig. 12.3).

The new model is inherently dualistic, taking into account the needs of the biological organism *and* the needs of the spirit or soul. This new model explains anomalies that plagued the original model. Rather than assume people have skipped levels to satisfy higher needs before meeting lower needs we recognize people operate on two separate pyramids. At the same time that lower level needs on one pyramid may not be satisfied the party may be working on a higher need on the companion pyramid.

In addition to helping us better analyze interpersonal conflicts, the second pyramid allows us to anticipate the inner conflicts that arise when needs on the two pyramids clash: when spiritual needs clash with mundane needs. When we consider both pyramids we end up considering a wider range of needs in our negotiation.

The second pyramid captures spiritual or transcendental needs to be considered when going *below the line*. The description of spiritual and transcendental needs provided is not meant to be comprehensive but rather suggestive. You will want to generate your own list of second-pyramid needs, using the category labels as prompts. The following discussion is a short introduction to possibilities, with an emphasis on how the pyramids relate to one another.

PHILOSOPHICAL DIFFERENCES. The second pyramid illustrates an important difference between the *Taming the Wolf* approach and other approaches. Spiritual needs are recognized as an integral factor in conflict resolution. We assume a dualistic model – biology *and* soul – best reflects the reality in which we encounter conflict.

When one party asserts that physiology drives all behavior and motivation, while the other party attributes needs to the soul, conflict arises over which interests should be considered valid. If we do not agree the other party's interests are valid the interest-based approach falters. We hit an impasse.

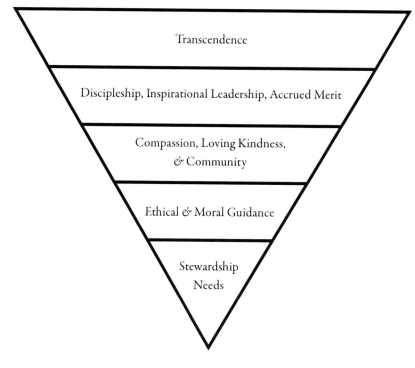

THE SPIRITUAL PYRAMID

Fig. 12.2. The Spiritual Pyramid

HUMAN NEEDS & SPIRITUAL NEEDS

Fig. 12.3. Human Needs & Spiritual Needs Pyramids

Ironically parties then take up positions with regard to the validity of interests. Positions develop over which below-the-line interests are valid for consideration. Each side takes the position that the other side's interests are not worthy of consideration. They apply opposing criteria to what constitutes a valid interest.

To overcome this dilemma core values of plurality and inclusivity must be shared. These values promote flexibility when it comes to considering the other party's interests. We do not abandon the paradigm of interest-based negotiation. We simply make sure we honor the values of plurality and inclusivity that dictate we consider our respective interests. Each party must come to see that if they want their interests considered they must consider the interests of the other. The Golden Rule, which possesses emotional and rational appeal to most people, is brought to bear on the impasse. The need for reciprocity is invoked.

Conflict over the validity of respective interests is typically grounded in a clash of worldviews. A short discussion of worldviews will make this clear.

Worldviews emerge from our needs and conversely needs arise from our worldview. For example, one party may argue physiological needs are the primary driver of their behavior; they may argue physiological needs define who they are and thus are not a matter of choice but rather a matter of biological imperative. Their worldview incorporates biological determinism, which says they have no control over who they are or what they do – as identity and behavior are dictated solely by physiology or biology. In this worldview physiological needs are the foundational soil from which all other needs emerge.

An opposing worldview considers the soul is the steward of physiology. Biology serves spirit. This view considers the free will of the soul negates deterministic models, it renders physiological needs subservient to higher purposes. Biological needs do not define our true identity; rather our spiritual essence defines our true identity. Those who hold this worldview argue that who we really are is a soul that transcends body death, rendering the body a less important aspect of identity but at the same time not negating the importance of our physical existence. The dualistic argument is not a dismissal of our biology but rather a moderation of the importance of biology in light of the existence of soul.

An additional difference further illustrates how the second pyramid explains first pyramid anomalies. The difference concerns altruism. A first pyramid anomaly results when we satisfy the needs of another instead of our own (altruism). Historically, all biological or evolutionary models have had difficulty explaining altruism as it contradicts the basic Darwinian survival of the fittest premise.

The second pyramid explains the anomaly – people sacrifice fulfillment of first pyramid needs in order to pursue second pyramid needs.

Stewardship extends beyond personal biology to a duty to relieve the physical suffering of others. An altruistic person does not leap up the levels of Maslow's hierarchy and skip over basic needs, but rather shifts focus to the second pyramid. You may recall times when your attention shifted from physiological needs to spiritual needs. Perhaps you were struggling to eke out a survival and you noticed another person starving – and you sacrificed what little you had to assist them. Satisfaction of stewardship needs trumped physiological needs. Focus shifted from first to second pyramid needs.

In your assessment, note such shifts – in either direction – that have occurred during your conflict. Such shifts may have confused the opposing party and may require explanation. Later on you may wish to use the illustration of the second pyramid to explain a shift that caused confusion. Explaining the needs you were trying to satisfy answers their challenge, What were you thinking?

Thus you will find it is important to analyze whether you and the other party face challenges when it comes to considering one another's interests. Do you anticipate difficulty in explaining interests you hope to satisfy? Will a difference in worldviews need to be acknowledged and addressed? Work out how you will explain your needs and interests to the other party in a manner that can be easily understood and accepted. If necessary prepare to explain how those interests fit into your worldview.

The following comparison of the two pyramids is meant to aid your attempts to explain interests and help you become more discerning in understanding the interests that drive the other party.

PHYSIOLOGICAL NEEDS / STEWARDSHIP NEEDS. The bottom of the new pyramid, stewardship needs, overlaps the original pyramid's base devoted to physiological needs (see fig. 12.4).

The lowest section of the second pyramid represents a need to nurture and protect physical creation, God's creation, which includes our physiology. We function as devoted stewards. Franciscans take this stewardship seriously. In his canticle, Francis wrote of Brother Sun and Sister Moon, and he called all creatures our brothers and sisters. He recognized the interconnected and interdependent nature of all creatures, and the resulting duty to be responsible for our actions toward all of creation.

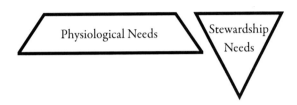

Fig. 12.4. Physiological Needs / Stewardship Needs

The inverted tip of the second pyramid acknowledges the interdependent nature of creatures and our spiritual need to steward the physical realm that includes our physical or biological existence.

While there is considerable overlap between the two pyramids – for example, both recognize physiological needs shape motivation – differences exist. With the first pyramid survival of the biological self drives all considerations; with the second pyramid our motivation is a call of duty to a higher power.

In Maslow's model physiological needs form the broad base of the pyramid and give rise to all other needs higher on the pyramid. In this view inhibiting the fulfillment of physiological needs leads to illness and pathology.

In the view supported by the second pyramid, transcendent or divine needs form the broad base at the top of the inverted pyramid. All other needs flow down from that base. In this view allowing physiological needs to reign unfettered and uninhibited leads to illness and pathology.

The second pyramid adds the assumption that a soul exists and that soul has a need to monitor, control, and steward the body, even to the point of suppressing physiological needs in the service of spiritual needs. Physiological aspects of life are subject to the control and stewardship of the soul.

Francis, more than most, focused on spiritual and transcendental needs. In the poverty of Francis we find an example of second pyramid needs trumping first pyramid needs. If one focuses on the first pyramid the choices Francis made can be counterintuitive. Thus we see how conflict surfaces when parties focus exclusively on needs on separate pyramids.

Clashes over the relative importance assigned to physiological needs lead to culture war skirmishes, especially with regard to sexual behavior. The conflict results from trying to satisfy needs represented on separate pyramids. One party believes physiological needs must be honored above all else, while the other calls for physiological needs to be set aside in lieu of spiritual needs.

At times conflict arises within a single individual when the urge to satisfy physiological needs conflicts with spiritual needs. Dramatic theatre often highlights this inner conflict in morality plays that examine crises of conscience arising out of opposing needs. In drama and in life when the urge to satisfy one need clashes with a desire to satisfy another conflict surfaces.

In some instances failure to satisfy a physiological need may threaten survival. If we lack food the body starves to death. At other times the failure to satisfy a physiological need does not threaten survival but rather results in a deficit of pleasure. When satisfaction of physiological needs relate to pleasure, parties may place very different values on needs. One party might argue they must satisfy their needs at all costs; another party might forego satisfying certain needs in order to satisfy others.

Confusion arises when different needs elicit different motivations for the same act. For example, the physiological need to procreate straddles both pyramids. Biological impulses that demand satisfaction on the first pyramid overlap stewardship needs associated with parenting and the creation of future generations. The motivation of the parties depends on their particular worldview.

In summary, the tip of the inverted spiritual pyramid overlaps the base of the original pyramid. Stewardship needs overlap physiological needs. In a dualistic model the soul seeks to steward the biological realm. This gives rise to motivations absent in a purely biological framework.

In your assessment of the needs and interests that you must satisfy, consider how the needs you identify on the first pyramid (physiological needs) and on the second pyramid (stewardship needs) overlap or clash. Unpack the motivation behind the actions that create conflict.

SAFETY & SECURITY NEEDS / NEED FOR ETHICAL & MORAL GUIDANCE. Safety needs (protection, stable social order, laws) on the original pyramid are overlapped by religious norms, codes, and commandments on the second pyramid (see fig. 12.5).

Needs associated with the aspiration to live an ethical life, with the goal of being acceptable in the eyes of God, parallel and overlap first-pyramid needs associated with meeting the societal demand to conform to legal behavior. While you may have a first-pyramid need to observe society's legal codes, you may also have a need to understand profound issues of good and evil – a need that lies on the second pyramid.

On the second pyramid there may be a need to know scripture that documents a divine plan that guides choices and behavior. In the Abrahamic religions the need to live in obedience and submission to God appears frequently.[8]

Fig. 12.5. Safety & Security Needs / Need for Ethical & Moral Guidance

In Judaism, Abraham's covenant with God is emulated: Jewish law lays out commandments that guide observant followers. In Christianity, Christ set a standard of ethical conduct for those seeking the spiritual kingdom, a standard that encompasses intentions as well as actions. The word *Islam* means submission, indicating the presence of a higher authority. Similar codes of behavior exist outside the Abrahamic religions; for example, in Buddhism, the Eightfold Path guides the religious in their quest for enlightenment through right action.

In these examples we find principles, axioms, or commandments designed to enhance progress toward understanding and achieving communion with the transcendent. While following these precepts may also contribute to a safe and secure society, their goal is spiritual in nature: the axioms focus our attention on our continued existence in a transcendent state.

If a mediator explores the second pyramid rules, codes, and commandments to which parties adhere she can be more helpful in resolving conflict. A mediator working in the courts may err by assuming the law dictates all decisions. A party's actual decisions may be guided by religious or spiritual codes rather than legal codes.

While the party may understand there are legal boundaries they must observe, they may view their conduct within a larger context, within a frame that encompasses the transcendent and spiritual as well as the civil. Mediation is an ideal process for those who wish to include such concerns in their decisions.

I am reminded of a mediation that reached impasse and was on the verge of collapse. The parties were preparing to depart without settling their dispute when I noticed a book hidden under a stack of legal briefs on the table. I asked if the book happened to be a Torah – it was. I asked the attorney if he consulted the Torah in his practice of law. "Quite often," he replied. My focus shifted to the second pyramid. I inquired into the religious principles that applied to the present case. Shortly thereafter the dispute was resolved. It was unusual to find an attorney openly operating on the second pyramid so the situation had escaped my notice. The experience illustrated that it pays for us to know all the interests in play during negotiation.

In a court trial, application of the law determines outcomes; in mediation, outcomes are determined by facilitated negotiation in which personal spiritual codes may play a major role. The second pyramid reminds us that when it comes to resolving disputes through mediation, even in a court setting, we need to be aware that religious codes may be more important than the law of the land. While a party may wish to contribute to a safe and secure civil society by adhering to civil laws, they may also have a need to live an ethical life within a spiritual or transcendent context.

Assess how you will meet your needs on both pyramids. Where will you seek ethical and moral guidance? What guidelines, codes, or axioms will shape your decisions? Weigh the importance you will place on using the law as practiced within the justice system versus the importance you will place on ethical codes that satisfy your need to live in right relationship to God.

For example, civil law may provide you with the right to punish the other party financially and seize their property but religious ethical codes may dictate forgiveness for transgressions. Your faith tradition may call on you to seek to transform the other party, nurturing repentance that results in non-coerced reparation. In mediation, unlike a trial, these interests are allowed to guide your decisions.

The two pyramids overlap. Satisfying our needs on one pyramid may strengthen our ability to satisfy needs on the other. In reverse when our needs on one pyramid are unsatisfied it may weaken our ability to satisfy needs on the other pyramid.

For example, we may depend upon constitutional law to protect the practice of religion. When the law protects freedom of religion we may then pursue the dictates of religious axioms, as long as they do not clash with civil or criminal law. When safety and security needs on the first pyramid are not met or when the law does not protect the practice of religion we may be persecuted, officially or unofficially, for practicing our faith and following our conscience. Thus, second-pyramid needs can suffer due to a failure to satisfy first-pyramid needs.

In a similar fashion the development of religious or spiritual codes of ethics and morality, a function of the second pyramid, may contribute to the formation of a civil legal system. When we have followed religious ethical codes that place us in right relationship with the divine we may be empowered and inspired to establish just civil law that monitors relationships with one another. In this manner a specific civil justice system created to meet the need for safety and security within a civil society may have arisen out of existing religious codes. Thus, satisfaction of our needs on one pyramid appears to increase the likelihood of satisfaction on the other pyramid.

There are those who will argue there should not be two separate systems of justice: some will advocate for a theocracy. They desire a system based on the rule of religious leaders who follow religious texts. Just as secular social scientists may consider there is only one pyramid, built on a foundation of biological needs, there are those who consider there is only one pyramid based on transcendent needs.

When we use the pyramids as conceptual tools to identify interests and needs that must be satisfied in order to resolve the conflict, we may come more quickly to a workable statement of differences. These conceptual tools may help us identify situations in which one group seeks to limit satisfaction of the needs another group considers valid. Conflict resolution demands we expand our view of the possible interests considered as we seek to identify the causes of conflict.

The idea that civil laws can exist alongside spiritually informed moral codes makes it possible for people of different faiths, who differ in their approach to satisfying second pyramid needs, to manage their mutual affairs. They recognize a common set of civil laws while retaining their own moral codes. They recognize second pyramid-based codes vary while a civil justice system addresses common interests and expresses collective agreement. The overlap of common interests, found in the public square, can be structured so as to not impinge on the needs of the second pyramid.

This approach, which honors diversity and plurality, proves valuable in conflict management, as long as civil law honors the individual's need for spiritual and moral guidance. If the civil (constitutional) law recognizes and protects diversity of religion, civil law can function as common ground. If satisfying the needs represented on *both* pyramids is recognized as an important factor in maintaining peace the dual system works. Mediation is particularly well suited to allowing parties to bring different principles to the negotiation. Thus, mediation is a valuable tool in the effort to insure peace and tolerance based on plurality and inclusion within society.

The above discussion is not intended to answer significant philosophical and legal questions on the relationship between law and religion. Rather, the discussion is intended to prompt personal assessment of conflict and cause you to ask, What will serve as my ethical, moral, or legal standard? What needs or interests with respect to religious views must I satisfy?

BELONGINGNESS & LOVE NEEDS / NEED FOR COMPASSION & COMMUNITY. On the original pyramid, *love and belongingness* tends to have a biological emphasis related to sexuality and the biological family, though it includes other types of belonging. On the second pyramid *spiritual love (agape)* extends to a broader community or all Mankind (see fig. 12.6).

Love on the second pyramid aspires to the unselfish; compassion and loving-kindness dictate empathy for others regardless of their past deeds or present status. The second pyramid focus on loving and being loved transcends self-as-biological-organism and takes on a mystical quality.

The premiere example of loving-kindness is found in the life and teachings of Jesus Christ who taught human beings to love one another, even one's enemies. He offered divine forgiveness for sins in an act of unlimited and unconditional mercy, grace, and compassion. This type of love is active, reaching out with compassion that becomes part of who we are as a spiritual being. It is not a series of biological reactions to situation-specific events as conceived on the original pyramid.

Fig. 12.6. Belongingness & Love Needs / Need for Compassion & Community

Participation in a spiritual community can satisfy interests located on both pyramids. First-pyramid needs for belonging can be met by membership in the faith community, in its role as a social network that satisfies our need to belong and be accepted by a social group. Attending social events such as church picnics, church events, or parish mission trips parallels social events in secular settings. Participation in a faith-based community satisfies a need for protection and support, as members care for one another's welfare, assist each other in difficult times, and collectively overcome challenges.

The needs satisfied on the second pyramid are less social in nature. They focus instead on sacred communion in which we are lifted up together in worship. The second pyramid need for belonging or community involves a spiritual family or *communion of the saints* with a transcendent focus. It includes relationship with God. Membership becomes a sacred endeavor in which we seek to satisfy a need for spiritual or transcendent love and eternal belonging. Second pyramid needs are met by participating in religious practices or sacraments, and in a life of humility and compassion.

This section of the second pyramid may include the need to apologize and the need to forgive or be forgiven so as to repair community.[9] Forgiveness is an expression of a willingness to cease resentment, release hatred, and abandon desire for retribution. This can include willingness to welcome back into the group a transgressor who has made restitution, thus restoring his or her belonging, and restoring the group to its former state.

Forgiveness grants that which is not earned, which puts forgiveness on the second pyramid rather than the first.[10] In Christianity, divine forgiveness is an act of God's grace and an expression of His unconditional love, which models how we are to treat our fellow brothers and sisters. The need to receive divine forgiveness can be found on the second pyramid. It is a need to be accepted back into the sacred community, into the Kingdom of God, after separation resulting from transgressions. Forgiveness expresses unconditional love that makes little sense within the evolutionary, biological frame of reference that dominates the first pyramid.

Apology also possesses a religious or spiritual flavor. In a religious context it is known as repentance. An apology requests of another that they *take away my guilt* at the same time I acknowledge accountability for wrongs committed. An apology is an attempt to restore belonging through acceptance of responsibility for transgressions – acts that have severed belonging, damaged community, and compromised the love shared. The apologizing party humbles himself before the party against whom he has transgressed. He acknowledges the worth of the other and seeks to make up for the disrespect inherent in his offenses.

In apology and forgiveness we find a willingness to sacrifice personal welfare or dignity in order to tend to the suffering or needs of the other. Thus apology and forgiveness are acts of love that restore community. While apology and forgiveness also take place in secular settings the spiritual aspects of apology and forgiveness distinguish them as responses to second pyramid needs.

The preceding touches lightly on needs related to compassion, loving-kindness, and belonging to a spiritual community. You will want to create your list of interests and needs in this category. In addition, consider what needs the other party may have for love and belonging that are not being met.

We can greatly reduce hostility by assuming that everyone has a need for love, compassion, and community and by making an attempt to meet that need. The power of divine love, ultimately, is the most powerful tool for dissolving hostility and bringing about reconciliation. When the other party is angry and upset it may be hard to imagine they seek your love and acceptance, yet that may be exactly what they need. We may be blinded to their need for love as a result of how difficult it is to see through the smokescreen of hostile emotions. We need to be sensitive when someone wants our love and approval but at the same time they are afraid to express that desire for fear of rejection. This sensitivity may be one of the most powerful factors leading to success in reconciliation.

ESTEEM NEEDS / DISCIPLESHIP, INSPIRATIONAL LEADERSHIP, ACCRUED MERIT. The needs for esteem on the first pyramid – the need to be seen as professional, competent, successful, the need to be seen as possessing influential status and wielding power – differs from the need for accrued merit on the second pyramid. Second pyramid needs typically forego power, prestige, status, success, and professional accomplishment, instead professing a selfless need to benefit the spiritual advancement of others or to be worthy in the eyes of the Creator (see fig. 12.7).

The second pyramid may include an aspiration to achieve understanding and competence in the practice of a faith tradition. Here one finds the devoted disciple: the monk, the nun, the friar, or the religious leader who aspires to live and model a spiritual or holy life. In this section we find the seeker or the mystic who gains religious insight – and here we find prophets.

Competence in achieving spiritual states of being may not be visible in an external fashion. The spiritual adept goes relatively unnoticed compared to the worldly esteem the competent professional acquires. Upon close inspection one finds a person is accomplished but does not seek attention, though on occasion inspirational religious leaders may attract a considerable following of those who perceive exemplary merit in their lifestyle or teaching.

Second pyramid esteem often does not emerge from our good works but rather relates to our state of being. We are esteemed not for our actions but for the presence of the Spirit, for our state of unity with the divine.

Fig. 12.7. Esteem Needs / Discipleship, Inspirational Leadership, Accrued Merit

Sometimes the mere presence of an accomplished religious leader is perceived as extraordinary, as with St. Francis. These leaders bring healing or understanding wherever they go. A spiritual leader allows the Holy Spirit to work through them to change lives. The competence for which they are esteemed may in large measure issue from this ability to invite and further the work of the Holy Spirit.

The need to attain such states of being or awareness may dramatically color how a party views conflict. In some cases, they may cling to the (false) idea that conflict is a sign of failure when, in fact, most religious leaders experience conflict – sometimes quite profound and extreme conflict, such as Gandhi or Mandela experienced. The primary difference is the manner in which spiritual leaders resolve conflict – usually through transformation of self and the other.

Conflict may arise when a person who has accumulated worldly esteem goes unrecognized by religious men and women or when people accomplished in spiritual disciplines are unacknowledged in secular society. The party with accumulated worldly esteem can be placed on Maslow's pyramid while the spiritually accomplished party can be located on the spiritual pyramid.

A divergence of needs represented on the two pyramids may pit those accomplished in business or politics against those pursuing spiritual merit or discipleship. Divergent needs may place leaders on opposite sides of a secular-versus-religious divide. At other times, such parties may seek rapprochement with their counterparts and may seek to integrate secular and spiritual needs.

Identify your efforts on the two respective pyramids. Determine if your opponent mirrors your interests or works from a different set of priorities. Determine if hostility has occurred as a result of a failure to recognize the need for esteem or the competence of the other party.

Self-actualization / transcendence. Maslow's revised model included self-actualization at the top of the hierarchy of the human needs pyramid. At this level, a person sought meaning, as well as cognitive and aesthetic fulfillment. On the second pyramid the top level concerns life as a spiritual being, as the soul or spirit that transcends the physical and enters into communion with the divine. Here we find needs and motivations that relate to the after-life or immortality (see fig. 12.8).

Both pyramids include the need for knowledge and meaning. On the first pyramid this level is summarized under the term *self-actualization*. On the second pyramid knowledge is revealed knowledge. Meaning arises from the supernatural. Transcending corporeal existence and establishing a personal relationship with God takes us beyond self-actualization and peak experiences. Knowledge on the second pyramid includes knowledge of self as a spiritual being that transcends the biological. It is knowledge of the transcendent true self.

When Maslow investigated peak experiences he frequently remarked on their spiritual nature.[11] However, as long as the first pyramid is limited by the constraints of naturalism (belief there are no supernatural causes or conditions), the spiritual aspect of these experiences remained unexplained. The peak experience was reduced to mysterious feelings or insights that could not be articulated. With the second pyramid we are able to provide a comprehensive model that includes awareness of the supernatural as well as the natural.

It is worth noting that for the purpose of mediation there is no need to debate the verifiability of the existence of the transcendental or supernatural. We simply acknowledge such concerns motivate parties and we understand an expectation of post-mortem existence shapes motivations. For example, acceptance of God's forgiveness plays an important role in how one conceives of a post-mortem future. This gives rise to a present-time need that must be met even though it concerns a future afterlife. In most religions, transcendental expectations actively shape present-time needs; preparation for postmortem existence colors present-time motivations.

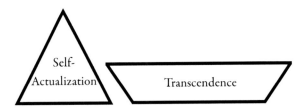

Fig. 12.8. Self Actualization / Transcendence

These powerful concerns play a role in how people address conflict. Some avoid confrontation, considering their opponent will be held accountable in the afterlife. They eschew violence as a solution to conflict, as violence detracts from spiritual merit. Yet others actively battle evil believing they gain merit through forceful action. When conflicts escalate into shooting wars these concerns become important. For example, a combatant may feel a need to sacrifice his life in a battle against evil in pursuit of transcendental goals, while another may sacrifice his life in non-violent protests against war.

Not all cases of motivation tied to the afterlife are as dramatic. In probate cases, the behavior of heirs may be monitored by their perception of the duty owed to the deceased. Those who view death as a complete annihilation of the person will harbor few concerns when it comes to violating the wishes of the deceased. Those heirs who consider there is continuity of life beyond death will consider they have a sacred duty to the deceased, a duty to honor obligations as part of an ongoing relationship.

You will want to assess how your needs and interests are driven by your view of the transcendent. Often these needs or interests operate far below the line, producing subtle and intuitive motivation. As you prepare for conflict resolution you may wish to surface these concerns, identify related needs, articulate interests, and understand how these factors affect positions.

At the same time it is worth approaching the needs and interests of the opposing party with the same focused curiosity. One asks the other party how transcendent interests affect their position. What worldviews – including views regarding the transcendence of the soul – do they bring to the table? Are those concerns acknowledged openly or do they operate in the background?

For those who hold secular views discussion regarding the peak experience may provide common ground for dialogue with those who hold spiritual views. Experience with heightened states of awareness, in which meaning takes on new dimensions and knowledge gains an intuitive or ineffable quality may provide a bridge to tolerance or inclusion. Such experiences may be all that is needed to create a dialogue in which parties acknowledge the importance of these needs in their lives.

SUMMARY. Working with two pyramids promotes a broader view of possible interests and needs. It brings the differences in how we assess our interests into the open and overcomes the situation in which parties talk past each other, failing to address the fundamental nature of their differences. The model is just that – a model – and its importance lies solely in its ability to enhance your personal assessment of interests and needs and to help you identify significant confusions that require clarification.

Interests & Conflicting Worldviews

In the process of mining interests we recognize our own needs and interests while seeking to understand the needs of the other party. When we ponder the task of building bridges we turn to mediation in earnest, searching for deeper answers. However, we may discover our worldviews are so dramatically opposed that differences appear impossible to bridge.

Our worldview relates to our needs and interests in two ways. On one hand, our worldview determines our interests and needs – as we take an interest in things that are consistent with our perspectives on life. If we value truth and integrity we likely have a need to be honest and an interest in being esteemed for our integrity.

Conversely, needs and interests shape our worldview. If our job requires accuracy and truthful reporting, then our worldview, which arises from our experience, is likely to honor and value truth and integrity. In the first scenario, our actions conform to our ideals; in the second, our actions give rise to our ideals.

In mediation we concentrate on the needs and interests side of this dual equation. We do not seek to overturn, dismiss, or deconstruct the other party's worldview. Instead we discover interests that can be satisfied at the same time each party continues to maintain their worldview. We attempt to satisfy the other party's interests without changing their values and beliefs.

Too often we approach a conflict with the premise that we must change the beliefs or values of the other party. This leads to impasse, as people do not easily change their values, beliefs, and worldview – especially at the behest of someone who opposes them. Often conflict persists because each party assumes they must convince the other to see the world as they see it: they expect the other party to honor the values they honor. However, it may be possible to satisfy both parties' interests without requiring they change their worldview. It is possible to move toward resolution by satisfying interests while also respecting different worldviews.

One solution is to not demand the other party value the negotiated outcome in exactly the same way we value the outcome. We only seek agreement that the outcome should satisfy our respective interests. We seek a resolution that acknowledges the values the other party holds while we maintain our values. We seek a solution that works *in spite* of differing worldviews. This is not always easy, but we greatly increase our odds of a durable resolution by recognizing and acknowledging our opponents' needs as they appear to them.

As you assess your approach to negotiation consider whether or not you have assumed you must force a change in the other party's worldview. Do you expect they will demand you change your view?

Materialism & the Second Pyramid

In extreme cases a difference in worldviews between the mediator and a party may make it difficult for a mediator to serve as an impartial neutral. There are people – psychologists, for example – who commonly assume there is no spirit or soul that transcends the life of the biological organism and who see spiritual needs as delusional at best.

This is an unworkable position for the mediator. As mediation prizes party self-determinism a mediator must consider a party's needs *as they exist for that party*. For this reason a mediator will want to recognize that spiritual needs often play a significant role in reconciliation and then not allow personal biases and prejudices to inhibit the process.

A mediator who finds spiritual interests incomprehensible should recognize and acknowledge his potential inability to remain impartial. Likewise, a party with spiritual concerns may not want to engage a mediator who finds it difficult to understand their interests. If a mediator finds it difficult to grasp a party's spiritual concerns it will be difficult for him to paraphrase or frame those interests in a neutral manner for the other party. For this reason a party with strong interests on the second pyramid should exercise caution in the selection of a mediator.

For example, in some venues statutes mandate court-based domestic relations (divorce) mediators receive mental health training rather than training in mediation. Such training frequently promotes materialistic views and bias against religion. If this is a concern parties may wish to engage the services of a mediator working outside the court who is sensitive to their needs.

Righteousness as a Barrier

While we must become aware of our spiritual needs, when we disregard or disrespect another's worldview we escalate conflict. Righteousness lacking in compassion tends to emerge when we fear the other party will disregard or disrespect our needs. When threatened, we may assert that our worldview is the only view possible; we may argue that all decisions should be based on our criteria alone. We move away from give-and-take relationship based on mutual caring and take up rigid and judgmental positions. We may cling to icons or idols against which all other views are judged.

This type of righteousness leads to us-versus-them scenarios. We abandon exploration of below-the-line interests; we fail to satisfy our needs; we fail to achieve our goals in negotiation. When we bask in the glow of self-righteousness our position becomes self-defeating. We provoke the wrong outcome, sacrifice our interests, and make it impossible for the other party to experience a transformation that might eventually bring them to consider our needs.

In some conflicts we have not sufficiently inspected the interests or needs that lie beneath the codes, commandments, or judgments we impose as criteria for resolution. When we look closer we may discover we have adopted rules or commandments out of context, in a self-serving manner. If we are to move forward we need to consider how our standards might appear to the other party. Do they even make sense to them? Have we communicated our views from our heart or have we delivered challenges?

The journey toward resolution of conflict requires us to consider that while the other party may not agree with our worldview they have legitimate needs they are trying to satisfy. In order to move ahead with below-the-line exploration, we must consider adopting additional values of pluralism and inclusion. We may be called on to consider other views and other interests and not leave the other party angry and resentful.[12]

Addressing the other party's needs and interests does not force us to abandon our beliefs or values, but requires us to ask how we can satisfy the other's needs within the context of our worldview. This may require humility, charity, compassion, and kindness. In this situation, we call upon the compassionate aspects of our faith to guide us in the effort to include the other and meet their needs, rather than employing judgmental aspects of our faith to exclude the other.

It is difficult to adopt an inclusive worldview. The challenge should not be underestimated. We have built a framework of beliefs and values that support and shape our life. A request or demand that seems to ask us to weaken this moral skeleton poses a threat. When we feel threatened, however, we must guard against the tendency to assume righteous positions based on counterproductive pride and hubris. When we temper righteousness with humility and compassion and listen with empathy the outcome can be significantly improved.

Nonetheless, compassion and inclusivity may not be easy to put into practice when closely held values are challenged. When the ground below our feet becomes unsteady, we tend to plant our feet more firmly, and hold our position steadfastly. Likewise, when our worldview is challenged we may have legitimate cause for alarm – but we must be mindful of how satisfying our interests may require we negotiate with an awareness of the interests of others. Our righteous position telegraphs take it or leave it. In contrast, a discussion of mutual interests allows the other party to find creative ways to satisfy our needs. We must provide options that allow them to meet our needs without severe Face Loss.

Nonetheless, there may be times when it is valid to stand on principle. It may be necessary to refuse to engage in settlement efforts that do not first and foremost acknowledge and respect our values. This is in keeping with party self-determinism. The critical question, however, is whether a principled stance will result in the best possible outcome. Do we achieve the results we intend?

It is valid to stick to principle and forego resolution – as long as we factor in the adverse consequences we generate. If we are willing to suffer those consequences and if we are comfortable with others suffering the consequences, the principled stand is valid. Too often, however, consequences arise that we have not anticipated. We suffer results that defeat our principled stand. We shoot ourselves in the foot.

When we stand on principle we often (unconsciously) make the decision to let power win the day – we intend to dominate the other party and coerce their behavior. If not now then once we have gathered sufficient power to overwhelm them. In other words, we make a decision to fight it out. Our vision is one in which we prevail and, if necessary, destroy the other party.

The decision to stand and fight, however, is usually the result of failing to take time to inspect the interests we are trying to satisfy. We have not asked an important question: What interest is served by holding firm to a particular value, belief, or worldview? The shift from positions to interests is a shift from the static, fixed, iconic, and rigid factors to flexible, creative, flowing, and living factors. It is a shift away from dead icons to the Holy Spirit working in its holy manner. This does not mean we succumb to moral relativity. Rather it means we become skilled in negotiating outcomes consistent with our values while avoiding rigidity that brings about outcomes that violate our values.

On occasion we mistakenly measure our faith by the degree to which we cling steadfastly to abstract concepts and impose inflexible rules rather than measuring our faith by the degree to which we open our heart to the Holy Spirit and its holy manner of working. There is a subtle but very important difference between taking a stand and simply holding firmly and quietly to compassion and love. In the former the other party engages our rigid stance with an oppositional embrace. In the latter the other party is enveloped by our compassionate love – and it becomes difficult for them to lock onto an oppositional embrace.

These issues are captured in the story of St. Francis befriending the Sultan Malik-al-Kamil, the ruler of Egypt, Syria, and Palestine at a time when

Muslims and Christians prepared for battle during the Fifth Crusade.[13] The story has relevance for our understanding of contemporary conflict among religions.[14] Taking advantage of a temporary truce in the midst of a war, Francis entered the camp of the Sultan empty-handed, as a peacemaker. His was a demonstration of seeking out the interests of the other party through direct conversation while honoring their Face, even though they practiced a different Faith.

Francis spoke passionately about his love for Christ but did not insult Islam, the Sultan's religion. Francis embraced the Sultan with the spirit of compassion and love even though, when he had first crossed enemy lines with his companion, Brother Illuminato, "[t]he men of God were seized in a violent manner by the sentries, assaulted, and bound in chains."[15]

Francis' faith was strong enough that he was able to continue to demonstrate brotherhood rather than righteous judgment. "Perhaps most importantly, as it turned out, Francis announced that his personal concern was for the eternal salvation of the soul of al-Kamil."[16] "The Sultan, impressed by the courage and spirituality of this inspired speaker, wished to hear more. The wolf had been transformed into a lamb, thanks to the influence of the Saint on the educated and open-minded Sultan."[17]

When the Sultan's advisers, the Imams, wanted to behead the friars, the Sultan refused, explaining to Francis: "You have risked your own lives in order to save my soul."[18] Thus we find a model in which concern for the interests and well being of the other serves to bridge a chasm separating worldviews based on religious beliefs. Francis provides us with a valuable model as he "did not directly attack the religion of Mohammed, but under the guidance of the Holy Spirit, continued to expound the truths of the Christian religion."[19] He did not relinquish his faith but rather allowed his devotion to be revealed through his passion and compassion. He allowed his faith to come alive in his concern for the welfare of the other party.

Francis, though personally able to establish a peaceful relationship with the Sultan, was unable to prevent the looming battle. This is not uncommon. Within religious communities the faithful can easily become attached to icons, rote codes of behavior, and doctrinal or political positions they feel must be defended at all costs. At the same time they inadvertently abandon the work of personal spiritual formation, work which changes hearts and nurtures unconditional love. In other words religion can easily become the source of conflict, rather than a source of inspiration for resolving conflict.

To address interfaith conflict it is especially important to go below the line to consider interests, for it is in the area of our faith-based interests and shared core values that we find common ground with people of other faith traditions, even in the presence of apparently differing doctrines.[20] Later in the book I will take up this issue in more detail.

Narcissism: Interests Gone Awry

Narcissism is an obsessive and aberrant need for esteem and self-aggrandizement. It is a condition in which the person is wholly concerned with self to the exclusion of others' interests. Narcissism is selfish on steroids.

The narcissistic person is unable to consider the world of the other person. The other person does not figure into their equation, except in so far as the narcissist adopts a manipulative strategy in order to convince (or deceive) the other party into serving the narcissist's needs.

Esteem for self becomes an overwhelming and all-consuming concern for the narcissist. Survival of self has been threatened to such an extreme extent that the narcissist is absorbed in an automatic, full-tilt defense, protecting the boundaries of self to the exclusion of all else.

Unfortunately, our culture, with its emphasis on self-esteem and its profound lack of attention to sacrifice, giving, and collaboration, promotes narcissism as a cultural norm. Generations raised on the philosophy that self-esteem is the paramount virtue in life may find they view the world through narcissistic lenses.

Narcissism as a way of life conflicts with spiritual paths in which I–Thou relationships become primary. Narcissists take offense at a request to extend their concerns to the other party's interests. They approach mediation as an attempt to obtain what they want, regardless of whether or not they are able to satisfy the other party's interests.

For a narcissist the best of all possible worlds is one in which they have the power needed to prevail over the other party, the power needed to assert their "rights" and protect their self-interest to the exclusion of others' interests. The narcissistic personality is often unable to enter into negotiation in good faith. This results in a failed mediation and a renewed effort to pursue a trial (or a war) in which the narcissist imagines they will be rewarded with the esteem they deserve.

They will find the zealous advocacy of an attorney to their liking, as hiring a "gunslinger" is consistent with their focus on serving only their interests. Unfortunately for the narcissist this approach does not guarantee a favorable outcome in front of a jury. While all participants in litigation end up spending considerable time and money, the narcissist rarely accomplishes his goals.

If a jury perceives a party has been unreasonable and disrespectful or if they perceive narcissism at work, they often punish the selfish party. The narcissist finds it difficult to turn off the "me-first" attitude in front of a jury and thus gives offense that leads to an undesirable verdict. The jury may concede the narcissist's claim has some merit and find in their favor but then they punish the narcissist by awarding minimal damages.

Paradoxically, concentrating exclusively on self-interest leads to self-destructive outcomes. In the end the zealous attorney has a difficult client on his hands when it comes to the narcissist, a client who is likely to turn around and pursue frivolous legal malpractice claims against the attorney.

In societies lacking an effective legal system, narcissism brings about extreme social and political strife. Wars have often been the result of narcissistic leaders refusing to relinquish control in countries struggling to implement democratic transitions of power. In such cases, the critical importance of a justice system becomes apparent. Where judicial institutions are corrupt or underdeveloped, narcissists wreak pain, suffering, horror, and widespread destruction on innocent populations.

The implementation of an interest-based approach to conflict resolution often serves to detect the presence of a destructive narcissist. If one discovers a party is incapable of considering mutual interests, very likely one has exposed a narcissist. This should provide a warning when it comes to how future events will unfold.

In the presence of a narcissist the opposing party should focus on discussing how self-interest is best served through collaboration. The adverse consequences of narcissism should be presented in detail allowing the narcissist to consider new perspectives. An education campaign showing the narcissist how to achieve the victory he feels he deserves should be launched to avert future difficulty.

Visioning Interests

There are many approaches to mining interests. You may wish to consult the business section of the bookstore for popular literature written by motivational experts on how to succeed, how to set your goals, or how to manage your way to success. *Mining your interests* overlaps with setting goals or finding your purpose. Or you may consult inspirational religious literature that addresses finding your purpose in life. These works can all function as prompts to inspire introspection and contemplation. Rarely do they offer a system that fits you perfectly but they can inspire your personal introspection and assessment. Too often we fail to engage the process and consciously determine our interests. We fail to prioritize interests. We bounce from situation to situation, from reaction to reaction, from one crisis to the next. We put out fires and fail to build our dreams.

When we are asked to identify our interests we are caught off guard. We vamp and improvise. In many instances, the short-term goal (end this conflict) may obscure the larger vision of possible outcomes that align with long-term goals. Thus it pays to periodically survey our highest priority interests in order to sustain a vision against which we measure our decisions during the conflict resolution process.

Robert O'Donnell of the Woodstock Institute for Negotiation suggests an approach to mining and prioritizing interests that keeps the process simple and workable.[21] In his visioning process we list thirty of our most vital interests then allocate 10,000 points to the list, assigning a relative value to each interest, after which we arrange them interests in a hierarchy. We rework the list multiple times until it faithfully reflects our priorities. The completed list is updated at least once a year to reflect changes in priorities (see table 12.1).

In constructing the list we state our interests with infinitives such as "I want to ..." This creates a list that is fluid and alive and reflective of our lived experience. Actors prepare for roles using similar techniques. Before putting a scene on its feet an actor reads the script and notes their character's motivation in each scene by writing, "I want to ..." They state the intention that plays beneath the dialogue. In the same way we state the intentions at play in our life.

When we enter a conflict resolution process this list of prioritized interests provides a set of criteria against which we measure negotiated outcomes. We determine whether a particular solution or offer is consistent with our long-term interests. Often we fight the good fight for a result that upon further reflection has little or no real importance in our lives. If we have created a vision list we can take a "time out" during conflict resolution to determine if the solution we are negotiating meets our more vital interests. Too often we become caught up in an oppositional embrace reactively or reflexively, only to later wonder what motivated us to engage the other party in opposition. With a list of our primary interests on hand we can evaluate whether resolving the conflict is important and what interests a resolution must satisfy to be of true value.

A list will have thirty entries with 10,000 points allocated to those interests. The following is an abbreviated example of such a list.

My interest is to ... (I want to ...)

Publish a book on conflict resolution	780
Manage a successful mediation practice	550
Practice my faith	500
Train mediators	435
Interview peacemakers	400
Fund a non-profit peace foundation	375
Consult with the local school board	250
Travel to sacred sites	175

Table 12.1. Interest List

We identify interests that warrant expenditure of time, effort, and money. We compare proposed outcomes in a negotiation with the list to determine if our primary interests are advanced or inhibited.

As a hypothetical example, imagine an executive of a non-profit learns he has been considered for the organization's leadership position. It appears a promotion might be offered within the year. A new member of the board, however, makes it known he supports an outside candidate for the position. The outcome of future deliberations among the board members is uncertain. It is clear the conflict will be nasty; no matter who wins, long-term damage to relationships will occur. Even if the executive obtains the leadership role, his ability to manage will be made difficult as a result of dissension among the board members. Nonetheless, he is ready to engage in a good fight to win the contest and secure a better life.

However, recalling an earlier period of self-reflection during which he assessed his desires, the executive takes a "time out" and retrieves the list of interests he previously drafted. At the top he finds "start an NGO (non-governmental organization) that utilizes my skill in designing high technology solutions for underdeveloped regions." Becoming the head of the non-profit with which he is currently working does not fully satisfy this interest. Discovering the mismatch between the list he created previously and his desire to win the executive position motivates him to slow down.

He takes time to meet informally with board members who support his candidacy for the top position with his current organization. In casual talks he discovers they would underwrite his dream venture – if he agrees to spend the next year in Africa supervising the drilling of wells in villages for his current employer. The assignment, they explain, provides an opportunity for him to accumulate credentials for on-site work that ultimately will convince them to fund his venture. Taking the assignment helps the current employer and allows him to realize his dream a year later. He agrees.

If he had not consulted the list of interests compiled during a period of introspection and contemplation, he might have done what so many of us do – he might have engaged in a intense battle to secure the contested position without realizing that such a victory would not meet his actual interests. If he persisted in pursuing the position and lost he would have burned bridges. As a result of going slow and carefully consulting his true interests, he was better able to satisfy his needs.

The process of uncovering and identifying interests may involve quiet contemplation, periods of solitude. The process may require conversations with significant others: family, friends, and associates. You may wish to make this process a part of a prayer retreat.

The first time you undertake the process you may be dismayed by the time required: the final product may only come together after a period of months during which you strip away layer after layer of interests that, upon further reflection, are false or empty. Rather than postpone completion until you feel certain about all choices it makes sense to set a deadline for a draft and allow for revisions over time. It is easier to maintain the momentum if you complete a list and then later revise and improve the list.

A Franciscan View

The second pyramid, a hierarchy of spiritual or transcendent needs, plays a significant role in the lives of most Franciscans. Stories that tell of St. Francis' love for all creatures and his eagerness to play the role of steward to the natural world – perhaps highlighted best by his preaching to the birds – are well known.[22]

The prayer attributed to Francis attests to the Franciscan focus on love and community.[23] Leonardo Boff notes, "Saint Francis wanted peace to be lived out in the relationships of his own companions. He always called them 'my brothers,' 'my most beloved brothers,' or 'my blessed brothers,' expressions of extreme affection that do not allow any room for divisions or exclusions."[24]

Perhaps less well known to the broader public is the Franciscan interest in the transcendent needs at the top of the second pyramid. Francis endowed the Order with a love of contemplation, setting an example by retreating into hermitage to seek union with the divine.

Saint Bonaventure, also a Franciscan, gave this aspect of Franciscan life a voice in *The Soul's Journey to God*.[25] In his introduction Bonaventure speaks to the priority he gives to interests on the second pyramid: "I propose the following considerations, suggesting that the mirror presented by the external world is of little or no value unless the mirror of our soul has been cleaned and polished."[26] For Bonaventure other interests only make sense in the context of the spiritual.

While we may not place the same weight or emphasis on our spiritual needs as Saint Bonaventure, we can recognize how profound these interests can be. Few take the daunting path of the mystic but many hear in their hearts the summons sounded from the top of the hierarchy of spiritual needs. It is a call that beckons us to communion with the divine.

Bonaventure not only trod this path, in *The Soul's Journey into God* he laid out the six stages of the journey. In the following passage we taste a flavor of the transcendent need that lifts the Soul toward the divine: "When finally in the sixth stage our mind reaches that point where it contemplates in the First and Supreme Principle and in the mediator of God and men, Jesus Christ, those things whose likenesses can no way be found in creatures and which surpasses all penetration by the human intellect, it now remains for our mind, by contemplating those things, to transcend and pass over not only this sense world but even itself."[27]

The writings of Bonaventure alter the landscape as we consider our needs. The transcendent is no longer merely a matter of blind faith but rather the destination on a very real journey we may be summoned to join.

Mystics who provide glimpses of the journey assure us the needs we feel in this regard are not mirages to be disregarded; they are not chimeras sent to deceive. "In this passing over, if it is to be perfect, all intellectual activities must be left behind and the height of our affection must be totally transferred and transformed into God. This, however, is mystical and most secret, which no one knows except him who receive it, no one receives it except him who is inflamed in his very marrow by the fire of the Holy Spirit whom Christ sent into the world."[28]

Franciscans are not alone in heralding these needs that reign supreme in the spiritual hearts of men. Trappist monk Thomas Merton wrote, with considerable insight, about the higher needs we encounter on the contemplative journey. The following passage echoes the ascension up the hierarchy of needs on the second pyramid: "The spirituality of Thomas Merton centers upon the fact that the whole of the spiritual life finds its fulfillment in bringing our entire life into a transforming, loving communion with the ineffable God. This communion is both the raison d'être and fruition of our deepest self. In fact, this communion reveals that we ourselves are ineffable, being made in the image and likeness of God and called to a union of identity with God forever."[29]

These sentiments may remind us that when we consider our interests and needs we may wish to plumb the depths and the heights of our divine nature in order to bring our divine self to the table as we seek resolution and reconciliation.

Scripture

Peter and John, however, said to them in reply, "Whether it is right in the sight of God for us to obey you rather than God, you be the judges. It is impossible for us not to speak about what we have seen and heard." (Acts 4:19-20)

Now the Lord is the Spirit, and where the Spirit of the Lord is, there is freedom. All of us, gazing with unveiled face on the glory of the Lord, are being transformed into the same image from glory to glory, as from the Lord who is Spirit. (2 Cor 3:17-18)

It is the spirit that gives life, while the flesh is of no avail. The words I have spoken to you are spirit and life. (Jn 6:63)

Finally, brothers, rejoice. Mend your ways, encourage one another, agree with one another, live in peace, and the God of love and peace will be with you. Greet one another with a holy kiss. All the holy ones greet you. The grace of the Lord Jesus Christ and the fellowship of the holy Spirit be with all of you. (2 Cor 13:11-13)

CHAPTER THIRTEEN

Managing Power

Francis could see that the wolf was only acting to fill his needs. He had made unfortunate choices that affected people of whom he knew nothing.

Through Francis the wolf was able to feel the pain of the people in Gubbio and he felt remorse. He was sorry for the pain he had caused, but he needed to eat. What could he do?

Mediation Principles

IN RESOLVING CONFLICT, understanding the use of power is vital. In this chapter our focus turns to how a party will use power to satisfy interests they have identified. We will consider the nature of power and the types of power at our disposal when it comes to managing and resolving conflict.

The use of power is so complex that a small library could be written on the topic. Therefore the following is not intended to be comprehensive but rather an introduction that helps you assess the role power plays in your specific conflict.

The Nature of Power

When we think of power in the context of human affairs, we may think of powerful leaders – presidents, dictators, monarchs, judges, mafia dons – who wield power over the lives of citizens or subjects, leaders who have the power to make decisions and issue edicts that control other people's behavior. While our attention may go to such high profile examples, we all encounter more subtle uses of power in our daily lives, uses of power that play a vital role in conflict.

Power can best be defined as *the ability to affect the decisions, actions, and behavior of others*. When we desire a particular outcome we exert power in an attempt to cause others to act, think, believe, or behave in accord with our wishes. A measure of the power we possess is our ability to *intend* and *determine* outcomes. When we possess total power we determine outcomes in their entirety – the resulting conditions are exactly as we wish them to be. When we lack power conditions and events are not under our control – others do not act, think, believe, or behave in the manner we desire.

Most conflicts involve power struggles, contests over who will determine specific outcomes. In power struggles we wrestle over who will dictate conditions, events, actions, and behavior. Power struggles attest to the fact that our lives are intertwined and interdependent. We co-exist in a complex web of cause and effect: we affect others, and they affect us.

When we unravel a conflict we become aware of our interdependent condition and we take stock of how we affect the decisions, actions, and behavior of others – how we use power – and the ways others affect our decisions, actions, and behavior – how they use power.

This mutual ability to create effects (use power) must be appreciated before one can resolve a conflict. In conflict the cliché "no man is an island" becomes painfully clear: the oppositional embrace brings us face to face with the power of another. This basic concept of interdependence is not easily grasped. We prefer to act as though we live in a vacuum, oblivious to the needs of others, oblivious to the effects we create. This lack of awareness of power relationships often brings about conflict.

Contrary to popular myth, power by itself is not intrinsically bad. Power is neutral. The manner in which we exert our power determines its value, as power can be used for good as well as evil ends. When we analyze our use of power we evaluate the effects we create on other people, good or bad. We assess how we are affected, good or bad, by the other party's use of power.

Coercion & Domination

When we react negatively to the idea of power we are usually responding to our experience with coercive power, those instances when force is applied to coerce us to comply with another's wishes. We also recognize we have used coercion to impose our will on others.

A brief example is warranted. Imagine you are hiking up a narrow path on the side of a mountain. A sluggish hiker blocks your progress and refuses to yield; all attempts to persuade him to move aside fail. You may eschew the use of force and sacrifice your desire to go fast. Or you may choose to employ coercive power: you may apply physical strength and push him ahead, forcing him to move at a faster pace. Or you may shove him out of the way even though there is a risk he will slip off the side of the mountain. You may coerce him to behave as you wish.

A more extreme example is applying lethal firepower. Two warring parties literally try to make nothing of each other; they each attempt to terminate their enemy's existence. Bullets are fired, bombs are dropped, and missiles are launched in an effort to obliterate the enemy. Direct physical force is applied to make nothing of the opposition. Power is used to dominate and coerce.

We may coerce another party without the immediate use of direct force. We might gain immediate compliance by threatening future negative consequences. We may issue a threat of impending punishment to be delivered using force. For example, if the hiker refuses to yield we threaten to ban him from the lodge mess hall at the top of the mountain. When we issue a threat, we use coercion indirectly. Later we may have to use direct force to enforce the threat – we may have to physically bar the hiker from entering the mess hall.

Using threat of future consequences to affect the decisions, actions, and behavior of others avoids immediate use of direct force, deferring the use of force to a later time. The promise of a negative consequence for non-compliance thus gains power from the promise that direct force will eventually be used.

For example, when a jury renders an award of damages, if the damages are not paid the sheriff uses physical force to remove the offender's property. We thus rely on threatened consequences to coerce the other person. We use power that depends on anticipated adverse consequences.

The preceding discussion introduces one way power is used – to coerce and dominate – that we tend to reject as undesirable, whether used for good or bad. Slavery is an extreme example of domination and coercion – but even when we are not literally enslaved we often feel like a slave when we are subjected to coercion and domination, when we lose our ability to act according to our free will.

In situations in which another person uses power coercively, notwithstanding our perception that their intentions are honorable, we typically become defiant or resentful. We chafe at the idea that our free will is trumped by another's use of power to constrain or dictate our choices and actions.

It is easy to make the case that freedom from domination and coercion is a universal human value. When we become immersed in conflict we become acutely aware of our loss of freedom as a result of the other party's attempts to dominate or coerce. It seems that if we could only escape the other party's coercive use of power and their attempts to dominate us we might enjoy a peaceful existence.

In his admonitions St. Francis advised the brothers to avoid attempts to dominate and coerce. He clearly understood that dominating another through coercive power does not lead to long-term peaceful outcomes. In his view a brotherly relationship built on unconditional love, in which each party grants the other the freedom to act in accord with their will, is preferred.

Francis' endorsement of the freedom to follow the dictates of one's heart was not a proposal for anarchy. Francis did not advocate an anything goes approach to life but rather saw the need for each man and woman to possess the freedom necessary to accept the divine guidance of the Holy Spirit, guidance that leads to a loving manner of being. In Francis' view free men become loving men – and loving men become free men.

Mediation parallels Francis' views on power, placing priority on party self-determinism while honoring the non-coercive use of power. This preference is not arbitrary but rather emerges from hands-on experience with successful strategies in conflict resolution. Power used judiciously and wisely produces durable outcomes with considerable party satisfaction, whereas, when power is used ineptly to coerce or dominate, impasse results.

Prior to convening, parties often express skepticism regarding mediation; they expect the misuse of power will render the process unworkable. A party often assumes the other party will ignore their needs and use raw power to defeat their interests from the outset. They may consider they possess insufficient power and they may assume the outcome will be dictated by the other party's coercive use of power. However, this is typically not the case. Mediation frequently is successful in averting abuse of power and moves the interaction toward more subtle and respectful uses of power.

Prior to mediation Party A may be aware that Party B has the power to affect their actions, but they frequently fail to understand the ways in which they also can employ power. Parties rarely understand that power is relative: one person may have power in one area offset by another's power in a different area. During mediation an exploration of the balance of power leads to a more nuanced approach that prevents power struggles.

The mediator guides the parties away from coercive use of power and toward principled negotiation. This may involve the use of procedural guidelines or ground rules that discourage the use of coercive power long enough for the parties to change gears. These procedural guidelines are introduced in opening remarks, at which time the mediator assures parties they will retain their option to exercise more coercive options *if* they do not reach a mutual agreement. However, the mediator explains, the procedures require that overtly coercive or violent means be set aside for the moment while the parties engage in a facilitated discussion.

This does not mean power is not a factor in mediation but rather that use of power becomes a matter for discussion and analysis. How we have used power in the past and how we will use power in the future becomes a topic of negotiation. A party may discover that, although they retain the ability to use force, the consequences of coercive power may not actually meet their needs. They may uncover a downside to the abusive or coercive use of power they had not previously recognized. Their understanding of how power can be used to reach an agreement that satisfies their needs may change during the process.

In spite of the mediator's explanation of process guidelines a party's unwillingness to set aside coercive power may persist. From their point of view, it will be necessary for them to use force to convince the other party to accede to their wishes. In their mind there is no alternative.

The mediator must overcome these fears and secure a preliminary agreement that temporarily suspends coercive use of power while the parties explore alternatives. He must convince parties to "lay their weapons on the table" in order to engage in a mutual exploration of less forceful solutions. When the conflict being mediated has already reached the courts, this cease-fire includes temporarily setting aside the power of the court to impose a solution in favor of the parties seeking their own solution. Such negotiation over the use of power is frequently an early step in mediation.

Negotiating Use of Power

Power plays a significant role in negotiation, even if its more forceful and violent expressions have been temporarily set aside. Coercive power remains in the background, operating in the context of projected consequences that must be taken into account should there be a failure to reach an agreement. When a party assesses their *best alternative to a negotiated agreement* (BATNA),[1] they must take into account the future use of coercive power to which they will be subjected.

At the beginning of the process there may be a need to remedy or acknowledge significant power imbalances. If the power imbalance is too extreme there is no negotiation: the powerful party simply states consequences that will result if their wishes are not honored. The discussion is over. It is difficult for mediation to get off the ground.

In response, the mediator accepts the more powerful party's assertion of future consequences at face value then begins an inquiry (in private sessions) into the degree to which the party has considered the consequences that will accrue should they make good on their threats. Is it possible they will also suffer adverse consequences? In private session the mediator reminds the more powerful party that coercive power does not exist in a vacuum – there are always consequences. He convinces the more powerful party to consider how a different approach might increase the possibility of a satisfactory resolution. When he assures the more powerful party they are not relinquishing their coercive power – should the mediation not be successful – the party often becomes open to mediation.

In the same manner the mediator works with the less-powerful party to bring about an understanding of possible consequences they might suffer should they refuse to respect the powerful party's interests.

I have encountered parties who stood to lose a great deal as a result of their unrealistic dismissal of the genuine interests of the more powerful party. They sustained the conflict through an unrealistic and at times deluded sense of power, which prevented them from engaging in realistic and fruitful negotiation. Though the weaker party had the most to lose if coercive power was used they nonetheless persisted on an aggressive path. When they finally jettisoned their unrealistic posture they found the more powerful party had no intention of overwhelming or dominating them. Rather the more powerful party had been mirroring the weaker party's aggressive posture.

When a weaker party asserts power that they do not actually possess it is not unusual for the stronger party to escalate their demonstration of power. The mediator must quickly orchestrate a Face Saving dance in which the ill-advised mutual show of force is abandoned in favor of more promising approaches to dialogue and conciliation – even if the change is promoted as a temporary and exploratory approach that can be rejected if it fails to bring results.

If and when parties reach an agreement that resolves the conflict it is common for that agreement to address the future use of power. This is particularly true if power has been abused in the past. With the mediator's help the parties build into their agreement provisions that detail the principled use of power to be used in the future to ensure compliance. During mediation parties become increasingly skilled at negotiating the use of power and thus are increasingly able to design a protocol that diminishes unnecessary escalation of conflict in the future.

As we consider the role of power in mediation we need to become aware of *the types of power used to affect decisions, actions, beliefs, and behavior* as well as the ways in which we use those types of power. In preparation for mediation you will want to list the types of power you will use, describe how you will use that power, chart the consequences, and assess your willingness to use your power in light of the anticipated consequences. The following discussion (and the discussion in the next chapter) assist with this task.

Types of Power

The following survey of types of power is not comprehensive but rather is designed to prompt consideration of power you will use. As you enter notes in the journal workbook include additional types of power if they better describe your situation. The following discussion includes categories Robert O' Donnell of the Woodstock Institute for Negotiation identified in his practical introduction to the use of power, "A Different Look at Power."[2] These categories are not mutually exclusive. When appropriate combine types of power in your analysis.

PROCEDURAL POWER arises from the process steps a mediator uses to guide parties to resolution of the conflict. As O'Donnell notes, this power is often overlooked or ignored, as we do not always appreciate that *how we proceed* affects our decisions, actions, and behavior.[3]

Mediation employs procedures and guidelines that help each party affect the other party's decisions, actions, and behavior. An example is the opportunity for each party to tell their story without interruption. This procedure empowers a participant: they are allowed to express what happened in its entirety, in their own words, with their own emphasis.

In the normal course of a conflict it is rare for a party to be given the opportunity to relate their story in full without interruption. If their entire story has not been heard it is difficult for them to change the other party's mind; they lack power to affect the other party. When they are allowed to share their story and insure they have been heard their power is increased; their ability to affect the decisions, actions, beliefs, and behavior of the other party is increased. Allowing uninterrupted opening narratives thus increases power through the use of procedure.

Another example is the use of *confidentiality provisions* that dictate contents of mediation shall remain confidential as far as the court is concerned. Events taking place in mediation or evidence prepared and presented exclusively for mediation cannot be used later in court.

Confidentiality frees parties to participate in a candid manner, fostering a higher degree of honesty and transparency. With frank disclosure of information and feelings, with candid confessions and apologies, and with heartfelt expressions of emotion – which would not be possible without confidentiality – parties increase their power to achieve a resolution. They increase their ability to affect each other's decisions, actions, beliefs, and behavior. Similarly, increased transparency, a by-product of confidentiality, increases awareness of factors contributing to the conflict thus increasing the party's ability to achieve the resolution desired.

Procedural power derives a portion of its strength from the parties' increased ability to accurately predict future events. Procedures bring order and discipline and channel efforts within agreed-upon boundaries of behavior. When a party enjoys increased ability to predict events that will take place during conflict resolution their fear of the unexpected decreases. Feelings of hope and safety, critical to mediation, increase.

In addition, the parties' experience in reaching an agreement on how they will proceed during mediation becomes practice for reaching future agreements. When parties enjoy success in formulating process guidelines it fosters hope that they will enjoy success in creating agreements on substantive issues.

It is important to corrrectly estimate the power of procedure. Carefully consider which procedures or guidelines will be helpful or vital in resolving the conflict. Analyze the kinds of procedures that will empower you to work toward a settlement. Consider procedures helpful in the past that might be helpful in the present. The mediator, who facilitates but does not dictate the process, will encourage you to offer suggestions regarding procedures.

PERSONAL POWER arises from personality assets such as charisma, charm, honesty, integrity, likeability, humor, and empathy. Personal power draws upon overlapping qualities of virtue, conscience, and character.

We may find our deepest reservoir of power in personal power, but we often fail to recognize the power that lies within, ready to be summoned or developed or recognized. Face-to-face with the other party we may feel powerless and tend to diminish our estimate of self-worth. Previously we may have failed to handle the other party's objections successfully, which leaves us feeling we lack sufficient ability to overcome their opposition to our wishes. Failed attempts to persuade the other party to see our point of view leave us feeling unable to reason with them. We fear we lack the rhetorical tools needed. When we extend a conciliatory hand and that hand is rejected it tells us our goodwill is insufficient.

The good news is the development of our personal power does not depend on someone else. On our own we can develop, nurture, and expand our personal power. We can make the choice to remedy the deficits in personal power we fear will undermine our efforts. While we may seek coaching or advice at the end of the day an increase in our personal power is in our own hands.

As we bolster our confidence we realize that, while personality, charm, and the humor we bring to a relationship play a role in how our requests are received, personal power is not limited to social artistry and polished manners. The ability to impart humble respect, calming empathy, and sincerity plays an even stronger role. These are qualities we can nurture.

We can also work diligently on self-assessment – when we are prepared we display certainty, calmness, and respect when facing the other party, qualities that increase our power to affect their decisions, actions, and behavior.

Personal power can also be enriched by spiritual formation. If we approach the other party with the face of a Franciscan and recognize the divine within them, their heart softens and they become open to dialogue, which gives rise to power that affects their decisions. I have added spiritual power to the list of categories later in the chapter, as this form of personal power deserves special focus.

REFERENT POWER derives its strength from a party's reference to an external standard or source of power. When a party refers to cultural standards of behavior, public policy, public opinion, or the laws of a state, nation, or international community, they are using referent power. In essence, with referent power one references a social or collective benchmark that guides decisions, actions, and behavior. The benchmark sets forth what *should* be done or what *should not* be done.

Referent power relies on agreement among the parties regarding the applicability of objective benchmarks. The law, for example, provides standards regarding right and wrong as seen through the eyes of society. Other less formal benchmarks tell us what a culture deems acceptable or unacceptable. The founder of a religious order such as Francis may put forth rules or admonitions that assist members to govern their affairs. These rules become benchmarks to which members refer. To the extent people agree that these collective benchmarks are fair and apply to the situation at hand they can be used as effective guides for decisions, actions, and behavior.

If the parties disagree with regard to the validity of laws, standards, or rules (or dispute their applicability to the instant case) referent power diminishes. It is not always necessary, however, for the other party to agree with the validity of the benchmarks *if* third-party enforcement exists – in other words, though the other party may not respect the law the court retains the power to enforce rulings and verdicts.

Likewise, a business can enforce its rules by firing non-cooperative employees or a religious organization may excommunicate those who violate its tenets. In many cases third-party enforcement gives teeth to referent power – the threat of enforcement affects decisions, actions, and behavior.

On the other hand, if a party does not respect a law, standard, ethic, or guideline, it is unlikely the referred power will factor into the *mediated* solution, except as a consequence that will accrue if the matter is returned to the court (tribunal, committee, council of elders, court of public opinion, etc.). During mediation the other party must accept the referent benchmark if it is to exert power over their decisions and actions.

In mediation parties commonly refer to the law, using expected litigation outcomes as referent means of affecting decisions, actions, and behavior. They predict how a jury or judge will decide the case, painting a picture of how the referred power will dictate consequences. However, if the other party's attorneys present different predictions regarding the trial outcome, or if they argue the law cited does not apply to the particular case, the law's referent power is diminished.

This same dynamic operates in other settings – parties debate how the referenced source of power will view the matter and how they will act to enforce rules, guidelines, or the founder's admonitions. For this reason the party that invokes referent power in mediation must take into account how the opposing party will view the source of referred power – how do they imagine the source of referred power, for example a judge, will view the issues.

Our acceptance of referent power varies considerably from situation to situation. Though the values guiding a small group may not be stated with the precision of legal codes, they may possess more power as a referent standard. Members of the group may agree more strongly on the validity of their moral standards than on the validity of civil law.

For example, friars in the Franciscan Order may consider the admonitions of St. Francis carry more weight than civil standards. They may engage in civil disobedience that protests war and violates civil law; they may place Gospel-inspired peacemaking above the law of the land as a standard to be followed. Likewise, a marriage may be based on values that are not reflected in the law, and when those values are violated the relationship ends. For this reason we find causes for dissolution of a marriage are not based on transgressions of civil law; dissolution is motivated by transgressions against the specific values and ethics accepted in the relationship. Such values and ethics may vary from relationship to relationship.

One cannot assume an authority will serve a referent function in all conflicts. For example, Party A may threaten Party B, promising to expose B's actions to the local Parent Teacher Association (PTA), causing B to lose the PTA's goodwill. This argument has power only if B has a son or daughter attending that school. If B is the head of a multinational corporation and has no children at the school, the sanction of the local PTA is not likely to be of concern – the reference lacks power.

Yet another example would be a situation where one party considers Biblical texts a valid reference but the opposing party, an atheist, dismisses their validity offhand. Because parties tend to attribute power to referred sources to differing degrees it is important for us to research the manner in which the other party attributes power to a source we intend to reference. Our use of referent power is contingent on the referred source being valid in the eyes of the other party or in the eyes of a third party who has the power to make binding and enforceable decisions.

When members agree to the values and rules of a group they acknowledge, directly or indirectly, the power of that group to punish their transgressions. But, at other times, we need to be cautious regarding the unintended consequences of referent power.

A party to a conflict might presume he possesses the power to coerce his opponent to accede to his wishes. In the process of mediation, however, the coercive party might realize his coercion will meet with disfavor if a group he values learns of his coercion – the group might ostracize him. He may recognize the gains he hoped to achieve through coercive measures are far outweighed by losses he will incur as a result of the group's disapproval. Faced with significant referent power, he must show respect to his opponent who previously appeared powerless. The example illustrates the power shifts that occur once the mediation is engaged. In the absence of mediation a power struggle may have ensued that would have resulted in adverse consequences to both parties.

When it comes to social justice issues we often find referent power at work in high profile cases. For example, international opinion regarding human rights violations may force a dictator to moderate his tyranny. The dictator may recognize that the threat from adverse international opinion may include embargos and trade boycotts, military or police actions, or prosecution before an international court. The potential adverse consequences provide his domestic enemies with referent power – he must restrain his actions in light of the potential response of powerful third parties.

A historical example of referent power is the pressure the international community brought to bear on South Africa's apartheid government. Groups dedicated to social justice, such as *Pace e Bene*, may organize public protests in an attempt to build referent power from a grassroots base.[4] Thus, as we assess referent power in our personal situation, we consider the broader connections we may call upon and we consider the ways in which we might generate referent power.

Borrowing power from a referred source is a viable option in the resolution of conflict, but one that must be pursued with skill. On the one hand, with research, you may be able to discover sources of referent power that will give your opponent pause. On the other hand, if you mistakenly believe your opponent will capitulate simply because you cite a statute, rule, or standard that you believe settles the case, you may be surprised to find your assertion has little actual power. In order to be effective you must find a referent power that is valid for all involved.

It is worth noting that referent power has a dark side – the use of peer group pressure to enforce anti-social behavior, as in gangs that specialize in violent coercion. Members face internal sanctions for failure to adhere to codes that demand violent persecution of outsiders. This turns referent power from a positive to a negative. Mediation in such a situation would involve engaging members in a prolonged analysis of their real interests, followed by discussion of long-term consequences that arise from coercive or violent approaches to satisfying those interests. Often the inability to think in a long-term, cause-and-effect manner leads to self-defeating actions and behavior.

While it has been argued that we should not try to change a party's values and beliefs in mediation, situations exist in which nothing short of a change of values and beliefs will make a long-term difference in resolving conflict. However, there is a primary difference between mediation and other approaches, a difference that arises from mediation's focus on party self-determinism. We start with an acceptance of the party's beliefs as they are and then we work toward a change in values, a change initiated and driven *by the party*.

We do not force a change of values from the outside. A mediator allows change to arise from within. This takes place in a process of examining consequences during creative problem solving.

The party looks closely at how their actions solve a problem or make it worse. Then they assign value to the outcomes. Mediation allows the party to analyze their values and beliefs within the context immediate choices and actions. This is accomplished during the creative problem-solving phase when values are tied to practical outcomes that satisfy interests. If values are self-defeating they are naturally discarded. It may turn out that a value or worldview was only an abstract thought, and had never been investigated in terms of real-world application.

In gangs, members most likely have not taken the time to assess the values they are honoring, implicitly or explicitly. Their life experience may not have allowed them to become aware that they *can* make choices and that they *can* exert their will in pursuit of values that meet deeper needs and interests. In this situation, the mediator assists in stripping away false assumptions that hold uninspected beliefs in place. They strip away negative referent power by inspecting the source of referred power (for example, gang leaders) more closely. Analysis of common-sense consequences diminishes the negative referent power, as the consequences typically fail to satisfy interests.

As you assess your personal conflict situation take the time to study the nuanced web of referent power that exists implicitly and increase your ability to use power by surfacing and recognizing power at your disposal.

EXPERT POWER involves the use of information, skills, and knowledge to influence decisions, actions, or behavior.[5] The expertise may be your own or it may be borrowed or hired from outside sources, such as expert witness testimony or reference to documented expertise in the form of reports or professional papers.

Expert power, like referent power, depends to a large extent on establishing agreement with regard to the validity of the expertise. How credible is the expert? If both parties agree the expert's views are valid then that knowledge or expertise has the power to affect their decisions. The recognized expert, whether it is you or an outsider, will be seen as knowing how things really are. This provides a basis for decision making.

As an example, imagine a man driving a car toward a precipice. A world-recognized expert in the back seat provides him with information on the braking distance for that make of car. Given the possibility the driver might plummet off the cliff if he makes a mistake, the driver listens to the expert and applies the brakes in a timely fashion. The expert demonstrates the power to affect the decisions, actions, and behavior of the driver based on his ability to predict consequences. When a party must understand the consequences of their actions or suffer harm they will listen to an expert known for accurately predicting future outcomes.

For example, if the mediator is a former trial judge who spent decades on the bench his prediction that a party will experience an adverse outcome at trial carries weight. The party will think twice before abandoning the conciliatory process and returning to litigation. The power of an expert lies in his or her ability to estimate the consequences of specific decisions, actions, or behaviors.

An expert may also be able to offer an opinion on what will be accepted as the truth when two or more parties argue over the validity of contested evidence. The expert serves as a *reality check* when parties need to arrive at a shared view of reality in order to make decisions. The expert provides an outside view that may be accepted as objective, allowing the parties to move forward.

Convincing the other party that your personal expertise is valid is more difficult. Nonetheless, your expertise may carry weight when it comes to predicting consequences. You might say, "I've been there before and I can assure you that if you do X the result will be Y." The other party may be persuaded by the manner in which you present your knowledge and may move closer to you in terms of the range of solutions considered.

For example, in a conflict over medical treatment that resulted in adverse side effects – a conflict that has the potential to turn into a medical malpractice case – the patient may defer to the doctor if the doctor carefully and convincingly explains that the medical result in this particular instance, though adverse, is within the range of possible outcomes. In other words, there is no way to avoid some risk. The doctor may advise the patient that the adverse outcome can be mitigated with subsequent treatment, which he is willing to oversee.

When the doctor appears to be respectful and caring, and offers an apology for harm done, his expertise may have sufficient power to affect the decisions, actions, and behavior of the patient. The patient may believe that the doctor knows what he is doing and may recognize that risks cannot be totally eliminated, no matter how competent the physician. Even in this very difficult situation a party (the doctor) may have personal expertise power, regardless of the assumption that past failure will invalidate that power.

There are other applications of expert power. When you have valuable knowledge or skills you may exchange such expertise as part of a negotiated solution. Imagine a conflict arises between you and your department manager. You strongly object to her management style, which you perceive to be destroying productivity and morale. As a solution you offer to manage your section of the department on her behalf, relying on your expertise with the day-to-day operations. You offer to lighten the manager's workload in return for increased autonomy. Once she assigns you the responsibility the conflict arising from her management style abates. Your expertise buys you the autonomy needed to resolve the conflict and improves your working conditions.

Self-knowledge (being an expert on self), though less obvious, should be considered a source of power. If you increase knowledge of your heart, you increase your ability to make clear decisions. A person who lacks self-knowledge waffles in the face of opposition or adversity. A person who has not become an expert on their interests finds it difficult to make decisions. They appear weak and ineffective and may sacrifice their interests when faced with a self-confident opponent with an aura of self-aware power.

The special type of self-knowledge that arises from spiritual formation plays a largely overlooked role. Knowledge of spiritual self arises from prayer, contemplation, meditation or other intense inner work that unveils one's true nature and brings one into relationship with the divine. This type of expert power, arising from deep spiritual knowledge, can be seen in the lives of Pope John Paul II, Mahatma Gandhi, Nelson Mandela, Martin Luther King, the Dalai Lama and other spiritual leaders. This special type of expert power, spiritual power, warrants its own category (discussed later in this chapter).

As you approach mediation take time to consider the expertise you bring to the process – either your own expertise or expertise you will need to borrow or hire. Assess the role expert power will play in resolving the conflict and assess what you might need to do to increase the expert power you will bring to the table.

RESOURCE POWER brings superior resources, such as time and money, to bear on the outcome of the conflict. Resource power arises from assets, tangible and intangible, that you can marshal for the purpose of resolving the conflict.

Conflict resolution that relies on expensive procedures, such as a court trial, requires adequate resources. The justice system is often criticized for being weighted against parties who lack deep pockets, as the procedural sophistication of litigation favors those with the significant financial resources required to wage legal battle. Such resource power imbalance affects outcomes: a party with abundant resources may intentionally litigate the other party into bankruptcy. One party may concede defeat when they no longer possess sufficient resources for their defense.

These imbalances lead to abuse of power and can damage the public perception of the legal system. Unequal resource power can lead to injustice and a pervasive perception that the system is unfairly rigged. The situation is worse in countries where wealthy litigants influence a corrupt judiciary. These conditions may lead the resource-limited party to turn to extra-legal methods of conflict resolution. They may turn to "self-help" options that turn violent.

When the imbalance in resources brings about a perception that institutional or systemic injustice exists the use of force and violence takes shape as a solution to a power imbalance. Thus, when a conflict concerns social injustice, the need to remedy power imbalance is a frequent and heated topic. Issues regarding the allocation of resources become contentious.

Mediation is a relatively inexpensive and viable alternative to litigation and thus can help balance resource power. However, the fact that mediation often balances resource power may, on occasion, lead the party with greater resources to avoid the process. The party with resource power fears they will lose the advantage they enjoy; they fear they will lose their ability to mount a legal offensive the other side cannot afford to defend.

Recognizing the tendency of the powerful party to avoid mediation in order to preserve an imbalance in resource power, a less well-funded party may turn to other types of power. For example, a less well-funded party may use referent power in the form of a negative public relations campaign designed to offset their resource power deficit. The well-funded party – who may rely on public goodwill to maintain wealth (resource power) – may be convinced to engage in a fair process by this use of referent power. In this manner a power imbalance is remedied by the use of an alternate type of power. When social activists take up the cause of the poor in cases of social injustice, they are attempting to use alternative power to remedy a resource power imbalance.

Resource power can also become a critical negotiation tool. It may play a positive role when resources are used to underwrite a settlement – the party with superior resource power may allow the opposing party to contribute other types of value to the settlement or may allow the opposing party adequate time to remedy shortfalls. For example, a lender or landlord with adequate financial resources may carry a creditor or tenant who possesses personal power in the form of trustworthiness or honesty. A party with ample resources may renegotiate the terms of a broken agreement, allowing the struggling party a second chance. On more than one occasion I have seen resource power allow a party to demonstrate compassion they would not have been able to show if they lacked resources.

In another example, a business relationship gone sour may be reconciled when a financier provides a new round of funding in return for an increased share of the business (exchange power), or when management is able to demonstrate expert power that assures a profitable future. Thus, using resource power in a positive manner, parties may move the negotiation past impasse.

On the other hand, most of us are familiar with the coercive manner in which resource power may be exerted. In a coercive use of resource power one party may promise to use resources to bankrupt or destroy the other party. Or the party with resource power may hold an inflexible position long enough to force the other party to capitulate and meet their terms.

In the dispute between Francis and his father, Pietro used resource power to demand obedience from Francis. He protested that he owned the clothes on Francis' back and demanded obedience in exchange.[6] Francis responds with a unique gesture: he disrobes on the spot. In one dramatic gesture his father's resource power evaporated. The father still had resources but those resources had no power to affect Francis' decision. Perhaps this abuse of resource power was the lesson that led Francis to a vow of poverty. It was not that Francis loved being without resources but rather he was led to a vow of poverty by his insight into how resources can be used to control our will and force our attention onto matters secondary to our spiritual life.

In some instances the dynamic is reversed and the party with fewer resources gains power to determine the actions of the party with superior resources. Take a case in which the party with fewer resources has damaged the more resourceful party and owes restitution, but lack of resources leaves them unable to pay and leaves the damaged party with little hope of being made whole.

In this scenario the party with resources faces a loss and the lack of resources becomes a source of power, although a negative power. Resolution may depend on an ability to creatively design other means of restitution, meaning the party lacking resources may need to satisfy the interests of the harmed party by using other types of exchange.

The allocation of resources is often the focus of the negotiation stage of mediation. Anticipating the importance of this aspect of the conflict resolution process, a party will want to complete a thorough assessment of resources they can bring to the table in order to resolve the dispute. They will also want to anticipate how the other party will use their resources in pursuit of reconciliation.

EXCHANGE POWER arises from the ability to trade or swap one thing for another in order to affect decisions, actions, or behavior. While negotiation may be a common skill for business executives, salespeople, or attorneys, for many of us the creative give-and-take of negotiating may be foreign and even threatening. We rarely practice the skills required to trade, swap, or exchange one valuable for another and this leaves us wary that another will take advantage of us. To offset this deficit a party may need to enlist the services of a lawyer or they may wish to study negotiation.

A mediator trained in negotiation will guide the process of finding a creative exchange. Nonetheless the mediator does not represent either party and cannot ethically negotiate with one party on behalf of the other. Thus, you may wish to seriously consider how you will bring exchange power to the process. Will you need assistance or will you be able to represent yourself?

The process of exploring mutual needs and discovering ways to exchange one value for another does not take place in the heat of a typical conflict. In order for exchange to occur there must be a degree of safety and hope. Exchange power may depend on procedural power to set the stage for an orderly and predictable process of trading value for value. This is one example of how different types of power may be combined; it is an example of how one type of power may depend upon the use of another type of power to set the stage.

It helps to conceptualize our ability to exchange with others as a power that allows us to affect the decisions, actions, and behavior of the other party. In many cases we do not recognize the value we possess that the other party needs. When we sit on the same side of the table and explore creative formulas for meeting our mutual needs, we often become aware, for the first time, of our potential exchange power.

In the previous chapter we worked on identifying our needs and interests and anticipating the needs and interests of the other party. Exchange power depends on the completion of such an in-depth inventory and analysis. The analysis should precede meeting with the other party.

Exchange power often depends on our trust in the medium of exchange. When we trust the currency – when we trust our money will be accepted in payment for goods and services – it is easier to utilize exchange power. When confidence in financial instruments wanes, it becomes more difficult to exercise exchange power. In developed societies with sophisticated means of exchange, the exchange power generated is evident in the emergence of a prosperous economy. When sophisticated mediums of exchange are compromised by betrayal of trust and fraud, exchange power is drastically diminished and the economy grinds to a halt, as though someone pulled the plug on a power generator.

In conflict resolution exchange power is often constrained by prior breaches of trust that must be repaired. So as you consider exchange power, assess the existing degree of trust between you and the other party.

In a later chapter we take a closer look at the negotiating process and the use of exchange power, but at this point assess whether or not the potential for exchange exists. Do not forget to include intangibles.

REWARD POWER employs a reward to influence the other party. O'Donnell notes, "It is usually granted conditionally, something is given if and only if a particular action, decision, or behavior is accomplished, made or exhibited by the other party."[7] He also notes that reward power is limited by two factors: the contingent nature of a reward makes it necessary to continually monitor performance and there is a risk the rewarded party will quickly become satiated and desire additional rewards, which can become costly.[8]

A reward is a special type of exchange, an extra value that goes beyond the bounds of a reasonable exchange, given for performance beyond the normal. It is an inducement that is not deserved on purely economic grounds but which reflects increased desire on the part of one party to bring about a decision, action, or behavior on the part of the other party.

The party offering the reward may not wish to pay the amount the other party demands, unless the other party performs beyond expectation. In this way, when the parties have reached a stalemate over the issue of exchange a reward, contingent on exemplary performance, can be used to break the impasse.

A reward can also represent a show of respect contingent on a party earning that respect by their subsequent actions. It may include a preliminary indication of skepticism regarding their performance or motivation. The reward may even be offered as an inducement to overcome a historical lack of performance. It may acknowledge that a party faces personal challenges with regard to the additional effort needed to overcome limitations. For example, someone with a substance abuse problem may be rewarded for overcoming addiction. The challenge they face is acknowledged with a reward for success. As in this example, the link between respect and reward is often strong.

Or a reward may simply acknowledge one party is about to do something beyond the ordinary – for example, delivering an order in a shorter time period than normal. The reward can be the respectful acknowledgment of challenges the other party faces in meeting our terms. It can be a way of acknowledging that our demands are tough to satisfy, while signaling we do not intend to take advantage of the other party by ignoring the additional effort required to meet our needs.

As noted at the outset reward power is useful, but caution is warranted. In addition to the drawbacks mentioned there is the potential the party to whom the reward is offered may consider the gesture disrespectful. They may consider the extra encouragement reflects a low estimation of their motivation. They may feel the party offering a reward has little faith in their motivation and is using the inducement to bypass their indolence. To avoid this problem the motivation for providing the reward should be clearly explained in a positive frame.

As you consider your use of reward power list the possible rewards you might give or receive that would make a difference in resolving the conflict.

HIERARCHICAL POWER uses senior position or superior status to influence the decisions, actions, and behavior of those holding subordinate positions or inferior status.

Hierarchal power can be abused easily given the inherent imbalance. Its use requires considerable skill, as it is easy to inadvertently render the other party powerless, leading to resentment. When resentment builds those lacking power seek covert means of exerting their will.

The naïve manager or executive may fail to discover hard-to-detect sabotage ruining his best plans and may never attribute the downturn in business or productivity to his abuse of hierarchal power. Taking this to the extreme, tyrants who use hierarchal power indiscriminately end up having to use more and more force to protect their position. They (correctly) imagine that those over whom they exert power have become covert enemies and assassins looking for any opportunity to destroy them. They do not realize that when they fail to curb their own abuse of hierarchal power or fail to curtail abuses committed by lieutenants, they are the engineers of their own demise.

Not all use of hierarchal power, however, is abusive or laced with danger. There are legitimate, practical reasons to operate with hierarchal structures. An organization with a clear command structure is often most efficient; the structure avoids confusion that results when leadership is diffuse and unclear.

However, when the use of hierarchal power exceeds its utility and when it is abused, leaving subordinates feeling powerless, trouble results. The purpose and utility of the hierarchal structure must dictate limits that curb misuse of position and status. Tailoring position and status to the organization's purpose helps prevent abuse of power. When leaders expand their power beyond what is needed to enhance the functioning of the group they stray into abuse of power.

Conflicts regarding hierarchal power are frequent, thus we find this topic is common in mediation, particularly when the relationship between the parties is expected to continue. A delicate balancing act is required: a party must show respect for status and position yet not abandon their own needs. The party with less power must use caution as they muster other types of power to bear on the negotiation. At the same time they attempt to remedy the power imbalance they must not cause Face Loss for the party with superior position or status. On both sides of the table there is a need to maintain respect and honor Face.

Likewise, the party with superior hierarchal power must not use position or status in a way that aborts the process. If the higher status party does not see the process to an end the less powerful party leaves harboring resentment that will manifest as covert non-compliance. The lower status person who is discouraged will resort to non-productive and counter-productive behavior or even violence.

One effective way to navigate this tightrope is to focus strictly on respective interests. The mediator facilitates a discussion of how the lower status individual can achieve satisfaction while the higher status party also satisfies their interests, all within the context of organizational purposes and goals. This strict adherence to interest-based negotiation, set within the context of the organization's goals, undercuts liabilities that arise in mixed-status negotiating. Nonetheless, skill is required to avoid triggering affronts to status or position – or one will push parties into the oppositional embrace of conflict.

In other cases, the primary focus may be on remedying abuse of hierarchal power. Misuse of position or status may have pushed an organization to the brink of ruin, necessitating an intervention that explores creative ways for parties to satisfy their needs within new organizational structures. Given the previous organization structure resulted in abuse, the parties explore how to restructure the hierarchy so needs are met and abuse is discouraged.

There are times when the higher status person assumes those with less power naturally resent his status and assumes they will rebel against authority regardless of his actions. He assumes people are naturally rebellious and undisciplined. When a mediator assesses the conflict he may learn that the person with less power actually appreciates the hierarchal structure. They prefer a leader who guides the ship but they resent power being used to rob them of self-respect, dignity, and opportunity. In such cases, the personal style of the individual with position or status may become the central issue of the negotiation.

When the validity of position and status are challenged conflict resolution focuses on the breakdown in consensus regarding hierarchal power. While hierarchal power may seem to rest entirely with the person who possesses status and position it also depends on the willingness of others to grant allegiance to the status or position. If a lesser status person does not consider the position or status of the senior party valid they may fail to comply and may challenge authority. This suggests hierarchal power depends, at least in part, on the perception that the higher status person has earned his position or status. Power must be deserved. Status must be earned. When this is not the case conflict results and the validity of hierarchal power must be reappraised and deficits remedied.

The subject of how to grant and maintain status, position, and hierarchal power consumes many of the best organizational minds. Opinion varies on how to best structure and operate a company (country, city, or household) and the topic of how to best govern collective efforts is a source of endless speculation. Thus one will encounter a great variety of views and circumstances when addressing conflict arising from organizational hierarchies.

Cultural differences also make a difference. The culture of Google varies considerably from the culture of IBM; the culture of an organization in India varies from the culture of an organization in Brazil. Differences regarding "how we organize" are not confined to the business world: the ways we manage status and position vary throughout all segments of society. The hierarchal organization of church leaders varies from denomination to denomination, church to church, parish to parish. Bishops vary from diocese to diocese. Even families vary in the manner in which they attribute status and decision power to their members.

The status attributed by high school students to one another provides a complex example of the pervasive role hierarchal power plays in all human endeavors. When we fine-tune our perception and appreciation of power that is based on status or position we find hierarchal power plays a role in most relationships. The role may be subtle or unacknowledged but it is always present.

In your assessment explore how position and status function in your conflict setting: How is power being abused by self or others? How do your efforts mesh with the hierarchal structure? What must be remedied regarding position or status? How does a lack of clear lines of authority create confusion and conflict? How does one manage issues regarding respect and disrespect? How does the culture view power imbalance in the workplace, government, home, or other setting? The resolution process will proceed more smoothly with an evaluation of these variables in hand, as the conversation will zero in on the precise problems giving rise to conflict.

PUNISHMENT POWER may involve brute force used to constrain, confine, imprison, injure, or destroy another party. It may involve using a third-party power, such as the police, to exact punishment. Or punishment may be more subtle: it may involve simply blocking fulfillment of the other party's desires. It may involve withholding or denying access to something valuable.

Punishment power frequently functions in conjunction with other powers. Examples of mixing categories include a boss turning hierarchal power into punishment power when he fires an employee; a party with resource power punishing the other party financially with a protracted and costly legal battle; a party who possesses personal power using public scorn and disrespect to punish another party with embarrassment or exclusion; or a party with referent power censoring another party causing them to be excluded from a group.

Punishment power may involve the use of physical power to inflict retribution through injury or pain. It can easily veer into the coercive and violent realm we hope to avoid in mediation but which nonetheless plays a role in conflict. The mediator, as an educator, facilitates understanding of the adverse consequences that may accompany the use of physical force to punish another. Adverse consequences include a destructive backlash. O'Donnell notes punishment power ... is very costly to the one who uses it, as it most often causes resentment and revenge.[9] The use of punishment may foreclose any future possibility of a negotiated resolution. Therefore, when possible, parties keep hope alive by avoiding the use of punishment power.

One characteristic of punishment power is the desperation that drives one person to punish another. The party using punishment typically has failed to control the decisions, actions, or behavior of the other person through other means and thus resorts to punishment as a last-ditch act of desperation. A deficit of other types of power leads a party to use punishment. For example, lacking other types of power, a bully resorts to brute force to punish those who cross him.

Wars often begin with one party's frustration over their inability to bring about change, compliance, or agreement, which gives rise to a desire to severely punish the enemy. In his desperate acts of violence the terrorist attests to his lack of power. The criminal justice system reflects at least some measure of societal desperation: the criminal, it appears, will not respond to other types of power, provoking punishment as a last resort. When we find the use of brute force to punish it pays to analyze prior failed attempts to use other types of powers to bring about peaceful co-existence.

Paradoxically, a party's refusal to *respond* to other types of power may arise out of their inability to *use* those other types of power. It seems a party must be able to exert power over others in order to respect that same power when it is applied to them. The person may (unconsciously) hold the position that if I cannot use the law to curtail the unwanted behavior of others, I should not allow the law to curtail *my* actions. This presents a challenge for the mediator: a party unable to use subtle types of power to satisfy their interests may not respond when the other party attempts to use those subtle powers. The mediator may have to point out subtle powers and explain how they might be used.

A mediator may also help remedy past upsets regarding the misuse of punishment power. A party may need to explore past uses of power and may need assistance in learning to trust more subtle forms of power, including powers they possess of which they have been previously unaware.

SPIRITUAL POWER draws on our divine essence. This power may come during prayer. It signals the presence of the Holy Spirit. It manifests as unconditional love, compassion, and divine understanding. This is the power realized by contemplative mystics – it is not the power of crusaders charging into battle. It is power that arises out of communion with the divine in which we discover our true self, the image of God within.

Here we find the power Francis wielded: power developed through prayer, meditation, and holy living. When we engage another person with our spiritual heart, when we come together in the I-Thou relationship, when we encounter the likeness of God in the other, when we meet each other in a spirit of loving-kindness and compassion, when we accept the presence of the Holy Spirit, we gain the spiritual power needed to profoundly touch another soul.

We travel beyond communication to communion, joining God-consciousness with God-consciousness, unleashing a power of which many remain unaware. We dive far below the line to unearth our most profound needs while being lifted up in divine communion. Inspecting our deepest needs leads to true satisfaction. Spiritual power, more than any other power, places us at cause over the decisions, actions, beliefs, and behavior of the other party. The tremendous impact of spiritual power leads us to recognize unconditional love is the most powerful force in the universe.

The spiritually transformative approach to conflict resolution depends on the presence of spiritual power. While we continue to use other types of power we recognize spiritual power provides the greatest satisfaction, the most durable outcomes, and the inner transformation required to resolve our current conflict. It fuels the transformation that allows us to become peacemakers.

One path to spiritual power is contemplative prayer. This is not an intellectual pursuit or the pursuit of mere experience. "Contemplation is not an experience to be gained but an eternal identity to be realized."[10] Contemplative prayer has to do with our knowing Who We Are when we share in the divine nature, the image of God. This concept is explored in "Merton's critically important yet little-appreciated notion *of the true self in God* as opposed to *the false self of egocentric desires.* The task before us is a prayerful asking of Who Am I, not relative to this or that aspect of my being, but rather whom am I *ultimately* before God?"[11]

When we acknowledge this power in the conflict resolution process we tap ontological roots and gain ineffable knowledge of our true essence. We arrive at the Mount to hear the Sermon. We let go of false selves. "This letting go in the moral order is the living out of the Beatitudes."[12] It is "an emptying out of the contents of awareness so that one becomes oneself an empty vessel, a broken vessel, a void that lies open before God and finds itself filled with God's own life. This gift of God is revealed to be the ground and root of our very existence. It is our own true self."[13] It is this true self that wields spiritual power, the power of unconditional love, a power that does not seek to dominate or coerce but rather to uplift.

In contemplative prayer we listen to our hearts and to the movement of the Spirit so that we might step forward into an I-Thou conversation. We leave behind the transitory and false and discover our capacity for love and compassion, we move beyond the confining borders of false self, the self-that-must-be-defended. The identity-that-must-be-protected diminishes in importance and is replaced by spiritual power that blossoms as a result of extending loving-kindness to others.

Brian Cox begins his engagements in faith-based diplomacy by sitting down with a participant for a spiritual conversation, a conversation that addresses matters of the heart.[14] This initial conversation provides an opportunity for a mediator (or diplomat) and the parties to share spiritual concerns, those things that matter most deeply to them. One might characterize this initial meeting as an opportunity to navigate the social landscape in order to find the fertile ground where an I-Thou relationship can take root. In such conversations fleeting moments of silence develop, moments in which we empty our minds and allow our true self to be fully present.

Thomas Merton provides a glimpse of the fruits of contemplative stillness: "At the center of our being is a point of nothingness which is untouched by sin and by illusion, a point of pure truth, a point or spark which belongs entirely to God, which is never at our disposal, from which God disposes of our lives, which is inaccessible to the fantasies of our own mind or the brutalities of our own will. This little point of nothingness and of absolute poverty is the pure Glory of God in us."[15]

If the spiritual conversation is preceded by the work of contemplative prayer the conversation invites stillness into the room, a stillness that allows divine providence to become a factor in reconciliation. A new dimension of conflict resolution that we may not have anticipated unfolds: a dimension in which spiritual power alters the balance of power in unexpected ways.

THE POWER OF DIVINE PROVIDENCE, closely related to spiritual power, concerns the power of God to affect our affairs. You will find different descriptions and understandings of divine providence in the religious literature and in works of theology. The approach in *Taming the Wolf* relies heavily on the mystical and contemplative tradition, on the heritage of Francis and Bonaventure, and on the wisdom of contemplatives such as Thomas Merton, St. Theresa of Avila, St. John of the Cross and others. You may wish to bring your own vision of divine providence to this journey. If your view differs from that presented here, substitute your understanding as you move toward reconciliation.

The power of divine providence reigns over the spiritual kingdom, a kingdom where we unite in unconditional love birthed in moments of transcendent unity or communion with the divine. Because the power of divine providence does not rely on domination and coercion it may seem counterintuitive, puzzling, and unfamiliar. It is a power rejected outright by many who cannot conceive of how the divine could possibly affect their lives, decisions, actions, and behavior.

While the power of divine providence has the potential of being universally understood, you will not encounter an acceptance of this truth on a universal scale at this time. Nonetheless, that lack of acceptance does not present an impassable barrier as you pursue this path.

Divine providence is truly paradoxical: it is at once personal and impersonal, temporal and eternal, immediate and transcendent. The power of divine providence emerges out of communion with the divine and thus is shared power that emerges when relationship becomes unity. When we stand separated, alienated, and alone we do not have access to this power; only upon achieving divine union does divine providence play a role in our life. While we cannot claim it as our personal power it is also not wholly other than ours, as divine providence works through us. It is not a power that overwhelms with coercion but rather power arising from the movement of our free will aligning with God's will.

James Finley captured an aspect of this paradox, "If in my deepest self I am a relationship to God – by whom, in whom, and for whom I exist – and if, from where I now stand, I am in ignorance of this relationship grounded in God, then it must follow that I stand in radical alienation and disorientation from my own deepest identity."[16] When, through spiritual formation and contemplative prayer, we dispel the fog of ignorance that obscures this relationship we engage the power of divine providence. The study we undertake to alleviate our ignorance is not an intellectual or theological exercise but rather contemplation that leads to communion with God.

This power, a mirror of spiritual power, also manifests in a form we recognize as unconditional love. While there is a distinction between the soul and God, "Merton holds for a perfect unity of love that amounts to mystical identification with God. Love makes us one spirit with God."[17] These seemingly paradoxical revelations of the mystic may give us pause. Language fails when it comes to describing that which is one and not one. And yet each of has experienced at least a glimpse of the truth of this union, a glimpse that motivates us to seek deeper understanding.

In order to gain access to clues that help us understand this unspeakable, ineffable divine relationship, we may seek the practical manifestations of this union. It is in union with others we achieve union with God. It is the loving person who is a religious person. While this sounds simple, it would be a mistake to underestimate the task. While we may have experienced love in our lives, we sense we are encountering a higher form of love when we come upon a saint who has entered into communion with the divine. We wonder in awe at the scope of the unconditional love they are able to bestow, at the ways divine providence informs their lives. In Francis, for example, we find divine providence emerging from his unending devotion to achieving unity with Christ. To this day, we find God working through those who turn to Francis to better understand how to follow Christ.

At first glance, before we explore the mystery of divine providence, we might consider divine providence to be a case of referent power. We may believe that we can refer to the power of God so as to cause others to think or act as we wish. This error is worth dispelling. With divine providence we do not hold up our view of God as a power another party must respect. Rather the power of divine providence works by infusing decisions, actions, and behavior with the divine spirit of loving communion. We do not invoke or summon divine providence but rather open the door to its influence by becoming still and allowing the Holy Spirit to infuse our lives.

We do not embrace divine providence with a banner that proclaims victory but rather on bended knee with a humble heart. We invite divine providence by opening ourselves to the influence of the Holy Spirit. This may seem counterintuitive. Some will turn away due to a lack of certainty as to how they might invite this power into their life. Such turning away is an honest response for that person. As noted, in mediation the party determines the manner in which they feel comfortable seeking reconciliation. We can suggest they consider the contemplative path but they may not be ready to walk it.

Though we may be uncomfortable and uncertain and not quite ready to engage this type of power, others may consider this is most important power to acknowledge. In Brian Cox's inspiring work on faith-based diplomacy the role of divine providence in human affairs is described and addressed in a manner that warrants inclusion in our analysis.[18] He recognizes a moral grain to the universe that warrants careful consideration as we attempt to integrate the spiritual into our daily life and into our attempts to resolve conflict.[19] This moral grain is not about rules or commandments as much as a divine presence that invites our participation. Inviting into our life the power of divine providence, which eschews domination and coercion, can be the ultimate use of power in conflict resolution.

The concept of obedience comes to mind when we speak of divine providence. Most often we conceive obedience to be a response to domination and coercion but unity with the divine invites non-coercive obedience. Ilia Delio, in *Franciscan Prayer*, sheds light on this meaning, "The root of the word *obedience* (*audire*) means to listen." She continues, paraphrasing Bernard of Clairvaux: "Obedience is listening to the breath of God's Spirit in our lives."[20] When we listen closely we begin to welcome divine providence into the conflict situation. As we turn toward the divine with a listening ear the Holy Spirit informs our decisions, actions, and behavior.

Parties taking this particular approach may wish to ask, how does this conflict appear from a divine perspective? Contemplative prayer, immersion in scripture, consultation with a pastoral counselor, and listening to the movement of the Holy Spirit frequently helps us gain a new perspective on the conflict ruining our life. We may discover we possess free will that allows us to choose to meet the other party in a divine relationship, and when we are reconciled with one another we reconcile with the divine.

Those who resolve long-term conflict and achieve reconciliation discover they are transformed spiritually. In the moment they embrace one another with compassion they discover the powerful simplicity of loving-kindness. In that moment all other concerns and interests recede in importance.

Paradoxically, at the same time divine providence empowers us to resolve conflict with another, the resolution of conflict lifts us toward union with the divine. In reconciling with another person we discover a profound communion that has its roots in the divine. We discover resolution of conflict is a divine act leading us closer to union with God.

A Franciscan View

Many of the lessons we learn from the life of St. Francis concern the use of power. On numerous occasions he faced misuse of power and he responded, in his words and actions, with spiritual power and the power of divine providence.

We, too, can choose to bring these more subtle powers to bear on our conflict. Francis reminds us to prioritize our use of power. Rather than depend on old patterns and assumptions regarding power, he invites us to explore new and unexpected ways of satisfying our interests and needs. We can enrich our journey with a few examples of how Francis collided with coercive power and turned to spiritual power to resolve the conflict.

When Francis' father, Pietro, attempted to control Francis with resource power, proclaiming in front of the bishop that Francis wore garments that he, Pietro, owned, Francis showed disdain for such coercion. "When he was in front of the bishop, he neither delayed nor hesitated, but immediately took off and threw down all his clothes and returned them to his father. He did not even keep his trousers on, and he was completely stripped bare before everyone."[21]

In one brash move Francis stripped his father of the coercive power he wielded unwisely. The onlookers gathered in the courtyard discarded the misconception that resource power was unassailable. They learned that a man willing to embrace poverty could break the chains others used to imprison him.

In a similar manner he disabused his followers of the notion that position, privilege, and status provided power worth pursuing. He rejected the negative aspects of hierarchal power in the name he assigned to the order – Friars Minoritas. He signaled his wariness of those who would use status to coerce others: "Let no one be called '*prior*,' but let everyone in general be called a lesser brother. Let one wash the feet of the other."[22]

In his fourth Admonition to the brothers, he echoed this theme: "1. 'I have come *not to be served, but to serve*' says the Lord. 2. Those who have been constituted in a position over others should only glory in that superiorship in the same way as they would glory if they were deputed to assume the office of washing the feet of the brothers (John 13:1-20)."[23]

To make sure that this theme of placing restrictions on hierarchal power seeped into the Franciscan culture he returned to the topic in Admonition 19: "1. Blessed is the servant, who does not regard himself better when he is glorified and exalted by people, as when he is regarded as vile, simple, despicable, 2. because how much a person is before God, so much that person is and no more."[24] In this rejection of hierarchal power Francis begins to signal his love for the power of divine providence. In his example, we see the shift from one type of power, used to coerce and dominate, to a different power that unites with love.

Francis expressed similar reservations regarding expert power as well as punishment power, eschewing both. He turned to the mysterious, at times paradoxical, always humble, power of the Spirit and divine providence, manifest in unconditional love achieved through union with the divine. Murray Bodo expresses this sentiment: "We live and move and have our being in God who loves us with an eternal, unconditional love."[25] In this union realized in contemplative prayer, "We become instruments of God's peace when we are so permeated that we do not even think about it. We radiate peace and good will, we communicate kindness and a loving attitude because God's peace becomes flesh of our flesh."[26]

These were not merely words to Francis. In the Earlier Rule he wrote, "Let them love one another, as the Lord says: *This is my commandment: love one another as I have loved you.* Let them express the love they have for one another by their deeds, as the Apostle says, *Let us not love in word or speech, but in deed and truth.*"[27] He lived this concept. Susan Saint Sing writes, "One of the reasons I believe in Francis' credibility with his relationship or his encounter with the Holy is that he never tried to impose his beliefs on others. He simply lived the gospel and proclaimed his message."[28]

His devotion to Christ led him to seek, through contemplation and hermitage, a union with the divine that fully informed his life. "In his preaching, he proclaimed peace, saying: 'May the Lord give you peace' (Matt. 10:12; Luke 10:5), as the greeting to the people at the beginning of his sermon. As he later testified, he had learned this greeting in a revelation from the Lord."[29]

Francis would retreat to the caves in the mountains above Assisi to seek solitude as, "He had learned in prayer that the presence of the Holy Spirit for which he longed was granted more intimately to those who invoke him, the more the Holy Spirit found them withdrawn from the noise of worldly affairs."[30]

We can follow his example and embrace silence and solitude when we wish to bring spiritual power or the power of divine providence to bear on resolving our conflict. In imitation of Francis we can nurture silence that allows us to listen to the Spirit.

Once Francis discovered the grace that came during silence it appears he was never far from this divine source of power and he was always attentive: "He was accustomed not to pass over negligently any visitation of the Spirit. When it was granted, he followed it and as long as the Lord allowed, he enjoyed the sweetness offered him. When he was on a journey and felt the breathing of the divine Spirit, letting his companions go on ahead, he would stand still and render this new inspiration fruitful, *not receiving the grace in vain* (2 Cor. 6:1)."[31]

As we study Francis and explore the teachings of other contemplatives we find clues to support the assumption that through moments of union with the divine we develop the ability to use spiritual power and the power of divine providence in our journey to peace. We observe a transformation to a peaceful nature achieved in stages. As Bernard Clairvaux observed, "A man is in a state of peace when he renders good for good, as far as it lies within him to do, and wishes harm to no one. There is another kind of man who is patient; he does not render evil for evil, and he is able to bear injury. Then there is the peacemaker, who returns good for evil and is ready to do good even to someone who harms him."[32]

The preceding description sheds light on the goal of our journey to reconciliation. Francis, in Admonition 27, captured the destination we seek through our contemplation: "1. Where there is love and wisdom, there is neither fear nor ignorance. 2. Where there is patience and humility, there is neither anger nor disturbance. 3. Where there is poverty with joy, there is neither cupidity nor avarice. 4. Where there is inner quiet and meditation, there is neither care nor unsettledness. 5. Where the Lord's fear guards *his courtyard* (Luke 11:21), there the enemy has no chance to enter. 6. Where there is mercy and discernment of God's will, there is neither excessive demands or hardness of heart."[33]

Scripture

But if you are guided by the Spirit, you are not under the law. Now the works of the flesh are obvious: immorality, impurity, licentiousness, idolatry, sorcery, hatreds, rivalry, jealousy, outbursts of fury, acts of selfishness, dissensions, factions, occasions of envy, drinking bouts, orgies, and the like. I warn you, as I warned you before, that those who do such things will not inherit the kingdom of God. In contrast, the fruit of the Spirit is love, joy, peace, patience, kindness, generosity, faithfulness, gentleness, self-control. Against such there is no law. (Gal 5:18-23)

As you enter a house, wish it peace. If the house is worthy, let your peace come upon it; if not, let your peace return to you. Whoever will not receive you or listen to your words – go outside that house or town and shake the dust from your feet. (Mt 10:12-14)

As he was coming forward, the demon threw him to the ground in a convulsion; but Jesus rebuked the unclean spirit, healed the boy, and returned him to his father. (Lk 9:42)

Where do the wars and where do the conflicts among you come from? Is it not from your passions that make war within your members? You covet but do not possess. You kill and envy but you cannot obtain; you fight and wage war. You do not possess because you do not ask. You ask but do not receive, because you ask wrongly to spend it on your passions. (Jas 4:1-3)

When Pilate saw that he was not succeeding at all, but that a riot was breaking out instead, he took water and washed his hands in the sight of the crowd, saying, 'I am innocent of this man's blood. Look to it yourselves.' (Mt 27:24)

Then Peter, filled with the holy Spirit, answered them, 'Leaders of the people and elders: If we are being examined today about a good deed done to a cripple, namely, by what means he was saved, then all of you and all the people of Israel should know that it was in the name of Jesus Christ the Nazorean whom you crucified, whom God raised from the dead; in his name this man stands before you healed. (Acts 4:8-10)

CHAPTER FOURTEEN

Use of Power

Hours passed as Francis prayed. The wolf watched closely, not fully understanding what was taking place, but sensing that Francis believed he felt remorse at having caused such pain.

Mediation Principles

THE USE OF POWER – the way we affect the decisions, actions, and behavior of others – plays a central role in our ability to resolve conflict. In the last chapter we explored the types of power that might be used during the negotiation stage; we now explore further the ways we use power to achieve our aims.

The Use of Power

The manner in which we use power is often apparent in the description of that power. When using exchange power, one trades valuables; when using referent power, one refers to outside standards or collective values; when using punishment power, one punishes the other party. In addition to these obvious uses of power there are additional ways we use power that need to be considered in order for us to fully prepare to achieve resolution and reconciliation.

In your personal assessment of how you will use power to bring about the decisions, actions, or behavior you desire, consider the following descriptions. Once again, I have turned to the work of Robert O'Donnell,[1] which identifies many of these variables, to which I have added additional descriptions.

COERCE. The use of force to impose a decision, action, or behavior on the other party may be the most appealing use of power, the most direct way in which to employ self-help. Personal physical strength may be employed to force the other to act or behave as we wish, or we may employ force indirectly, relying on a third party, such as the police or the military, to use force to realize our desires.

When we talk about power often what comes to mind is this type of coercive and violent force. As described earlier, with this extreme use of power – for example, when we bomb our opponent into submission – we negate the other party's efforts, negate their self determinism, dismiss their interests, discount their humanity, and literally make nothing of them. This represents an extreme on an imaginary scale that measures the use of force.

At the same extreme end of the force continuum there are other uses of power that do not result in obliteration of the other party but which incapacitate them or push them into servitude. The use of force can render the other party unable to be who they want, unable to do what they want, or unable to have what they want. They are compelled by force to be who we want them to be, to do what we want them to do, and to have only that which we want them to have.

Examples include the use of lethal force against citizens or authorities by drug lords, extremist militias, or gangs intent on coercing behavior to satisfy their cravings. While a few of their victims are killed, the primary effort is to terrify others into submission. Another example is an illegitimate government that uses thugs to control the lives of citizens: they kill, maim, or imprison their political opposition – and thus terrorize those who might consider opposing their rule. When we think of conflict, we often think of these extreme situations in which the use of violent force plays a central role.

Such use of force has negative consequences. Though one may overwhelm the opposition in the short run, in the long run force inspires opposing force. The warlord finds himself the target of drone-operated missiles or rivals that use deadly force to usurp and supplant his power. The use of force prompts revenge. The young kid whose father was murdered by the drug lord lies in wait for decades and then strikes.

Nations that employ the threat of nuclear weapons to exact compliance eventually find themselves targeted by emerging nuclear powers. Conflicts escalate to the stage of threatened mutual annihilation. This escalating spiral of force-against-force is often what concerns us when we think of conflict. If one extrapolates the consequences of the use of brute force a picture of widespread destruction emerges. Entire civilizations crumble into barbaric conditions, their lofty aspirations, ideals, and values are buried under the rubble. The wars of the twentieth century remind us of how easily violence spirals out of control.

Negative consequences are not restricted to the scale of national or regional powers: they accrue at the personal level as well. The use of coercive and violent force – an option positioned on the self-help end of the continuum of conflict resolution – exacts a steep price. Relationships and lives are destroyed. The cost of using force is almost always prohibitive. Those wielding power as well as their victims suffer unintended adverse consequences. The family or the community turns violent and disintegrates; hardship and ruined lives become the norm.

In order to satisfy long-term interests and needs we must learn the skill of engaging power in less destructive ways. As long as our popular culture remains impoverished with simplistic tales of violent means of resolving conflict we can expect increased suffering and a disintegrating society.

In preparation for mediation, review the history of your conflict, noting times when you used force or the other party used force. If harm resulted, assess the steps that will be needed to heal wounds in order for the process to go forward. Make a plan for how you will set aside force during the mediation process. If force has been used in the past usually you will need to pay considerable attention to issues of security and safety that you will need to address.

THREATEN. We can use our power to threaten the other by expressing our intention to cause harm or bring about unwanted conditions they will suffer.

The use of a threat may appear to be a straightforward use of power that will get the job done, but it possesses significant potential liability. Once threats have been used, building a golden bridge over which parties may travel to come together becomes significantly more difficult. Threats escalate the conflict to the point where mutual destruction eventually appears to be justified, foreclosing the chance for peace.

When you issue a threat you risk the other party will issue a counter threat; tit for tat is a common response to a threat. Furthermore, when you issue a threat you harden your own position needlessly. After issuing a threat you feel a need to Protect Face by backing up your threat. Inadvertently, by issuing a threat you set up a situation that forces you to carry out the threat or accept Face Loss. Short of apologizing for the threat and accepting the other party's forgiveness, you have become trapped in an aggressive posture. When you threaten another you fabricate a barrier to your own happiness.

A more effective use of power involves using a reality check in which you discuss the consequences of the other party's actions without issuing a threat. You avoid attacking the other party with a threat, and instead calmly and rationally describe consequences that will emerge in the absence of a mutual agreement.

If the consequences you describe in a calm and logical manner appear to the other party to be a threat, you simply ask the other party how they would respond if they were in your position. "If you were trying to satisfy the interests I am trying to satisfy, what consequences might arise if your interests were blocked?" In this way you substitute a reasoned discussion of consequences. You invite the other party to join you in exploring appropriate responses to their behavior. In a detached manner you explore cause and effect relationships between their actions and your responses.

Another downside to using a threat arises when you become identified, in the eyes of the other party, with the harmful act you threatened. When a threat is issued it becomes difficult to separate the threat from the person making the threat. The focus turns from interests to people – this is the exact opposite of what we hope to bring about in principle-based negotiation.

After a threat has been issued it becomes more difficult to rewrite the shared narrative with a collaborative theme, as the narrative now includes the other party in the role of the *evil enemy who threatens us*. The threatened party has a difficult time recasting the threatening party in the role of a collaborator.

Essentially, a threat is a notice of a future consequence delivered with anger. It is an invitation to resume the oppositional embrace. When your fists are clenched it is difficult to hug another; when fists are waved, both sides pull back, ready to attack and defend. But when you assume the role of a dispassionate collaborator analyzing possible outcomes you allow the opposing party to consider you are *someone I can work with* rather than *someone who will cause me harm*.

Evaluate the threats you might have issued or the threats directed at you in this conflict. What will need to be done, if anything, to take those threats off the table while you mediate? Will there be any reason to use threats during the conciliation process, or will you refrain from making threats? How will you respond to threats?

MANIPULATE. We may also incur liability if we use our power to manipulate the other party, using unfair means to gain an advantage. In manipulation we try to satisfy our interests at the expense of the other party's interests using trickery.

The master negotiator skilled at manipulating the other party achieves his goals with little concern for the other party. Buyer beware applies when one is faced with a manipulator who employs misdirection, deception, and tricks. For example, an expert may use his expertise in a manipulative manner rather than to aid a collaborative settlement. A lawyer who drafts an agreement with provisions that intentionally work to the detriment of the other party fits in this category.

Studio executives who deceive a filmmaker by applying dubious accounting procedures when computing profit participation are found in this category. A party with hierarchal power who pulls strings for self-gain rather than for the good of the company uses manipulation. Those with position or status who use their power to reassign employees in order to silence and discredit whistleblowers depend on a manipulative use of power. You may be able to add dozens of examples of your own in which manipulation is used in tandem with a legitimate power.

There are those who see virtue in manipulation. They even blame the party they cheat for not being smart enough to catch their manipulation and duplicity. In their view, if you are unobservant and can be manipulated by their misdirection, deception, or tricks, you *deserve* an adverse outcome because you failed to protect yourself, not because their manipulation is unethical.

Those who accept this view of ethics imagine manipulation is the natural state of affairs and hold to the axiom that the most skilled manipulator deserves the spoils. In their worldview manipulation has positive value as it maximizes self-interest. This point of view is much more common than we would like to accept. Perhaps one of the most important factors to assess as one enters negotiation is whether or not one is dealing with someone who believes they have a right to use deception and manipulation.

Using manipulation to exert power and arrive at unfair agreements has drawbacks. If the relationship extends over time the manipulated party may develop hard feelings and may refuse to remain in the relationship. They sever ties and abandon the friendship. Trust disappears. In the future the manipulator will have an increasingly difficult time convincing others to enter into relationships that require trust. The manipulator limits their own future ability to use persuasion or collaboration, as the other party distrusts the manipulator and refuses to sit on the same side of the table.

If the manipulator intends to never see the manipulated party again he may consider there is little risk. This dynamic may lead manipulated parties to conclude it is best to only do business with those one knows well. This increases the value and power of social networks, which provide a firewall against the manipulator.

After a society has been the victim of manipulators for a considerable period, the general trust level plummets and its members begin to take defensive positions. It becomes much harder to engage in productive activity due to the increased need for vigilance that requires multiple layers of security. An overall downward spiral in production takes place. Families, businesses, organizations, regions, and nation-states succumb to the adverse effects of tolerated manipulation and deception. When the culture values deception and trickery, when the deceiver and manipulator become folk heroes, hard times lie ahead.

Assess the role manipulation has played in your conflict and the role it might play during negotiation. What will you need to do to investigate and verify claims or promises?

GIVE UP OR GIVE IN. We may give up or give in and thus abandon the pursuit of our interests. This may seem a counterintuitive way to exercise power, but as O'Donnell notes, when one gives in, one leaves the other party with a feeling that they owe something in return, which should be paid in the future.[2]

There are times when giving in does not produce a positive or beneficial effect: the other party takes advantage of our retreat and we walk away feeling abused. At other times, however, if we give in with the grace of true non-attachment, results may be positive, for example, when the other party feels an obligation to reciprocate later.

After we give in the other party might feel they have taken unfair advantage for which they must make amends. The time frame of this urge to make amends varies greatly. The response may be immediate: the other party may refuse to allow you to give in and may insist on making a new offer that better satisfies your needs. At times this quick reversal in their position arises out of a sudden recognition that they are about to cause unwarranted harm – and they are not ready to carry the burden of having committed an injustice.

In other cases the realization that there is a need to make amends may take years or even decades. It may have to wait until a time when the other party looks back on their affairs and arrives at a new tally of the moral or ethical balance sheet. Thus, with this use of power the one who gives in must be patient, seeking equity and justice in the long term.

The natural tendency for us to want what we cannot have and reject what we can have plays a critical role in the give up or give in use of power. The other party may be willing to fight with you as long as you passionately pursue your interests and they are able to deny satisfaction. Solely because you want something they oppose you. Once you stop pursuing your interests, once you offer no resistance, they may suddenly feel compelled to reverse direction and help you satisfy your interests.

This can be observed when children fight over a toy. When one child finally walks away from the contested toy, the other child often tries to share the toy they previously withheld. They practically force the toy they hoarded on the other child. There is a dramatic reversal in the pattern. This is part of the reason the give up or give in use of power proves effective.

Assess whether giving up or giving in can meet your strategic needs. Where have you focused your resistance? What might happen if your resistance suddenly disappeared?

DEFER. Our use of power can include going to a third party for a decision the other party will be forced to accept. This parallels referent power as it is an appeal to a higher authority such as the courts. One uses resources, expertise, status or position to enlist a powerful authority to play a judicial role. This is similar enough to referent power that we will not discuss it further here.

EMPOWER. We can entrust the decision to the other party by choosing not to use our power.[3] In this approach we extend trust to the other party. This differs slightly from giving up as we remain engaged in the process and grant power over the outcome to the other party. We make a gift of power to the other party. We don't walk away. We give the other party something valuable – the power to make the decision.

This approach – holding our power in abeyance while trusting the power of the other party – may seem counterintuitive. How do we use our power by not using it? This simple idea – allow the other party to make the decision – is similar to *turn the other cheek*, a profound but extremely difficult technique to apply. We are putting ourselves in the other's hands after releasing our resistance to their efforts, intentions, or desires. This creates a dramatic shift away from the oppositional embrace in which we push or pull against one another.

Entrusting the decision to the other party demonstrates unconditional love by granting them total respect and autonomy in their decision-making. In essence, you convey respect and love by trusting the other to use power. In many cases a conflict hangs up over the use of power, over who decides the outcome. A classic component of conflict is the power struggle over who has the right to dictate what happens. Each party demands the right to determine outcomes and conditions – they battle over who gets to determine future reality.

In the resolution process the power struggle may subside, at least temporarily, with the introduction of the idea that parties will collaborate. Unfortunately, the power struggle often continues at a covert level. Before progress can be made parties must achieve a willingness to temporarily relax control. When one party ends the struggle by entrusting the other party to make the decision considerable forward momentum results.

One might assume that giving the other party the power to make the decision would result in one's interests being blunted, but this is not necessarily the case. The result may be adverse if one accommodates out of apathy or fear or a compulsive need to play victim. The result can be surprisingly positive if one accommodates from a position of strength, and if one releases rigid attachment to being in control. When you entrust the decision to the other party they feel respected may feel a reciprocal desire to meet your interests, even if they don't understand the impulse.

When we attempt to exert power over the outcome we often find the interaction locks up in the oppositional embrace. When we detach the embrace is released. Up to this point the other party may suspect you are not really ready to collaborate. Only when you relinquish power do they trust your intentions. This approach may seem paradoxical – in order to achieve your goals you let go of your goals – but there is ample evidence to support the validity of this approach.

When we consider St. Francis' vow of poverty in the context of the use of power we recognize his vow involved more than meets the eye at first glance. His vow was not an expression of a love for deprivation but rather a deeper understanding of Christ's teachings. He came to know that we gain what we really need (the spiritual kingdom) by ceasing to cling to possessions with no inherent value.

The compulsion to control others may be a "possession" we need to release. When we release our desire to dominate or coerce we often find the other party no longer seeks to force their decision or their control on us. A new level of mutual respect allows for collaboration. While Francis' poverty and lack of attachment may seem terribly mysterious, particularly within the framework of our present culture – which hammers home the virtues of possession, control, and defense of property – such lack of attachment may give us the ability to entrust power to the other party, which can be remarkably rewarding.

Consider what aspects of the negotiated outcome you might entrust to the other party. Consider how you might be clinging to control you no longer need to exert. How might you turn the other cheek in a show of non-resistance?

INFLUENCE. We can influence another without using overt force with indirect means that call upon subtle techniques to affect the decisions, actions, and behavior of others.[4]

Influence is considered a sufficiently vital tool in mediation that one school of mediators specializes exclusively in the study of influence taught by Robert Cialdini.[5] Drawing upon research in social psychology Cialdini explains the vital role played by influence variables – factors such as reciprocation, commitment and consistency, social proofs, liking, authority, scarcity, and automaticity. If you do not make your living influencing others, if you are not in a selling profession, Cialdini's work can provide you with the intellectual framework needed for negotiation. If you feel awkward or unprepared to negotiate on your own behalf this introduction to influence is worth acquiring.

In some instances influence may accrue from position or status, at other times it may arise through resource or expert power, but the *ability* to use influence extends beyond the presence of these forms of power. Influence calls upon intangible relationship skills.

Parties who come to the table with hierarchal, resource, or expert power may squander those powers through inept handling of influence variables. They may be unaware of the subtle (and sometimes deceptive) techniques of influence they might use to impact the decisions of the other party. They may be unaware of the techniques the other party uses to affect their decisions.

A good example is Francis' father, Pietro, who possessed influence within the town of Assisi, but who misused his power and failed to anticipate Francis' response to his display of authority. Pietro failed to understand how to use his paternal authority when faced with the influence Christ had on Francis. He failed to understand the persuasive power of liking and the power of reciprocity that would have made possible a more productive interaction with Francis. He failed to recognize Francis' commitment to live a life of devotion to Christ, in imitation of Christ. He failed to grasp Francis' need to behave at all times in a manner consistent with his devotion to Christ. In spite of continuing to possess superior resource and hierarchal power Pietro found his influence dwindled immediately and never recovered.

As you assess your approach to negotiation consider how you might influence the decisions of the other party. If you are not certain how you might use influence, take time to explore the resources mentioned above.

PERSUADE. We can persuade the other party to accept our position based on evidence, facts, logic, or other convincing presentations that support the merit of our position.[6]

During facilitated negotiation offers and demands are exchanged, sometimes directly between parties, at other times they are shuttled back and forth by the mediator. These demands or offers rarely stand on their own: they must be accompanied by a reason. *Why* should the other party accept the offer or demand? What reason justifies taking the deal? Without a reason an offer or demand fails to impinge on the other party, and it fails to excite their attention. An offer or demand without a reason is easily swept aside and quite often triggers resentment.

A reason provides an anchor in the psyche of the party that receives the offer or demand. A reason communicates that you respect the knowledge and intellect of the other party. It demonstrates a willingness to submit your plan for their appraisal, thus reinforcing their right to self-determinism. Persuading the other party with argument or logic is one way we use power.

In some negotiations, however, reasons may not be the most important persuasive factor. Persuasion may tap emotions, intuition, or spiritual insights. Nonetheless, even when persuasion captures emotions or intuition rather than intellect, being presented with a persuasive reason allows us to feel comfortable with our emotional or intuitive decision. In other words, though effective persuasion may speak to the heart we must supply the mind with a parallel rational motive. Though our decision may be based entirely on emotion we want to feel *as if* we acted rationally. The persuasive reason provides a higher comfort level. Hours or days after we conclude a negotiation, emotions may ebb; then we look back to the reason behind our decision.

This is especially true when we must report our decision to friends, family, or other stakeholders not present in the negotiation, as it may be difficult for us to express intangible emotions or spiritual intuitions that prompted agreement. We may find ourselves at a loss for words that convey the subtler decision-making that took place. It is much easier for us to explain our actions with a logical reason, even if that reason was tangentially or minimally involved in our final decision.

In one mediation I witnessed this dynamic. A party arrived at a settlement agreement but after the other party departed she turned to me and asked me to help her prepare an argument she could present to explain to her boss why she had settled the case. Her boss, she explained, was unreasonable and not amenable to settlement, so he would query why she settled rather than pushing for a trial. She wanted an argument based on hardcore self-interest that her boss could accept within his aggressive worldview.

In that particular case the task was not difficult. I helped her explain to her boss that, given this particular case was unusually weak and offended the conscience, if they brought the matter before the judge they risked prejudicing future cases (with merit) that would be tried in front of that particular judge. They would not only lose the present case but they would negatively prejudice future decisions. Armed with a rationale that spoke to the way her boss viewed the world, armed with a rationale that spoke to his self-interest, she left pleased with the resolution she had negotiated.

In some negotiations emphasis may be on the persuasiveness of arguments presented. The challenge for the mediator is to recognize when the persuasive argument is critical and when it is a subtle cover for emotion and intuition. Lawyers, who specialize in persuasive argument, sometimes focus on their reasoned presentation of the case to the detriment of their client. They may fire away at opposing counsel with arguments that miss the emotional, moral, or spiritual core of the conflict. A perceptive mediator senses when the time has come to move away from attempts to persuade with legal argument and to move toward exploration of more intimate and less logical factors of persuasion.

As a party to negotiation, it is important for you to prepare persuasive reasons that explain concessions you offer or accept – even if the real motivation is less logical or reasoned. The other party's apology or compassionate gesture may touch your heart, persuading you to offer concessions that violate the legal strategy you spent hours hammering out with your attorney. When that happens you may wish to supply a rational reason that satisfies your lawyer, as otherwise he may continue the good fight long after you have turned in another direction. Unless you persuade your attorney you are satisfied, with reasons he can understand, he will continue his zealous advocacy.

I have witnessed a client ready to enter into an agreement – his needs satisfied by an offer – while his lawyer remained on the battlefield waging litigation war to the bitter end. A mediator becomes skilled at recognizing this situation and works to bring the party and their representative to a unified position, though at times the attorney may fail to fully reconcile his approach with the client's views. The personal dynamics may cause a client to defer to the lawyer, even though he has found a new solution. Most mediators can relate stories of clients dragged down the costly and painful litigation path simply because they could not persuade their attorney to change course.

Attorneys are not the only allies with whom we must reason. Friends, family, or significant others must be convinced we have protected our interests. In one case a young plaintiff received a very generous settlement from an insurance carrier. I expected she would be quite pleased with her ability to persuade the other side of her rights and needs. When she signed off on the deal she wore the long face of dissatisfaction, which was puzzling.

I became worried something had gone terribly wrong. I did not want the deal to go forward if it caused such visible dissatisfaction. I called a time-out and went into private consultation with the young lady. After querying her state of mind I realized *she* was pleased with the settlement but feared presenting the outcome to her father (waiting at home) who had an inflated jackpot justice view of the case.

In his mind the lawsuit was going to result in a bonanza that would support him for years to come. His daughter, the litigant, was struggling with how she was going to present her success in a way he would understand, in spite of his unrealistic expectations. She faced the unappealing prospect of disappointing his false expectations, expectations that rendered her success an embarrassing failure. Her dismayed look reflected her inner search for persuasive reasons that would quell the anger that would erupt from his disappointment.

Another way to use persuasion is to clarify communications. Our power to affect the other party increases when we bring about clarity regarding events, intentions, and possible future plans. A powerful example of the use of communication to clarify issues can be found in the task of uncovering deception. When we suspect the party with whom we are negotiating is deceptive we use communication skills to shed light on their intentions. We ask them to clarify the principles on which they are operating and ask them to clarify their interests. We use our ability to communicate clearly and persuasively to draw the other party into dialogue that results in a clear statement of intention. We then commit this statement to writing so we have a record to which we can return if the other party strays from agreed-upon principles. When we possess their clear statement of intention and principle we can use the statement to persuade them to adhere to their agreements.

As you head into mediation you will want to consider how you will persuade the other party that your plan for resolving the conflict has merit. Will you persuade them with the rhetoric of a sound argument or will you persuade them with emotion? You may wish to assess whether there is any argument the other side can present that will persuade you to settle the conflict.

COMPROMISE. We may satisfy our interests through the use of compromise, in which we make concessions and agree to take less than initially required. Compromise, like collaboration, is one of the primary approaches to resolving conflict. It is also a way to exercise power – with compromise we affect the decisions, actions, and behavior of the other party.

For example, we may find ourselves in a situation in which we have resources that allow us to take a partial loss; we have the option of using the power of compromise to bring the conflict to an end. We use compromise in order to turn our attention to more productive endeavors or to save the relationship. We may choose to compromise when we discover the conflict is drawing negative responses from bystanders whose favor we value.

On occasion we may reach a moment in negotiation when we realize our aspirations will not be met: our interests simply cannot be satisfied with the resources available to the other party or the goodwill of the other party has boundaries we did not anticipate. It becomes clear that full integration of our interests with the interests of the other party is not possible. In this situation we decide to divide the fixed pie. After cutting the pie both parties walk away both partially satisfied, partially dissatisfied. We use the power of compromise when there is wisdom in walking away with a partial success.

Compromise is most useful when we do not expect to continue the relationship. Compromise works best when the end of the conflict is also the end of the relationship. In this situation we are prepared to accept dissatisfaction in exchange for the psychological satisfaction of release from the burden of the conflict. In relationships that are expected to continue, the lingering dissatisfaction may be a lasting negative factor – this warrants the extra effort needed to find a more collaborative outcome.

COLLABORATE. We collaborate by integrating our interests with another's interests to arrive at a solution that provides maximum satisfaction to all involved. Collaboration was identified as a style of conflict resolution consistent with integrative bargaining. Collaboration can also be considered a way to use power – a way to affect the decisions, actions, and behavior of the other party.

In most instances, mediators coach parties to use collaboration, as collaboration provides the most durable and satisfactory outcomes. The work done in integrating our needs with the needs of the other party pays dividends. But you may ask, how do I begin to collaborate with someone with whom I can barely stomach having a conversation? In the heat of a conflict the idea of collaboration sounds preposterous.

This is when our earlier work in addressing emotional upsets, communication breakdowns, false attributions, and other barriers pays off. Once we drain negative emotion, heal wounds, and repair broken communication, a renewed sense of purpose appears. The renewed purpose fuels a desire to work toward resolution rather than escalation.

At this point, after employing personal or spiritual power to overcome personal barriers we may decide to use the power of collaboration to affect the decisions of the other party. Collaboration does not usually spring from a sudden outpouring of brotherly love between the parties but rather as a conscious choice, a decision. Taking a collaborative approach is an act of will in which one moves past residual hostility to join the other party on the same side of the table. It demands we choose how we will affect the other party.

Taking a collaborative approach may seem daunting, and the idea of collaboration generating power may seem foreign. But sometimes collaboration is the most effective use of power. When we collaborate we orchestrate all the types of power at the table to affect decisions, actions, and behavior. When we are open to co-authoring the outcome we change the conflict dynamics and generate the power needed to make things happen. When we collaborate we mirror the interdependent nature of our existence. We honor our connectedness.

PRAY OR MEDITATE. We engage in contemplative prayer or meditation as a way to engage spiritual power and to open our hearts to the power of divine providence. In contemplative prayer we discover the power of the loving Spirit and we find the inner strength to seek union with the other party. Through contemplative prayer we use spiritual power to affect the other party's decisions, actions, and behavior in a profound and peaceful manner.

Franciscan scholars have noted that finding the path to healing division in our daily lives begins with a search for the spiritual in life. "We, too, are called to find this union in the ordinariness of our lives if we allow ourselves the freedom first to find the Christ center within us, then to follow Christ by trusting in God's unconditional love."[7] Using contemplative prayer we seek this union.

Too often we create a divide in our minds and in our lives – on one side we place our mundane struggles; on the other side we place our pursuit of spiritual matters. We segment and compartmentalize our lives. At the local parish we present a smiling and contented face; in our daily business we worry and seethe with resentment or anger. With the use of prayer or meditation we seek to transcend our segmented condition and bring about a union of the divine with the ordinary. With the recognition of the divine in the ordinary we gain insight into "a humble God bending low."[8]

When it comes to conflict resolution we use contemplative prayer to tap spiritual power that brings forth the sacred perspective of seeing the divine within the ordinary. Delio counsels, "We can do it if we relinquish our idols, our need to control, our frenzied impersonal activity and allow ourselves to enter the still point of our lives wherein lies the seed of eternity."[9]

The use of contemplative prayer to release the spiritual power of compassionate love is a core concept in spiritually transformative mediation. This approach relies on the example of St. Francis who guides our steps as we go forward in search of peace and harmony. As you evaluate your conflict resolution approach consider the ways you might use contemplative prayer to invite the divine into the process.

SUMMARY. The preceding discussion of the use of power is not exhaustive. You may recognize additional ways of using power that apply to your particular situation. Each conflict situation and conflict history is unique and requires you to identify the ways power will be used.

Keep in mind, as you work through the prompts in the journal workbook, that this discussion is not meant to create rigid boxes that limit your choices, but rather to suggest paths of inquiry that expand your options. Where previously you may have felt hemmed in by limited options, after responding to the prompts, you will feel an increase in freedom and heightened optimism.

As we explore the use of power we come to see that categories overlap: effective strategies involve multiple types of power used in concert. The skilled negotiator brings the entire tool set to the table, employing a wide range of options to reach an agreement.

One use of power, nonviolence, has not been addressed as a separate topic, as the nonviolent approach is a hybrid use of influence, collaboration, giving in, entrusting, persuading, and prayer. Those who practice nonviolent activism tend to use a mosaic of types of power with the common factor being a lack of violence. The nonviolence movement approaches a conflict from the point of view of how can we affect the decisions, actions, and behavior of our adversary without resorting to violence?

Negotiating the Use of Power

When we think of negotiation we usually think of back-and-forth dialogue regarding substantive outcomes. Our attention goes to the substance of the negotiation – who is going to get what? Equally important, but often overlooked, is the underlying negotiation regarding the process – the negotiation that determines how we will go about negotiating. This preliminary negotiation addresses procedures and guidelines to be used during negotiation. It addresses how we will behave toward one another during the conflict resolution process. This negotiation, whether implicit or explicit, determines how we will use our power during the process.

Agreements concerning the use of power may involve substituting one power for another. For example, a party may have the finances (resource power) required to wage a costly court battle but agrees to suspend costly litigation in favor of a more collaborative approach such as mediation. The substitution rests on the idea, "Let's give this a try. Let's see if we can do better." During this give-and-take process the mediator shepherds the parties toward a collaborative use of power.

The satisfaction we seek in mediation is not limited to *what* we achieve – *substantive satisfaction* – but also concerns *how* we achieve the outcome. The party must feel the process was fair and just in order to be satisfied – they must experience *process satisfaction*. They must also feel *psychological satisfaction*; they must feel they were empowered and respected.

These three types of satisfaction – *substantive, process, and psychological satisfaction* – can be represented as the legs of a triangle. How we use power affects satisfaction, especially process and psychological satisfaction. The manner in which power is used determines how we feel about the fairness of the process and how we feel about the way we have been treated. The manner in which power is used to affect the decisions, actions, and behavior of the parties determines the quality of the post mediation relationship. If we resolve the conflict with an agreement, but we feel we have been treated unjustly or disrespectfully during the process, we depart dissatisfied.

A mediator monitors the use of power and promotes collaboration. Highlighting collaboration is not an arbitrary choice. Collaboration produces the best results, perhaps because it accurately reflects the ontological importance of relationship. Collaboration goes with and not against the moral grain of the universe. When we collaborate we honor and respect the other party and create shared compassion. We open the door to the possibility of discovering the divine within each other. When we exercise our free will in concert with another, inviting their needs into our heart, we co-author the relationship and share in each other's divinity.

Delio writes, "We are called to be co-creators of the universe, to 'christify' the universe by our actions of love."[10] The exercise of our free will in concert with our use of spiritual power, which relies on love and compassion to affect decisions, actions, and behavior, creates the ongoing, shared narrative of this universe. When we co-create (collaborate) with another person in a loving manner, we take on the likeness of the loving and humble God who bends low to embrace us in our fragile human condition.[11]

A Franciscan View

Franciscans commit themselves to a path of nonviolence in their affairs and invite others to share in this principled commitment to the absence of violence, force, domination, and coercion. Michael Crosby, a Capuchin Franciscan, in *The Paradox of Power* writes, "Nonviolence is a way of ordering our lives so that everyone will be empowered; it refers to people who discipline themselves to be gentle rather than severe."[12]

The idea of empowering others parallels the idea that participants in mediation need to recognize the power they possess and learn how to use that power gently. The use of spiritual power – the ability to affect the other party through love and compassion – leads to an embrace of a gentle power so effective it trumps all others. Crosby continues, "When this happens, gentleness becomes the positive face of nonviolence."[13]

Nonviolence, from a *Taming the Wolf* perspective, is not one particular approach, but rather a guideline or personal ethic one honors while eschewing the desire to coerce and dominate. We advance with the gentle face of a Franciscan that welcomes the other into dialogue and collaboration. Nonviolence practiced in this manner becomes a state of being.

The Greek word for nonviolence "was used to describe a wild animal who had been tamed and made gentle."[14] By definition, *Taming the Wolf* is the study of nonviolence but I hesitate to use the term, as mediation involves more than simply eschewing violence. And a mediator does not engage in protests common to the nonviolence movement. Rather mediation is a process consisting of proactive steps that move us beyond the need for violence, mediation is a process of taming the wolf with gradual steps that empower the wolf to become a peacemaker.

This journey requires we use power tempered by discernment. Making peace involves recognition of the use and abuse of power, followed by building a bridge to reconciliation. Though foundations of this bridge may be planted in the rocky soil of coercive use of power, the bridge's span rises to an apex where we find gentle use of power.

The metaphor of a bridge tells us the process involves spanning differences to restore relationship. In the legend, Francis not only tamed the wolf, he tamed the hearts of the citizens of Gubbio. He mediated differences and brought the parties into new relationship. As he walked with the wolf and the citizens of Gubbio on the metaphorical bridge they rose higher and higher. They lifted themselves above violent uses of power to find a gentle power based on collaboration, exchange, and divine providence.

When we protest in the spirit of the nonviolence movement, extreme caution is warranted, as we face a complex web of cause and effect. We do not exist as dispassionate outsiders; we are enmeshed in an interdependent universe. When we protest the acts of another person or group, it is easy to overlook that which exists within our group or within our heart that also warrants protest.

In *The Remembrance of the Desire of a Soul* by Thomas of Celano, we find the story of "How [Francis] Knew Someone Considered Holy Was a Fraud."[15] In the story we learn of a brother who "to all appearances, led a life of extraordinary holiness," but "while everyone was commending and praising the man, our father [Francis]" held a contrary view.[16] Francis said, "Don't sing me the praises of his devilish illusions," and he called the man fraud.[17]

The brothers were upset with Francis' analysis. They challenged him, "How can lies and deception be disguised under all these signs of perfection?"[18] Francis focused on one telltale sign: the man never went to confession. The brothers, following Francis' directions, invited the holy man to partake of confession – as Francis predicted they found the man refused. Soon after, the man left the order.

Francis leaves us with the following lesson: "Realize the power of a good confession. It is both a cause and sign of holiness."[19] Francis advises us to prepare ourselves to enter conflict resolution through tending to relationship while simultaneously recognizing the multiple factors to which we must tend – some of which live within us.

Scripture

Small and great alike, all are greedy for gain;
*   prophet and priest, all practice fraud.*
They have treated lightly
*   the injury to my people:*
"Peace, peace!" they say,
*   though there is no peace.* (Jer 6:13-14)

He then addressed this parable to those who were convinced of their own righteousness and despised everyone else. "Two people went up to the temple area to pray; one was a Pharisee and the other was a tax collector. The Pharisee took up his position and spoke this prayer to himself, 'O God, I thank you that I am not like the rest of humanity – greedy, dishonest, adulterous – or even like this tax collector. I fast twice a week, and I pay tithes on my whole income.' But the tax collector stood off at a distance and would not even raise his eyes to heaven but beat his breast and prayed, 'O God, be merciful to me a sinner.' I tell you, the latter went home justified, not the former; for everyone who exalts himself will be humbled, and the one who humbles himself will be exalted." (Lk 18:9-14)

Chapter Fifteen

Making Decisions

When Francis emerged from his contemplation, he quietly suggested an answer to the dilemma. It was a suggestion that could meet the needs of both the town and the wolf.

Francis understood the wolf's concern and assured him he would present the idea to the townspeople in such a way that the wolf would be forgiven and welcomed into the town.

Mediation Principles

ST. FRANCIS BEGINS the next step in the conflict resolution process – seeking creative solutions. In previous chapters, we analyzed and assessed the conflict and we may have discovered that previously our faulty decision-making prevented the resolution of the conflict. In order to avoid additional miscalculations and to prepare for the search for creative solutions, we seek to become aware of how we make decisions, how we predict outcomes, and how we respond to risk.

Hundreds of authors offer advice on achieving success in relationships and business. You may have visited the business section of the bookstore and found titles that appealed to you. Management experts spend their careers gaining proficiency in these skills, so we realize we are not going to become professional negotiators overnight, nonetheless, if we become aware of a few basic concepts we will be sufficiently oriented to the process to insure our satisfaction with the outcome in most cases.

In this chapter we will explore negotiation and decision making basics and look closer at how we approach the task of sitting down at the table with the other party.

Mediator Assistance

A mediator assists in the decision-making process just as Francis assisted the wolf. She listens closely and asks questions that peel away layers of accumulated habit or bias. She helps us analyze our responses to offers or demands and helps us ground our thinking in sound reasoning that aligns with our interests.

As noted in an earlier chapter, mediators bring different styles to this task: they may facilitate without offering opinion or advice; they may evaluate, providing assessments and possible solutions; they may direct the process toward an outcome. Others nurture transformation that unleashes the party's own creative abilities.

Francis takes a mixed approach: he facilitates the process; becomes a creative participant and evaluates options; directs the process and suggests he carry a solution to Gubbio; and he transforms the hearts of the participants. He does not demand that the wolf accept his solution as the only way to proceed. Instead he defers to the wolf's self-determinism. As you prepare, consider the style you prefer and how much or how little input you desire.

The *Taming the Wolf* approach relies on transformation, which some might argue is the only approach that guarantees lasting change and durable outcomes. In the past we may have responded to other's needs in ways that generated conflict; we may have been disrespectful, inconsiderate, or even deceitful. The manner in which we handled matters of exchange may have contributed to conflict.

In order to overcome past upsets we must experience an inner change that allows us to see ourselves and the other party in a new light. Facilitative, evaluative, and directive approaches do not necessarily bring about such a change. When the relationship is not expected to last this may be okay but, in most other instances, transformating the relationship is vital. If mediation fails to transform the heart of the individual and the nature of the relationship, conflict will continue. The mediator will handle one dispute, only to find another will take its place.

If disputants are comfortable with a facilitative, evaluative, or directive process and they reach a negotiated settlement, the process is valid. For disputants seeking lasting change in the way they manage conflict and relationships the transformative approach offers the greatest benefit.

As you head into the negotiation stage also consider the style your representatives, for example, lawyers assisting with negotiation, bring to the table. Assess to what extent you are comfortable with your representative guiding your decisions. Do you want a take-charge representative who leads, or do you prefer a client-centered representative who facilitates your decision-making process but leaves decisions fully in your hands?

Consider how your representative's style integrates with the styles of the mediator and the other party. In some cases, an aggressive lawyer may so offend the other party that progress becomes difficult and time consuming. If your lawyer's aggressive style derails the process, a different approach is needed. On the other hand, if an aggressive style is needed in order to force the other party to take you seriously, it is a wise approach. If the aggressive attorney prolongs a negotiation, costing you time and money, you may want to mitigate his influence with your style. These dynamics are not limited to attorney representatives – in non-legal settings similar concerns apply to those who assist or represent you.

In some situations you may encourage your representative to take a tough stance as part of a good cop/bad cop tactic. You allow the attorney to hold a hard line while you soften at the first sign of a concession by the other side. There are many variations on how to work together, so you will want to discuss your approach in advance and find the best style for the situation.

Francis, who begins to imagine possible solutions, engages with what John

Paul Lederach has labeled "the moral imagination."[1] Lederach notes, "The moral imagination develops a capacity to perceive things beyond and at a deeper level than what initially meets the eye."[2] "A defining characteristic of the moral imagination" is "the capacity to give birth to something new that in its very birthing changes our world and the way we see things."[3] Francis engages the moral imagination, while the wolf, suffering under the burden of conflict, relies on Francis for possible solutions.

Francis, though inspired by moral imagination, does not force a solution – no matter how creative – on the wolf. He allows the wolf to embrace the creative vision and make it his own. If the wolf is unable to draw Francis' suggested solution into his heart the brainstorming process continues.

Settlement Criteria

Prompts in the journal workbook prepare us to consider criteria we use to evaluate proposals – whether the proposal is a settlement offer, terms of a new relationship, ethical codes for future business dealings, agreement regarding restitution for damages, or other types of proposals containing negotiated terms that resolve the conflict.

Previously we detailed our interests and speculated on the other party's interests and we identified concerns that will be important in the negotiation. We may have developed an agenda to guide exploration of below-the-line interests. At this stage we call upon our moral imagination for solutions that resolve issues and satisfy interests.

An example of an issue is whether or not an employee will receive an annual pay raise. An exploration of interests reveals the employee has a need to cover increased healthcare bills due to a recent illness. As a result of exploring interests, the issue is reframed – it is changed from a demand for a raise to a request for help paying for healthcare. The new frame may inspire a solution. The company purchases increased healthcare coverage at a rate lower than the employee would pay individually. The total cost of this solution to employer and employee is lower than a pay raise; the cost for additional coverage is less than the increase in pay the employee would need to cover his costs if he paid individually. Moving from (above the line) issues to (below the line) interests clarifies the goal of the negotiation. Going *below the line* makes it easier to set criteria.

As we prepare to negotiate, we consider criteria we will use to evaluate a proposed solution. We shape criteria against which we evaluate proposals to see if they truly satisfy our interests. At first glance this step may seem tedious but in the long run it saves time and produces better results.

The prompts in the journal workbook direct you to list criteria you will use. Even with such a list we can make errors that sabotage an outcome. To avoid or minimize errors we take time to study our personal decision-making style.

Making Decisions

Though we have identified interests and set criteria for evaluating proposals, we need to assess the types of errors in decision-making that typically sabotage our attempts to reach a satisfactory resolution.[4]

One possible error is **accepting the first proposal** that satisfies our minimum requirements. We err in accepting a proposed solution that fails to satisfy most of our criteria, a solution that fails to produce the highest overall benefit. We jump at the first opportunity for a resolution and fail to explore additional options that provide greater satisfaction.

This error may be motivated by an attempt to move through the process as quickly as possible. Even though we have agreed to mediate we may feel uncomfortable facing a party with whom we have been in conflict. Rather than taking time to process all relevant information, we streamline the process in order to get it over with. Prompts in the journal workbook help us avoid this potential misstep, as we give prior thought to outcomes that satisfy our interests. Those who arrive at mediation without the benefit of preparation are susceptible to accepting the first proposal that meets a single minimum criterion.

The opposite error is **eliminating options that do not meet *all* criteria.** This approach may result in our rejecting all possible proposals, as it is rare for one proposal to satisfy *all* criteria. A more efficient approach is determining which proposal satisfies the greatest number of criteria. First, we assign relative values to the criteria. Then we compare the two most promising proposals against the criteria. We add up the assigned values of criteria and determine which proposal garners the higher score.

I do not mean to imply this approach relies on mathematical science that will result in a scientific solution. Rather, assigning relative values and weighing our choices is beneficial because it slows the process and forces us to take time to evaluate proposals on the table. We do not seek scientific objectivity but rather the best subjective evaluation we can muster.

In spite of our intention to be thorough in this task, we commonly employ methods that speed up and simplify decision-making. These mental shortcuts or problem-solving models are called *heuristics*. They aid in making sound decisions when time is limited. These shortcuts, however, become ingrained in our thinking – eventually, we may no longer be aware of the thought process that originally created the heuristic model. The downside to such homegrown shortcuts is inadvertent bias that introduces error.

For example, we often make judgments based on our memory of **recent and/or vivid events**. When we compare the current situation to our experience the readily available points of comparison are events that happened recently or events that are vivid and easy to recall. These experiences may not provide an accurate model for the current situation. We fail to estimate how likely it is that recent or vivid events will repeat in the future; they may be anomalies unlikely to repeat. In selecting recent or vivid events we introduce faulty data into our calculations.

This same miscalculation may occur even when we carefully match the current situation to a more extensive recall of our past experience. We may access additional memories but those memories still may not be representative of the current situation. The decision we face may not be reflected in our past personal experience; our experience may provide an *inadequate sample* of typical outcomes and may reflect unusual or rare events.

To arrive at a good decision we may have to expand our knowledge by consulting the experience of others who have faced these types of decisions. We can prevent errors caused by using **inadequate samples of experience** by taking time to honestly consider whether or not our past experience provides the information we need. As our personal experience is inevitably tainted, it becomes necessary to pause and assess the biases we import into the current decision-making process. Only after we double-check the relevancy of our personal experience and strip away bias does the past experience become reliable for evaluating future proposed solutions.

Another heuristic concerns the way we anchor decisions to **reference points or baselines**. We may select a baseline against which to evaluate a proposal, but if the baseline reference is invalid we err. Suppose our expectation for the quality of our marital relationship is referenced to the baseline of our parents' relationship2 but our parents maintained peace by limiting their interaction and living separate-but-parallel lives. If we choose this baseline we miss the opportunity to create a dynamic and productive relationship. Our baseline reference is so far from the ideal we do not even consider the heights of satisfaction to which we can rise.

The opposite can occur. We can set our baseline too high. If our baseline reference for a monetary settlement is lifted from a newspaper article about a hundred-million-dollar jury award in a high profile case, we can make unreasonable demands that will never be met.

There are no magic formulas for computing valid baseline references. Even with careful consideration we may adopt a baseline that introduces error. Slowing the process allows time for us to eradicate most obvious errors. If we are aware that personal bias distorts baseline references, we will take time to explore baseline measures others have used in similar situations. This exploration allows us to compare and contrast those references with our own references to expose obvious bias.

Overconfidence also causes miscalculation. We may become overconfident in our ability to predict future events based on our heuristic models and then later discover errors that result from *using the familiar to judge the unfamiliar*. Overconfidence occurs frequently when litigants estimate how they will fare before a judge or jury. One researcher found "individuals are systemically overconfident in estimating the position of a neutral third party and in estimating the likelihood that a third party will accept their position."[5]

A plaintiff may read about a high-profile jury award and incorrectly assume the award is a norm that represents the verdict he can expect. Or he may proceed with litigation bolstered by unwarranted confidence based on his experience debating politics over the family dinner table, unaware that procedural rules in effect at the dinner table bear little resemblance to the procedural rules of the court.

Overconfidence and bias take over when an information vacuum exists. As conflict escalates we cease communicating with the other party. In the resulting vacuum, we lack reality checks. As a result, our personal narrative reflects a self-serving evaluation of our conflict behavior, which we consider to be more constructive and benign than the behavior of the other party.[6] Silence begs us to insert our bias into the information vacuum.

Social pressure increases bias. Groups to which we belong exert pressure on our thoughts and actions. Vested personal interests within groups – for example, our concern with maintaining leadership positions – may strongly influence our decisions, creating a stubborn form of bias. We may fail to acknowledge the power of social pressure.

The influence of the group may represent a legitimate need of stakeholders or an illegitimate demand that biases decisions. We must evaluate the situation. If we act out of a need to appease others we may fail to satisfy our own interests. If we ignore legitimate needs of stakeholders we also fail.

Strident **over-commitment** to an earlier position is another source of error. In conflicts that have escalated, we often over-commit to earlier positions when those positions are no longer compelling or cogent in light of new evidence and changing circumstances. During conflict we often take a stand and vow we will not budge. Over time we execute a few minor shifts in position and with each new position we issue a new commitment to hold to that stance. Our movement is not in the direction of a more flexible relationship but rather in the direction of a series of postures to which we become overly committed.

Social psychologists note a common pattern in the shift to over-committed postures: "[A] party's concern with maximizing winnings, which was first replaced by a concern with minimizing losses, is now supplanted by a determination to make certain that Other loses at least as much as Party."[7] The position, *the other party must lose as much or more than I have lost* becomes resistant to change – even when we recognize the other party's loss will force an equal or greater loss on us. This type of over-commitment leads to mutual destruction.

As we prepare to negotiate we should review the wisdom and durability of earlier commitments. We should inspect our positions to see if we are overly committed to a stance that no longer has merit. Our thinking must catch up to the present circumstances so we are not anchored to a no-longer-relevant past.

Though we proceed slowly, exercise caution, and make sure we are informed, we still commit errors as a result of **selective information processing** – which means we seek information that confirms our assumptions while ignoring information that counters our assumptions. It is natural for us to form hypotheses and then discover evidence that confirms those hypotheses, while overlooking contradictory evidence. We have a *I am right* bias that blinds us to actual evidence. Unless we tame this propensity to view the world through the lenses of our hypotheses, we can still fall short even though we remedy other errors in our decision-making.

Exploring and inspecting information that contradicts our views is not easy. To understand the difficulty, select a topic that is important to you and then consider ways in which you might be wrong. Consider how an opposing view might be correct. Most of us can only take a few minutes of such torture before we give up and proceed with our default position of trusting our views are accurate.

One way to escape the dilemma of not being able to explore all possibilities is to engage a trusted adviser to play critic. Select a devil's advocate to play your opposition. Choose a lawyer, pastoral counselor, friend, or spouse and give them permission to challenge your views, assumptions, and biases. Grant them permission to *make you wrong*.

They do not have to believe opposing views are correct; they simply have to represent those views persuasively. The purpose is not to win the argument. The exercise simply allows you to hear yourself argue against other views. Do not accept a new view or justify your position on the spot. Simply allow the experience to filter through your consciousness.

A trusted adviser advocating for alternative positions during role-playing provides a golden opportunity. Nonetheless, allowing anyone free rein to challenge our assumptions will be painful. Some parties will not easily tolerate the emotional discomfort. Those who are able to engage the exercise, however, will benefit greatly. The experience will imbue your decision-making process with texture and richness.

In preparation for negotiation, a party who has difficulty hearing other views may turn to prayer, and seek an opportunity to become humble in the presence of the divine. This may open their hearts to new perspectives and new creativity. Prayer may fire the moral imagination.

When we combine the words *moral* and *imagination*, we begin to understand Francis' special role as a model mediator who invited the divine into his peacemaking efforts. John Paul Lederach writes, "Theologically this notion is found in the Word that becomes flesh, the moment when potentiality moves from the realm of possibility to the world of the tangible. In other words, the moral imagination finds its clearest expression in the appearance of the creative act."[8] St. Francis, with his heart open to the Spirit, was able to engage the moral imagination, aligning his prayerful thoughts with the divine Word. He nurtured the transition of potential into the tangible through his brotherly actions.

The critic who will most seriously challenge our assumptions is the other party to the conflict. They will harbor few reservations when it comes to pointing out how wrong or misinformed we are. Nonetheless, if we have engaged in the humbling process of allowing an adviser to challenge our assumptions, our presentation will convey a reasoned and humble presence. Our delivery of proposals will sound a note of quiet confidence and certainty.

As a bonus, evaluating criteria and eliminating biases will prepare us to identify the biases and decision-making errors the other party demonstrates. Our preparation may allow us to move to the other side of the table to collaborate in evaluating solutions. Our preparation makes us a better collaborator.

Facing Risk

In negotiation we encounter comfort or discomfort with risk. Research provides evidence that people tend to be *risk averse*.[9] When people are given an opportunity to risk losing a small certain gain in return for the chance to obtain a large gain, they usually decline to take the risk. They walk away satisfied with the smaller but certain gain. If a party is assured of a $1000 gain, they will choose to hold on to that gain rather than risk losing the $1000 by taking a chance they might receive $3000.

People also tend to be *loss averse*. They tend to abhor the idea of loss. Faced with a certain loss they will risk suffering an even greater loss if they might avoid the existing loss. If they have lost $1000 they will risk losing another $3000 in an attempt to erase the $1000 loss.

In summary, we tend to refuse risking current gain to achieve a larger gain. Rather than risk what we already have to achieve a larger gain, we protect what we have. But we will risk losing more in an attempt to erase an existing deficit. Rather than suffer a loss we will risk losing more in an attempt to eliminate the existing loss.

If a party recognizes risk aversion and loss aversion tendencies, they will frame offers or demands in terms of gain or loss. For example, a party may offer $20,000 as compensation for property damage valued at $30,000. The party receiving the offer can view the $20,000 in two different frames. They can see $20,000 as a $10,000 loss (given damages were $30,000). In this case, they refuse the offer and attempt to secure the entire $30,000. They want to avoid the perceived loss of $10,000. To avoid a certain loss of $10,000 they risk losing the $20,000 already on the table. They turn down the offer and demand $30,000.

If, on the other hand, they view the $20,000 offer as a gain they must protect, they are unlikely to risk walking away with zero. They hesitate and do not demand $30,000. In this frame the $20,000 is seen as a gain. It is money they did not have before negotiations started. If they accept the offer they have realized a certain gain of $20,000. They will be averse to risking the $20,000 gain to seek a greater gain of $30,000.

A mediator, perhaps aware the party making the offer cannot come up with $30,000, may frame the offer as a gain and suggest the other party consider the offer carefully. He might ask, Do you really want to walk away and leave money on the table? However, if the mediator knows the party making the offer is prepared to make up the damages in full he may frame the offer as a $10,000 loss. This might motivate the other party to hold out for the entire sum in an attempt to eliminate all loss.

However, a mediator must not breech his duty of impartiality by tilting the negotiation one way or another. For this reason, most skilled mediators advance both frames simultaneously to allow parties to arrive at their own perception of events. When a party views the offer as a loss, the mediator suggests they look at it as a gain; when a party sees the offer as a gain, the mediator suggests they also look at it as a loss. Moving back and forth between frames the mediator helps diminish reactive risk and loss aversion. The party may then base their decision on other criteria. Or at least they are aware of the bias due to risk aversion and loss aversion. In your negotiation, be aware of the frame you place around offers and demands. Make sure the framing does not unduly prejudice your decisions.

For the party making the offer the opposite framing applies. Payment of $20,000 might be seen as locking in a gain of $10,000, the amount saved by offering $20,000 rather than $30,000. In addition, if a settlement is reached, they will not incur legal fees related to trial. This outcome can be framed as a gain. "You will pay only a fraction of what you might have been forced to pay. You're ahead." If they proceed to trial, they will risk losing the certain gain to achieve additional gain – perhaps the court will award no damages. That would be seen as a $30,000 gain (minus legal fees). But there is a risk that damages will exceed $30,000 plus lawyer's fees. The party most likely will not want to risk the $10,000 gain by proceeding to trial in pursuit of a larger gain. They will be risk averse.

If we employ the opposite frame, the payment of $20,000 is considered a loss. The party will have $20,000 less in the bank. Given they have an aversion to loss they may proceed to trial in an attempt to erase the $20,000 deficit. They will risk the greater possible loss should the court award damages of $30,000 or more plus legal fees. They show an aversion to loss.

Thus, the manner in which the $20,000 offer is framed affects whether or not the party chooses to settle. If they feel they have realized a gain, they may not wish to risk losing that gain. If they feel they have suffered a loss, they will want to risk more in an effort to wipe out the loss.

A mediator pays attention to the manner in which the attorney frames the choices to their client. The attorney may be helping their client see the different frames in order to make the best decision. Or the attorney may be using the frame to move the client toward a particular outcome.

The examples provided take place within the context of the litigated case but the dynamics apply to all contexts in which negotiation regarding valuables, tangible or intangible, takes place. A teen may have negotiated moving his curfew from 10 o'clock to 11 o'clock, but this achievement falls short of the midnight curfew he desired. Does he settle, not wanting to risk his one-hour gain by shooting for a midnight deadline? Or does he consider he has lost an hour (compared to his goal) and risk further debate? (The risk would be the parents feeling he has pushed the negotiation beyond a reasonable point, which might cause them to walk away from the negotiation, leaving the status quo in place.)

Consider the following advice: "The framing effect suggests that in order to induce concessionary behavior from an opponent, a negotiator should always create anchors that lead the opposition to a positive frame and negotiate in terms of what the other side has to gain."[10] In other words, as you negotiate consider how you can put a positive frame on offers and demands. Consider how you will convince the other party they have realized a gain they will want to protect.

When a party provides a rationale that supports an offer or demand or a rationale that supports their response to an offer or demand, they should consider how their language frames the situation. A poorly constructed rationale can create a frame that causes the other party to refuse what might otherwise be reasonable. The other party may translate careless statements into an incentive to maintain risky positions. They may fear they have suffered losses. They may renew their commitment to the fight as they consider they have lost too much to give up.

We do not want to box the other party into a position that persuades them to assume a negative frame. One article suggests, "Strategically, then, a negotiator should avoid inducing the opponent to make statements or behave in any way that would create the illusion of having invested too much to quit."[11] Mediators understand they must keep hope alive in order to keep the negotiation going. They realize a big part of keeping hope alive is avoiding negative frames. As a party you will also want to be aware of the need to keep the dance going.

While many factors contribute to our decision to accept or reject a proposal, the factors discussed above are those that tend to operate below the surface of our awareness affecting our judgment without our knowledge. For this reason, try to surface these factors in preparation for negotiation. Your ability to satisfy your interests will improve to the extent that you identify errors you tend to make and to the extent that you spot biases that color your decision-making. After reviewing previous errors, design a personal approach to decision-making that protects against your common biases and errors and helps you navigate past flawed reasoning.

Values, Beliefs, Reasons

In mediation, our values and beliefs, packaged as worldviews, are typically considered non-negotiable. Nonetheless, we need to be aware they play a role in decision-making. Values and beliefs are not errors – as they are intimately tied to our identity and often accurately reflect our needs and interests. Uninspected worldviews, however, can skew decision-making, resulting in outcomes that do not serve our needs.

While it is not the role of the other party to attempt to alter our values and beliefs in negotiation, we should make sure our values and beliefs are well reasoned and well founded. During conflict resolution we may experience challenges to our values and beliefs, challenges that demand we engage in introspection, contemplation, or dialogue with a pastoral counselor.

Differing values usually surface during a conflict – perhaps the conflict started when values clashed. We may assume such clashes doom mediation to failure. However, the presence of differing views does not mean resolution is impossible, rather it means we must find a single solution that is valid from opposing worldviews. This is not easy, but not impossible.

As parties share their values and beliefs with each other they can be coached to no longer see those values and beliefs as incompatible biases that must be eliminated. Rather they see worldviews they can accommodate *within the context of the core value of pluralism.* This assumes they have adopted pluralism as a core value. The path to acceptance of pluralism is the Golden Rule: *Do unto others as you would have them do unto you.*

If you want the other party to accept your values and beliefs as valid for *you*, it is incumbent upon you to accept their values and beliefs as valid for *them*. The need to impose our worldview can be a fundamental barrier to peace. When we force another party to believe as we do we seek to dominate and coerce, we seek to control the minds and hearts of others. When we inspect this urge closely, we find the impulse can be reduced to a need to coerce and dominate.

When we seek to impose our worldview we need to ask if we have an unrecognized need to coerce or dominate. We ask ourselves clarifying questions that explore the deeper interest we are trying to satisfy by imposing our worldview on another. We are coaxed to ask, When we coerce and dominate another do we really satisfy our interests? Or do coercion and domination foster consequences that ultimately inhibit or destroy our ability to satisfy our interests? Does seeking coercion and domination set in motion consequences that ultimately punish us?

The Golden Rule may attest to a fundamental and universal dynamic in which we reap the fruits of the seeds we sow. If we sow seeds of domination and coercion we reap the sour fruit of domination and coercion directed toward us. We must consider the adverse consequences when we abandon compassion and love to satisfy a need to dominate and coerce one another.

Plurality means we accept the fact the other party holds values and beliefs that work for them. Plurality calls on us to eschew domination and coercion, to refuse to crush or dismiss or invalidate the other party's values and beliefs. It calls on us to share our views in respectful dialogue. This may produce unexpected results.

If Party A shares their values and beliefs with Party B, Party B may come to recognize the values of those beliefs. B may find merit in A's beliefs; they may subsequently share those beliefs. This is not a case of A forcing a value or belief on B but rather an instance of B adopting Party A's value or belief as their own. Thus we return to the core principle of self-determinism – the party adopting a new value or belief has done so on their own initiative and on their own determinism.

The mutual respect that accompanies plurality promotes dialogue and exchange of views. While plurality honors diversity, paradoxically it provides the best opportunity for unity, because plurality is a value stripped of a need to dominate or coerce. Plurality dictates you will honor each individual's values and beliefs as valid for *them*. With plurality we have a primary core value that opens the door to conflict resolution and reconciliation.

Thus, we need to practice the Golden Rule and unconditionally honor the other party's worldview. When we reject plurality we reject lasting peace. No matter how lofty our values and beliefs may be, if they do not include plurality they lead us away from peace and unconditional love. The move from exclusivity toward a compassionate inclusivity is vital in peacemaking.

As an absolute minimum for conflict resolution, we must add to pluralism the desire to collaborate to find a solution that best satisfies the interests of both parties. Combining pluralism, the Golden Rule, and collaboration as core principles we find ways to frame solutions that meet respective needs within the context of differing worldviews.

Though we view the world from separate and unique perspectives, we can find common solutions. These solutions may carry different meanings within each party's unique worldview. However, we remove value and belief labels from the common solution so each party can affix their own labels. We cease arguing about labels, satisfied with the negotiated solution.

There are three minimum values parties must agree on in order to find common solutions: pluralism, the Golden Rule, and collaboration. As you assess the role that differing worldviews play in your conflict, assess the degree to which pluralism, reciprocity, and collaboration will allow you to overcome worldview differences.

The Best Alternative to a Negotiated Agreement

A *best alternative to a negotiated agreement* (BATNA) represents an "if everything fails" option. It is the option that generates freedom to step away from coercion or domination. The BATNA is the alternative to which you turn *if negotiation fails to satisfy your needs*. You resort to this option when the other party offers less than your bottom line or demands more than your upper limit.

Carefully designing a BATNA prevents you from entering into an unsatisfactory agreement as the result of believing you have no alternative. The other party may invest effort in causing you to feel you have no choice; they may want you to believe your only option is to accept their offer. The BATNA provides you with the needed alternative and thus preserves your freedom of choice.

The BATNA is worked out prior to negotiation and provides a frame of reference that empowers us to remain thoughtful throughout the process. During the heat of negotiation, when tempers and emotions flare, when we worry that our needs will not be met, we tend to lose sight of the big picture. An overbearing opponent might convince us we have no other choice than to accept their demands. Or, feeling buffeted by argument and contention, we may slam on the brakes and decline offers that actually meet our needs. Entering a negotiation without boundaries and guidelines is a recipe for disaster.

A BATNA describes the option one will exercise if negotiation fails; it serves as an anchor in a storm. It is not a plan hatched in the emotional moment but rather a well-thought-out arrangement that has consequences with which we can live.

At the same time, we must not allow rigidity to creep into the process by setting an unrealistic BATNA. If we become rigid our BATNA functions as a take-it-or-leave-it position that inhibits creative negotiation. Nor should we allow the BATNA to serve as a bottom line that leads to premature compromise. A BATNA is the plan you put into effect *after* a negotiation fails and a settlement is no longer possible. It is the plan you activate in lieu of a negotiated agreement.

When you have a sound rationale and a realistic plan as an alternative, you do not lose hope and negotiate against your self-interest. A BATNA inspires you to deliver a confident presentation that differs from boastful threats. The other party will be able to sense you have devised a reasoned plan, a plan you will put into play to meet your needs should mediation fail.

As noted, it is important to work out the BATNA in advance and then work with the mediator to fine-tune parameters. The mediator can provide a reality check that helps you determine if the BATNA is a legitimate option. The only caveat to consider is that a mediator typically does not want to know your bottom line. The mediator knows that should he become aware of your bottom line he might unconsciously work to satisfy that benchmark rather than allowing the process to determine the outcome, which might be better than your bottom line.

Francis invoked his BATNA when his father called into dispute the ownership of the clothes on his back. Pietro implied Francis was not free to act as he chose as long as Francis wore clothes Pietro supplied. Francis was not about to let this issue abort his freedom of conscience and stifle his freedom of action: he stripped off his clothes and broke the bonds of ownership his father claimed. He invoked his BATNA. We might ask ourselves, When a party demands more of us than our conscience can authorize can we walk away naked?

Brainstorming

A technique used to expand our options and broaden our perspective is brainstorming. It is a technique in which we consider all solutions that come to mind, without evaluating or judging their merit. We do not censor our thoughts. No matter how outrageous or impractical, we add all possible solutions to a list.

In brainstorming we may generate dozens of options with little value. However, we may also arrive at genuinely unique and appropriate solutions as the technique frees up our creativity. In addition to the possibility of hitting upon an ideal solution, we reason broadly on issues that previously shut down our thinking. As a result, we enter into negotiation with confidence in our ability to participate in a fluid process. The initial phase of brainstorming is performed individually; later, the process may be engaged jointly.

After we generate a list of options we engage our critical faculties and evaluate their merits, selecting solutions that meet minimum criteria. We may piece together more than one solution if we discover solutions listed are fragments of a larger, more comprehensive multi-part solution. In the evaluation step we select two, three, or four possible solutions that show the greatest promise. We then re-evaluate these solutions in the light of new information we gain from the other party. If we narrow the list too severely, we lose the flexibility and creativity we gained by brainstorming.

Framing Revisited

A party may reject an offer simply because the opposing party suggested the solution. When a party dismisses or devalues offers simply because they come from the opposing party we call it *reactive devaluation*. In their mind, any suggestion from the opponent must be flawed.

We can avoid reactive devaluation by having the mediator frame a proposal as his own. The mediator presents an offer as tentative: "Here is an idea I would like to explore." Or he may say, "I have been listening to both parties and I wonder if this idea might meet your needs." In reframing the offer or demand as at least partially his own, the mediator moves the process forward. You may want to consider if it is advantageous to have a third party front a solution you would like considered.

Values may also be framed to avoid triggering escalation. During mediation we learn that the frame of reference used to evaluate decisions can become more malleable than we first imagined. Mediation helps us embrace movement and flexibility. Rather than bracing our defenses at the first sign of differences we embrace the views in play with genuine curiosity. In a nonthreatening setting we are free to get inside the other party's head and test drive solutions from their point of view. After we release the tight grip of the oppositional embrace we learn to dance rather than wrestle. The ability to frame values and beliefs in ways that do not give offense improves our ability to "dance."

Francis, a peacemaker, viewed the world through a different frame of reference than that held by the wolf and the citizens of Gubbio. This is not uncommon. Their experience of successful resolution allows mediators to frame offers, demands, reasons, values, and behavior in ways that promote hope. They provide the glue that holds the process together during early stages when the parties cannot always see their actions and options in a positive frame.

Francis assures the wolf he will present the proposed solution in such a way that the idea will be seriously considered by the townspeople. He is confident that he possesses the skill needed to frame the solution so it will be acceptable to the citizens of Gubbio.

A party begins to see how careful framing avoids emotional triggers and obstacles, and begins to view the process as a journey that demands skill and finesse but nonetheless a journey it is possible to complete. In providing hope, the mediator performs one of the most important tasks in mediation.

Negotiation

When St. Francis suggests a solution to the conflict he kicks off the negotiation phase. For the first time we hear of a possible end to the conflict. Yet conflict resolution remains a possibility, not an actuality. Hard work remains – the hard work of negotiation.

Many parties do not know how to negotiate, while others are sophisticated negotiators. Numerous books and academic texts are devoted to the subject of negotiation; they are recommended for those who wish to become proficient. While we cannot cover the topic in thorough detail, we can introduce key concepts.

Negotiation is a process wherein two parties attempt to reach an agreement to exchange something of value (tangible or intangible) on terms suitable to both. They discuss valuables they are willing to *give up* and valuables they would like to *receive*. A critical focus is balancing the value exchanged – how do we balance what we give with what we receive? The exchange may involve tangible goods such as money or property or intangibles, such as respect, status, apology, power, or promises of peace.

In conflict resolution, negotiation often addresses the need to repair imbalanced, inhibited, or non-existent exchange. In most conflicts give-and-take has gone awry. Conflict originates when Party A wants something Party B possesses, which B refuses to give to A. Party A may want a job that B can award, but B refuses to grant the job to A. Or conflict results when B forces A to have something they do not want; for example, B demands A remain in an abusive relationship that A would like to terminate.

These issues of exchange – things we want but cannot have or things we do not want but are forced to have – parallel issues of domination and coercion. In healthy, low-conflict relationships, exchanges are balanced and freely given, but where we have conflict we typically have imbalanced or non-existent exchange. We often find an earlier negotiation has caused a problem with exchange and we now seek to remedy that prior failed negotiation with a facilitated negotiation (mediation) that brings exchange back into line.

In earlier discussions we introduced two basic types of negotiation: *distributive bargaining* in which a fixed pie is divided among the parties and *integrative bargaining* in which parties seek to integrate their respective interests to maximize benefit to both. In negotiation we may divide the pie, expand the pie, or both.

Distributive Bargaining

Distributive bargaining is often called *the dance*. One party makes a demand and the other party responds with an offer that generates a new demand or counter offer. This continues until parties successfully arrive at an agreement. The process is characterized as a dance because of the back-and-forth nature of the process in which one step motivates a matching step.

You may have been raised to avoid bartering – as I was. For many years I held the view that there is one price and that is it. I don't bargain or haggle. Yet we all engage in negotiation every day without being aware of it. Life is filled with the dance of negotiation. We engage in a dynamic give-and-take. We live in an interdependent condition, we are brothers and sisters to one another. Thus we must negotiate a constant give-and-take.

Even if we successfully meet our needs in day-to-day affairs, most of us remain unskilled in the formal dance of negotiation. Past upsets with exchange inhibit our participation. While this give-and-take may not be our natural strength it is a mistake to bail out or shortcut the process. We serve others and ourselves better by preparing to play an active role. The dance has hidden value that comes to light with experience. We gain increased comfort with the process as we take part.

One hidden value of negotiation is the dialogue that accompanies offers and demands. When we present a demand or an offer, we typically present a reason we believe that demand or offer correctly values the exchange. When the other party rejects our demands or offers, they express their views regarding value. As we consider counter offer after counter offer, as we complete dance step after dance step, we refine our understanding of the value assigned to the tangibles and intangibles involved.

At the conclusion of negotiation the effort we have expended leaves us feeling we have hammered out a fair exchange. If the other side accepts our first offer, we worry that we offered too much – would they have taken considerably less? In contrast, engaging the process provides certainty that we have crafted the best deal possible: we have not offered more than absolutely necessary nor accepted less than necessary.[12] When the music ends we leave the table understanding how we arrived at the values reflected in our agreement.

Realizing we will be engaged in negotiating offers and counter offers, we often wonder whether or not we should make the first offer and how we will determine the appropriate starting figure. While many people believe it is best to wait for the other party to make the first move – as that provides information on how they value the exchange – it is also true that the first number, if reasonable, tends to anchor the negotiation.

If you make the first offer and start low, the range of offers might fall within a lower range. There are limits to this anchoring effect. The first offer must fall within a *reasonable zone*. Offers or demands outside that zone – offers that are too low or demands that are too high – will be considered an insult. Insulting offers or demands will be disregarded and not considered valid. The insult given may slow or derail the process. This suggests we should spend time, in advance, estimating the reasonable zone.[13] If we are confident in our knowledge of the reasonable zone, we make the first offer and anchor the negotiation closer to the end of the zone we prefer.

These and other considerations go into the process of reaching an agreement with the other party regarding exchanges that satisfy our interests. In the negotiation we allow the dialogue regarding value to determine a fair outcome.

Integrative Bargaining

When we move to integrative bargaining and adopt an interest-based style, discussion goes beyond dividing the pie to include plans and projections for how we might increase the total benefit stream in order to satisfy both parties' needs.

For example, an employee may desire to significantly increase their income. If management considers the customer base is fixed, which limits revenue, there is a clash between the employee's need to earn more and management's need to hold down costs. In integrative bargaining the employee reveals he has unique marketing skills that will allow him to significantly increase the customer base and company revenue. Management agrees to underwrite the marketing plan and to pay him a significant bonus for additional customers. With the new plan both the employee and employer benefit from increased business, from an expanded pie.

When one moves to integrative bargaining the number of possible outcomes skyrockets. The focus becomes collaborative – how can we work together to increase the benefits available so we can all meet our needs and interests? This creative collaboration process removes barriers to expanding the pie; increased value emerges; communication is restored.

When parties trade their respective bargaining rationales they understand each other better. Previously, parties may not have understood the value their counterpart attributes to the tangibles or intangibles for which they are negotiating.

The personal transformation we experience during the conflict resolution process elevates integrative bargaining into a creative co-authoring of the future. In the *Taming the Wolf* approach this is accomplished with the collaborative affinity of the I-Thou relationship. A shared future emerges from mutual recognition of the interconnectedness of "brothers and sisters" who recognize the presence of the divine in one another.

Satisfaction as a Measure of Success

St. Francis seeks to meet the needs of both the wolf and the townspeople, but how will he measure success? The measure of success is *party satisfaction*. Francis orients the parties to the concept that *both* must be satisfied if there is to be peace. A third-party observer cannot truly judge success – as the observer's criteria for satisfaction may not match the criteria of the parties. An outsider cannot know accurately what will bring the parties satisfaction. An objective measurement of success cannot be found; subjective satisfaction determines success.

Satisfaction can be represented by a triangle in which the sides represent substantive, procedural, and psychological satisfaction.

Substantive satisfaction concerns the substance of the agreement – was the party satisfied with the exchange of valuables, tangible and intangible? Did the outcome meet his needs?

Procedural satisfaction concerns perception of the process – was it fair and just? Procedural satisfaction exists when the process, the manner in which the outcome was achieved, is judged to have been fair and equitable.

Psychological satisfaction results when a party feels they have been treated with respect and their emotional needs have been honored. When empathy for feelings and concerns has been shown a party will rank psychological satisfaction high.

When you know the goal of mediation is satisfaction in these three areas, it becomes easier to prepare. You know where to focus your attention. You know the objectives that must be met. Rather than focus merely on the substantive outcome you hope to achieve, you realize how you go about achieving the outcome matters, and how you treat the other party matters. Only when all three factors are considered do you achieve a satisfactory outcome that will endure.

Tactics

When we consider negotiation we often think of tactics used to achieve an advantage. This raises a number of questions: Should we be skilled in the use of tactics? Must we be skilled in defending against tactics? When do tactics become deceptive and unfair and when are tactics valid means of procuring the best deal possible?

In the negotiation literature, tactics are frequently addressed in the context of how lawyers should ethically represent clients. The consensus in the legal community appears to endorse the use of aggressive, self-serving tactics.

These tactics may deceive the other party regarding one's true intentions. They may deceive the other party regarding the value of the exchange. But such deception must not cross the line into *material misrepresentations*.

When one misrepresents a material fact such as the square footage of a property or the actual mileage on a used car that misrepresentation can be discovered later, providing the other party with verifiable evidence of wrongdoing and wrong dealing. Short of such violations, the legal community appears to support tactics that defeat transparency. There is little call for transparency. In fact, a lack of transparency is often honored as a necessary aspect of negotiation. I tend to disagree with this point of view, though I realize drawing clear lines of proper disclosure in a highly subjective endeavor such as negotiation is difficult if not impossible. While complete transparency may be overly idealistic and even impossible that does not mean an intention to deceive is the best approach.

I would argue that the I-Thou relationship we are trying to achieve as we seek reconciliation depends heavily on transparency, honesty, and caring for the other. Attorneys, who are less concerned with reconciliation, often take a different view. The following quotes capture the dilemma of an adversarial view of negotiation: "The critical difference between those who are successful negotiators and those who are not lies in this capacity both to mislead and not to be misled.... To conceal one's true position, to mislead an opponent about one's true settling point, is the essence of negotiation.... Of course there are limits on acceptable deceptive behavior in negotiation, but there is the paradox. How can one be 'fair' but also mislead? Can we ask the negotiator to mislead, but fairly, like the soldier who must kill, but humanely?"[14]

The concept of zealous advocacy – getting all you can for your client – drives the dilemma. Another article clarifies the position of the Bar: "The *Model Rules* adopt the hard-line position that when negotiators make assertions about their settlement authority or the legitimacy of demands they are making, they do not vouch for the truthfulness of their assertions, regardless of how sincere they may seem. If a gullible person on the other side of the table believes a negotiator's false statement about a bargaining position, the fault lies with the person who is ignorant of the rules, and not with the one who intentionally misleads."[15]

It is vital we understand the consequences of this view (common in Hollywood, on Wall Street, and in Washington). While some might consider this approach maximizes the rewards an individual enjoys, such views may be shortsighted. If we argue that the party who is deceived is to blame for his failure to recognize he is being deceived, in essence, we argue that trust plays no role in negotiation. The minute we abandon trust as a fundamental principle, cultural institutions crumble under the weight of corrupt practices justified as good negotiation.

In the long run, when trust crumbles, systems that depend on trust cease to work properly. The citizens of entire nations suffer as global and national economies seize up and the willingness to do business – willingness to exchange one valuable for another – diminishes. As we map the consequences that lie beyond short-term individual gain, the common argument found in the legal community warrants skepticism.

Another article helps shed light on the purpose of tactics: "The essence of much bargaining involves changing another's perceptions of where in fact one would settle. Several kinds of tactics can lead to impressions that are at variance with the truth about one's actual position: persuasive rationales, commitments, references to other no-agreement alternatives, calculated patterns of concessions, failures to correct misperceptions, and the like. These tactics are tempting for obvious reasons: one side may claim value by causing the other to misperceive the range of potentially acceptable agreements."[16] In a competitive negotiation, which is where most mediation begins, the idea of causing the other party to misperceive value seems natural. If one seeks a larger piece of the pie or to have one's interests satisfied to the exclusion of the other, using tactics makes perfect sense.

However, as we move toward a collaborative approach we see less need to claim value by causing the other to misperceive value or our intentions. In fact, the opposite is true: both sides benefit by gaining an accurate understanding of the value each places on tangibles and intangibles to be exchanged. The collaborative approach leads to durable settlements, as those settlements are based on accurate information and clear intentions.

Nonetheless, when one sits at the negotiating table the decision becomes difficult. Should you engage in tactics to better your position? To what the degree should those tactics be deceptive? Our natural approach to negotiation starts on the competitive end of the scale, which involves tactical planning. The unanticipated factor that changes the equation is the manner in which our relationship with the other party develops. As empathy and compassion increase, as mutual caring and respect improve, and as willingness to collaborate grows, tactics and deception feel increasingly out of place.

However, if we are unable to provide a firm and accurate statement of the value we place on something this does not mean, necessarily, that we are being deceptive. Many times we are not being deceptive as much as engaging in bargaining as a method of *clarifying the value* something has for us.

At the outset, we may believe we have a firm value in mind based on a factual appraisal, but our perception of value is always tentative, always subjective. The final value can only be determined by give-and-take bargaining. As we negotiate, the true value emerges out of the interaction. The value we perceive becomes a function of the value the other party attaches to the same tangible or intangible property. Our changing appraisal, by itself, is not an indication of deceptive tactics but rather a natural part of the search for an accurate appraisal of value.

The more competitive the negotiation, the more likely tactics make sense; the more collaborative the process, the less likely tactics make sense. The downside to tactical negotiation, particularly the use of deceptive tactics, is their long-term adverse consequences. When we negotiate to our advantage without considering the satisfaction of the other party we engineer an outcome that may fail to endure. When deceptive representations or false information come to light, as they must in the long term, confidence and trust are diminished or destroyed. Future conflicts become harder to resolve.

As I write this chapter a financial crisis threatens the globe. A perception of widespread corruption on Wall Street and in Washington exists. The credit markets, suffering a loss of confidence, have been rocked. To a significant extent this crisis is the product of a powerful lawyer class acting on the (mistaken) belief that if a person suffers a loss as a result of another person's deceptive representations the person who was deceived is at fault. The fault lies with the person who was cheated, who simply wasn't smart enough to protect their interests. (Or the person who hired lawyers that weren't smart enough to protect them). The party who successfully deceives is honored, while the party deceived is labeled gullible. This idea – that the party who was deceived deserves the blame – is an ethic that degrades an entire culture. When social trust is betrayed conflict escalates and ruins lives.

The *Taming the Wolf* approach endorses collaboration in which parties are candid, honest, and transparent. It involves respect for the divine in each other, it acknowledges our interdependent condition. A culture suffering a breakdown in trust and transparency must be mended with a new cultural ethic that recognizes the brotherhood of Mankind.

Renegotiating the Social Contract

Taming the Wolf, though written with the individual in mind, also applies to the need to renegotiate the social contract that binds us as brothers and sisters. This contract can no longer celebrate deceptive tactics. It can no longer celebrate the falsehood that individuals bear no responsibility for our mutual fate. When Jesus delivered the Sermon on the Mount he spoke to all times, all places, and all people.

When St. Francis followed Christ with a passion that placed all other relationships in their proper perspective, he was not offering irrelevant poetry lacking in substance. He honored the need for us to embrace each other as creatures of God with compassion in heart and deed, to set aside attachment to material possessions, and to elevate the Spirit within to its proper place in our lives. He spoke to the heart of our social contract, recognizing that contract is a harmonic of our divine contract.

Renegotiating our social contract is not something to be done abstractly. It is an action we take by negotiating anew our relationship with every person we encounter. When we meet the Other whether we acknowledge the fact or not, we negotiate the respect and love we are willing to exchange. We also negotiate the degree to which we are willing to enter into relationship with the divine – as the divine manifests in the heart of the other person. Day-by-day we negotiate our journey toward the spiritual kingdom. When we deceive ourselves or deceive another, when we use power to dominate and coerce, when we seek to gain an unfair advantage in possessions and position, when we excuse our use of tactical deception in our dealings, at that time we negotiate into existence a hellish condition in which crisis after crisis delivers suffering.

Taming the Wolf focuses on handling conflict that ruins our lives. The focus is on the crisis that takes shape when our needs and interests clash with those of another. Focus is on the acute pain conflict causes. We must remember these tools play a role in our daily living. We are continually negotiating relationship with each other and with God. We come to this sacred negotiating table knowing we want more, knowing we can give more.

Good Faith

In preparation for mediation you may want to commit to paper your personal ethical rules for negotiation. This short document, comprised of fundamental ethical axioms to which you will adhere during negotiation, may include statements regarding trust, lack of deception, values, the Golden Rule, and respect. It may be culled from scripture or may be drawn from personal policy you have adopted for conducting your life.

Use this list to draft process guidelines that will make mediation safe and effective. Procedural guidelines may concern the manner in which parties address one another, confidentiality and public disclosure, setting agendas, scheduling and logistics concerns, the role of the mediator, and the identification of stakeholders.

A common agreement is that parties show up prepared for *good faith* negotiation. Good faith is somewhat vague but commonly assumed to include honesty with regards to facts, truthfulness, and the absence of behavior that could be considered *bad faith*. You may want to codify acceptable good faith behavior by discussing the following: issues regarding discovery procedures; how you will encourage a frank and candid exchange; confidentiality regarding information revealed exclusively for mediation; procedures for disclosing positions, interests, concerns; agreements regarding caucus (private session) procedures; agreements regarding confidentiality of private sessions; housekeeping issues such as schedules, locations, contact information. Take up any additional concerns unique to a particular conflict that can be addressed while setting procedural ground rules.

You might suggest principles that can be used to monitor the relationship. For example, Francis developed admonitions designed to help friars manage their personal relations.[17] In some instances the conflict history may include offensive or harmful behavior. Good faith may need to be defined as a cessation of such hostility that might include name-calling, disrespect, physical abuse, or other threatening actions.

I have witnessed situations in which one of the parties has engaged in innuendo and character assassination in an attempt to rob the other party of reputation and power. In such cases, at the beginning of mediation the party who was slandered may request that such slander – reports not accompanied by verified facts – be excluded from the discussion. The slandered party may request the proceedings be captured in written minutes or on video or that a witness be present to prevent future distortion and misrepresentation of the events that transpire.

While often it makes sense to hammer out procedural agreements, this step can be overdone, stalling the process. The best policy is to set the minimum procedural guidelines required to enable the process to begin. The mediator, listening to the parties, should have a good sense of how far she should go in facilitating negotiation of procedural guidelines during the opening, as opposed to negotiating acceptable behavior during the process. This is a judgment call and is subject to error, so it helps for you to suggest guidelines you require to feel safe and willing to engage in the process.

A Franciscan View

The Franciscan worldview colors the *Taming the Wolf* approach to conflict resolution. Ilia Delio, in *The Humility of God*, describes the Franciscan focus on nurturing relationships. "The necessity of the other for Francis thrust him into radical poverty whereby everything that hindered his relation to the other was stripped away."[18]

It is not hard to imagine Francis setting aside all concerns except the satisfaction of the other person, even when the person sitting across the table held different views, for "the difference of the other … was not an obstacle for Francis but rather a celebration of God. For he found his identity in God, and he found God in the ordinary, fragile human flesh of the other."[19]

This did not mean Francis lost the ability to discern differences during negotiation for "although Francis' world with Christ as center attained a unity and harmony, it was not a totalizing unity of sameness but rather a unity of difference."[20] Unity, in the Franciscan view, does not demand the other party conform to a vision of sameness but rather includes a celebration of differences.

For example, "Bonaventure indicates that the fullness of the mystery of Christ is the fullness of otherness and difference."[21] We discover a worldview grounded in unity that embraces pluralism and inclusivity. We find these views expressed by one of the first Franciscan theologians: "In Bonaventure's view, the word 'God' denotes inexhaustible love in which love of the other is love of God. This love is nothing less than the humility of God's goodness shining through everything that exists, including the fragile things of creation."[22]

Earlier in this chapter, we discussed the role of pluralism and inclusivity in allowing us to overcome barriers erected by differences. The practical application of pluralism and inclusivity, however, may give us pause. The task is not easy. To discover potential paths around the barrier of differences, we turn to the concept of shared core values: "Various scholars are pointing out today that other religious traditions do embody the core values of the Christ mystery without naming them such as love, compassion, mercy, forgiveness, reconciliation, peace, enlightenment."[23] Our ability to embrace shared values may depend on our acceptance of a concept grounded in Franciscan history: "It is not important that Christ be named. It is important that Christ be lived."[24]

While Francis inspired with his preaching – even the birds would grow silent and listen – it was the way he lived in devotion to a Gospel life that moved others to join him as brothers and sisters. Yet Francis did not demand that friars copy him; he did not insist they be exactly like him. Rather, he embraced diversity. "Francis prayed day and night that God would give all men the courage to be themselves instead of what others expected them to be."[25]

His mission was to liberate men and women from attachments that kept them chained to suffering. "He did not want all men to enter the brotherhood or to join the Lady Clare and her sisters. He only wanted them to be free, to be what they wanted to be in their own hearts."[26]

Francis loved with his eyes. His glance could set others free from suffering and yet "civilization dulls this power of the glance. A part of the education the world gives us consists in teaching our eyes to deceive, in making them expressionless, in extinguishing their flames."[27] When we harbor a Franciscan worldview our glance instead imparts love. When resolution of conflict depends on our ability to tear down walls of separation, "if we truly see and love what we see then the walls that separate – culture from culture, religion from religion, people from people – must crumble. Where there is Christ there can be no hatred or jealousy or anger or bitterness. There can only be love, the love that unites not by clinging to things for themselves, but by giving itself away, by suffering and death for the sake of the greater union."[28]

We may be challenged by the paradoxes inherent in Francis' devotion to Lady Poverty who "was *the* symbol of the paradoxes of the Gospel; richness in poverty, life in death, strength in weakness, beauty in the sordid and shabby, peace in conflict and temptation, fullness in emptiness, and above all, love in detachment and deprivation."[29]

But when we become confused, we may turn to the following, "Man is complex and God is simple and the closer one approaches God, the simpler one becomes in Faith and Hope and Love."[30] When worldview differences impede our ability to reconcile we seek such simplicity. At such times we consider, "Perhaps there [is] a great chasm between piety and goodness. Piety, after all, [is] something mainly external and goodness was in the heart."[31] With increased introspection, we may discover we have saddled ourselves with external expectations that inhibit our ability to act from our heart.

Francis was not naïve when it came to the hostility that might erupt from those who do not understand or respect our worldview. He was the target of ridicule and hostility simply for following his dream. "He was shabby and unkempt and the crowds hissed and mocked that the son of the richest man in town should go begging for stones to repair churches."[32] In his poverty, however, he came to recognize more clearly the spiritual conditions that surrounded him: "It was marvelous how people became who they really were once you reached out your hand to them in the gesture of a beggar."[33]

He came to know with certainty that "when the secret desire for appropriation is thwarted, agitation, irritation, anger, and rupture are the result. Francis rightly saw, too, that man on his own cannot overcome this desire and liberate himself from this shrinking back on himself and his own works."[34] The remedy, he understood, was the power of the Gospel on display in the life he led with the Friars Minor.

This insight continues to live in the example of the Friars Minor, as we find in a handbook that addresses peace and justice efforts: "For the knowledge of suffering to move us to work for its elimination, it must have an effect on us, it must reach down to the depths of our being, to the heart, and move us to compassion. We truly know only that which we endure or, better still, that which is shared suffering. For the Christian the only genuine knowledge is that which moves us to compassion."[35] In these words of contemporary friars, we find the charism of Francis.

In the guidelines for contemporary Friars we find a worldview that honors peace and justice, a worldview that recognizes the importance of social justice. The following excerpts express these values: "6. The friars must defend the rights of the poor in a spirit of minority, renouncing all temptation to power and violent action (GGCC 69,1) and being sure to neither despise nor judge the powerful and the rich (GGCC 98,1). 8. The friars should devote themselves to establishing a society of justice, liberty and peace, together with all people of good will. 10. To 'those people who threaten life and liberty' the friars are 'to offer them the good news of reconciliation and conversion (GGCC 98,2)."[36] And, "1. All the friars should be agents of peace."

The guidelines illustrate the demeanor we might expect from a Franciscan: "(e) Dealing with conflict through dialogue and not through power and manipulation; not leaving aside those who are intellectually less gifted or those who are physically weak, but caring for them lovingly (GGCC 44). (d) Promoting ecumenical and inter-religious dialogue and collaboration (GGCC 95, 1-3). (h) Humbly exhorting the rich and powerful, inviting them to practice solidarity and justice, and calling to conversion those who threaten life and liberty (GGCC 98,1-2)"[37]

Assuming an attitude of humble love does not mean we capitulate to injustice. Rather, the quoted advisory points to a style of being at the table. Duplicity and manipulation are eschewed. "Francis feared duplicity and hypocrisy more than anything in all the world. It was against hypocrisy that Jesus had railed again and again in the Gospels, and Francis was sure Jesus would never speak harshly against anything unless it spoiled the human heart and made the Holy Spirit's entry there impossible."[38]

We can imagine Francis would hold firm in his effort to expose and expunge duplicitous tactics from the proceedings. This does not mean he dismissed valid differences. Current guidelines tell us otherwise: "All activities, both fraternal and pastoral, should be reviewed so as to eliminate any hint of intolerance, division, exclusion, or lack of equality. Following Jesus is authentic when we recognize the value of each person, and when we practice mercy, reconciliation, forgiveness, etc."[39]

Scripture

Immediately the one who received five talents went and traded with them, and made another five. Likewise, the one who received two made another two. But the man who received one went off and dug a hole in the ground and buried his master's money. (Mt 25:16-18)

He made a whip of out cords and drove them all out of the temple area, with the sheep and oxen, and spilled the coins of the money-changers and overturned their tables, and to those who sold doves he said, "Take these out of here, and stop making my Father's house a marketplace." (Jn 2:15-16)

Still God had regard for their affliction
* when he heard their wailing.*
For their sake he remembered his covenant
* and relented in his abundant mercy,*
Winning for them compassion
* from all who held them captive. (Ps 106:44-46)*

CHAPTER SIXTEEN

Apology

He knew [the people of Gubbio] could let go of their fear and hate if they saw the wolf ask for forgiveness and accede to a peaceful relationship.

Francis extended his hand. The wolf showed agreement by placing his paw in Francis' hand and Francis began to call him Brother Wolf.

Francis and Brother Wolf walked back to Gubbio.

As they neared the gate, the citizens could not believe their eyes.

Francis and Brother Wolf continued to the town square, although the Mayor and the entire town watched with hate and fear.

Brother Wolf had to keep his eyes on Francis to still his fear.

Francis called out, "Come, the wolf will not hurt you. Let us talk in peace. I have spoken with Brother Wolf and he apologizes for his actions and wants to make amends."

Francis told them Brother Wolf's story.

Mediation Principles

FRANCIS RETURNS TO GUBBIO to facilitate the negotiation between Brother Wolf and the people of Gubbio. The citizens are not emotionally prepared to hear directly from Brother Wolf; their wounds and hatred make it difficult to listen with their hearts. Brother Wolf, who also experiences trepidation, is in no emotional condition to present an opening offer in his own words. Therefore, Francis, framing his effort as an invitation to talk peace, delivers Brother Wolf's offer: an apology and a promise of amends.

The townspeople, though skeptical, are willing to listen, as they have learned to trust Francis. This is common. When a neutral mediator, who has agreed to entertain a party's concerns and fears in a fair and just manner, delivers the opening offer that offer is more likely to be considered. When Francis delivers Brother Wolf's proposal he establishes the emotional space needed for hope to take root. If the townspeople were forced to listen to Brother Wolf hope might be blunted by painful emotions. Francis, who speaks with compassion and a loving heart to his brothers and sisters, delivers the narrative in a manner that penetrates emotional defenses. He speaks to hearts as well as to minds.

When Francis then meets with Brother Wolf and the townspeople in private sessions, he delivers carefully framed messages to the parties. He shuttles demands and offers. His presence allows the parties to slowly break away from the oppositional embrace and to hear suggestions. The mediator may forego shuttle diplomacy and facilitate face-to-face exchanges as such joint sessions are preferable when possible. However, while face-to-face negotiations have benefits – for example, they prepare parties for future dealings when the mediator is no longer present – it is not always possible or wise to convene joint sessions.

These initial negotiations rarely proceed without challenges. A common barrier is a lack of apology and forgiveness. Until the relationship is restored through apology and forgiveness, agreements on matters of substance remain out of reach. In this chapter, we consider the role apology plays in building bridges. In the next chapter, we consider forgiveness.

Building Bridges

Francis has garnered a preliminary understanding of the conflict. He now begins to construct a metaphorical bridge over which parties may travel as they seek reconciliation. He must span the divide with mediation techniques. His demeanor becomes important as he forms the temporary link that sustains the dialogue as parties test whether or not it is possible to reconcile differences.

At this stage, mediators like Francis who have personally experienced spiritual transformation tend to infuse the process with a contagious form of unconditional love. They model a forgiving heart and patient humility, qualities used to shape a temporary bridge that arcs over existing barriers.

After establishing this temporary bridge the mediator facilitates the construction of a more permanent bridge that will remain standing after his work is completed. Until the parties find the inner strength needed to support their own bridge, the mediator sustains the process. He is analogous to a construction foreman: he helps parties locate appropriate building materials and provides a blueprint for the construction of a safe and secure bridge.

As the process advances, parties recognize their responsibility for mining bridge-building materials. The mediator prepares them to accomplish the heavy lifting that is required to build a lasting structure. The bridge-building process rarely proceeds without interruption or challenges. Barriers materialize and block the path; impasses spring up and halt forward progress; construction stalls. The mediator guides parties past impediments and roadblocks until they gain the skill necessary to plot their own detours around barriers.

Perhaps the most common barrier is the lack of apology. Extending an apology may seem a simple matter – most of us have had to say, "I'm sorry" – yet the subject turns out to be more complex than is apparent at first glance. The following discussion: (1) clarifies the elements of a successful apology; (2) describes how an apology functions; (3) explores the value an apology brings to the conflict resolution process; (4) exposes errors that can cause an apology to be rejected; and (5) suggests ways to avoid common errors in making an apology.[1]

Value of an Apology

A successful apology imparts a medley of benefits. The following descriptions unpack these benefits into categories that will aid your planning. The more benefits an apology contributes the more likely the apology will be accepted. As you read, consider how you will structure an apology that fits your situation. Keep in mind the words of Brian Cox: "A proper apology can be the most powerful and liberating component of healing a relationship."[2]

[*Note*: I use the terms *offender* and *victim*. This implies one party has committed a harmful act and the other party has been damaged, but this is rarely accurate. A clean dichotomy between offender and victim is unusual. In most conflicts both parties commit harmful acts. Apologies are owed on both sides of the table.]

AN APOLOGY SHOWS RESPECT. When we admit transgressions we humble ourselves; we lower ourselves and lift up the other party in a show of respect. Admitting misdeeds honors and restores the other party's dignity, which has been diminished by our harmful actions. When we harm someone we rob them, intentionally or unintentionally, of pride and dignity – as a harmful deed communicates we do not value their feelings, identity, or needs.

Apology reverses the implicit or explicit invalidation of the other party's worth. It communicates and demonstrates willingness to suffer shame and humiliation in order to validate their worth. An apology expresses willingness to shift focus from our needs to the needs of the other person. We bend low on one knee and bow our head before the *divine within the other*; we place their worth and interests on a level equal to or above our own. An apology conveys we are willing to show them deserved respect and restore their stolen dignity.

Errors that sabotage an apology include all the ways we fail to show respect. Apologies delivered with a superior attitude and apologies mumbled as an aside not only fail to provide needed respect, they convey additional disrespect. An apology that attempts to maintain a dominant or coercive position – which leaves the offended party in the position of a victim – will fail.

The act of conveying respect requires us to lift up the other person, not to keep them down. If we do not lift them up we do not satisfy their need for respect. If we fail to bend down before them and beg forgiveness, we communicate our intention to revive our status instead of acknowledging their status.

In order to avoid these errors we ask ourselves if we actually respect the other party enough to deliver a sincere apology. Can we assume a humble attitude that lifts them up? Can we look them in the eye and acknowledge we caused harm? Can we can bend low on one knee, literally or metaphorically, and solicit their forgiveness? Can we show respect by giving them choice over whether or not we are to be forgiven?

In the course of the conflict we may come to perceive the other as so evil or low that kneeling before them creates dissonance so strong we are paralyzed, unable to act. We find it difficult to imagine ourselves in a renewed relationship. We hesitate. If the task appears overwhelming, it may be necessary to address our feelings toward the other party in more depth. We must complete additional inner work before we attempt to structure an apology.

One approach to overcoming reticence is concentrating on seeing the divine within the other party and experiencing the humility we feel when we kneel before God. In this way, we may discover that aspect of the other party we *can* respect, that part of them we *can* lift up above us. Connecting to the *divine within the other* may provide the spark needed to enable a show of respect. This approach may require us to see everyone as brothers and sisters as Francis did.

AN APOLOGY IS AN EMPATHETIC EXPRESSION OF CONCERN. An expression of apology demonstrates empathy; it tells the offended party we are capable of feeling their pain and suffering. When it comes to empathy it does not matter if the harm suffered was a direct result of our actions or whether our deeds were intentional or unintentional. When we experience empathy we recognize and feel the other's pain and suffering.

Without this expression of empathy the other party is not certain we truly "get it." In the victim's mind, if we do not feel their hurt we might not have sufficient reason to avoid causing them pain in the future. Thus, in the absence of an apology the victim harbors doubts about the wisdom of collaboration. They are not eager to come to the table to work on reconciliation. A sincere apology offers the victim hope that we can see the world in the same manner they see the world – complete with hurt and humiliation.

Possible **errors** include delivering an apology that communicates we do not understand the severity of their pain. A breezy, glib, or abstract apology fails to connect with the hurt they feel. A rote or glib apology will not convince the victim we grasp the harm suffered. In contrast, an empathetic apology connects at a feeling level. It is not easily faked, as counterfeit empathy rings false and sounds hollow.

The harvest of a non-empathetic apology is an awkward cessation of dialogue. The process grinds to a halt while the cause of impasse – a lack of empathy – goes unrecognized. The victim, upon receiving an unfeeling apology, may strive harder to make the offender feel their pain. They may desire to inflict pain that forces the offender to feel what they feel – they may drag out costly litigation designed to make the offender suffer financially.

A similar but more egregious error is for the offender to question the victim's suffering – to imply the victim could not possibly suffer as they claim. The common response to this error is an emotional storm that ends with the victim demanding the conflict resolution process be terminated immediately.

A solution for lack of empathy is to approach the victim in the manner of St. Francis, as though the victim is a brother or sister. The imagined affinity automatically opens a non-verbal connection that allows empathy to work below the surface. This intuitive approach, which has the quality of a silent prayer, can be a challenge. It is difficult to see others through the eyes of a Franciscan. For this reason it is important to practice greeting others with the face of a Franciscan each day. Then, when we are faced with a difficult moment that requires empathy, we will be up to the task. In other words, we learn to recognize the movement of the indwelling Spirit through daily practice as we interact with others.

When we are challenged to show empathy, we are challenged to perceive the feelings of the other person and care about those feelings. This may be as simple as recalling a time we were in the same position. Or we may seek to discover a spark of divinity in their gestures, their eyes, or in their voice.

At times we may notice the other party is afraid of us. For a fleeting moment we see ourselves through their eyes – as someone to be feared. We are humbled when we recognize we caused harm. We experience empathy, knowing we would not wish to suffer the harm we caused. Unless we are sadists or psychopaths we are saddened to learn our presence causes the discomfort of fear. Our empathy lets the other person know we understand their suffering, and we are concerned.

AN APOLOGY EXPRESSES ACCEPTANCE OF RESPONSIBILITY. Accepting responsibility for pain, suffering, loss, or other unwanted condition experienced as a result of our actions is an important factor in a successful apology. This aspect of an apology addresses our causative role in another's suffering. As Brian Cox notes in *Faith-Based Reconciliation*, "it requires a willingness to be held accountable for one's actions toward God, toward the victim, and toward the larger community."[3]

If we omit a statement of responsibility and omit a recitation of details regarding our transgressions the other party doubts our sincerity. They worry that we will inflict additional harm on them, as we have not properly understood how our past actions caused pain and suffering.

A failure to acknowledge we are responsible for our actions communicates that we suffer an inaccurate perception of causality. In our victim's eyes, if we lack awareness of the effects we caused, we are prone to causing additional harm. When we commit harm for which we do not recognize we are responsible we become a continuing source of danger in the eyes of the other party. The victim, with good cause, assumes our lack of insight into our responsibility might be the soil in which future harm takes root.

In contrast, if we accept responsibility and detail our role in causing their suffering the other party gains comfort. They see we are sufficiently cognizant of our actions to avoid future wrongdoing. When we take responsibility we acknowledge we are aware that we possess free will and that we are able to exercise discernment and choice. When we assume responsibility we tacitly agree that we will make better decisions and exert better control over our actions in the future.

Errors include apologizing for the wrong action or apologizing for actions of little import (actions that carry minor sanction), while neglecting more important misdeeds (for which we may be punished). When we deflect blame by attributing other cause to the harm we delivered we undermine our apology.

The most extreme case of deflecting blame occurs when we argue the victim caused themselves the harm they suffered. This deflection of blame might be phrased, "I'm sorry you suffered, but you know your suffering was the result of your own doing, right?" This egregious error occurs when you express regret then lecture the victim on why they should not have put themselves in harm's way. For example, you might explain that if they had not trusted you they would not have been hurt. Other variations include blaming chance, nature, or even God for the misfortune that befell the victim.

Additionally, if you acknowledge your acts caused harm but then claim you were not in control of your actions, that you were impaired, your apology will fail. An extreme version of this error comes from those who invoke an ontological defense claiming there is no such thing as free will – their actions are simply predetermined by biology or unknown forces operating in the universe. "It wasn't my fault, the Devil made me do it."

A subtle dodge occurs when a party promises they will take responsibility *if* the other party also takes responsibility. While there is validity in the idea that most conflicts involve mutual responsibility, this type of statement is an attempt to mitigate responsibility and diffuse blame. It fails to reach the level of a valid apology.

Deflection of responsibility provokes the harmed party to undertake new efforts to demonstrate, through the imposition of penalties and punishment, that your actions have consequences. The more unwilling you are to recognize and acknowledge responsibility, the more they wish for you to suffer consequences that will teach you a lesson.

It is difficult to accept responsibility for causing harm. There are no easy answers to this challenge, as our minds, chattering like monkeys who sense danger, refuse to be calmed. The harm we have done is the last thing we want to sit with. Our natural impulse, when it comes to harm we have done, is to cover up the memory with a blanket of forgetting.

If we were not locked in conflict from which we seek respite, we would certainly head for the hills in avoidance or beat our chest in a show of aggression against intruders inquiring into our transgressions. In most cases, we furiously rewrite the narrative in order to justify our behavior with a story that places our white hat back where it belongs. We script accounts that excuse our failings with all manner of artful justification.

When the other party wants us to sit with those harmful deeds and claim them as our own, we struggle mightily. At times, when we embrace our misdeeds, a host of other misdeeds come into view. A house of cards collapses. A tsunami of sin is unleashed that threatens to drown us. The overall task of repentance may be greater than we anticipated. To recover our balance we need time for contemplation and prayer, time to delve deep into our souls to truly understand the causes of our wrongdoing. At these times we sense a need to know how we arrived on the wrong side of righteousness.

One solution to being overwhelmed is to narrow our focus to the exact deed or deeds that weigh against our merit in this particular conflict. We ask the other party to describe the actions for which we are responsibile. Their analysis will differ, sometimes significantly, from our analysis (and may even differ from the facts); nonetheless, their perception of our transgressions is a good starting point. Quite often it turns out they have a more limited view of our wrongdoing than we have. Their response helps us define and limit our apology. Upon listening closely, we may discover we can apologize, at least in part, for actions they consider our fault.

When our view of our responsibility does not match the other party's account, it can be helpful to apologize for those things we honestly perceive to be our responsibility. Our apology, though it does not match their grievances, nonetheless demonstrates willingness to offer considered and sincere remorse for events as we see them.

Our sincere apology for misdeeds the victim does not consider fundamental to the conflict is preferable to an insincere apology designed to appease the victim. They want us to know that what we did was wrong; they do not desire mere acquiescence to their view. Parties tend to accept that different perspectives will be present. The sincerity of the offending party in acknowledging their version of wrongs is more important to the offended party than words meant to please.

In many cases, the victim wishes to see us struggle with our sins. They recognize considerable pain is involved in our inner journey to come face-to-face with the person we are ashamed to be – the person in the mirror who deserves to be punished. If they see us struggle, they may feel suffering has been balanced, at least partially.

A word of caution: We can too easily focus on transgressions and on violations of the law. When we focus on flaws we risk losing sight of the magic taking place – the transformation of the individual and the relationship.

The process of identifying transgressions in an apology is not an end in itself but rather a means by which we achieve reconciliation. In the humble witnessing of our misdeeds before another, the primary goal is to draw close to them in reconciliation. It is important we do not lose sight of this goal.

In *Things Hidden: Scripture as Spirituality*, Richard Rohr discusses tension between the law and grace, which Paul addresses in Romans and Galatians.[4] He reminds us that by over-emphasizing deviations from the law we risk veering away from a process designed to elicit grace, mercy, and forgiveness.

APOLOGIES INCLUDE EXPRESSIONS OF REGRET FOR WRONGDOING THAT VIO-LATES THE MORAL GRAIN OF THE UNIVERSE. An apology expresses the sentiment that events have occurred which should not have taken place. Things have been said or done which should not have been said or done. The apology acknowledges the existence of a moral perspective – a way things should be. It acknowledges the existence of a moral grain to the universe and acknowledges wrongdoing violated that moral grain.

The acknowledgement that morality guides our behavior reassures the victim our future actions will conform to an acceptable range of behavior. It provides the other party with a starting place from which to rekindle a desire to restore the relationship. It sets the stage for a shared expression of right and wrong upon which we can build future agreements.

In using the phrase *moral grain* I am not speaking of rules, codes, and prohibitions that sometimes serve as a version of religion that diverts our focus from divine relationship. Rather I speak of the Holy Spirit that pervades the consciousness of the spiritually aware person. I refer to the sanctity of the divine relationship between individuals united by the Holy Spirit. When that sacred relationship is violated, the moral grain has been disturbed.

Jesus taught in the Sermon on the Mount that our attention should not turn to rules and commandments but rather to the intentions that fill our hearts.[5] This finer-grained morality resonates in a palpable manner when one discovers the I-Thou relationship. When we consider apologizing in a way that recognizes the moral grain of the universe we ask, *Are we tending to the divine relationship between us?*

Errors include expressions of regret detached from moral relationship – regrets that express cynical sympathy that the universe dealt the victim a bad hand. Moral relationship presupposes the individual possesses free will to honor a relationship with love, respect, and caring.

Those who refuse to acknowledge they possess the freedom to make moral choices find it difficult to express regret at having violated a moral relationship. Their mental and emotional disconnect from the exercise of free will is a cause for worry on the victim's part. The person wronged is robbed of the security that comes with knowing moral concerns will guide the offender's actions in the future. The victim has reason to worry the offender does not value compassion, love, fidelity, honesty, transparency, caring, or other factors that provide a foundation for a moral relationship. If the offender disowns the power of moral choice his or her future actions are thereby rendered unpredictable.

Thus, the focus is not on the violation of rules but rather on the *violation of relationship*. In a sense there are no absolute rules, as rules are relative to situation and time and place.[6] The absolute is found in the transcendent unity of relationship with God. When I speak of the moral grain of the universe I am advocating relationship-based morality not rule-based morality.

This does not mean we toss out agreements, rather it means we judge what is important, in a moral sense, in the context of relationship. Rules or agreements exist only to support the relationship. An example of a rule based on relationship is the Golden Rule: if an action is harmful when done to me then I should not act in that way toward another. The Golden Rule exists within the context of divine relationship. When we stress a rule for the rule's sake we move away from morality based on relationship.

When we negotiate a resolution to a conflict, we realize adherence to a negotiated settlement agreement will rely to some extent on the parties' intention to abide by its provisions. If the concept of a moral relationship is foreign, the necessary trust and confidence is missing. If the offending party does not subscribe to moral principles as guides for relationship we do not know how he will make choices in the future. The wronged party, faced with an offender who does not recognize the moral grain of the universe, may abandon mediation and bring the dispute before a tribunal, such as a court, which possesses the power to coerce compliance.

One solution lies in taking time to contemplate our moral foundations. The moral grain is about divine relationship – it addresses good or evil within the context of relationship. We know those who blindly follow orders can cause harm; unintended consequences arise out of good intentions when they become a crusade no longer moored to divine relationship. Thus we need to monitor our focus, and make sure we do not substitute rote obedience and rule for the compassion and love of the I-Thou relationship. The moral grain is not determined by rules or orders; it is dictated by whether our action helps or harms the other with whom we are in relationship.

An apology, to be effective, must recognize the moral grain of the universe grounded in relationship.

AN APOLOGY MAY SIGNAL THE OFFENDER SEEKS FORGIVENESS. An apology may be a plea from the offender that asks the victim "to take away my guilt."[7] With an apology the offending party expresses a desire to jettison the burden of guilt. They wish to shed their role as a wrongdoer and cast off their identity as a sinner or transgressor. The apology expresses a desire to be reinstated to one's former position as a respected participant in a relationship.

An apology may be a request for help in transforming a harmful self into a repentant self worthy of acceptance into a renewed relationship. The apology communicates: "I need your help to be made whole again." An apology can be a hand extended in a humble request for friendship and love, a request to be lifted up and out of the role of transgressor into a union of brotherhood.

This form of apology may seem to focus entirely on the needs of the offender but this is not the case. The victim receives a considerable boost in dignity and self-worth when their help is solicited – sometimes the best compliment we can pay someone is to acknowledge their help has value to us.

Errors include focusing too narrowly on the offender's need for redemption to the exclusion of concern for the harmed party. While the act of asking the other for forgiveness automatically involves humility and respect, there are times when an apology must focus on the victim. Otherwise it can backfire. When an offender's need to release his burden of guilt overshadows the offended party's need to receive restitution the apology may seem self-serving. When our feelings of guilt appear to obscure our awareness of the pain of the victim the redemptive aspect of an apology is compromised.

Miscues can be avoided by paying close attention to timing. One must honor the needs of the victim when raising the issue of unburdening guilt. Concerns regarding absolution must be balanced with restitution. One can avoid misperception on the part of the victim if one clearly grants the victim the power to refuse to grant forgiveness. One should not assume the apology automatically warrants or earns forgiveness. When you seek help in absolving your guilt do not give the impression you believe the task is accomplished by apology alone.

Nonetheless, when the offender grants the victim the right to judge the worthiness of their apology they restore dignity and demonstrate respect that warrants serious consideration of their request to be absolved. The power of a request for absolution should not be underestimated.

AN APOLOGY EXPRESSES WILLINGNESS TO MAKE AMENDS. An apology can express willingness to provide restitution or reparations. The apology sets the stage for the offender to make up damages in a manner that restores the relationship. In a humble gesture the wrongdoer promises to endure the burden of restoring the balance between the parties. The apology expresses a desire and willingness to take on the task of making up damages – it is a pledge to make the world right again. The pledge should be accompanied by details – how does the offender plan to make the harmed party whole?

Restitution may correct an imbalance in a direct manner. For example, if one caused a loss of money the money is replaced. In other instances intangibles such as reputation are lost, thus restitution cannot provide a one-for-one return of that which was lost. Instead, restitution may be an acceptable alternative the victim agrees will restore the balance.

In some instances, the victim may only be interested in knowing the offender is *willing* to make an effort to offset the damage done. Willingness to make up damages may be more important than actually mending the damage. In most cases, however, actual restitution and reparation are critical. The mediated negotiation can be a lengthy process of determining an exact restitution plan with appropriate contracts, payment schedules, accords, treaties, or other instruments that formalize the agreement.

Errors include the failure to offer reparations for damage caused. Offering restitution to the wrong party is another possible error. For example, one may pay restitution to the state but not to the individual harmed. Restorative justice – in which offenders make amends directly to their victims – is an attempt to remedy the error of restitution made to the wrong party.

Another error is to make a general sweeping statement of an intention to provide restitution while failing to offer a plan grounded in reality. Failing to consult with the victim about the nature of restitution they deem appropriate is an error. We may arrive with a fixed idea of proper restitution but it may differ from the victim's concept of appropriate reparation. We may come unprepared to negotiate restitution in good faith.

Also, a failure to engage in the hard work needed to arrive at a negotiated agreement regarding restitution is an error. We might arrive at mediation prepared to make up the damages but in the back and forth of negotiation we forget our initial intention. We grow weary, abandon the process, and reassume our conflict posture.

In order to prevent errors a party making an apology will want to carefully consider the appropriate amount and type of restitution and design a tentative plan should the offer be accepted. This planning does not negate the need for collaborative negotiation during the conflict resolution process, but does allow the offender to back up an apology with a substantive reparations offer.

If an offender has given no thought to what is appropriate or how to deliver reparations their restitution offer may appear insincere, an afterthought. Frequently, the process of determining the exact amount of reparations takes place separately from the initial apology, but having worked out a tentative plan communicates you have come prepared to negotiate appropriate reparations. A willingness to negotiate in good faith regarding appropriate restitution goes a long way toward making the apology acceptable.

AN APOLOGY SIGNALS A DESIRE TO RECONCILE. An apology signals a change of heart. It says the offender is willing to Restore Other Face in order to change the conflict dynamics. The party who offers an apology as a Face

Saving gift signals the relationship is of sufficient value to warrant a humbling act of self-accusation.

An apology may be an offer to enter into a truce, a willingness to cease hostilities and change the course of events. An apology can be a subtle concession that states implicitly (rarely explicitly) that you were right and I have been wrong. This type of apology is not a statement of culpability but rather a congenial and conciliatory movement toward reconciliation. In this type of apology you wave a metaphorical white flag and communicate you are willing to concede your pride to make it possible for the other party to come to the table. Frequently, there is an expectation that a reciprocal concession will be extended and the other party will offer a matching apology.

Errors include failing to send a message that accurately communicates a desire for reconciliation or failing to make sure the message is actually received. It is possible the apology will be perceived as an attempt to manipulate if the apology appears insincere or tactical. This results in the victim challenging the apology and demanding further proof of remorse. The demand for a show of sincerity, delivered in a confrontational manner, pushes the party who apologized into a defensive posture and the process hits an impasse.

The skeptical victim who detects even the slightest insincerity may spend too much time analyzing the apology, seeking to detect the apologizer's ulterior motive or strategy. The victim's skeptical response, which challenges the sincerity of the apology, communicates the wrong message to the party who apologized – it telegraphs that his good-faith concession will not be reciprocated. The apologizing party incorrectly assumes that the victim, who has become suspicious, is refusing to come to the table in good faith, whereas in fact the victim simply desires additional proof of sincerity. The resultant misunderstanding renews opposition and hostility.

To prevent errors the party offering an apology offers a disclaimer: they realize their apology may not end the conflict but they have a personal need to change the tone of their presentation. They make it clear they wish to apologize for their previous behavior or attitude during the conflict, sending the signal that they have had a change of heart.

They may ask the other party to grant them the courtesy of an audience for their apology, thereby inviting the other party to collaborate in the role of the listener. In other words, they offer to apologize in return for the other party listening with close attention. The parties exchange intangible valuables – an apology in exchange for respectful attention.

If you add that you do not necessarily expect to be forgiven you take the edge off the other side's fear. When you claim your main purpose is a self-initiated desire to modify your behavior (with no expectation of reciprocation), you remove much of the other side's fear that you seek tactical advantage.

AN APOLOGY REMOVES THE INSULT FROM THE INJURY. In many instances, the conflict may not have escalated if an apology had been offered at the outset. We hurt from the injury we suffer but we also hurt from damaged pride, from the insult attached to the injury. The need to Protect Face may drive a conflict that otherwise might have been resolved by addressing substantive issues alone. The insult becomes tangled up in the substance. An acknowledgment of the harm done to Face highlights the lingering emotional upset and the resolution process gains speed.

Errors stem from failure to separate substance from psychological needs. While we may quickly assess substantive issues that must be negotiated, we are slower to recognize psychological and emotional damage requires healing. We concentrate on fixing the disagreement over substance and fail to fix the person. I have watched the relative importance of substance and psychology become inverted. We assume the substance of the conflict is why we are here and yet the contested substance turns out to be minor, while the emotional pain looms large.

As discussed earlier, an attack on our identity resonates as an attack on our survival, causing minor hurts to take on exaggerated importance. When we offer a narrow apology that stingily addresses substance and withholds apology for insult given, our apology fails. Sometimes the offending party offers a narrow apology, which is rejected, and then complains, "I apologized. What more does the other side want?" They assume the harmed party is unreasonable but miss the fact an apology is owed for insult given.

Another source of possible error is the tendency for the victim to avoid admitting they suffered Face Loss. If they admit they were hurt they add yet another layer of Face Loss. For this reason, they hold their emotions in confidence, making it difficult for the offender to recognize Face Loss is a hot-button issue.

Errors can be avoided by asking, with a show of concern, if our actions have given insult. The query may be worded: "I sense I have insulted you during this conflict. Am I right?" This communicates that you recognize harm done beyond substantive issues. It conveys the message that the offender is willing to hear the victim express personal, heart-related grievances. An offender's expression of remorse at having offended the victim's dignity may elicit revelations from the victim – the offender can then respond with a detailed apology for the suffering caused.

In many instances, it is difficult to anticipate the exact manner in which a victim perceived insult. Thus it pays to ask the offended party to share their hurt. However, they may respond with hesitant denial, as they would rather not confess weakness. In this case, the offender offers a blanket apology, "I realize what I did must have been insulting and caused you pain. I cannot imagine how you felt, but I know it cannot have been pleasant, so I wish to say I am sorry for causing any discomfort you might have experienced." Such an apology, delivered with sincerity, evokes the victim's understanding and appreciation, freeing them from the need to admit weakness or vulnerability. Later, they may feel more comfortable in discussing the specifics of the insult they felt in order to clear the air and set the stage for reconciliation.

AN APOLOGY MAY PROMISE THE HARM WILL NOT BE REPEATED. In acknowledging wrongdoing the person who apologizes communicates to the victim that he has regained control over his actions and he makes an implicit promise the harmful acts will not be repeated.

An apology that signals the offender has suffered mental anguish in the form of guilt or an apology that signals the offender has shouldered the burden of repentance conveys the message that the offender also suffered as a result of his actions. He expresses the realization that a repeat of past transgressions will cause him additional pain, thus he has a selfish reason for not repeating past harmful acts. The offender's realization that it is not in his interest to cause additional harm may reassure the victim. A further apology that explicitly promises destructive acts will not be repeated carries considerable value for the victim.

An apology enables a victim to distinguish between an uncaring sociopath and a remorseful offender. The person who injures us and apparently does not care is dangerous. A sociopath unable to feel the pain he has caused is likely to hurt us again. A sociopath or narcissist not only finds it difficult to apologize, they have a tough time understanding why there should be an apology. They will find it difficult to deliver a valid apology that meets the victim's needs.

On the other hand, people of good heart and good intention want to apologize; it will be a natural impulse, though the delivery may be challenging. In order for a victim to feel safe in a continued relationship they must determine the offender's true intentions. In the past they may have failed to recognize the danger the offender presented, but now that they have been stung by conflict they are more observant and more discerning. Before they renew the relationship or agree to collaborate they want to know the nature of the person with whom they are dealing. An apology that promises no future harm will occur is vital when it comes to distinguishing a remorseful offender from a sociopath.

Errors include promising harmful actions will not be repeated even though the current conflict resulted from repeated past harmful behavior. The victim rightfully wonders if they can expect a change when none has taken place previously. The apology must recognize past negative patterns and include a plan for terminating the repetitive behavior.

The apology can also fall short if the offender appears to underestimate how difficult it will be to change their behavior. Most of us recognize it is not easy to change. Awareness of the difficulty must be acknowledged or the apology will be evaluated as glib.

Recognition by the offender that repeating the behavior will cause herself additional harm may carry weight with the other party, but only if it seems the offender cares about the price he will have to pay. If the offender offers an apology and promises his behavior will not be repeated but the apology lacks humility and satisfactory reparations, the apology will be judged inadequate.

In summary, a party who apologizes must present a cogent and convincing argument that assures others their harmful acts will not be repeated. An apology can be improved by adding a realistic expression of the degree of difficulty the offender expects to encounter as they change their behavior. This expression may be accompanied by proof of current attempts to change with the help of others, for example, with the aid of a priest or counselor or by enrollment in a program that addresses the problem with which they struggle. There may need to be an agreement that the offender will be monitored for a period of time, or an agreement that sets stiff penalties for future violations.

A sincere willingness to pay a higher price than requested as a way of making amends for the current transgression may overcome suspicion, as it offers proof of a strong personal effort to reform. It may be necessary to plan the apology with an advisor in order to insure your presentation does not inadvertently appear glib, especially when it comes to promises to make changes.

AN APOLOGY IS AN EXPRESSION & ACKNOWLEDGEMENT OF FREE WILL. A confession extracted under duress does not rise to the level of apology. An apology should contain a brief explanation of the factors that motivated the offender to apologize. The story should recount their exercise of free will in choosing a humble admission of wrongdoing for which they are sorry. The apology that includes an expression of free will, with a description of the choices that led to an apology, signals to the victim that the offender comes to the apology freely, consciously aware of his choices.

If the offender does not recognize the need to apologize on their own, it is unlikely they felt the suffering of the victim sufficiently for their apology to matter. In contrast, an apology given as a matter of choice establishes that the offender recognizes he exercises control over his actions. The party that cannot conceive that they control their actions, the party that considers events just happen, has a difficult time offering a convincing apology.

Errors include giving any indication the apology is not freely given, but rather results from other forces, even duress, over which the offender has no control. If the apology does not originate with the offender's free will the victim doubts its sincerity and harbors concerns the harmful act will be repeated.

While responding to the prompts in the journal workbook, contemplate the degree to which you exercise choice over your decision to apologize. If you find you have a tendency to attribute your apology to outside forces you may want to reconsider. Perhaps the apology is premature; perhaps there is a need to further analyze the conflict. Maybe you do not really wish to apologize and you are doing so to satisfy the demands of others. Your task is to search your heart to see if you can discover a desire to apologize. This inner work may become part of the story of the apology's origin that you later share with the offended party.

AN APOLOGY PROVIDES AN EXPLANATION OF WHY THINGS HAPPENED. When the offender delivers a detailed account of his actions as he perceived them and provides the victim with clues to the reason events happened, he satisfies the victim's need for understanding. Clarification of that which was previously a mystery reduces uncertainty and allows the victim to move forward feeling they have a good grasp on reality.

This is important as, when you are harmed, you often experience a lingering sense of unreality that limits your confidence. A victim of a harmful act, even if the harm was minor, feels out of synch with life and fears her perception of reality might be tenuous. This occurs because rarely do we conceive ourselves to be the justified target of harmful deeds. Thus, when another harms us we become confused and the experience seems unreal. It doesn't make sense.

An apology detailing clear explanations for harmful acts committed helps a victim rewrite the historical narrative in a way that makes sense. Knowing *why* an offender acted as he did dispels mystery. Often the victim discovers the transgression had nothing to do with him or with his actions but arose out of conditions in the offender's life. When it is possible to piece together events in a comprehensible narrative we regain our grounding in reality and we can make sense of our life.

Errors occur when the explanation for a transgression is unclear or illogical. A lack of clarity or logic deepens the mystery rather than dispelling it. Convoluted reasoning diminishes the value of the apology. Covert accusations against the victim, buried in the explanation of events, also render the apology suspect. An explanation that lacks sufficient detail reflects a lack of introspection.

It is common for offenders to detour around the heart of their wrongdoing and attempt to Save Face with an account that veers into justification and defers blame. Apologies heavy on justification and denial do not explain misdeeds as much as they attempt to explain them away, which diminishes the effectiveness of the apology. When one has deceived the victim it is particularly important to clarify acts of deception, allowing the victim to put missing or incongruous pieces of the narrative into proper perspective.

To avoid these errors if you are offering an apology, you should contemplate why the transgressions took place as they did – what chain of causality determined events? If you have come to understand the causes make sure you can describe them in a clear manner.

Consider whether your explanation contains sufficient detail to be of value. Does it connect the dots in a way that brings renewed clarity? If the explanation avoids an accounting for the actual events that took place, the narrative warrants a deeper look. You will want to see if you can understand core reasons unwanted events took place.

If the apology claims "It wasn't my fault" or becomes a laundry list of reasons the offender should not be held accountable it most likely will fail. It is better to offer a self-accusatory account of a few misdeeds for which you can take full responsibility than to offer an account filled with justifications or denials that explain away your actions.

If you can take full responsibility for at least one aspect of the harm done you meet the other party's needs more than if you offer a self-excusing narrative. It is even more important to avoid attributing blame to the other party.

AN APOLOGY PROMOTES SPIRITUAL GROWTH. Those who practice a faith tradition are often aware of the value repentance brings to their spiritual life. To repent is to turn toward the divine and away from alienation and wrongdoing. Repentance is an act of reestablishing relationship. Jesus was reported to have said that he came not to call the righteous but rather to call sinners to repentance.[8] He implored us to renew our relationship with the divine.

When our actions and thoughts are a source of dissatisfaction, when we feel disconnection and alienation from our true nature we seek transformation. In repentance we turn toward the divine for forgiveness and our turn toward the divine culminates in union and atonement (at-one-ment).

In the act of taking responsibility for misdeeds we embrace humility, which is paradoxically uplifting. When we bend low to repent we are lifted up in our divine nature. As we confront that which is *not who we truly are* we gain insight into *who we can be*. As we denounce our actions with repentant self-accusation, we peel away false self to reveal true self – our spiritual essence in union with the indwelling Holy Spirit. When we repent and offer apology we turn toward the divine and are transformed.

When we owe an apology we need not wait for the other party to signal their willingness to forgive. We step forward and take a risk. We may or may not be forgiven. "Repentance, like forgiveness, is personal to one side and doesn't demand the other's cooperation. Repentance begins with a changed heart, which results in changed thinking, and, ultimately, changed behavior."[9] The choice that launches our spiritual growth is ours alone to make.

When we think of repentance, apology, and confession, however, our thoughts are often shrouded in dark shadows cast by the blackness of our deeds. With apology we seek to dispel these shadows and journey into the light that brings transformation. Our attention shifts to our final destination – sacred reconciliation. When we become mired in the darkness of our misdeeds we risk missing the purpose of repentance and apology, which is to be uplifted through transformation. Here we find paradox. We lower our eyes to gaze up at the divine; we take on a burden that lightens our soul; we humbly acknowledge our imperfect nature and thus reveal our made-in-the-image-of-God nature.

We repent and wipe away the residue of wrongdoing that obscures our vision of true self; we repent and wipe grime from the mirror in which the image of the divine is reflected. We discover we have not lost the true self within – the image in the mirror has not disappeared but has simply become distorted by the dirt from our accumulated misdeeds.

Healing occurs in relationship. The journey from guilt to repentance draws both parties into an I-Thou relationship. Reciprocal humility develops. In accepting an apology, if only at the level of close listening, the victim joins the offender in the spiritually uplifting act of atonement. Perhaps the most important value created as a result of apology is renewal of a sacred relationship, the reciprocal recognition of each other's divine nature, which arises from the divine act of repentance.

Errors include not endowing an apology with the respect it deserves. When we deliver a glib, perfunctory apology, we neglect its spiritual nature. We err when we do not listen to our heart as we prepare an apology, when we do not recognize how intensely the act of apology resonates within our soul.

If we see the act of apology as a degrading act of submission rather than a humble act of contrition we are not lifted up. If we consider apology to be an act that proves to the world how wicked and evil we are, rather than a gesture that lifts us above our flawed nature, we fail to realize its full potential. If we omit an attitude of humble compassion, we fail to realize an apology's full potential. If we do not see our apology as a step toward divine relationship we minimize the power of apology.

To overcome these errors we refuse the temptation to toss a glib apology or to use apology as a political tool. Instead, we seek the deeper meaning of apology and embrace repentance as a healing process. We recognize and acknowledge our flawed nature in the context of our journey toward a Spirit-filled existence. We strive to accept grace that heals our wounds and transforms shortcomings into wisdom. We recognize and embrace spiritual growth that arises out of the painful and humbling task of apologizing. We use conflict resolution not only as a method of removing barriers to our happiness but also as a path to spiritual transformation.

APOLOGY PROVIDES AN OPPORTUNITY FOR CONFESSION. On more than one occasion a party has turned to me during mediation and offered a significant confession. At times they confessed an act over which they have suffered silently for years. Such unburdening moments usually arrive unexpectedly. It seems that all of a sudden they can no longer bear the burden and they must tell their story.

Prior to that moment they had not found a setting in which non-judgmental trust was present. They had not encountered anyone who would hear their story and accept their contrition without judgment. Those who have the opportunity to participate in the formal *Sacrament of Reconciliation* may not have such pressing needs. Nonetheless, with most people I have found that when such a moment arrives during mediation the need to unburden becomes overwhelmingly strong.

Such confessions, delivered privately to the mediator, do not form an apology; nonetheless, if the party so desires, the confession can be structured and framed into an appropriate apology. Such confessions of wrongdoing can be a first step toward apology but at other times molding the confession into a formal apology may not be necessary, as the private unburdening alone often results in a dramatic change of demeanor that conveys, nonverbally, the presence of a new heart. The offender, once aggressive, is contrite. The change can be so dramatic the other party recognizes and accepts transformation has taken place.

At other times, an impromptu confession delivered to the harmed party may morph into an apology on the spot, though this is less frequent. In other instances, a mediator may choreograph a confession-and-apology moment using a formal reconciliation service or ritual of reconciliation. The results can be remarkable when these healing moments take place – party to party. We witness the pinnacle of the reconciliation process.

Errors might include the mediator missing the exact moment when the confession is ripe or not making sure he has heard the entire confession. These moments are extremely fragile and hinge on a look, a pause, a quiet moment when the party recognizes it is safe to unburden. If the mediator is rushed or distracted with the details of the negotiation or if he lacks a feel for the quiet moment of contemplation the pregnant moment passes. If the mediator is too quick to acknowledge the confession and interrupts the narrative in mid-delivery the confession is aborted and rendered incomplete.

In the less frequent case of a confession delivered directly to the other party, the victim may commit the same errors of inattention and premature acknowledgment. However, as there is less expectation that the other party will be skilled in handling emotional moments the damage may be less.

When there are multiple parties a reconciliation service may be specifically designed to enhance confession and empathetic listening. The service may be structured to allow for a collective process of repentance that lifts up the entire group and fuels their passion for the pilgrimage of life.

To avoid errors the mediator maintains an attentive and prayerful posture. When a mediator respects party self-determinism he or she is willing to listen closely for clues to the party's desires. In contrast, when the mediator over-directs the process the more subtle moments may not ripen and may fail to lead to transformation.

A skilled mediator recognizes that when a party is actively looking for an opportunity to unburden they continually evaluate the mediator's ability to listen without judgment. They assess whether or not they can trust the mediator to hear their concerns. Their attention focuses on clues to mediator sensitivity. They want to know if the mediator is aware of the more subtle and spiritual aspects of the conflict.

The mediator invites challenges and questions regarding his views on difficult topics and expects a party will attempt to catch him off guard or provoke a reaction. He expects they will test the waters to determine if they are safe in his hands. This testing is a prelude to a confession and a request for help in structuring an apology.

SUMMARY. The preceding discussion provides glimpses of why and how we apologize. It helps us consider how we satisfy the other party's needs as well as our own. From the viewpoint of mediation apology overcomes barriers and releases impasse. From a psychological perspective, apology reestablishes respect, dignity, and emotional tranquility. From a negotiation perspective, apology helps us move to a realistic appraisal of restitution required and makes possible a settlement that insures a more peaceful future. Most importantly, apology fosters spiritual transformation.

As you prepare your apology, should one be needed, revisit this discussion as you respond to the prompts. Make sure you have delivered all value possible. Delivering an apology is not necessarily as easy as one might assume. Dashing off a simple I'm sorry may result in rejection and continuation of the conflict. A more careful and considered approach moves the process toward reconciliation.

Should you expect to be the recipient of an apology, use the above discussion to analyze feelings of dissatisfaction you may encounter. Even if you are concerned about maintaining a collaborative spirit do not accept an apology you feel is manipulative and/or insincere, as your unexpressed resentment will eventually hinder the process. Rather than accept an apology that does not meet your needs take time to expand the discussion of the other party's apology in light of the needs you hope to satisfy.

Partially Hidden Guilt

An offender suffers a particularly painful form of guilt when they are uncertain whether or not the victim knows they are responsible for harmful acts.

The offender may assume their role in causing harm was hidden or unknown, but at the same time they may fear their misdeed has been secretly discovered and not openly acknowledged. The offender is trapped wondering whether or not the other party knows the exact nature of their actions.

The offender's thoughts alternate between "they must have found out" and "they could not possibly have found out." The anxiety can be brutally taxing. Caught in this dilemma, they may become erratic, alternating between hostility and propitiation. They experience intense mood swings and their anger may become extreme. They frequently threaten to abandon the conflict resolution process.

Thus, if the opposing party accuses you of wrongdoing but their anger seems over-the-top and their accusations are illogical or non-factual, there is a high probability they suffer uncertainty as to whether or not you have discovered *their* misdeeds. They are beside themselves with uncertainty regarding the state of your knowledge of their transgressions. This phenomenon can give rise to a very erratic, unpredictable, emotional, angry, and distracted condition.

Litigation and other adversarial processes, with their adversarial discovery phase, exacerbate this phenomenon, provoking increased hostility as lawyers strive to uncover evidence of wrongdoing. Litigants suffer and worry. What do *they* really know? What remains hidden? When a lawyer advises their client to be less than forthcoming – at the same time the opposing attorney attempts to expose wrongdoing or dishonesty – the client can suffer a painful form of guilt anxiety. They wonder and worry if they have been found out. The anxiety drives hostility and anger.

There is a solution to this dilemma: be forthright in stating what you know and do not know. Reveal your concerns about their behavior. You may say, "I don't know what you think I might know, but here are the issues about which I have concern." Or, "I know you have committed (specific misdeeds), and I am willing to discuss how that affected me if that is important to you." Or, "I know it can be very uncomfortable to not know what someone else knows about you. If there is anything you want to ask, I will be honest regarding what I know. If there is anything you need to tell me, I will listen." Yet another approach is to take the mediator aside and let them know you suspect the other party has not disclosed transgressions that are weighing on their conscience, and thus they need an opportunity to meet privately to discuss their concerns.

The mediator who recognizes anxiety exists over what is known and what is not known regarding transgressions should create opportunities to clear away uncertainty. He may say to an agitated party, "Sometimes things we have not been able to tell the other party cause discomfort. If there are any concerns you need to raise, let me know how I might help you." This may bring considerable relief to the offender and allow the process to move forward.

Yet another solution is for the mediator to overtly state the dilemma to both parties: "There may be harmful things each of you have done and said and each of you are uncertain what the other party actually knows. We will have an opportunity for each of you to tell your story so we can clear up these mysteries. Is that okay with you?" This provides a context in which an offender can bring to light hidden deeds in the course of a narrative that includes apology.

Why People Do Not Apologize

On occasion one or both parties will refuse to apologize. In some instances, the impasse is temporary, but at other times the impasse may end the reconciliation process. In *On Apology* Aaron Lazare describes the paradoxical nature of a refusal to apologize: "We are left with the paradox that the two major motives for many people to apologize – changing the external world and relieving their inner feelings of guilt and shame – are the same reasons why others avoid apologizing – fearing the reactions of the external world and suffering from the emotions of guilt and shame."[10]

Paradoxically, we must go through the fire in order to not get burned; we must take the action we fear in order to avoid the outcome we fear. When we apologize we move through our fear, change the external world, relieve feelings of guilt and shame, and increase the odds that we will reconcile with the other party. There is no quick, easy, and painless way to accomplish these steps and, as a result, some parties balk and refuse to move ahead.

On occasion, both parties acknowledge their refusal to apologize. For practical reasons they agree on a compromise that allows them to go their separate ways, agreeing they have no desire for a future relationship. They express an intention to walk separate but parallel paths and are satisfied with a minimalist process that satisfies non-relational immediate needs without apology.

A mediator hopes to guide the process to reconciliation but must recognize some parties simply wish to disentangle, conclude their business, and move on. This is better than achieving no result; nonetheless, it falls short of a durable settlement and improved relationship. The mediator first acknowledges the limitations at the present time and then suggests adding to their negotiated agreement a provision that allows parties to re-engage the process at a later date, should they have a change of heart.

In other instances, party ego needs may prevent them from humbly admitting wrongdoing. They may anticipate that the act of repentant apology will be so degrading it will cause significant and lasting damage to their identity. Therefore, they cannot bring themselves to submit an apology. They cling tightly to false self, unable to turn toward the divine.

They anticipate their self-image will suffer irreparable harm. They fear the other party will think so much less of them they will refuse to continue the relationship. In such instances, the risk of ongoing tension and conflict appears less formidable than the risk of irreparable loss of face. Further spiritual formation and letting go of ego in a safe setting is needed; they need a setting where Spirit-inspired relationship is nurtured. They may not have experienced unconditional love and compassion previously. They may not be familiar with these qualities that make it possible for them to apologize.

Lacking experience with unconditional love and compassion it is hard for them to imagine their apology will garner forgiveness. They may see only the darkness of their deeds and expect retaliation; they do not see the light of divine compassion that dispels shadows. For this reason it may be necessary to structure conflict resolution to allow time for a spiritual retreat during which inner transformation catches up with unfolding events.

Another barrier takes shape when a representative, such as an attorney, advises against making an apology, fearing the apology will be used in court as an admission of guilt. While this concern is valid, safe methods of apologizing within the legal setting exist. In most states mediation provisions provide confidentiality protection.[11] Or your attorney may construct an apology that navigates around unwanted legal exposure. If your representative expresses concern regarding the expression of apology, you may ask them to consult the article "Advising Clients to Apologize."[12]

When an abusive opposing party views our apology as a weakness to be exploited we may legitimately decide to withhold apology. This fear is usually overblown but, when the mediator also senses danger, it may be best to defer apology. For example, in cases involving an abusive spouse, bringing an end to the abuse takes precedence over the need to apologize.

When a genuine threat exists the mediator may suggest the threatened party seek help in another venue. Unfortunately, more coercive processes aimed at handling abuse, such as court-based restraining orders, do not always provide safety. Sometimes mediation is the best option. In the special case of abuse only skilled professionals who use extreme caution should guide the process. Most likely a team of professionals working in tandem will provide the best approach.

As mediation continues to gain recognition and acceptance I foresee the development of sophisticated techniques for handling the abusive party through carefully choreographed shuttle diplomacy with a heavy emphasis on individual transformation. Improved processes that minimize the immediate danger but allow a mediated dialogue to take place – for example, holding separate sessions at a distance through electronic media – will be designed.

Another barrier to apology takes shape when an obsessive need to be right offsets the desire to apologize. As discussed earlier, being right can equate with survival at a primal, unconscious level. To admit we were wrong may make us feel, at a deep emotional level, that we will cease to exist. A party trapped in an obsessive need to be right may not be able to articulate their fear or misgivings when it comes to offering an apology. Their emotions may obscure their ability to look inward to locate the source of their resistance to apology. The party may even agree that their refusal to apologize and their refusal to admit they were wrong are illogical and counterproductive, but they are simply unable to get past the barrier.

In order to address the barrier of *must be right* the party may need adequate time to sit with their emotions during contemplative prayer in which they wrestle their fears and shine light into the shadows. A spiritual counselor may help them recognize the death they face is an ego death that gives birth to a new spiritual self, a self consistent with who they really are, not the false self in which they have been trapped.

They may need help addressing compulsive and judgmental righteousness. They may need to consult scripture that teaches our flawed nature is a fact of our human condition, scripture that assures we are forgiven in spite of our flaws. It may be important for them to engage in spiritual formation, during which they learn apology, confession, and repentance are ultimately about our turning toward our true nature through divine relationship.

Healing Historical Wounds

It is worth noting that apologies from one group to another play a critical role in ending cycles of revenge. The group member who directly caused harm may deliver the apology or an individual who represents the group may offer the apology. The apology may concern harmful events that happened a generation or more in the past that gave rise to a wounded memory that has been carried into the present.

An example can be found in Truth and Reconciliation hearings held in the wake of violent cultural and political upheaval, as in South Africa.[13] In large-scale conflicts peacemakers have learned the importance of providing victims with a full accounting of crimes perpetrated in a repentant and truthful recitation delivered by those who committed violent acts. This type of apology – in which perpetrators of violent ideological or hate-based crimes are called to account before officials and victims – is a carefully managed process that attempts to prevent cycles of violent revenge in order to heal society.

The process meets victims' need to understand exactly what happened. Victims may satisfy their need to see offenders humbly take responsibility for misdeeds. Apologies delivered by a representative not directly involved in the offense rarely satisfy the victim's need for an apology – the victim usually has a need to hear from those immediately responsible. The institutional apology rarely provides insight into the perpetrators' motives and cannot adequately demonstrate shame and guilt. It cannot deliver the specificity needed to purge all lingering pain. Nonetheless, such apologies can restore dignity, acknowledge a common moral vision, and promise a future free from harm. Such apologies begin to mend the relationship between peoples. They heal historic wounds, avert future conflict, and lower the level of resentment and hatred.

In the wake of the success of the South African hearings, truth and reconciliation hearings have been employed in other venues with success. Thus we should not overlook institutional efforts to heal historic wounds. While all of the victim's needs may not be met and results may vary, the degree of satisfaction is significant enough to warrant support for the process.

Institutions that recognize lingering historical wounds have resulted from their members' actions have learned the value of offering formal public apologies. Brian Cox, author of *Faith-Based Reconciliation*, writes: "Deep historical wounds that remain unhealed can cause communities and nations to become captive to a bitter history and unable to live in peace with others."[14] The institution may collectively assume responsibility for the actions of predecessors or ancestors, actions that took place generations ago. The effort is one of healing and to accomplish healing one must understand the needs an apology serves.

Major conflicts too often are the result of a lingering sense of injustice handed down generation to generation. When anger over perceived insults of the past are inflamed by new events, violence erupts. Genuine apologies that do not attempt to bury the past and instead honor the memory of those who suffered restore the dignity of the offended people, heal wounds, and prevent new outbursts of violence.

This type of healing prevents future conflict and, thus, in this context, peacemakers inherit a mandate to heal history.

A Franciscan View

Francis prepares us for the challenge of apology through his instruction in humility. In naming the Order the Friars Minor he signaled the importance of stepping down from positions of power in order to acknowledge our flawed nature, a nature that frequently leaves us with a need to apologize to those we have harmed.

Francis understood the repentant heart turns away from self-importance to seek a closer relationship with the Divine. He was aware of the need to engage in periods of hermitage during which solitude prepares us to seek repentance.

Murray Bodo, in *Francis: The Journey and the Dream*, provides an account of this seeking, as undertaken by Francis: "At first, this inner search was a painful and terrifying look at himself, at his weakness and sinfulness; and the journey was a downward dive that made him feel that he was drowning in some vast, bottomless lake. But as he persevered in prayer, he came at last to something like a great, silent, waterproof cavern in which the sound of his own voice seemed mellow and deep, and there at that depth within, Jesus spoke softly to him and made his heart burn with love."[15] Francis's example teaches us that, as we struggle with the need to apologize, we need to set aside the time to participate in a spiritual retreat for "the conquest of ourselves can be perfected only in the Spirit."[16]

As is often the case, we set out to follow Francis, determined to conquer the obstacles that stand in our path, only to find that the challenge is greater than anticipated. Francis himself was humbled by the advice he gave the brothers: "He remembered his pious words to the brothers that sadness and melancholy were the devil's work; and if any brother were dejected, he should go to Confession. What a laugh! How different things look when *you're* the one who's depressed."[17]

At the very moment we elevate Francis to the role of a model to be followed, he assures us, humbly, that he is but a little poor man, and he invites us to walk by his side. He talks about the brothers, knowing the words apply to us as well: "In each of them there was the Dream of discovering within themselves a secret source of energy, a Presence that would transform their lives and restore the harmony of the Garden of Paradise."[18] Our thoughts, however, waver and we are beset with worry over our violations, transgressions, and violence. We embrace regret but also fear humbling ourselves before another. It is not easy to admit we are not who we hoped to be.

Our internal judge places us on trial. At the same time, we anticipate the sting of the other party's judgment, aware that we will be judged as we have judged others. We may sense this path of judgment leads nowhere, for "when we lead off with our judgments, love will seldom happen. If the mind that needs to make moral judgments about everything is the master instead of the servant, religion is almost always corrupted."[19]

We are not the first to be confused or frightened by the call for humble repentance. The words of Richard Rohr capture our quandary: "The relationship between grace and law ends up being a central issue for almost anyone involved in religion at any depth. Basically, it is the creative tension between religion as requirements and religion as transformation."[20] As we grapple with our transgressions, we face this choice between religious requirements and religious transformation.

In order to maintain our ego we carefully tally our score and our opponent's score with respect to fulfillment of edicts and rules. But we know transformation involves change rather than scorekeeping. It calls on us to turn toward the divine seeking repentance and union. Our salvation is not contingent on a scorecard but rather on the love that fills our hearts as we seek union with the divine presence in the other party.

We cling steadfastly to our false self, our ego, but we know that eventually we must let go or we will drown. "Our problem is not our shadow self nearly as much as our over-defended ego, which always sees and hates its own faults in other people, and thus avoids it own conversion."[21] Ironically, our ego, which appears to be a life jacket, is an anchor.

As we enter the silence of contemplation we hear echoes of the words of disparagement we have spoken about the other party. We recognize in our words of disparagement a hidden account of our own transgressions. We avoid uncomfortable truths that soil our ego, but "Jesus is not too interested in moral purity because he knows that any preoccupation with repressing the shadow does not lead us into personal transformation, empathy, compassion or patience, but invariably into one of two certain paths: denial or disguise, repression or hypocrisy."[22] Instead, He waits patiently for us to enter into a relationship with Him.

As we seek the spiritual path to apology and redemption, we rediscover the dirt path above Assisi that winds up Mount Subasio to the caves where

Francis found solitude and the religious experiences that enflamed his soul. Rohr underscores the value of this experience: "Until people have had some level of inner religious experience, there is no point in asking them to follow the ethical ideals of Jesus. Indeed, they will not be able to understand them. At most they would be only the source of even deeper anxiety. You quite simply don't have the power to obey the law, especially issues like forgiveness of enemies, nonviolence, humble use of power and so on, except in and through union with God."[23]

Always moving forward, never stopping, we seek union with God and long to know the reality that lifted Francis upward even as he fulfilled his earthly pilgrimage: "Oh, how sweet were the ways of penance and sacrifice! They filled the heart with new strength and the spirit with a determination that transcended every bodily weakness and cowardice."[24]

We strive to understand the simple yet profound knowledge Francis acquired through a lifetime of devotion: "It was all so simple when he thought about it now. Love comes to those who have Love already. You find what you bring with you in your heart. God has first loved us and that gift is ours before we ever set out to find it."[25]

Scripture

God has overlooked the times of ignorance, but now he demands that all people everywhere repent . . . (Acts 17:30)

"I tell you, in just the same way there will be more joy in heaven over one sinner who repents than over ninety-nine righteous people who have no need of repentance." (Lk 15:7)

The Lord does not delay his promise, as some regard "delay," but he is patient with you, not wishing that any should perish but that all should come to repentance. (2 Pt 3:9)

CHAPTER SEVENTEEN

Forgiveness

He has the same needs as you and only wants to eat and not go hungry. Can the people of Gubbio feed him if he promises to never again take the lives of the people and their animals?

Remember, our Savior taught forgiveness. He taught us to love our enemies.

Mediation Principles

ORGIVENESS MAY BE the most elusive and difficult step in reconciliation. Scholars and theologians have devoted careers to understanding the nuances of forgiveness. A considerable portion of the Gospel is dedicated to explaining what it means to forgive. We find books that focus exclusively on the topic.[1]

Francis, in living a Gospel life, came to know the vital role forgiveness plays in reconciliation. It is easy to visualize Francis approaching Gubbio, Brother Wolf at his side, knowing he would soon be called on to guide angry and grieving citizens on an emotional journey in search for their forgiving hearts.

In this chapter, we follow in Francis' footsteps to discover what will be needed for you to discover your forgiving heart. The sheer scope of the topic makes it impossible to present all there is to know about forgiveness in a chapter. In addition, forgiveness is so uniquely personal that perhaps only firsthand experience allows us to fully understand the topic. Nonetheless, the concepts presented in this chapter will serve as valuable navigational aids you can use to map your personal route to forgiveness.

Before beginning you might ask: Is it mandatory that we forgive the other party in order to resolve a conflict? Is forgiveness absolutely necessary? Or is it possible to skip forgiveness and still resolve a conflict?

It *is* possible to *resolve* a conflict without achieving forgiveness. While forgiveness is a prerequisite for reconciliation, resolution is another matter. Parties may resolve conflicts or settle disputes without extending forgiveness; they may resolve their conflict and go their separate ways, stopping short of reconciliation.

If parties desire more than mere resolution and settlement, if they desire the fruits of a restored relationship, if they wish to reconcile, they will need to address forgiveness. If they hope to realize the spiritual transformation that is the cornerstone of the *Taming the Wolf* approach, they will need to seek the divine magic of forgiveness. When we wish to move beyond the conflict ruining our lives to secure our future happiness, forgiveness is vital.

Forgiveness Is Not Contingent on Apology

Previously we noted an apology was not contingent on a promise of forgiveness. An apology is offered regardless of whether or not the offended party grants forgiveness. The same dynamic holds true for forgiveness: forgiving is not contingent on an apology. We can forgive another even when the offending party refuses to apologize for harm they have done.

While either an apology or an expression of forgiveness can stand alone, most often the two are linked in the reconciliation process. A legitimate, heartfelt apology prompts the harmed party to consider forgiveness. An apology opens the door to in-depth expressions regarding what happened and how that made us feel – and those heartfelt exchanges draw parties closer together, allowing the desire to forgive to take root. This reciprocal give-and-take of apology and forgiveness advances the process toward reconciliation.

Reciprocity may be important for additional reasons – as we struggle with the decision to forgive, we may recognize a fundamental need *to be forgiven*, which may make us hesitant to *not* forgive the other. If we refuse to forgive another and we turn them away we risk being turned away when *we* need forgiveness.

This need to reciprocate, however, only serves to give us pause – the fear of not being forgiven is insufficient motivation for us to forgive. Such fear-based motivation does not arise from our compassionate heart; therefore it will not provide the immense inspiration needed to lift us up sufficiently to forgive. True forgiveness demands we go beyond fear-driven motives.

We forgive, not from weakness or fear, but rather out of a compassionate desire to bestow a sacred gift on the offender. The considerable value that being forgiven holds for us causes us to recognize the value our gift of forgiving holds for another. Ultimately, however, forgiveness is a gift freely bestowed with love.

As you prepare for reconciliation ask yourself if your forgiveness will need to stand alone, absent the other party's repentance and apology. Will you be able to extend forgiveness to another who refuses to repent? Will reciprocity of apology and forgiveness play an important role? Or will you be able to give that which has not been earned? Will you be able to freely give the gift of forgiveness?

Barriers to Forgiving

As we approach the moment when forgiveness becomes vital we often find our progress slows to a halt. Self-created barriers impede our progress. During the conflict we may have taken actions that appeared, at the time, to be solutions that would restore our personal contentment and happiness, but now those solutions appear in a different light: they become barriers that prevent forgiveness.

Previously it may have seemed that payback (revenge or retribution) would restore peace and contentment. It may have seemed we could teach the other a lesson that would resolve the conflict. We assumed our opponent would get it and back off. However, we discovered retribution or revenge generated adverse consequences and we backed away – but we never totally abandoned the idea. We set aside our immediate urge for revenge but at a subtle and barely conscious level we remained invested in the possibility of revenge.

Now, as we try to forgive, desire for revenge resurfaces and becomes too intense to be set aside easily. Revenge scenarios haunt our daydreams. An inner voice whispers, return the blow and make them pay. The desire becomes visceral. We hunger to make those who hurt us feel the pain they caused. Dreams of revenge block our path. We discover how truly difficult it is to abandon the thirst for revenge once we sipped its addictive poison.

Another faulty solution for restoring personal contentment and happiness that we may have adopted is turning away from the other and refusing to acknowledge their existence. Given that in most cases we cannot obliterate them physically we vow to obliterate them from our mind – we seek to make nothing of them in our mental space. The offender no longer exists for us: he or she has become a non-person.

This method rarely works. A ghostly image of the offender strolls the halls of our mind, appears uninvited in our dreams, disturbs our peace in quiet moments, or jumps out of the shadows when least expected. In our attempt to escape we shutter our consciousness with help from drugs, alcohol, or the stupor of depression. Ironically, in our attempt to disappear the offender *we* begin to disappear ourselves. We become less vital, and less present to others whom we love. In our impaired state of lessened consciousness we find it difficult to grasp the logic of forgiveness. Our diminished consciousness has become a barrier.

Or we may have tried a third possible faulty solution in which we convert our wounded nature into our identity as a victim. We no longer seek to heal our wounds but rather display them as symbols of who we are – a victim. We invite the world to see our wounds and to know us by our wounds. As we approach forgiveness this solution becomes an impediment.

We cling to a victim identity, which has become valuable, much as a crutch is valuable to an injured man. Intuitively we realize forgiving the other means we must set aside this victim identity. We must abandon the public display of our wounds and leave a cherished part of our ego identity to perish. In many cases, we are unwilling to jettison the victim identity we carefully crafted. Victimhood thus impairs our ability to forgive.

There may be other similar solutions we employ in our attempts to restore the happiness conflict has stolen from us. During your preparation for mediation, add to the list any solutions you employed that have morphed into barriers to forgiveness and reconciliation. If you wish to reconcile you will need to dismantle these barriers; you will need to gain an intimate knowledge of how your choices impede your progress. The three examples of solutions-become-barriers – lingering desire for revenge, diminishing consciousness, assuming a "victim" identity – provide prototypes for the following discussion on how to dismantle barriers.

Analyzing & Dismantling Barriers

As we consider forgiving another a voice inside says, "Yes, but …" Our tentative vision of forgiveness fades. This signals we must turn our attention to dismantling barriers that block our vision and our progress.

REVENGE. Even when we previously dismissed acts of revenge as unrealistic and suppressed our initial impulses, as the pain of injury or injustice lingers, the impulse resurfaces. The quest for revenge may begin to appear logical and sane, though we know that when we hurt another, even in an act of justified retribution, we accrue adverse consequences – not the peace and contentment we seek.

If we truly desire reconciliation we must recognize the revenge impulse creates an impediment not a solution. Revenge is not an alternative to forgiveness; it is not a matter of choosing one or the other. Rather, the urge for revenge is a barrier we overcome to free up our ability to make a choice – to forgive or not forgive.

Dismantling the revenge urge does not take place in one easy step; it is a repetitive endeavor completed over a long period. Each time the thought of revenge resurfaces we perform a cost analysis, greeting emotion with cold logic. Rather than suppress the emotion we accept and acknowledge the urge as natural, even expected. Then we apply a rational analysis to determine if following the urge will result in satisfaction.

Consider the following example. We assume revenge will satisfy an immediate need to get even and make the other party experience the pain we *felt* but: (a) it will leave us struggling under a burden of guilt for the pain we *cause*, (b) it will result in low self-esteem after we dispense injury or harm, and (c) it will result in remorse when we watch the other party stagger from the physical, emotional, or mental wounds we deliver. We add up costs, assess the outcome, and ask: Will the burdens of guilt, low self-esteem, and remorse be too high a price to pay for satisfying our urge?

As we evaluate anticipated satisfaction of revenge we project anticipated consequences into the distant future and compute a long-term cost/benefit analysis. We may anticipate that after we take revenge, as our anger subsides, we will realize what we *really* desired was our own happiness, not the other's suffering. While we may dream that the other party's suffering will translate into our happiness, we realize it is highly unlikely we will derive genuine happiness from the suffering of another.

Instead, our analysis warns that once we engage in revenge, even small acts of revenge, we risk sliding into chronic hatred. We may agree with the following sentiment: "If you start to hate, you can never stop. You burn yourself from the inside. To retain one's personality, to survive, simply to keep common sense, one has to kill hatred. Immediately."[2]

As we tally possible consequences we realize it is not only *our* hatred we must anticipate; revenge leads to repeated rounds of reciprocal retaliation. Though Hollywood films celebrate characters who exact brutal revenge on their enemies, providing vicarious release for audiences who dream of taking revenge without suffering negative consequences, in real life we do not walk away, arm around the girl, enjoying bliss after butchering evildoers. Unlike the hero of the Hollywood drama we face reciprocal revenge that launches a cycle of reciprocal retribution in motion.

Sripted drama may satisfy our need to see the scales balanced with an act of revenge, but we know this is rarely possible, as the other party does not view our attempt to balance the scales in the same light we do. Individuals see the world from different perspectives; they inevitably value their own hurt as more costly than the hurt another suffers. From the viewpoint of the other party, our acts of revenge exceed the proper measure of fairness. From their viewpoint, they are justified in evening the score. As soon as they have healed from the injury we caused, their focus turns to making *us* pay a price.

Revenge escalates in a seemingly endless game of tit for tat. Sometimes we even hand down the task of delivering revenge to the next generation. The result is violence that continues long after memories of the initial circumstances fade from memory.

When we perform an honest appraisal, we see the potential cost of revenge mount. Guilt, remorse, low self-esteem, a descent into chronic hatred, and continued cycles of revenge drive the price to towering heights. The urge to take revenge may be so strong we are swayed to set aside our cost analysis. We fool ourselves into arguing that our revenge is not meant to meet our needs but rather is meant to teach the wrongdoer a lesson. We argue that taking revenge is altruistic, and worthy of our sacrifice.

Retributive punishment, however, rarely educates anyone: pain, suffering, and degradation do not fuel insight. As a general rule, pain and suffering *diminish* awareness. Pain does not teach us to reason, it teaches us to react. Pain makes us dumber, not wiser. A person consumed with pain acts from a stupor. The cumulative long-term result of the pain and suffering of retributive punishment is a less aware culture, a people confused about what matters in life, a people acting from a state of semi-consciousness. Our altruistic lesson, financed with our sacrifice, fails to produce desired results.

As you respond to the journal prompts consider the ways your emotions cause you to accommodate a desire for revenge. Switch gears and assess the burdens you will assume by exacting revenge. Inspect closely the needs you will satisfy. Will revenge actually lead to satisfaction or is the perceived satisfaction an enticing mirage? This step may need to be repeated numerous times, as the urge for revenge does not abate easily.

DIMINISHED CONSCIOUSNESS. Banishing the offender from our mind might seem likely to result in contentment and happiness. Rarely, however, are we able to erase the offender and their harmful acts from our consciousness. Trauma lingers. Wounds received – emotional, mental, or physical – become frozen in mental images that take on a life of their own.

These mental imprints anchor pain and suffering in our psyche and have the potential to replay without end. The memories are encysted with negative emotions that are triggered when we happen on similar circumstances or upon subsequent encounters with the offender. Our ability to respond to the present moment with enthusiasm, caring, and love is diminished, as the imprints cause our thoughts to wander in the painful past.

During attempts to resolve conflict the buried negative emotions are triggered repeatedly; we relive the pain, which convinces us to abandon forgiveness. But, as the late theologian and ethicist Lewis Smedes writes, "The only way to heal the pain that will not heal itself is to forgive the person who hurt you. Forgiving stops the reruns of pain."[3] Ironically, painful memories, mental imprints encysted with pain, block the path to the very forgiveness that would heal the pain.

The decision to banish the hurt from our mind often results in the pursuit of diminished consciousness through the use of drink or drugs or by retreat into the stupor of depression. Unconsciousness, however, never actually erases pain and suffering: it simply clouds our reality and buries our upset. "The pains we dare not remember are the most dangerous pains of all" for they lie in wait and resurface to cause more pain.[4]

When we resort to diminished consciousness to dull our pain we drape an imaginary black veil over that which we do not wish to view. Unconsciousness, like revenge, is paradoxical. While it seems to remove our hurt, it actually retains the hurt in a form that later seeps back into our lives to wreak havoc. The shrouded mental record of pain continues to exist but, hidden behind a mental black curtain, it exists as something we dare not view. Rather than improving our ability to inspect, clean, and heal our wounds, diminished consciousness allows those wounds to fester in the dark, releasing poisons that make us ill.

Pushing the harm we experienced out of sight into unconsciousness thus fails as a strategy for restoring peace and contentment. In order to heal we must bring truthfulness and specificity to the process of forgiveness. We start with truthfulness, identify our real intentions, accurately recount events, and strip away all bias, alteration, and justification. Truthfulness calls for "harmony between the message you give to the outside world and the feelings you keep on the inside."[5]

Then we turn to specificity as forgiveness demands full awareness of that which has taken place. When we forgive, we forgive with specificity.

Mediator Ken Cloke calls for a forthright and accurate account of the harm we suffered: "Only by acknowledging the crime can we consciously choose forgiveness and avoid the appearance of cowardice in the face of evil."[6]

When we turn away and seek diminished awareness we invite evil to shadow us on our life journey. If we are to move past our impulse to diminish our consciousness, we need to retrieve the pain and suffering we shoved into unconsciousness, where it now acts as an impediment to our happiness. We turn away from the impulse to obfuscate history and instead seek an accurate account of its details.

In mediation preparation we assess the ways in which we have employed diminished consciousness as a strategy. We carefully analyze the methods we employ, intentionally or unintentionally, to shut down awareness. We invite truthfulness and no longer pretend that what happened did not happen. We address the details with specificity so we can erase lingering harmful effects. We clean the wound to insure we will not suffer from an infection that renders the soul ill.

VICTIM IDENTITY. If we use the third coping strategy, taking on the identity of a victim, we repeatedly trigger wounds and wear wounds as a badge, as a statement of who we are rather than viewing them in a manner that diminishes their hold on us.

When we play victim others may sympathize initially and even take up our cause, but eventually they lose interest in our victim status. They may fall into the trap of treating us like the victim we claim to be. They may direct abuse in our direction; they may perpetuate the unhealthy condition. Michael Henderson observes: "One answer to the question why some forgive and some do not may lie in the company one keeps. If you move with those who constantly remind you how much you suffered and how bad the other lot were, it is hard to break free."[7]

Caution is required when we assume the identity of a victim: the identity may be difficult to shed. We may attribute considerable value to our victim identity. Victimhood may appear to serve us well, but in the end it almost always betrays us. Before we can forgive we must lose our attraction to being seen as a victim, we must surrender our victim identity.

Upon surrendering this identity we may be forced to carry our burden in silence. Brian Cox, in *Faith-Based Reconciliation*, notes that a victim may reach the point where they must simply carry the burden of having been harmed and "the act of burden bearing is the singularly most difficult and courageous act by a victim."[8] If we are unwilling to let go of being a victim, if we are unwilling to carry that burden, we balk at forgiveness.

The victim identity generates value in other ways: when we act as a victim, we implicitly name the offender as evil. Public shaming of the offender through the public display of our victim status has a value we may be reluctant to abandon. This is a particular type of revenge: our public status as a victim exacts the revenge of negative public opinion on those who harmed us.

Just as we may be reluctant to let go of our need for revenge, we may hesitate to jettison a victim identity that punishes our adversary. The cost of forgiveness is losing any currency we derive from punishing the other party through public display of victimhood. Dismantling this barrier involves an honest and accurate assessment of the benefit we derive – we need to check closely to see if we are purchasing freedom and happiness, or bondage.

SUMMARY. The preceding discussion touches on dismantling common barriers we may have built inadvertently with our coping strategies. As you assess factors that stand in the way of forgiving, you may discover you have adopted other unique solutions that have become impediments to forgiveness, obstacles that obscure your vision and block your path. Our task is to dismantle these barriers and glimpse the possibility of forgiveness, after which we follow our vision to reconciliation.

Fairness

There is one additional common barrier worth special attention: our concern with fairness. Our sense of fairness is deeply offended when we comprehend that our attempt to even the score leads to adverse consequences *for us*. When our attempts to make things right cause *us* to suffer, life seems terribly unfair. We may become bitter and unwilling to consider forgiveness that comes at such a high price.

This dilemma is significant. If each time we seek to set things right we are doomed to sink into guilt and remorse or we are doomed to become prisoners of endless cycles of eye-for-an-eye revenge, then how can we possibly make this world fair and just? If our avenging actions create new imbalances, which lead to additional rounds of vengeance, how do we escape the vicious circle? If our attempts to defeat evil trap us in evil, are we forever doomed to endless rounds of pain and suffering? It appears we stand powerless in the face of evil, caught in a double bind. We protest from deep in our soul: *This is not fair!*

Our protest against a universe we perceive to be unjust blocks forgiveness. We consider forgiving, but we see only injustice. The situation would be hopeless if not for a special teacher, Jesus, who taught *turn the other cheek*. His extremely counterintuitive lesson of nonviolence calls on us to reverse the normal flow of events. We might be tempted to consider the phrase *turn the other cheek* to be a lovely sentiment that cannot possibly be put into action. Do we *really* want to get hit again? Of course we do not want to suffer additional pain but that concern misses the point of the lesson.

When we turn the other cheek we release our resistance to pain, suffering, and evil. If we resist and fight back we become stuck to the evil we fight – we experience the embrace of conflict. As an analogy, consider pushing down firmly on sticky flypaper. The paper sticks to your hand. With revenge the results are analogous: fight the other party and we become stuck to them. Evil is analogous to superglue: it binds us to the other party. We struggle to escape but our bondage becomes increasingly secure. We renew attempts to destroy the other party and become more firmly cemented to them.

Those who undertake righteous crusades, those who are all fired up and ready to strike blows against evil end up unintentionally causing more evil. Collateral damage is one side effect but, more importantly, the righteous warrior ends up destroying himself.

In conflict the solution we *really* seek is slightly different than we imagine – the outcome we seek is *to no longer be stuck*. The goal is not to overcome or punish the other party but simply to be freed from being held captive in the oppositional embrace. *Turn the other cheek* is refusing to press down on the flypaper. We release the impulse to fight back that keeps us locked in an endless spiral of violence.

At first glance, turning the other cheek may seem to be the approach of the weak and powerless, a form of avoidance. Upon closer inspection we discover turning the other cheek is the only answer to this paradox. It is the *only* response that sets us free from entanglement. This solution taught two thousand years ago turns out to be more than mere philosophical platitude. Turn the other cheek is down-to-earth practical advice and an important prelude to forgiveness. In preparation for granting forgiveness we let go of our resistance, disengage from the oppositional embrace, release our desire to strike back, and abandon our obsession with measuring fairness.

For the sake of illustration, consider evil to be a character with a face. If we observe closely, we can see how evil taunts us and invites us to throw a punch. Evil *wants* us to strike out. Evil knows that when we strike we end up trapped, and we will struggle harder and harder to escape entanglement, only to become more and more ensnared. Evil wins every time we lash out, as the blow we unleash entraps us in the very thing we seek to destroy.

Evil is the ultimate sticky paper, the quintessential quicksand. When we strike back in retaliation we end up dancing with the devil. As Smedes notes, "Monsters who are too evil to be forgiven get a stranglehold on their victims."[9] He adds, "When we refuse to forgive monsters, we give them exactly what they want. Monsters do not want to be forgiven."[10] This analysis captures the nature of our dilemma: evil feeds on our inability to release our resistance to that evil and forgive.

There is no doubt that striking a blow against evil feels good and satisfies deep needs. Inherently there is nothing wrong with getting even or destroying harmful entities. The instinct to destroy evil, to destroy that which causes harm, is laudable, but force-based attempts fail to actually make evil go away. Attempts to destroy another person pile hurt on top of hurt. We are led to believe that one more destructive blow, one more bomb, one more enemy slain and we will be free. But freedom eludes us.

This is the ultimate unfairness against which we protest: *fight back and you lose*. Does this mean we should surrender in the face of evil and face an eternity of suffering? That is not the intended lesson. Instead, we need to pay close attention to options that allow us to defeat evil – those options are not what we might think. Our own defeat is *not* inevitable. Defeat only appears inevitable when we approach evil in the wrong manner.

We must ask what hidden or missing options should be explored in our search for a way to overcome evil. One option that solves the dilemma – turn the other cheek – leads to an understanding of forgiveness. With forgiveness we accept that we will not be able to balance the scales. We release our impulse to strike back, we forego dreams of extracting an eye for an eye. When we choose forgiveness, we free ourselves from the oppositional embrace. We recognize the false promise that accompanies measuring and doling out retribution. We recognize the divine promise of unconditional love that transcends tests of fairness and defiantly changes the nature of the game.

But, you may protest, how can a world that does not allow us to strike a return blow be fair and just? There are times when it seems we must forgive the world for its inherent unfairness. Richard Rohr expresses this vital concept: "To accept reality is to forgive reality for what it is."[11] Once we recognize that our view of fairness is not reflected in reality we can protest, but it may be in our best interest to cease protesting and investigate other solutions such as turning the other cheek and forgiveness. I doubt there are many people who turn the other cheek because they find the idea inherently appealing. Rather, they come to this approach after encountering failure with other approaches. They come to His lesson from a practical need to reduce their suffering. From the point of view of fairness, *turn the other cheek* is an objectionable affront; from a practical view, it is golden wisdom.

The picture I hope to paint is not yet complete. There are many questions to be answered before we fully embrace this counterintuitive stance. I shall return later in this chapter and in the next chapter to the question of why the oppositional dance with evil can be solved only by forgiveness. However, at this time, while we are removing barriers to forgiveness, we simply need to recognize our protest against unfairness prevents us from considering forgiveness. As you assess your personal barriers, pay close attention to the intensity of your protest and inspect how that protest impedes your desire to grant forgiveness.

Forgiveness Defined

After you clear away barriers and impediments that make it difficult or impossible to even consider forgiveness, you will want to dig deeper into the nature of forgiveness itself. You will want to ask, when we forgive, what are we actually doing?

Forgiving another is not an act that occurs magically or fortuitously. Forgiveness is not a warm fuzzy feeling arising mysteriously from distant shores of our psyche. It is not a sudden cognition emerging, unbidden, from our subconscious. *Forgiveness is an act of the will.*

Forgiveness does not just happen. We must actively decide to forgive those who inflicted the harm we did not deserve. Forgiveness is not something we owe: the party who hurt us does not deserve our forgiveness. Forgiveness does not right the scales of justice or balance wrongs; it is not a *quid pro quo*. Rather, forgiveness is an affirmative act, a compassionate giving of ourselves that disregards balance and measure and debts paid. This does not mean apologies and amends do not sometimes contribute to our willingness to forgive – they often do. However, though an apology and/or amends may open our heart they are not prerequisites for true forgiveness.

Revenge attempts to even the score; forgiveness tears up the scorecard. When we are harmed we experience being made less: our physical, emotional, and mental states are reduced, our identity diminished. With revenge we seek to reduce the condition of the offender; we seek to lower their status; we seek to make the offender less – physically, emotionally, and mentally.

In contrast, when we forgive *we lift the offender up*. With forgiveness we make *more* of the offender. Instead of increasing the offender's suffering and diminishing their well being, we pull back from retribution. In the face of our own hurt we defy natural instincts and increase the amount of compassion and love in the world. We actively lessen the overall suffering in the world and increase peace, happiness, and contentment. When we forgive we give witness to the divine within. With an act of forgiveness, we turn away from our flawed human nature and toward the redeeming presence of the sacred, the divine. *We increase divine presence through an act of free will.*

In the conflict resolution process we learn to control our free will, placing forgiveness within our grasp. One might assume, incorrectly, the effort involved is simply "positive thinking"; but we do not think positively when we are wounded by the acts of another; we cannot think positively when our heart is filled with hate. When I speak of an act of the will, I need to qualify the phrase: forgiveness is an act of the *divine will* with which we have been endowed.

Forgiveness is not about using the power of our will to coerce the other party. When we forgive we do not engage in the use of force designed to dominate. In contrast, the exercise of free will that summons forgiveness requires humility and requires we let go of control over the other. When we forgive we accept the other as they are, including their flaws and shortcomings. Forgiving requires an act of divinely endowed compassion that relinquishes the exercise of power used to exact consequences. Forgiving does not require an act of will that demands results, compliance, or conformity, but rather an act of will that sets aside the other's transgressions and failings. We do not use our will power to overwhelm or overcome the other party, but rather to transform our own nature, to call forth the loving compassion that is our divine heritage.

When we engage in the pursuit of humble, loving, and compassionate ends, we discover our will is naturally endowed with divine grace. We discover a humble type of power we previously did not recognize. While you may choose to view these dynamics within a different paradigm, I believe that only when we recognize our essential divine nature, only when we invite the indwelling Spirit to play a role in our lives, do we find the power to forgive.

In forgiveness we find a uniquely spiritual task that calls on us to channel divine grace received into the grace we bestow on others. When we forgive we become a conduit for divine presence in the mundane. When we forgive we turn against the natural order of things and affirm a different measure of success, one that asks if we have increased the total measure of lovingkindness and compassion in the universe.

When we go against the natural order we discover the defiant quality of forgiveness. Forgiveness is not a cowardly alternative to vengeance, rather forgiveness defiantly affirms a divine reality. In choosing forgiveness we make a dramatic decision to change ourselves, change the other, change the relationship and the world. We defiantly build a future of love. We discover, after much searching, that unconditional love, manifest in the form of forgiveness, is the most direct path to reconciliation.

False Self / Divine Self

To clarify the spiritual transformation that leads to forgiveness and then reconciliation, it helps to use a model that conceives our nature to have both a false or evil side and a true or divine side. The model requires language that is not quite metaphor but also not quite literal.

I will call our evil side our false self. This is the home of ego, lies, clinging, anxiety, hate, defensiveness and a host of other negative intentions and emotions. The false self considers we are justified in dominating and coercing others. It seduces us into believing we are justified in grasping and hoarding in a survival of the fittest competition. The false self is the bounded self that refuses connection, harmony, and unity, a limited self that turns its back on collaboration and mutual benefit. It honors separateness and division, hierarchy and status. This ego-driven self does not recognize interconnectedness or the possibility of transcendent union with the divine.

That which we might call our true or divine self resonates with the indwelling Spirit and is capable of discovering and engaging the indwelling Spirit found in others. This divine self recognizes its transcendent nature and honors the communion of souls realized through loving compassion.

This divine self is unbounded, unlimited, and exists in knowing and loving divine relationship. This divine self embraces I-Thou relationship. As we assume Francis discovered, one might consider the true self or divine self to be who we really are when we have transcended earthly trials and recognized our place in the spiritual kingdom.

While the model of a false self and a divine self risks being too black and white, omitting nuances between the two poles, it has value for the purpose of our assessment. While more often than not we balance both dark and light in our struggle to know our divine nature, for the purpose of illustrating forgiveness we will assess whether it is our false self or our true self that drives our views and decisions.

As we chart our actions we evaluate which self, false or divine, results from our exercise of free will. In our personal assessment we acknowledge that we may use our freedom to choose the path of the false or divine. Delio captures the challenge, "We need the freedom to be ourselves as God has created us and loves us, and we need the courage to live in God's love humbly, attentively and with compassion."[12] Using this model we assess our successes and failures when it comes to living humbly as our divine self in God's love.

When we find ourselves trapped in the oppositional embrace of conflict, we inevitably discover the situation has arisen as a result of entanglement between our false self and the false self of the other. Experience teaches us that all conflict involves a battle between two false selves.

When we seek to forgive we must turn away from our false self in an act of free will. As a result of abandoning that which is false we gain the freedom to cease our conflict embrace. We slip the knots of entanglement. If we continue in this direction we also slip past the false self of the other party to connect with the image of God within them.

Thus, a spiritual transformation ends the contentious embrace of false selves and gives birth to a sacred connection. This divine interaction in which we become open to the other has been called I-Thou relationship.[13] Miroslav Volf in a quote from *Exclusion and Embrace* observes, "A self that is 'full of itself' can neither receive the other nor make a genuine movement toward the other."[14] When we empty ourselves of that which is false we create space for the other to enter.

Thus, forgiving is not a passive series of events. We actively step out of our false self and aggressively circumvent the false self of the other. We seek to enter into an I-Thou relationship from which we can generate forgiveness.

In your conflict assessment become familiar with the quality of your false self. Become mindful of your thoughts and behavior when you are being and acting from that bound and limited point of view. Detect anger, hate, and defensive posturing that are telltale signs of the false self we have built out of fear and ignorance. Become aware of being invested in protecting your ego and keeping others in their place.

When we act from this limited self we fail to achieve harmonious relationships, as the false self demands division and separation and insists we defend ego with domination and coercion. False self does not forgive. It is made up of emotional and mental patterns we develop to protect our identity, which appears to be under siege. False self is a decoy we have created that allows us to operate in a world that apparently does not value or need us for who we really are as spiritual beings. We recognize the presence of false self when we remark, "I was not being myself" or "I don't know who I was being" or "That wasn't really me."

At other times, when we have an uplifting religious experience, we feel *this is who I really am*. Such conversion moments provide contrast to the false self we construct as a shield to protect our inner nature. The religious experiences of transcending the limited and small self provide a benchmark to help us discern false from divine self. As we become more and more mindful of the differences, we can document in our journal the aspects of false self that must be cleared to the side as we seek reconciliation.

Reconciliation depends on restoring relationship based on the divine within, no matter how fleeting that connection may be. For reconciliation to occur we must include the other in our circle of sacred affinity. The importance of inclusion is captured by Richard Rohr: "After all, our task is to *separate* from evil, isn't it? That is the lie! *Any exclusionary process of thinking, any exclusively dualistic thinking, will always create violent people.*"[15] Violent people are those who operate from the defensive shell of an identity created to do battle with all that we fear. All that does not participate in God's love.

We begin to recognize the importance of a type of inclusivity that makes it possible for two divine selves to embrace and discover sacred unity – but we also recognize the accompanying need to separate from the false self.

Thus we have a two-step process. First, we separate from false self and become more fully who we truly are in essence – our divine self made in the image of God. When we recognize falsehoods our spiritual vision – with its obscuring impediments wiped away – sees past the false to the truth of divine self. Once we accomplish this task we proceed to the second step: we extend our spiritual vision past the false self the other is being to discover the divine self within them. We discover the image of God and realize it is possible for us to unite with them – at this level.

In summary, we cut bonds that tether us to false identity then, with the torch of compassion, we sever bonds that tether us to the false self of our opponent. Our spiritual eyes see past falsehoods to perceive the divine within the other. Escaping the limitations of false self, we intend our communication to speak to the other's divine heart. The ensuing I-Thou dialogue removes entanglements that tether false selves in opposition. Walls become bridges.

We are released from the oppositional embrace that binds false selves in conflict to discover the honesty, authenticity, and compassion of a relationship grounded in the love of God.

Ability to Forgive

When we first decide to forgive we suffer doubt. We are not certain we will be able to forgive, even when we express a strong desire to do so. It feels like we are being asked to go out on a ledge and jump. However, the decision to forgive sets in motion a transformation from false self to divine self. This transformation gives us an ability to forgive we did not previously possess. We find an ability that is not possible for a limited and bound self; we find an ability that is only possible when we operate from awareness of our true nature.

In other words, the *decision* to forgive, which we make when we are uncertain we are actually able to forgive, fuels inner transformation that taps divine resources. After we jump we grow wings. The decision – an act of will – sets the process in motion. Faith that our decision will propel us beyond our limitations emerges. We have faith that after we jump we will learn to fly.

Why should we harbor such faith? Because the ability to forgive is a natural property of divine self, a sacred property with which we are endowed. When we give ourselves permission to step out of our false self we regain an ability to forgive. When we discard limits and boundaries and welcome the freedom of the spiritual nature with which we are endowed we find ways to forgive. The latent ability has always been there; only the faith needed to engage that ability has been missing.

Doubts tend to arise because the decision to forgive is paradoxical, counterintuitive, illogical, and difficult to comprehend. It flat out does not make sense within the context of our normal rational thinking. When we struggle with the decision to forgive we are pushed to seek contemplation and stillness; we are forced to transcend human logic and tap divine resources.

When we wrestle with the decision to forgive we seek to understand the nature of the indwelling Spirit. Forgiveness, like apology, is redemptive. We do not ordinarily consider granting forgiveness an act of redemption. It is the offender who seeks redemption through our forgiveness. Nonetheless, in making the transformation from false self to divine self we are redeemed as well.

When we reluctantly recognize in the process of forgiveness that our false identity with its flaws and shortcomings (sins) has played a role in the conflict we recognize a need to be forgiven as well. Our actions during the conflict are actions of false self, ego self. Even if we were not the original offender, once conflict began we contributed to its escalation. Our decision (conscious or unconscious) to interact from the point of view of false self contributed to the continuation of the conflict. When we faced off with the other party as our false self we brought on our own suffering. When faced with opposition we responded as our false self and failed to embrace the other party from our divine essence.

Before I explain the model further it is worth consulting the thoughts of Thomas Merton, the Trappist monk who has done so much to help us better understand our faith. James Finley, in *Merton's Palace of Nowhere*, describes Merton's explanation of the false self:

> … Merton equates sin with the identity-giving structures of the false self. This in itself is significant. The focus of sin is shifted from the realm of morality to that of ontology. For Merton, the matter of who we are always precedes what we do. Thus, sin is not essentially an action but rather an identity. Sin is a fundamental stance of wanting to be what we are not. Sin is thus an orientation to falsity, a basic lie concerning our own deepest reality. Likewise, inversely, to turn away from sin is, above all, to turn away from a tragic case of mistaken identity concerning our own selves.[16]

He continues,

> This then is the false self. It is a tragic self, in that it ends up with less than nothing in trying to gain more than the everything which God freely bestows upon his children.

> The false self is a whole syndrome of lies and illusions that spring from a radical rejection of God in whom alone we find our own truth and ultimate identity.[17]

When we play the part of a victim or are unwilling to forgive we are clinging to this false self. A preliminary step in forgiveness is humbly asking divine forgiveness for our having greeted the world with a false identity – an identity that sprang from a rejection of God. In response, we receive the grace of divine forgiveness that inspires us to discover and engage the divine nature of the other party. We seek that which is God in the Other. Then we forgive as we have been forgiven.

In the same way the grace of divine forgiveness we receive allows us to step aside from our false self, the forgiveness we bestow on the other party allows them to step outside their false self. When the indwelling Spirit transforms our heart, we are empowered to transform the heart of the other.

As a result of this transformation we see clearly how we have been fighting in our adopted role of false self against another party who has also adopted the role of a false self. This new perceptual altitude allows us to see we have been allowing mutual puppet selves (false selves) to fight a proxy battle when our true selves (divine selves) are absent, hiding, or lost in darkness. We have been engaged in a battle of lies, fighting shadows alongside our opponent who also fights shadows.

We begin to wonder, "*What* were we doing?" It is then we step away from conflict embrace with humble apology and forgiveness. We experience a profound new awareness. We know that what really matters is reducing the sum of lies in the world and increasing divine presence. We reduce the separation that is sin and increase the presence of God that is love. We realize, just as Francis taught, that what matters most is (divine) brotherhood.

The process of forgiving motivates us to understand the full story of how we descend or fall from our true identity as divine self endowed with the image of God into playing the role of a false self that obscures our true nature. We begin to sort out how we become entangled in the pain and suffering of conflict. Thus, forgiveness may initiate one of the most significant spiritual transformations of our lives. When we are called upon to imitate Christ's forgiveness we open a door that leads to an understanding of unity with Christ. We begin to glimpse the mystical heights Francis came to know.

At first glance the decision to forgive appears to rest on our perception and evaluation of the party who offended us. It appears our forgiveness must emerge from taking measure of the worthiness of the other party who harmed us. It appears we must ask, "Is he worthy of forgiveness?"

We soon learn, however, that forgiveness demands we address our estrangement from our divine nature. Forgiveness takes place within the context of a relationship. Lewis Smedes wrote, "You can reverse your future only by releasing other people from their pasts."[18] We must also release self from the past. In the spiritual transformation of reconciliation, we come to realize that in the past we were acting as other than our self formed in the image of God. The other party suffers from the same predicament. We both have been estranged from who we really are. While it was not apparent earlier we now discover that as we forgive we are forgiven.

We do not ask, "Is the other party worthy of forgiveness" as much as we ask, "Am I worthy enough to forgive?"

Forgiveness Takes Time

With heightened perception comes the humbling insight that the falsehoods in which we find ourselves entangled are too extensive to erase overnight. Stripping away the entanglements of false self takes considerable time. It is easier to understand the dynamics that are in play than it is to complete the hard work required to untie all the knots. While we may experience the grace of moments of great freedom and significant lucidity the overall task of becoming free from entanglement in lies and falsehoods requires patient persistence. It requires committed contemplative prayer.

We Do Not Excuse, We Forgive

Blaming the other party for their condition seems almost foolish once we become cognizant of the falsehoods accumulated on both sides, leading to conflict. Instead, we may find we feel sympathy for the other party once we discover the challenges they face and the ways life has overwhelmed them.

Yet we do not blindly dismiss their condition – after all, they are responsible for making the decision to cling to a false identity and deny their divine self. For this we do not excuse them, but we forgive them. "You do not excuse people by forgiving them; you forgive them at all only because you hold them to account and refuse to excuse them."[19] If we excuse the other party we make them less than they are – less than made in the image of God. When we hold them to the standard of their divine self we refuse to render them less than they actually are. We hold the divine self accountable for clinging to false self and we know "forgiving is fair to wrongdoers because it holds them to the incriminating touchstone of their own free humanity."[20] We honor the free will with which they have been endowed, and hold them accountable for their decision to abandon awareness of their divine self created in the likeness of God. We hold them accountable for retreating from their true nature into falsehoods (sin).

Our upset with the offender is fueled by our knowledge that they possess choice. The decision to turn away from our divine nature is perhaps what we really mean by sin. Sin can be seen, not as an infraction of rules, but rather as clinging to a false identity while denying one's true nature. "Our hate tells us that this person has a will and he used this will to harm us."[21] In reconciliation we see the full potential in their free will, the potential to discover their divine nature. We witness to their divinity through forgiveness that compassionately conveys that we understand – as we have walked the same path. While we were trapped in conflict we disparaged, belittled, and degraded the other, but now, in forgiveness, we turn toward them with a compassionate gaze and admire them. We actively lift them up with forgiveness.

If you find false self and divine self too metaphorical or too inexact, simply assess aspects of your life that seem false and aspects that resonate with truth and compassion. Set aside the aspects that seem false while strengthening those that seem truthful.

Self-Forgiveness

For some people, the attempt to leave that which is false behind may surface an additional barrier: lack of self-forgiveness. When we cannot forgive self it becomes nearly impossible to forgive another.

One reason we have trouble forgiving others may seem puzzling at first – the anger we feel often has its roots in *our own transgressions*. We ordinarily assume a person who is angry has been harmed by another. We witness their anger and assume they suffered at the hands of the person with whom they are angry. The truth is often the reverse.

Ironically, harmful acts *we have committed* cause anger toward others. This requires explanation as the idea may seem strange or even offensive to those who see it as blaming the victim. The concept, however, rests on observations a reader can verify with their own experience.

Consider the following sequence of events. When we commit a misdeed our identity suffers. When we harm another it is difficult for us to accept our actions. A self-image that includes inflicting harm on others is not an image we can sit with comfortably. We do not wish to see ourselves as bad or evil. We do not wish to be seen as one who harms others without reason. In our constant battle to maintain a positive self-image our commission of harmful acts presents a serious threat. We threaten our own self-image.

In our effort to maintain a positive self-image – after we have harmed another – we alter (in our memory) the sequence of events. We reinvent our motivation for having committed a harmful act; we write a story that is consistent with the self-image we wish to maintain. We conceal our sleight-of-hand redrafting of our story from ourselves. Approaching the task in a semiconscious manner we mask our duplicity with a swirl of disturbed emotions that blur reason. Our emotional state becomes a smokescreen that blurs reality, making it possible for us to redraft and alter our narrative.

In an attempt to preserve self-worth we fabricate justifications for our misdeeds and argue the person we harmed *deserved* harm – *they had it coming*. Our acts were justified. In order to preserve a sense of our goodness we fabricate a narrative that frames the evil nature of the other person as justification for our causing them harm. Time becomes jumbled in our emotionally blurred memory. The harm the other allegedly committed is conceived to have happened *before* we harmed them. Our acts – we tell self and others – were justified reciprocal actions taken to punish the other party for their misdeeds.

If an advantageous time shift in our story is not possible, if we cannot mask the true timeline with a swirl of heated emotion, we conjure a preemptive strike rationale. We claim to have successfully detected their intention to do us harm, which justified our punishing them before they could act. In *Things Hidden* Richard Rohr recognizes the pervasive nature of this problem: "The human delusion seems to be this: We seem to think someone else is always the problem, not me. We tend to export our hate and evil elsewhere. In fact, this problem is so central to human nature and human history that its overcoming is at the heart of all spiritual teachings."[22]

Thoughtful responses to the journal workbook prompts help you assess the degree to which you have justified your misdeeds with anger toward the other party. Untangling this bramble bush is not an easy task but a task that grows easier with experience. When we turn to an analytical process such as responding to prompts, rather than immersing ourselves in dark or unsettled emotions, we buy time to truthfully and accurately sort out chains of causality. We learn to catch ourselves in the act of redrafting.

Absent such introspective discipline, our anger and rage ratchet up in direct relationship to how badly we harmed the one against whom we complain. We offset the guilt that threatens us by balancing our story with a tale of a commensurate wrong they must have committed. In other words, the more harm we have caused the more justified anger we must show. Our narrative must demonize the other in order to justify the punishment we delivered, thus keeping our white hat image intact.

In our narrative of outrage, we explain how we were forced by the other party's dreadful nature to take action. We explain how we are not typically that type of person but we had no choice when confronted by their misdeeds or evil intentions. However, we first committed an offense for which we now seek justification. Though *we* committed the harm we angrily point out the other party is in the wrong.

Angry justifications and altered narratives erect mental barriers that protect us from being forced to recognize our flaws. Unfortunately, barriers that protect us from admitting and owning our harmful acts also prevent us from forgiving the other for the *actual* harm they have done. If we forgive the other party, we remove them from the category of evildoer to which we have assigned them in our attempt to justify our harmful actions. If we accept their apology and grant them forgiveness we can no longer justify our actions as responses to their evil. Our harmful acts must be viewed in their true light and we must come to grips with the task of repentent transformation.

Intuitively, we know that if we forgive them we will be forced to come to grips with our own harmful acts in a more realistic manner. When and if we forgive them we might be forced to reveal (to ourselves) that we have transgressed. To protect self-image, we maintain our demonization of the other – our un-confessed misdeeds bar us from participating in reconciliation.

If we cannot admit we caused harm and if we cannot repent and forgive ourselves we find it impossible to forgive the other. "One reason it is difficult to mediate forgiveness is that doing so forces parties to take responsibility for their actions and inactions, to recognize that they contributed to the problem or allowed it to continue."[23] The reconciliation process grinds to a halt as, "the pain we cause other people becomes the hate we feel for ourselves.... We judge, we convict, and we sentence ourselves. Mostly in secret."[24]

In order to move beyond this impasse we must gain the ability to admit we are flawed and in need of forgiveness. In reality, most times we do not apologize or forgive alone: "The story is not usually about an innocent lamb and a bad wolf. Most of us have to do our forgiving while we are being forgiven."[25] In forgiving self we acknowledge our imperfect nature, accept divine grace, and recognize we have the potential to rise above our flawed nature. We can achieve redemption. "The moment you become whole and holy is when you can accept your shadow self, or, to put it in moral language, that is when you can admit your sin. *Basically we move from unconsciousness to consciousness by a deliberate struggle with our shadow self.*"[26]

As we consider forgiving the other party we may discover we need to first forgive self, and only then do we become free to forgive another. If we refuse to forgive self it becomes hard to forgive another. Forgiving self may seem akin to narcissism but narcissism is love for false self and we are pointing to love for the divine self. When we forgive and show love for the divine within, we also show love for God, whose nature is to love unconditionally and whose gift is forgiveness.

It is important to realize self-forgiveness is not about producing an excuse or justification that lessens your misdeeds. It is not about explaining away what you have done but rather it is about seeing clearly that you have harmed another. "Self-esteem is not the same as self-forgiveness. You esteem yourself when you discover your own excellence. You forgive yourself after you discover your own faults."[27]

Self-forgiveness has its foundation in Divine forgiveness – when we repent for deciding to be other than divine self, we experience rebirth as divine self and in the transformation from false self to divine self, we receive God's forgiveness. The transformative experience of Divine forgiveness inspires us to grant forgiveness to the party who harmed us. We are lifted up so that we might lift up another.

Self-forgiving that lifts the burden of harm we have committed does not replace the forgiveness we seek from the other. We do not forgive self and automatically achieve reconciliation. Self-forgiveness simply eliminates the need for us to harbor hostility we use to justify our harmful acts. Self-forgiveness is a prerequisite to forgiving the other.

The angry, offended party, upon forgiving self, slowly begins to reveal their transgressions and unburden guilt. They may say, "Look, I realize I have not been an angel either. I need to apologize for a few things myself ..." This is not yet forgiveness, but rather reciprocal repentance. They do not start by forgiving the other who has already apologized. First they mirror the apology and *then* they extend forgiveness.

The reciprocal apology may imply forgiveness – the apology offered in return for an apology may say, "Your transgressions are washed away by my understanding that I have also done harm." Mutual forgiveness emerges from reciprocal apology. The mediator must pay close attention as forgiveness may take place nonverbally during the recognition of mutual culpability. There may be an instantaneous recognition of entangled false selves and a lightning-fast connection at the level of true selves. Mutual forgiveness may take place quickly.

In your analysis and assessment do not overlook the subtle factors of *omission* and *complicity*. There are times when we become embroiled in conflicts we did not originate and for which we assume we have nothing to repent. Nonetheless, once a conflict starts, we often act in ways that later cause shame and embarrassment. Our conflict-induced behavior (insults, harmful acts, disparaging statements, hostile thoughts) becomes a source of guilt that shuts down our ability to reach out to the other.

Do not sweep the hidden influence you exert under the carpet. Although you may not have initiated the conflict, upon closer inspection you may discover the ways in which you positioned yourself to be swept up in conflict. Your involvement may have come about through your covert influence, as a result of omissions or inaction, or with your quiet complicity, all of which necessitate repentance and forgiveness.

In summary, when the moment to forgive arrives, if you find only anger and hatred in your heart, inspect your conscience. Do you need to confess transgressions and seek forgiveness? Is there a lack of self-forgiveness? Richard Rohr cleared the overgrown brush on this path with the following words, "on the cross of life we accept our own complicity and cooperation with evil, instead of imagining that we are standing on some pedestal of moral superiority."[28]

It is difficult, maybe impossible, to achieve reconciliation with a guilty heart. Thus we benefit from a retreat to solitude where we can descend from our pedestal of moral superiority to spend time inspecting our conscience. One who deceives their own heart risks ruin. Lies we use to protect our self-image create a foundation of sand in the path of storm-blown surf. A more solid foundation is found in repentance and self-forgiveness.

For many, unraveling transgressions in a process of self-forgiveness is a tough road to travel. We have our reality set in concrete. We wear the "white hat," we know the other is to blame, and we know there is no reason to dig up old bones. It is too painful. While it is true that the process is not accomplished without discomfort, that discomfort is always less than the pain that arises from unresolved conflict that ruins your life.

Practical Steps

An excellent, practical presentation of forgiveness, which deserves study, can be found in the late Lewis Smedes' *Forgive and Forget*.[29] He identifies stages we encounter on the way to forgiveness: we *hurt*, *hate*, *heal*, and *unite*. This is an excellent place in this chapter to catch up on the work you are doing in the journal workbook, and to open the journal to the related prompts for the following discussion.

Hurt can range from slight offenses we quietly endure, to egregious harm suffered, to grave wounds – all are hurts we worry will never heal. The *degree of hurt* can be charted from mild to severe.

A second scale charts *the degree to which the hurt was deserved* – we may be innocents suffering hurt that shocks the conscience or we may ourselves be guilty of wrongdoing. While most hurts offend our sense of fairness, there are times when we feel we deserved the harm we experienced more than at other times.

A third scale charts the *degree to which the hurt was personal and intended.* We may have been in the wrong place at the wrong time, or we may have been specifically targeted.

Assessing the severity of hurt, the degree to which the hurt was deserved, and the extent to which the hurt was personal – forces us to become specific. We may complain, "You caused me to suffer tremendously, which I did not deserve, and you hurt me intentionally. You targeted me." Or, "I may have deserved to be hurt, but what you did was beyond fair. I think you took it out on me personally because you don't like me." Another response might be: "I know you did not mean to hurt me personally and I realize I was at the wrong place at the wrong time but, still, it wasn't fair for you to hurt me that badly."

Smedes notes, "The hurt that creates a crisis of forgiving has three dimensions. It is always *personal, unfair, and deep.*"[30] Charting these three dimensions in your journal workbook will give you a good start in your assessment. As we identify specifics of our hurt, stored up negative energy releases and burdens lighten. Although this is a crucial step in the right direction, we must continue the process and confront our hate.

We **hate** in varying degrees from *passive hate* (we simply do not care what happens to the offender) to *passive aggressive hate* (we hope they are harmed but we do not wish to deliver the blow) to *aggressive hate* (in which we actively and directly attempt to bring about the other's demise). Hate may be overt or covert. When we fear the other party or fear the opinion of onlookers, we hate covertly. In other instances, we hate overtly and make our enmity well known.

When we hate, our intentions and actions are directed toward damaging, lessening, or destroying our relationship with the other – we refuse to perceive or acknowledge the offender's divine nature. Hate infects us with disease and poisons our heart, yet it is a stage we must pass through as we come to own our troubled emotions. "When we deny our hate we detour around the crisis of forgiveness. We suppress our spite, make adjustments, and make believe we are too good to be hateful."[31]

We also balk at letting go of our hate when it serves our needs. For example, we may hold onto hate when we choose to be a victim and avoid admitting the ways in which we were complicit. These detours from honesty prevent us from reaching our goal of reconciliation. Thus, in the effort to dismantle barriers to forgiving, do not skirt the step of owning your hate.

In your assessment be sure to distinguish anger from hate. Anger drives us to change that which is wrong whereas hate does not want change. Hate wants to make things worse through revenge. "Anger is a sign we are alive and well; hate is a sign that we are sick and need to be healed."[32] The journal prompts will ask you to discern anger from hate and will help you unpack these views and emotions.

Our hate needs **healing**. Healing is not forgetting. It involves removing the imprint of the wound by coming to know that wound in detail. We cleanse the wound with attention to accurate details, by seeing events as they are. Healing involves separating lies from truth. In order to heal – in order to resurrect true self – we may have to experience the death of the ego self or false self.

Healing requires we move forward with calm determination, intending to invest the world with divine presence. In order to heal we become present to the wounded world that hates. We expose false self that hates and we heal by turning toward our divine self. We may then discover additional layers of hurt and new layers of falsehood, which prompt us to start over and continue to heal. "When you forgive someone for hurting you, you perform spiritual surgery inside your soul; you cut away the wrong that was done to you so that you can see your 'enemy' through the magic eyes that can heal your soul."[33]

Healing comes to fruition when we **unite** under an umbrella of grace. "The one who knows all and receives all, as a mirror does, has no trouble forgiving all. It's not a matter of being correct, but being connected."[34] Whereas previously we were silent, we now restore our ability and willingness to communicate. We discover and enhance common, shared views of reality. Our ability to love is resurrected as we extend a kind word, a heartfelt gesture, a glance of admiration, a shared laugh, a handshake, or a hug. "You will know that forgiveness has begun when you recall those who hurt you and feel the power to wish them well."[35]

Assess the degree to which you must hurt, hate, heal, and unite. Track your progress and repeat steps as necessary. Achieving the ability to forgive does not happen overnight. The task resembles chipping away at a boulder lying in the road blocking our path.

When Evil Overwhelms Us / Transcending Evil

There are times when our pain, hurt, dismay, and anger cannot be sustained by our focus on the individual offender. As we begin to recognize the offender's weakness, frailty, and flawed human nature, our ability to hate and blame the offender fades.

Yet we continue to hate and hurt. We continue to feel events were unjust and unfair, but the individual offender no longer embodies sufficient evil to warrant our continued hatred. He seems small, perhaps foolish, but our pain is great. In our eyes he becomes a symptom of a more profound evil. Behind that frail offender must lie a more worthy villain – we may elect fate as the mega-offender, or we may turn our hatred toward the creator for allowing bad, even horrific, things to happen.

However, when we elect fate, evolution, or the creator as the ultimate offender, we sink into apathy and our hate festers. Like an injured wolf snared in a trap who faces a slow, lingering, and painful death, we bare our teeth and threaten to maul anyone who attempts to help.

Our ability to forgive fades – we no longer see the offender who caused specific harm as an appropriate target for hate *or* forgiveness. We perceive the individual offender incapable of doing other than they have done as a result of that which made them what they are – fate, evolution, or a creator. Our blame is too vague and dispersed to allow for forgiveness and reconciliation. We no longer focus on specific acts that must be forgiven. We protest all existence. Such generalized hate defies forgiveness. As a victim we strike out and pass the hurt to others (who do not deserve the hurt) and thus exacerbate the conditions against which we protest.

When we thrash about madly like a drowning person and curse the entirety of existence as the source of our suffering, we are in need of rescue. The lifeboat we need so badly may be spiritual formation.

Paradoxically, to defeat the siege of evil trapping us in unwanted conditions we must gain in-depth understanding of our flawed nature then come to know the power of our free will to lift us up. This dual task – exploring our greatest failings at the same time we discover divinely endowed free will – begins with small decisions made in minor moments and leads to the discovery that we can change conditions and hearts.

In other words, though we suffer with flaws, we possess the freedom to mend our shortcomings and transcend our flawed nature. We are not helpless victims, but rather active participants in creation. Our lives are not predetermined.

Spiritual formation may require the assistance of a pastoral counselor or spiritual director who helps us take note of our daily exercise of free will. The pastoral counselor assists us to become mindful of our moment-to-moment choices. We reverse course as we are transformed from a victim of evil forces to an active participant in divine creation. This progression from darkness into light is gradual, accomplished in small steps.

To reach an understanding of evil requires a lifetime of work and yet, while we wrestle with that task, we are called upon to forgive. "We start over, too, in the semidarkness of partial understanding. We will probably never understand why we were hurt. But forgiving is not *having* to understand. Understanding may come later, in fragments, an insight here and a glimpse there, *after* forgiving."[36]

Through the work of reconciliation our understanding accelerates – moments of insight deepen and we sail ahead with grace. Too often we hope we will first become enlightened and then, bestowed with wisdom, we will confront the mundane matters of transgression and reconciliation. The opposite appears to be the case. While we are coming to grips with transgressions and working toward reconciliation, we gain wisdom – not the wisdom of data and facts, but rather the wisdom of presence, dialogue, relationship, transcendence, and ineffable or mystical union with the divine. The wisdom of the Holy Spirit.

In becoming mindful of our exercise of free will, which determines much of our future, we become aware of the history of our choices, including transgressions. This exhumation of the past need not be forced; as one ponders current decisions, old decisions come to view.

In our review and assessment of the past we may become aware that we obscured the degree to which free will shaped our lives. We may find we mentally covered up our causal contribution – in an attempt to dodge responsibility for harm we caused. Previously, when we exercised free will and caused harm to self or others we ducked responsibility and assigned cause elsewhere. We argued the cause of harmful events was beyond our influence. The source of evil was out there. Eventually, in order to avoid being called on to take responsibility for adverse events, we adopted the belief that things just happen. A vicious, self-fulfilling prophecy ensued: the more we refused responsibility, the more other factors determined our fate. To avoid responsibility we handed off cause over our life to others.

This cycle transpired in the following manner. First, in order to abdicate responsibility and avoid blame, we conceive we are not a causal agent. We act as though we have no responsibility, as though we are puppets under the control of a puppet master who pulls the strings. When we suffer negative consequences we complain and curse the hidden evil influences that yank us about on the stage of life.

Eventually, as a result of our covert effort to avoid blame, we postulate hidden influences that sabotage any awareness of free will we might have had. In order to assign blame elsewhere we rig the game so we could blame fate, evolution, or the creator. We point the finger elsewhere, but in doing so we elect ourselves the effect of mysterious evil beyond our control.

When we consider or review our personal history, we discover a tendency to edit our causal role in order to avoid self-condemnation. We resort to blaming the other, as "scapegoating or sacralized violence is the best possible disguise for evil. We can concentrate on evil 'over there' and avoid our own."[37]

We fashion our self-image as an innocent leaf bobbing up and down on the turbulent surface of a stormy ocean, tossed about by other people and random events. As our mindfulness increases, our memory returns and our thought processes become more transparent. We begin to take more responsibility for the moments in which we exercise free will. We begin to see that as we move up and down with the waves we contribute to the motion that lifts us up and sets us down. We exist in an interdependent state. We affect others. They affect us.

As we begin to make conscious choices in the present we experience success and failure, which often place our attention on our past failures. We begin to recognize the burden of accumulated sins that crushes us, often in moments of unresolved conflict. We come to recognize with fresh eyes the self-fashioned burden we secretly decided to endure. As we set that burden down and sort through its contents we recognize signs that point out this is the work of our own hands.

After we experience positive results in exercising the free will with which we have been endowed, we possess the power to forgive self for previous wrongs. This self-forgiveness comes after we recognize we abandoned our divinely endowed nature and sacred free will. We drag ourselves out of the ditch we excavated. We crawl up its slippery slopes and lift ourselves out from under the shadow of evil we assumed would always overwhelm us. We recognize deep in our hearts that we pulled this shadow close to obscure our misuse of divinely-endowed will. With this inner transformation we accept it was not God who abandoned us – rather the blame lies with the way we exercised free will, with the way we sullied the image of God in which we were created.

Along the way we may study the Gospel narrative of forgiveness, a narrative that challenges the view that creation is rigged to cause pain and suffering. In studying the Gospel story of the unconditional love that flows from God we may come to grasp the magic of forgiveness that becomes a blowtorch we use to cut chains that bind us.

In the conflict resolution process we realize those who stand opposed to us also possess free will, and we recognize God is not orchestrating our suffering or theirs. Rather we have brought about suffering through individual and collective choices. As we mature in spiritual formation we find we have always possessed freedom to act either as false self or the divine self of a saint. We begin to discern the role our choices play in the divine plan – a plan that begins with endowed free will and ends with the unity of divine love as we become co-authors of loving-kindness and compassion.

As we develop increased mindfulness we invite the presence of the in-dwelling Spirit to become our companion in the journey out of the desert, out of bondage. During our contemplative anticipation of eternal life we discover our unforgiving human nature (false self) represents an incomplete and limited perspective. We discover grasping the magic of forgiveness requires we view from the transcendent perspective of the Resurrection. We begin to glimpse, perhaps dimly, that the way lies through the Cross.

Following in the footsteps of Francis we contemplate the forgiveness Jesus bestowed as He was on the verge of entering the spiritual kingdom. While we may not fully appreciate how forgiveness looks from the point of view of resurrection into eternal life, we strive to catch glimpses of this profound perspective.

During our spiritual transformation, when the exercise of our free will resonates with and aligns with the will of God, we discover divine grace flows in our direction. We learn we have been endowed with free will that allows us to choose to unite with the Divine. We are granted freedom of choice; we can choose to repent. We become conscious that "evil is not overcome by attack or even avoidance, but by union at a higher level."[38] We stumble upon the revelation that grace and divine forgiveness exist without end, without limit. We learn to partake of that grace by moving toward unity with Christ in an exercise of free will guided by indwelling Holy Spirit.

Upon our transformation we no longer see ourselves surrounded and trapped by an evil world. We turn our attention to the divine, rather than to the evil in the world. Richard Rohr captures this transformation, "I believe Jesus is teaching us that *if we put our energy into choosing the good – instead of the negative and largely illusionary energy of rejecting the bad – we will overcome evil in a much better way, and will not become evil ourselves!*"[39]

Rarely do we remain free from the snares of the false self for extended periods. Moments of liberation are fleeting. Those moments, however, are frequently long enough for reconciliation to take place. As we repeat the rec-

471

onciliation experience over the years of our life, we gradually become more and more divine self – *we become a forgiving person.*

In summary, learning to forgive to the extent that we become forgiving persons requires us to discover the divine within. We must come to understand "created in the image of God." One of the most powerful messages in all sacred texts is that through divine forgiveness we are granted salvation and are made new. In the experience of accepting divine forgiveness an important truth is revealed: though we are imperfect in our human nature, grace reveals our divine essence. The experience of receiving compassionate forgiveness – being forgiven when we do not deserve to be forgiven – sparks spiritual rebirth.

The path to reconciliation, for many, includes what may seem to be a major detour into pastoral counseling, contemplative prayer, confession, meditation, and hours spent in front of the mirror. When we struggle in the quicksand of cynicism with a loss of faith, this detour may seem to be the least likely route to bring about a cessation of our suffering. Prior betrayals and previous dead ends in our religious or spiritual life may have caused us to turn our gaze away from God. Divine grace may appear to lack a pragmatic foundation. We turn away from the possibility and promise of unity to wander on our own. However, when we become embroiled in conflict, and need to be forgiven and need to forgive, we discover, perhaps to our surprise, that the most pragmatic route to restoration of happiness and peace of mind is through spiritual transformation.

The Healing of Forgiving

In another paradox we find forgiveness meets the needs of the forgiver as much as the forgiven. "Forgiveness is not something we do for someone else, but to free *ourselves* from unhealthy pain, anger, and shame.... Forgiveness is a gift to our own peace of mind, our self-esteem, our relationships with others, and our future."[40] Forgiving another lifts our burden of hatred.

We enjoy a spiritual rebirth when we align our will with God's will, which graces us with unconditional love in all moments for all time. In Henderson's *Forgiveness*, Olgierd Stephan offered a similar insight: "A person is at his or her fullest when offering forgiveness; then we are most truly 'in his image.'"[41] Henderson goes on to write that "the act of forgiveness has a dual effect of freeing the injurer from his guilt and remorse, and freeing the injured from negative feelings toward that person, and quite often toward himself."[42]

These are difficult seas to navigate. One needs a mediator with more than ordinary skill or a spiritual adviser as a member of the conflict resolution team.

Historical Wounds & Forgiveness

While our primary focus has been on the individual, groups may need to forgive one another in rituals of collective forgiveness. We may belong to a group or a nation that has wounded other groups or nations, resulting in historical wounds that keep conflict simmering with an ongoing potential to erupt into serious hostilities. In regions such as the Middle East, historical wounds keep violent conflict alive for generations. In these situations, just as with a conflict between individuals, reconciliation and peace depend on collective repentance and apology, followed by forgiveness.

Our collective false selves must give way to a collective embrace of the divine in life. Often we sense we are trapped in a web of collective false identities, in false self-images that do not include "in the image of God." As an individual, although we may seek to forgive and reconcile, we may be limited in our forgiving and reconciling by a web of relationships and allegiances. Aspects of our interdependence speak most loudly to our false self.

As forgiveness requires specificity to be effective, a web of collective causes presents considerable challenge. Victims and perpetrators exist on both sides of the conflict; confusion obscures events; truth is elusive. Brian Cox introduces the task ahead: "Facing the truth about history is a complex process of having an honest conversation about the past, where informed and morally courageous people determine the past hurts and injustices that must be healed. Hence, acknowledgement begins with research into the specific events, people, and places associated with historical wounds."[43]

The Truth and Reconciliation hearings in South Africa, partially chronicled in Michael Henderson's *Forgiveness*, became a model upon which others have designed processes needed to handle the horrific results of violent conflict.[44] The South African Truth and Reconciliation Commission had a "fourfold agenda: the establishment of as complete a picture of the past as possible; the possible granting of amnesty for crimes committed during the anti-apartheid struggle; the restoration of the human and civil dignity of victims; and the compilation of a report of what went on as well as recommending reparations."[45]

This approach addresses the solutions-become-barriers paradigm discussed earlier, including overcoming the urge for revenge and the allure of diminished consciousness. "Archbishop Tutu, who headed the Commission, called it a compromise 'between those who want amnesia and those who want retribution.'"[46] The hearings, in addressing specific acts committed by specific offenders against specific victims, avoided the problem presented by diffuse responsibility that one so often faces in healing conflicts between groups and nations.

We risk losing authenticity of apology and forgiveness due to a lack of specificity with regards to responsibility. Nonetheless, we cannot avoid responsibility for actions taken in our name; we are accountable. Cox notes the challenge an individual faces: "I have to realize that the actions of my community or nation, which are taken on my behalf, invariably affect my relationships with other individuals, communities, and nations. Therefore, as a member of a community or nation, I must share in the collective responsibility for actions taken on my behalf."[47]

This is true of forgiveness as well. While it may make no sense to forgive those who are no longer present, those who may no longer be alive, collective forgiveness signals a desire and willingness to move into the future free from burdens of the past. In order to accomplish this goal there is a need for public rituals of apology and forgiveness that educate entire communities regarding historical wounds given and received, rituals that provide opportunities for an exchange of promises of peace and brotherhood.

Forgiveness rituals must be sufficiently memorable to linger in the collective cultural mind and offset memories of wounds suffered. They must be meaningful enough to allow future generations to escape the burden of revenge. The narrative myths we use to position and maintain the Other as our enemy must be dismantled; the characters in our narrative must be rewritten to fit the future we dream. Ancient heroes who destroy opponents with swift swords must give way to heroes who destroy evil with compassion. The heroic Francis who suited up to go to war is replaced by Francis the peacemaker dressed in a simple habit. Just as Francis rewrote the narrative of his life, we must rewrite the collective narratives of cultures in conflict.

Within various religious communities leaders have called for us to abandon the culture of exclusion based on us-versus-them thinking. They call on us to embrace inclusivity in our ever-contracting global village. In living with the values of inclusivity and plurality, we look for that which connects rather than divides. Rather than dismiss others because they differ we embrace them. We recognize that only human arrogance allows us to believe we can dictate to God the manner in which he reveals Himself to all people.

Holding a posture of inclusivity and plurality we initiate "spiritual conversations about matters of the heart."[48] We engage in storytelling aimed at remedying cross-cultural, cross-border, and cross-generational disputes; we pay special attention to how stories teach forgiveness. "There is a redemptive remembering. There is a healing way to remember the wrongs of our irreversible past, a way that can bring hope for the future along with our sorrow for the past."[49]

Artists have an important role to play in crafting narratives that cleanse and heal wounds, and lead to enduring forgiveness. They may design memorials and museums that capture our wounded past while presenting forgiveness narratives.[50] As cultures become interdependent and interactive, on-line "memorials" may acknowledge wounds of the past, provide platforms for apology and forgiveness, and help incubate new narratives, giving birth to storytelling that promotes peacemaking.

A Franciscan View

In the story of Francis, in the events of his life, we find an example of a profound spiritual transformation. After Francis recuperated from his year in prison in Perugia, he vowed to do great deeds. Giving in to vainglory and vanity, he signed on for a military exploit promoted by a young nobleman who "was furnishing himself on a large scale with military weaponry and, swollen by the wind of empty glory, ... asserted solemnly that he was going to Apulia to enrich himself in money or distinction."[51]

Shortly thereafter Francis had a change of heart that led to his transformation. He gave away the trappings of a warrior and returned to Assisi where he quietly began to follow his spiritual heart. "Thus he retired for a short time from the tumult and business of the world and was anxious to keep Jesus Christ in his inmost self."[52] Francis traded the sword of the warrior for the heart of the Prince of Peace.

The transformation was startling in its intensity and breadth. He now walked the Gospel path with its emphasis on forgiveness. We can safely assume he learned that "as long as you deal with evil by some other means than forgiveness, you will never experience the real meaning of evil and sin. You will keep projecting it over there, fearing it over there and attacking it over there, instead of 'gazing' on it within and 'weeping' over it within all of us."[53]

Ilia Delio writes beautifully of Francis' transformation: "Only in relation to the other did his weaknesses become strengths, for it was in naming his weaknesses that Francis matured in authentic human love. Because of the mystery of Christ, Francis' personhood developed, from a self-centered 'I' to a relational self, an 'I' in need of a 'Thou.' ... As Francis deepened his relationship with Christ, the other became less outside Francis as object and more related as brother."[54] The turn from false self – the vain Francis mounted on a warhorse – to the divine self – the humble Francis spreading the Gospel in word and deed – can inspire our transformation as we seek healing.

The healing that comes from forgiveness takes on a special significance in the Franciscan tradition: "We think that Christ saves us *from* the world and we find it hard to believe that Christ saves us *for* the world, that is, Christ heals us of our divisions so that we may be reconcilers and peacemakers for humankind and the earth itself."[55]

Francis calls out to us to become reconcilers and peacemakers, a journey that starts from our place of suffering. The words of Delio shed light on our condition: "Suffering is not the consequence of sin but the place of transformation. It is a door by which God can enter in and love us where we are, in our human weakness, our misery and our pain. When we let go of our defenses, our egos and our walls of separation God can embrace us in the fragile flesh of our humanity."[56]

The Franciscan tradition, modeled after Francis's loving heart, leads us to divine unity and knowledge of divine love. It teaches us to discard our judgmental attitude, much as Francis discarded the garments of his father. "When forgiveness becomes largely a juridical process, then we who are in charge can measure it out, define who's in and who's out, find ways to earn it and exclude the unworthy. *It makes for good religion, but not at all for good spirituality.* We have destroyed the likelihood that most people will ever experience the pure gift of God's forgiveness."[57] Yet the pure gift of God's forgiveness is the cornerstone of reconciliation and, as Francis demonstrated, forgiveness is the elixir that restores our health and lifts us up.

Francis taught us to seek the heart of Jesus when we are faced with the need to forgive and to include the other. When we have been lifted up and awareness of our divine origins has been restored. We are prepared to turn to the other party and recognize their divine essence. We are empowered to lift them up in the glory of divine communion. The importance of inclusion to a Franciscan is captured in the following: "This is Jesus' simple message: Holiness is no longer to be found through separation or exclusion of, but in fact, the radical inclusion (read 'forgiveness') of the supposedly contaminating element. Any exclusionary system only lays the solid foundation for violence in thought, word and deed."[58]

Francis, the Universal Brother, taught us to greet everyone as brothers and sisters. Delio writes, "all are taken into the embrace by being forgiven and called 'brother' or 'sister.' We who have been embraced by the outstretched arms of the crucified God open our arms even for our enemies, to make space in ourselves for them and to invite them in, so that together we may rejoice in the eternal embrace of the triune God."[59]

Scripture

Finally, all of you, be of one mind, sympathetic, loving toward one another, compassionate, humble. Do not return evil for evil, or insult for insult; but, on the contrary, a blessing, because to this you were called, that you might inherit a blessing. (1 Pt 3:8-9)

All bitterness, fury, anger, shouting, and reviling must be removed from you, along with all malice. [And] be kind to one another, compassionate, forgiving one another as God has forgiven you in Christ. (Eph 4:31-32)

"Stop judging and you will not be judged. Stop condemning and you will not be condemned. Forgive and you will be forgiven." (Lk 6:37)

[Jesus] said to them again, "Peace be with you. As the Father has sent me, so I send you. And when he had said this, he breathed on them and said to them, "Receive the holy Spirit. Whose sins you forgive are forgiven them, and whose sins you retain are retained." (Jn 20:21-23)

CHAPTER EIGHTEEN

Impasse & Evil

The citizens of Gubbio asked Francis to talk privately with them, to help them understand his suggestion. The Mayor guaranteed no one would hurt the wolf while they conferred.

The people of Gubbio talked with each other for hours. Relatives of the dead were the hardest to convince. They harbored a hard place in their hearts for the wolf.

Francis wept with them and touched them in a way that softened their hearts.

Mediation Principles

ARTIES TO A CONFLICT who have moved through the stages of conflict resolution, including the forgiveness step, will be well on their way to reconciliation. They will go on to formalize their agreement and engage in rituals and celebrations that acknowledge a healed relationship, activities that will be addressed in the following chapter.

For others, however, forgiveness may have presented too much of a challenge. The process may have ended without resolution of the conflict, or the parties may have reached a resolution but stopped short of reconciliation. Those who failed to resolve their conflict may be ready to seek a decision or verdict from a judge, jury, elder, or other third party. Or they may be ready to take matters into their own hands, regardless of the pain and suffering they will cause themselves.

Throughout the process a mediator maintains a neutral position with regard to the outcome. She avoids imposing a resolution on the parties and she is aware that not all attempts to resolve conflict end in success. This does not mean the mediator does not show care and concern. She will continue to assist the parties with attempts to overcome impasse while adhering to the principle of party self-determinism, which dictates the parties themselves will decide whether to continue the process or not.

At this stage, when it appears all further effort is futile, the mediator does not fault the parties for failure to achieve reconciliation; instead, she works, mostly in private sessions, to understand the impediments causing impasse. She reminds participants that conflict resolution is not easy and that the most significant gains often emerge as we overcome the most daunting challenges.

In contrast to the mediator's encouragement, a weary, disillusioned, and discouraged party may regard forgiveness and reconciliation as unachievable. They may consider further talk of such endeavors to be the musings of a mystic. For them, reality is quite different. In their view, they face intractable evil and a conflict that is not amenable to resolution. This chapter addresses seemingly intractable barriers that call on us to go beyond normal efforts toward resolution and reconciliation.

Perhaps the most important barrier to be overcome in conflict resolution is the *hidden negative influence of a destructive third party*. Paradoxically, given this barrier is invisible, it does not appear to be a barrier. Yet it is perhaps the most significant factor in conflict resolution failure. The destructive third party is the antithesis of a mediator. Rather than trying to resolve a conflict, the destructive third party is invested in keeping conflict alive. When the reason for impasse is puzzling the hidden and destructive third party is the first factor to be assessed.

I will also address the situation in which a party's fear is so deep and so pathological that they resist any attempt to reconcile and instead respond with intentions to destroy. In this case, the party who faces what appears to be intransigent evil evaluates the limits of their ability to handle evil. Based on a realistic appraisal of their skills they choose either to continue conflict resolution work or to disengage from the process and sever relations with the other party, even if they must take a loss in the process.

In other cases, the impasse may be related to unhealed wounds that leave a party unable to participate with full self-determinism. The diminishment of their faculties may necessitate a time-out while they remedy deep-seated problems. We will consider the difficult decision a mediator must make regarding whether or not a party troubled by emotional or psychological wounds should continue the process or seek outside assistance.

We will also consider impasse arising from a persistent power imbalance preventing a just outcome, an impasse that forces the oppressed party to use nonviolent protest, resistance, or non-compliance in order to remedy the imbalance. The situation in which injustice is institutionalized will be discussed and I will compare and contrast the work of the nonviolent activist and the neutral mediator.

While we often focus our attention on the other side of the table, it pays to assess whether or not conflict on the same side of the table fuels the impasse. For this reason, the importance of procuring stakeholder consensus will be discussed.

Hidden Influence of the Destructive Third Party

One special barrier to reconciliation deserves considerable attention – the hidden influence of the *destructive third party*. The destructive third party is the antithesis of the mediator, a *constructive third party*. The destructive efforts of the hidden third party directly oppose the mediator. The mediator assists parties in resolving conflict while the destructive third party covertly promotes conflict. A mediator facilitates resolution of conflict as the parties:

- identify and remedy miscommunication and misunderstanding;
- identify interests and motivations;
- design creative solutions that satisfy interests through collaboration;
- heal the hurt suffered;

- recognize and admit transgressions;
- structure and deliver apologies;
- find their forgiving heart;
- extend forgiveness to those who caused harm;
- plan for a future based on mutual caring;
- draft guidelines or settlement agreements;
- acknowledge reconciliation through ritual.

The mediator seeks the highest level of transparency possible and strives for full disclosure. He or she nurtures active participation and party self-determinism. This is the work of a constructive third party.

In contrast, the destructive third party precipitates and perpetuates conflict. Reverse the actions of a mediator and the result will be the predictable behavior of the destructive third party who:

- intentionally creates miscommunication and misunderstanding;
- causes confusion regarding interests and motivations;
- defeats attempts at collaboration;
- exacerbates pain and suffering;
- discourages and sabotages apology and forgiveness;
- actively blocks reconciliation efforts.

The destructive third party strives to defeat self-determinism, seeking covert control over others. He passionately avoids transparency, operates in the shadows, and covertly foments conflict. In the destructive third party we find an agent that actively, albeit covertly, seeks to create and promote conflict.

All conflict is the result, to a greater or lesser degree, of such destructive hidden influences. While an old saying claims it takes two to tangle, most fights result from three agents: two parties locked in conflict and a hidden destructive third party.

The unseen or hidden nature of the destructive third party causes conflicts to rage even when the warring parties wish to put an end to hostility. The disputing parties can never quite get to the bottom of their difficulty; they never quite achieve an accurate assessment of factors causing their clash. The invisibility of the hidden influence automatically introduces mystery and confusion.

Take a case in which siblings Susan and Mary are embroiled in a dispute over their father's estate. In a private session, Susan tells the mediator how horrible Mary has been to their father. In a separate private session, Mary informs the mediator that Susan has been terribly hurtful to their father.

Each sibling relates a story of how bad the other has been to their father. Therefore, each feels they deserve the bulk of the estate. When the mediator asks them, individually, to explain how they came to know about the horrible deeds of the other sibling, they both explain they learned about the other's harmful acts from their father.

They tell the same story: their father took them aside and told them how much he appreciated them and told them how much pain the other sibling had caused him to suffer. Susan and Mary heard the same exact story, but with the other sibling cast in the role of villain. However, they do not realize their father told them the same story because the destructive third party, the father, swears both to secrecy. This makes it difficult if not impossible to detect the source of their negative views toward each other.

As time passes they typically forget where they heard the whispering campaign against the other. They integrate the falsehoods into their view of reality. They *know* with certainty that the other sibling behaved badly. Each feels fully justified in making sure the other never sees a dime, as each knows the other is an undeserving villain.

I have witnessed such duplicity reach an extreme in a case in which a parent retained two separate lawyers who drafted two separate wills, with neither lawyer (and neither sibling) knowing there were two wills. Upon the parent's passing, the siblings were left to unravel contrary legal facts that left them hopelessly locked in an expensive probate battle.

In the hypothetical case of Susan and Mary each seeks their father's favor (even after he passed) by punishing the other sibling. Once this dynamic is set in motion the result is a nasty conflict from which siblings rarely recover – sometimes remaining estranged for their entire lives – unless the hidden influence of the destructive third party comes into view.

In conflicts that have gone on for considerable time the influence of the destructive third party becomes buried under subsequent hostilities. It becomes difficult for a party to recognize the role the underlying hidden influence plays, as their attention is locked on the subsequent acts of hostility by the other party. The destructive third party fades into the background and becomes a *hidden influence*.

For example, a stepfather and stepson may be pushed into conflict by the wife/mother who complains to her husband about the son and complains to the son about his stepfather. After the mother warns her son to behave because the stepfather is unfair, unloving, and biased against him, the son adopts a surly and hostile manner toward his stepfather. After hearing from his wife that her son has problems with discipline and lacks respect for authority, the stepfather treats the stepson gruffly, demanding unerring obedience and strict adherence to rules.

From the beginning the way they treat each other is premised on the mother's negative comments. When the stepfather, anticipating disobedience, barks a command, the stepson assumes this is proof his mother was right – the stepfather *is* unloving and uncaring. The stepson shoots the father a look of defiance that aggravates the stepfather and verifies the son is inherently disrespectful, a view planted by his wife.

The conflict escalates and the relationship deteriorates as a result of the destructive third party (the wife/mother) planting false attributions in the minds of the stepfather and the stepson. Years later, when a mediator attempts to sort out the resulting family conflict, the stepfather and stepson find it difficult to recognize the underlying cause of their conflict was the mother acting as a destructive third party. She has become a hidden influence.

When the mediator suggests they consider the hidden influence of the mother they protest and point to each other's hostile actions. The father focuses on the time the stepson swore at him and failed to come home that night. The stepson focuses on the times the father treated him harshly and unfairly, times when strict rules crushed his freedom. They both relate specific incidents to back up their complaints about the other – but those specifics obscure the precipitating reason for the conflict: the hidden influence of the destructive third party.

Considerable effort is required for the mediator to guide them past the offending incidents to locate the first time the stepson thought the stepfather was uncaring and unloving and to locate the first time the stepfather thought the son was disobedient and disrespectful. When they finally locate the original cause of their antipathy, their perceptions clear up and they recognize the good qualities in each other that had been masked. The stepson recognizes the stepfather is a loving and caring father while the stepfather recognizes the stepson actually wanted to please him.

Conflicts of all sizes are driven by such hidden and destructive third-party influences. These dynamics play out whether the conflict is a family matter, an office quarrel, a business dispute, a public policy dispute, or a clash between nations or civilizations. A skilled mediator employs calm persistence, insightful diligence, acute perception, and considerable skill to uncover these hidden causes of conflict.

When faced with a conflict that defies resolution it pays for a party to uncover such triangulation by locating the hidden destructive party who foments conflict. These sources of triangulation are not abstract concepts or opinions that sway one's judgment, but rather actual people acting as hidden, destructive third parties. To clear up the situation one locates exactly who was the negative influence.

A mediator listens closely and guides an exploration of the sources that have formed each party's views toward the other. She detects signs that a hidden and destructive third party has been (and continues to be) a factor in the conflict. She casually poses questions aimed at discovering where the party learned negative information about the other party or where they learned of generally held disparaging opinions with regard to that person.

She listens for names of sources that influence a party's views, perhaps asking a party to list common friends, acquaintances, co-workers, or associates. The mediator explores situations in which a friend in common has caused each side to doubt the other. Her questions are not posed in a challenging or accusatory manner, but rather are advanced with a casual but interested demeanor. She repeats the process with the other party.

She asks both sides, "Who will benefit if you continue to fight?" Rarely will the parties be able to answer this question immediately. Their concept of benefit will not include the subtle psychological benefit a destructive third party derives when others are distracted or battling one another. The parties usually do not see the psychological benefit the destructive third party acquires when each of the embattled parties seeks the third party's private counsel. They do not make out the subtle benefits that accrue for the destructive third party. And because they are so embroiled in conflict they do not see the destructive third party's misdeeds.

For example, if the boss is tied up in constant conflict with Office Worker A the sub-standard work of Office Worker B goes unnoticed. If two siblings battle each other they do not have time to pay attention to problems their mother wants to keep hidden. Two nations at war cannot devote their resources to competing with a third nation that covertly promoted the conflict. In each case, the destructive third party slips under the radar as a result of a conflict they have promoted between two other parties.

A mediator may approach this type of situation by asking what outside party would be most threatened if the parties in conflict were to reconcile. He might ask: Who might lose the most if you two heal the relationship and become friends? Who might suffer feeling excluded? Who might consider their status threatened? Who might no longer be valued as a source of inside information? Gentle and curious probing assists the parties in discovering the influence they have previously overlooked.

When the parties successfully locate the hidden destructive third party they will be amazed at how quickly the conflict resolves. After a relatively short period of reflection and discussion they will recall times when they became distrustful of each other because of a whispered secret, a dropped hint, or damaging innuendo delivered by the destructive third party. As they recognize the degree to which they have been influenced unwittingly the conflict unravels with amazing speed. Clarity descends over the proceedings and it becomes clear that reconciliation is within reach.

The hidden and destructive third party can be a neighborhood gossip, a co-worker skilled in office politics, or a sophisticated intelligence agency mole dispatched to disrupt another government. They can be found in every walk of life and at every level of society. Their motivation is fear laced with paranoia; they fear they will be rejected and become an outcast if other people enjoy close, loving relationships.

The happiness of others is perceived as a threat to the welfare of the destructive third party. The young lady who fears she is not sufficiently attractive or interesting pits two friends against each other, hoping to covertly defend against the fear of being ostracized due to a weak social position. She reduces the perceived threat to self-worth by entangling others in conflict that lowers their esteem. In her mind, if her friends distrust and dislike one another she benefits from increased attention and, conversely, if her friends enjoy a close relationship she will be abandoned.

The *chronically evil destructive third party*, a special case, experiences constant fear not tied to a specific situation. This tormented individual typically harbors fears that everyone (yes, everyone) rejects them. Everyone is out to do them in. This pathological fear (rarely admitted overtly) drives their every action. As long as everyone else is kept off balance they feel safe. They fight a constant offensive against the welfare of others with a focus on sabotaging relationships. They eschew any form of transparency as they fear they might be discovered by others to be deficient or evil.

The chronically evil destructive third party experiences generalized fear, distrust, and paranoia, which pushes them to secretly promote conflict and confusion wherever they go. They maintain their power by covertly undermining the power of others. One reason they are so difficult to recognize in the course of daily affairs is that most people cannot begin to imagine fear so irrational. Such extreme and pervasive fear makes no sense; it is so illogical that it goes unnoticed by those trying to make logical sense of a situation.

Fortunately, the number of people afflicted with such all-consuming fear is small. Unfortunately, the destruction they cause can be significant. We all experience bouts of insecurity and on occasion act out of fear, but these normal experiences do not begin to compare with the mindset of the pathological hidden destructive third party who must compulsively destroy relationships.

Whereas you might become aware that you have acted unfairly due to insecurity and fear, and you may experience a desire to remedy the wrong you have committed, the evil destructive third party does not experience such doubts or desire for repentance – for them, the need to covertly attack and undermine others is real, necessary, and all-consuming. They do not consider they have done wrong. They perceive they are under constant attack and are justified in constantly responding with destructive counter-measures.

Another example is the character assassin who traffics in misinformation and negative public relations, using rumor and innuendo to destroy reputation and honor. They mount whispering campaigns to destroy a targeted enemy. These covert operators can be uncovered through an in-depth investigation of the source of discrediting information. The covert operator can be drawn into the open and exposed by implementing a policy of transparency.

Character assassins commonly operate on a number of fronts at once, engaging numerous targets simultaneously. However, one must proceed with diligence, as the character assassin may not be the actual destructive third party – the actual destructive third party may be using them as a tool. Investigation may reveal the character assassin was carrying out the instructions of a destructive third party who remains hidden. The solution is the same: discover and expose the hostile hidden influences not present at the table.

Perhaps one reason mediation is successful in resolving so many conflicts is that the mediator plays the role of a *positive* third party in counterpoint to the *negative* third party who is active in almost every conflict. The antidote to a negative third party is a positive third party. Whereas the hidden negative third party has the goal of keeping the parties at one another's throats, the positive third party, the mediator, works to reconcile the parties. While the destructive third party works to keep his or her intentions hidden or obscured the mediator stresses transparency. Destructive efforts that survived in the shadows are exposed to light and their effect is diminished or vanished.

Unfortunately, the hidden destructive third party sometimes intervenes in conflict resolution, assuming the role of mediator while covertly making the situation worse. As the mediator they promote the fight not the fix. In these cases, the person who seems to be resolving the conflict is the same person who worked behind the scenes to fuel the fight in the first place. The conflict escalates and it appears mediation does not work. For this reason, it pays to use a mediator previously unknown to the parties.

This does not mean no member of the party's intimate community can serve as a mediator, as most people have good intentions and (with some training) are able to help. However, there is a significant risk that one will inadvertently fall prey to a destructive third party masquerading as a peacemaker. Caution is warranted.

The other liability that comes with assigning the mediator role to a member of one's intimate circle lies in their inability to identify the destructive third party. Someone from the inner circle will have blind spots or prior allegiances that prevent them from rooting out hidden influences. A destructive third party is likely to exert a covert influence that extends throughout the entire group, making it hard to find a true neutral within the group who will expose their influence.

While irrational fear is the typical motivation for the destructive third party, pathological greed can also lead to a strategic use of divisive tactics. An arms dealer might meet secretly with two neighboring countries. He tells each faction his work takes him behind the scenes into the enemy camp where he has gained valuable insights he is willing to share. With feigned reluctance he conveys the news that the other side has recently increased their stockpile of armaments.

When each side hears of the other side's activity, they increase their store of weapons and become hypersensitive to signs of hostility. They begin to misread intentions – the slanted reports of the destructive third party plant false attribution. The most innocent events take on a threatening tone in light of the third party's back-channel information, which cannot be verified. Already on edge, the parties erupt into violent conflict at the slightest provocation and the greedy third party benefits. A persistent mediator, searching for the underlying causes of impasse, searches out greed-driven destructive third parties as well as the more common fear-driven destructive third party.

As these dynamics operate in all conflicts the mediator's task is to create sufficient trust for parties to name the sources of things they have heard about the other party. As the parties become more interested in discovering the truth they cease protecting secret or previously hidden sources. Usually they reveal the source privately to the mediator, hesitating to reveal (to the other party) sources that have sworn them to secrecy, sources they consider valuable back channels, or sources they want to protect from retribution.

When the mediator points out that the party's cherished sources may be playing a duplicitous role, the party typically becomes interested in exploring the situation. When the parties divulge their previously unrevealed attitudes and perspectives and the hidden source of such attitudes their antipathy for each other vanishes quite dramatically. It can seem magical.

They slowly recognize the reasons behind their negative or fearful view of the other; they realize those views were planted for the benefit of a destructive third party. They share their mutual embarrassment at having been duped. Effusive apologies are usually exchanged for the harm they have done as a result of negative gossip or accusations. They realize they acted on negative views without having given the other party the proper opportunity to defend themselves.

After you discover the damaging hidden influence of the destructive third party and after you have experienced the healing that emerges from the discovery, you will not see gossip and character assassination in the same light. After you have gone through such an experience you will become astute in assessing sources of information that affect your views. You will become alert when you begin to suffer adverse feelings against another.

The destructive third party should be expected to counter the efforts of the mediator, while trying to remain hidden. You may discover the identity of the hidden destructive third party by noticing who opposes the reconciliation efforts – you note who in the immediate environment talks down the process. Some hidden influences are less disguised than others: the arms dealer is fairly obvious; the jealous admirer lurking in the shadows is harder to detect; the dear friend who smiles and hides their paranoia while destroying relationships may be quite difficult to detect. As the motivation will usually be illogical or insane, the casual observer will commonly overlook their influence. Once we recognize their deep-seated fear and obsessive need for covert control the picture comes into focus. Taking time to respond to the prompts in the journal workbook should result in considerable progress.

Destructive Third Party: Additional Handling

In most instances, when parties step away from a destructive third party their negative influence ceases. But what happens, you might ask, to the destructive third party? How does a mediator respond when a party asks for advice regarding future dealings with them?

Most likely the destructive third party will not cease operating out of fear and paranoia; they will continue to attempt to undermine the relationship, the business, the parish, the organization, the movement, or the nation. They will view the parties who resolved their conflict as a new threat and they will sink further underground. They may turn up the heat, intensifying underhanded efforts to stir up discord in other quarters. The parties who successfully resolved their conflict may unexpectedly find conflict springing up with others in the family, group, or business.

There are a number of approaches to handling the situation. The parties may invite the destructive third party to a special mediation session where the parties engage in a frank discussion of the destructive influence the third party exerted. They can ask them to explain their behavior and disclose the interests they were trying to satisfy. The destructive third party can be invited to participate in brainstorming how their interests might be met in more transparent and productive ways.

The mediator might ask what would have to happen for the destructive third party to feel more secure. What would have to change? They might be guided to adopt less destructive approaches for dealing with insecurity. The parties may be asked to share ideas regarding actions they might take to diminish or eliminate the threat they inadvertently pose to the destructive third party. If the institutional structure is a source of threat strategies for reducing the threat may be proposed and adopted.

In a small percentage of cases this approach will result in improvement in the relationship and in reconciliation between the destructive third party and those he or she harmed. The hidden destructive third party may have been pushed into fear-driven behavior by situational factors that generate insecurity, for example, an institutional environment that promotes cutthroat politics. Or they may have suffered a short-term bout of fear and insecurity based on a misunderstanding. In such instances healing and reconciliation take place.

Usually, however, the destructive third party's fear is irrational and is not based on an actual threat from the environment. You will not know which situation is in play – situational threat or irrational fear – until you actually attempt to handle situational factors. If the handling fails you are facing irrational fear that is difficult to manage. If this is the case, the destructive third party will protest and refuse to seriously engage a process intended to improve situational factors. They will adopt a defensive posture of denial, blame, and non-compliance. Their fears are too deeply entrenched and will not be easily dissipated.

The problem becomes more difficult when one considers the viewpoint of the hidden destructive third party who acts on evil impulses. Love shown toward someone who is so deeply threatened and extremely insecure will be seen as a ploy designed to undermine their power. Expressions of love and compassion will be viewed as strategic moves designed to circumvent defenses. To someone who is deeply and existentially threatened, unconditional love appears to be a Trojan horse designed to fell their defenses.

This presents an immensely difficult challenge for the party seeking reconciliation – ironically, *the love needed to heal the fear is feared*. They fear the love that will heal them. The medicine that will cure the illness is refused; they fear the medicine itself causes illness. This conundrum is taken up in the following section on wrestling with evil.

Increasing transparency is one strategy that makes it difficult for the hidden influence to continue to cause upset and damage. When the first approach – handling situational, organizational, or environmental factors – comes up short, the mediator suggests the family, group, or business adopt new guidelines for acceptable behavior with emphasis on increased transparency.

For example, when the adverse effects of negative hidden communications threaten to wreck a relationship or organization, the group adopts clear policy that disallows whisper campaigns and character assassination. Parties craft a policy that honors transparency and open dialogue. They ask members to agree to conduct themselves in a principled manner, honoring the right of each individual to know what is said about them.

If methods for resolving disputes are missing or are not well known within the group, such methods can be formally introduced and adopted as part of day-to-day operations. The family, group, or organization is encouraged to become dialogically active and mediation friendly. They may send a representative to train in conflict prevention and resolution skills. This approach has the advantage of establishing clear principles of transparency to which individual members must adhere as well as establishing ongoing remedies for breaches.

The unrepentant destructive third party will find the new policies and guidelines intolerable – the power of their cunning political manipulation is undermined by such policies. They may soon depart, leveling accusations that other group members are overly rigid, prudish, suspicious, or oppressive.

A third way to approach the impasse a destructive third party presents is to maintain a persistent focus on their interests. Their tangle of fears must be unraveled through persistent and compassionate pursuit of their interests, even though their interests may ignore and exclude the welfare of others, and even though their interests may appear anti-social or even insane.

After a full exploration of the destructive third party's interests the mediator makes the case for the interdependence of the destructive third party's interests with the interests of the other parties. He demonstrates how their personal interests are inexorably intertwined with the interests of others: if they please others they will be pleased in return. In other words, the negative third party is gradually educated regarding the interdependent nature of relationships.

When the mediator links the destructive third party's interests to the interests of others a challenge arises – the third party may experience interdependence as a threat. It fuels their fear. The idea that they depend on others is intolerable if they perceive others are out to do them harm. If they perceive others are out to destroy them, learning they must depend on others presents a troubling conundrum – they must depend on enemies for survival. This can be extremely unsettling. Transforming their perception of relationship from a perceived threat into a perceived asset is difficult and may or may not be possible.

The mediator may also focus on proposing and designing institutional safeguards that provide comfort to the fearful third party – finding ways to reduce fear and insecurity with agreements that emphasize their right to survival and success. This requires constant affirmation and assessment of their welfare. Over time these positive affirmations and assessments create a disconnect between the positive effect of their present well being and tne negative effect of the accumulated fear driving their insecurity.

This approach separates the safe and hopeful present from the dangerous past. But the approach is time intensive. You are constantly throwing the insecure person a lifeline and drawing them into the present, taking time to help them view the present as it is – not as the past tells them it is. Few enterprises have the resources needed for this type of remedy yet if one desires peace the time spent may be necessary.

A fourth approach is to remove the destructive third party from the group. They can be asked to leave. Others can refuse their communication. The group can shun the destructive third party, though it is best to leave the ex-communicated party a reentry path into the group. You may want to give them instructions regarding repentance and amends.

Dismissal is viable at times but in other instances you may encounter obstacles in the form of rules, regulations, or laws that demand just cause for dismissal. The sly destructive third party operates in the shadows as a hidden influence, making their covert mischief difficult to document. They claim they are entitled to express their disruptive opinions. What happened to free speech? they protest.

Often, at the same time well-intentioned people who violate minor codes or make mistakes are dismissed the truly destructive person rises in the ranks. The destructive person often is the cause of the mistakes others make – the destructive third party creates disturbances that result in others making mistakes. The solution is to adopt a policy that clearly prohibits gossip, whisper campaigns, character assassination, hidden adverse influence, and office politics. St. Francis took this approach in his admonitions.[1]

As one works through challenges associated with inspiring a group to foster and honor transparency, disclosure, and the I-Thou relationship, one might uncover a situation in which the institutional structure itself creates an environment that nurtures destructive third parties. As noted previously, there is a difference between individuals pushed into destructive roles by organizational factors and individuals who inherently struggle with overwhelming paranoia resulting in destructive behavior.

In the first case, individuals respond to new structures with relief and a change of behavior; in the latter case, changes in policy do not bring about transformation. As you respond to the prompts determine the nature of the relationship or organizational situation you face. If your situation involves structural or institutional factors that drive insecurity, fear, and destructive third-party behavior, see the section later in this chapter that addresses social change. If the problem lies with an individual the sooner one recognizes the situation the quicker one can remedy the destructive individual's problems or disengage from the individual altogether.

Wrestling with Evil

The hidden destructive third party who cannot find a path out of the trap of fear and paranoia, who cannot abandon the need to harm others is what we usually consider evil. They are people intent on destroying others – physically, mentally, emotionally, and spiritually. The common factor is a profound existential fear – everyone is out to destroy them. The fear-driven person assumes that if others become happy, powerful, creative, successful, loved, or admired, the successful party will use their good fortune to trample the existence of the fear-driven person.

The "evil" person knows with certainty their only hope for survival is to sabotage and undermine the power of successful people. Their only hope is to gain absolute power over all beings – to render others powerless, to reduce others to a state of degradation, apathy, and unconsciousness. Their only hope is to render others powerless and harmless. The good fortune of others is a direct threat that must be countered – in their eyes.

The type of jealousy they experience is not petty longing for another's possessions. It is a profound jealousy that views another's good fortune or good nature as a prelude to their demise. They do not experience trivial or banal envy; they experience a deep, ontological jealousy. This is not a trivial matter related to manners or polite company – this is a matter of life and death.

We all experience fear, defensiveness, and jealousy. We all live with a shadow side that haunts and troubles us, and we all commit harmful acts for which we must repent. We all slip up on occasion and cause others pain and suffering. Few of us, however, can comprehend the depth of fear, jealousy, and profound desire to see others suffer that we find in those who engage in evil with an unrepentant heart, those who see no possibility of release from their need to fend off others through evil intentions and actions.

The profound extent to which the few truly destructive beings manifest evil can be truly difficult to comprehend and confront. We are stunned, shocked, and unable to wrap our minds around the evil some men commit. We cannot fathom the heart that can torture and hideously maim another human being. We find it difficult to imagine being trapped in a mindset in which we are unable to see a single other person as a source of love and sustenance. We find it difficult to imagine the frame of mind that dictates one must destroy all others in order to survive.

These factors correspond to what some have called spiritual warfare. Agents of evil conceive themselves to be locked in a battle against any power that might uplift or free another being. This includes divine power that frees the indwelling Spirit, the divinity within us. The presence of the Holy Spirit presents a serious threat to the agent of evil. The movement of divine self is toward relationship and unity, but the agent of evil cannot tolerate relationship and/or unity – as such constitute a perceived threat to their existence.

The agent of evil fails to realize the power granted through divine grace is the power of love and compassion, a power that by its very nature does not seek destruction of the other. The soul trapped in profound fear is unable to grasp this concept. The idea of humbling self in order to enter into communion with the divine other in an I-Thou relationship is terrifying. Opening one's heart to the other, in their view, allows that other person unfettered access to destroy them. For the person wracked with deep existential fear, establishing a relationship based on compassionate love allows the other person too much power – in their mind such vulnerability will result in their demise. Becoming open to the other is to invite certain destruction.

Too often we validate the fears that haunt them when we set up good-versus-evil paradigms and set out to defeat evil. Warrior language and a warrior attitude confirm their suspicions – others are obviously out to destroy them. The zealous crusading warrior confirms the fears of the agent of evil and proves to them they are not paranoid. They are shown their fears are justified. They know innately they are not without sin, so they view noisy attempts to destroy evil as efforts to destroy them.

They do not see their "fear that becomes evil" condition as a trap from which they can be freed. They do not see that war is not being waged against *them*, but rather against the very condition that entraps them. They do not see the effort to overcome evil as an effort to break down the walls of the jail in which they are confined; rather they see it as an offensive effort targeting their survival.

An analogy is a man who has fallen into the grip of a large boa constrictor. The snake is squeezing the breath of life from his body. When help arrives and rescuers attempts to kill the snake to free him, the man believes the rescuers are attempting to murder him and he fights off those who would rescue him. He mistakenly identifies with the snake choking the life from his body.

A problem when it comes to unrecognized and refused assistance is the use of inappropriate language. Language that communicates judgment and aggression toward evil does not signal rescue but rather danger. In our attempt to rescue another from an evil condition our sloppy language tends to create polarities or dichotomies that pit one identity against another, setting in motion the oppositional embrace of conflict in which two false selves become locked in combat.

The path out of this conundrum may consist of a healing process designed to mimic mediation, a process of spiritual transformation specially designed to unlock the inner oppositional embrace. In such a path to spiritual transformation the person is separated from the condition he suffers – he is separated from a condition in which evil and destructive acts have been accepted as the solution to survival. When evil and destructive acts are accepted as a solution to the problem of *everyone is out to do me in* then, before evil can be addressed, the divine self must be freed from both the problem (everyone is out to do me in) and the solution (destructive acts). In other words, we cannot convince someone to cease committing evil and destructive acts unless we first free them from the condition they suffer – a perception that everyone is out to do them in. This is precisely the problem Francis faced when he went out to meet the wolf – what would he need to do in order to not appear to be a threat to the wolf? How was he to move past fear that would cause him to be viewed as a threat?

This recommends we all consider, How can we move past the existential fear of all existence that traps an agent of evil? What is the "sign of the cross" that makes this possible?

The path of advanced contemplative prayer and meditation addresses this issue. Unfortunately, the availability of spiritual direction and training in advanced contemplative prayer is far too limited. Retreat centers with this focus are sorely needed. Francis relied on devotional solitude extensively, spending time in contemplation on Mount Subasio and Mount La Verna. He leaves a model we can follow, provided availability to such resources is increased significantly.

In the short term, during the heat of conflict, a party will need to assess whether or not they can provide the inspiration and guidance required to bring about a spiritual transformation that will free the fear-driven destructive person. In some instances, a party may feel up to the task, they may feel they truly can love their enemy. They may feel they can maintain sufficient compassion to weather the storm of negativity and hostility that will be unleashed in their direction.

At other times they may realize they do not possess the steady compassion and lack of fear required to transform the evil they face. They may be forced to wisely acknowledge they are unprepared to handle the situation. They must walk away. Perhaps they forfeit the substantive gains they had hoped to realize in mediation. But when they walk away with peace within, knowing they are no longer entangled in a situation they cannot transform or heal, they realize a gain. It is vital to our future happiness that we carefully and accurately assess our ability to handle these very tough challenges.

Walking Away

When we have encountered fear-driven evil and have become entangled in a situation beyond our personal ability to transform, we may choose to walk away, wiser for the experience. This option may seem to be little more than a surrender and acceptance of loss and defeat. Nonetheless, the outcome is not entirely negative. We walk away having learned vital lessons that will serve us in the future.

When we find we have become engaged in an oppositional embrace with evil beyond our ability to handle we are presented with an opportunity to recognize the causal factors that precipitated our entanglement. We have an opportunity to inspect how our decisions led to entanglement with evil.

When we analyze our behavior we may recognize there were times when we had misgivings, times when our intuition told us to avoid becoming involved, but we ignored the warning signs. When we accurately assess our personal responsibility we realize events would not have taken place in the manner they did without our complicity.

Our failing may have been as simple as lack of attention or we may have compromised our values in an attempt to gain possessions to which we were overly attached. We learn from the experience how to avoid those situations in the future. We acquire increased ability to correctly perceive someone who is troubled. We recognize that if we become involved with a person in a state of fear-driven evil our sole focus must be on their recovery and transformation. If they are not healed attempts to engage in other activity lead only to conflict that ruins our life.

The experience may transform the depth of our spirituality. While we may not possess the personal resources needed to inspire a spiritual transformation in the other party, the encounter motivates us to devote time and effort to our own spiritual formation so that, in the future, we can assist those trapped in the hell of *fear that becomes evil*.

Perhaps we experience a wake-up call that motivates us to augment our spiritual resources. Perhaps encountering intractable conflict makes us realize we have been lazy in our spiritual development and we are unprepared to handle life's most difficult moments.

When We Cannot Walk Away

There are times when we cannot walk away. The other party may be so bent on causing us pain and suffering that they continue to stalk us, forcing us to address their fear-driven needs. It may appear only raw force will extricate us from the situation. That raw force may be our own or it may be the resources of the courts, law enforcement, or the military.

Yet we realize retribution or revenge will backfire. The narrow choice we face is whether or not we will use force to restrain those who would do harm. Will we use force to restrain an offending blow? This decision is personal; there are no rote formulas. The primary deciding factor may be certainty that the force is actually defensive – not a justification for our desire to harm another.

Some will decide they cannot be certain of the moral validity of using force to defend self or others, so they abstain from all use of force. Some parties, recognizing the liability of mounting a defense, may decide turn the other cheek. Yet others employ force minimally to defend self and then increase significantly their use of compassion and love to steer the situation toward reconciliation.

A party may choose to act forcefully in self-defense while simultaneously offering an olive branch. Recognizing the liability involved in the use of force they may employ force in the least measure required to halt immediate destructive actions aimed in their direction. At the same time they honor the hostile party by offering them an opportunity to collaborate on resolving contentious issues.

One strategy is to use force in a tit-for-tat manner: we defend against the destructive party when they take destructive action and extend positive options when they cease. At the same time we defend ourselves we communicate key principles of collaboration. A minimal amount of defensive force may bring about conversation that promotes collaborative solutions, with special attention on reducing causes of real or imagined fear. The hostile party may be restrained long enough to allow them to engage in spiritual transformation, which redirects the interaction in a positive direction.

On the other hand, if the reason we cannot walk away lies in our own attachment to a particular outcome – whether that outcome involves obtaining possessions we desire, teaching the other a lesson, defending our ego, defeating evil, or simply blind hatred and desire for revenge – it is time we sort out the factors that control our lives. What false self are we honoring? What wounds remain unhealed? What fears have not been laid to rest? What desires own us? We may realize our own spiritual formation is incomplete, we may seek pastoral counseling.

Healing Personal Wounds

While the majority of impediments to reconciliation are rooted in fear, unhealed wounds, which are closely related, may also impede reconciliation. While it is possible to resolve a conflict in the presence of unhealed wounds – parties often resolve the dispute and go their separate ways – it is not possible to reconcile if wounds are unaddressed. (This does not mean reconciliation must wait for full and complete healing but rather that parties must first acknowledge the wounds and healing must begin.)

In the legend the victims' hearts hardened. The pain of having lost loved ones is too intense for them to consider direct dialogue with Brother Wolf. Prior to their wounds being acknowledged, prior to the initiation of the healing process, the idea of a relationship with Brother Wolf is unimaginable. When hearts harden, healing is required. In cases where wounds have been acknowledged, yet parties remain stalled at the apology and forgiveness stage, a deeper level of healing is needed.

While the legend does not provide details of how Francis worked with the suffering of the townspeople, we can imagine he greeted their pain as his own – in contemporary language, he empathized. He took their wounds into himself – in the same manner he embraced Christ's wounds – and he cleansed those wounds with boundless compassion. His cleansing of wounds through sacred empathy made healing possible. Some mediators possess such skills; many do not. When those skills might not be present a party may wish to seek trauma care from a pastoral counselor.

On occasion a caring party may suggest to their wounded opponent that they are willing to postpone or delay the process if time is needed for healing. Or the mediator may decide healing should precede mediation. The mediator may realize the process will be unsafe or unproductive in the presence of unhealed emotional wounds. In this case, the mediator and party must decide if trauma care is a solution.

An unhealed emotional wound need not necessarily be the result of the present conflict. A wound that impedes reconciliation may have been suffered in prior incidents at the hands of other parties. The current conflict may have caused the old wound to reopen. It is not uncommon to find a party fighting old battles through the guise of the current conflict. Essentially, they are fighting a proxy battle. They may have lost a prior contest of wills and may be trying to overcome the earlier defeat by picking a fight with anyone who will engage. When the party realizes the actual battle they are trying to resolve lies in earlier events (with people not now present), the current conflict may resolve quickly.

Healing and catharsis are important aspects of conflict resolution, but if a party experiences difficulty a mediator must call for a recess to allow them to seek help elsewhere. When people resolve conflict, catharsis and healing take place naturally. The mediator does not practice therapy even though resolving conflict is therapeutic. When emotional wounds become barriers to reconciliation, a mediator must carefully judge the party's ability to continue the process. He must decide if a separate parallel process aimed at healing emotional wounds is necessary. The guiding motto is *do no harm*. If impasse can be overcome by the mediation process and parties remain actively involved on their own initiative it makes sense to continue. The guiding principle is party self-determinism.

If the previous emotional trauma incapacitates a party, rendering them unable to participate with full faculties, it makes sense to delay mediation until emotional healing has been addressed. If a party suffers in a way that prevents self-determinism or if they are battered by extreme emotions to the point of losing control, emotional wounds may need to be healed in a different venue.

Trauma care is not something the mediator provides; mediators are not therapists. It would be an error for a party to expect the mediator to act as a therapist. Working through conflict may make a party feel better and they may achieve psychological satisfaction – but this is not the same as resolving long-term psychological problems.

Some might argue that most conflicts are rooted in psychological problems. They might argue, with good cause, that the other party's psychological problems gave rise to the conflict. If the other party had not been troubled no conflict would have arisen. On occasion, this is a valid argument that posits a correlation between psychological problems and the presence of conflict.

The important determination to be made when considering whether or not mediation is appropriate is whether the party is able to assume control of their current actions and decisions and are able to exert self-determinism. The self-determined party who possesses the ability to resolve a conflict is best served by mediation. The party who cannot operate in a self-determined manner may need other types of support before engaging the process.

While a conflict can arise solely out of the present situation, as mentioned, a conflict may arise as a result of past emotional wounds that have so damaged a person that their relationships with others are constantly besieged by conflict. The unfortunate party who has become embroiled in conflict with a person suffering such emotional wounds may be correct in asserting that healing the past may be not only beneficial, but absolutely necessary.

Such assistance is not something that can or should be imposed on a party. The mediation ethic of honoring party self-determinism dictates that a party must choose to handle their wounds in a time and manner of their choosing.

If a party does not choose to address those wounds and yet those wounds stand in the way of reconciliation, the opposing party may acknowledge their inability to handle the situation and may choose to walk away.

The opposite danger, perhaps more frequent, is the tendency to patholo-gize normal responses to conflict. A party involved in conflict suffers dif-ficult moments: they experience turmoil and challenges to their identity, they suffer anxiety and trepidation, and they grapple with disappointment. When they face an opposing party in conflict they experience a wide range of human emotions and they are faced with a spiritual challenge that calls for transformation. When we do not allow them to work through the process and find their own strengths and truths, but rather label or diagnose their uncomfortable feelings as mental illness, we abort their opportunity for im-portant growth and transformation.

The mediator may choose yet another path when faced with unhealed wounds that give rise to unusually difficult emotions. Rather than terminate the mediation process and fail to resolve the conflict, he may compartmen-talize issues and narrow the focus to allow for limited resolution. He controls and limits the agenda. When he perceives a party is troubled (lacking control over decisions), he may decide to move ahead with a narrow definition of the conflict. He avoids issues that cannot be addressed without extensive heal-ing of emotional wounds. The decision to compartmentalize the dispute and empower a party to focus narrowly allows the process to proceed.

In other cases, he may decide that working through the conflict will re-sult in healing and reconciliation. He may anticipate resolving the current conflict will aid in healing the past. He may observe that one party possesses qualities that will help the other party if they are allowed to work through the conflict and reconcile their relationship.

For example, one party might possess a compassionate and forgiving at-titude that becomes the catalyst for dialogical healing. The subsequent reso-lution of a life problem (the conflict) may provide considerable benefit. The success achieved in resolving the current conflict may provide the confidence and optimism the challenged party needs to handle other interpersonal prob-lems. Success in resolving the current conflict may thus help heal wounds as-sociated with past failures to handle conflict.

Non-Violence

When injustice or evil has become institutionalized or ingrained in the larger culture the individual conflict resolution process suffers. The powerful party may see no need to work with the interests of the weaker party and no need to collaborate, as their position provides them with a surplus of power that allows them to determine outcomes in a manner that pleases them.

In these instances, the oppressed party faces overwhelming odds against reaching an outcome that provides substantive, psychological, or process satisfaction. In these situations, a quiet and mostly hidden form of violence overrides attempts at collaboration, empathy, or mutual satisfaction. The overwhelming power of one party makes remedying the power imbalance a nearly insurmountable task.

One solution for the weaker party is to adjourn the mediation and employ nonviolent tactics that escalate the conflict by garnering public attention and support. The focus changes to tactics that make the injustice or abuse of power broadly known, increasing referent power. While it may seem paradoxical that a party seeking peace must create conflict in order to resolve conflict, this dilemma exists when power imbalance negates the resolution effort.

Mohandas Gandhi and Dr. Martin Luther King Jr. are perhaps the most well-known and successful practitioners of nonviolent protest, resistance, and non-compliance. Both men, faced with widespread cultural injustice, resorted to the nonviolent practice of standing up to injustice by placing their lives and the lives of their supporters on the line.

Their nonviolent approach, inspired by the life and teachings of Jesus, eschews violent means while demanding presence and action. Nonviolent action does not rely on raw force to overcome the opposition and does not rely on sabotage to bring the oppressor to the table, but rather relies on amassing other legitimate forms of power, such as the power of public opinion, or the moral power that arises from common, shared values regarding justice.

Nonviolence employs the power of presence and witness and rests on principles. Nonviolent non-compliance employs principled refusal to acquiesce to unjust demands or orders. It invites the other party to use force that will backfire on them. The nonviolent activist allows the adverse consequences of violence to accrue to the oppressor; they exhibit patience and allow the oppressor to suffer, directly or indirectly, from his own misdeeds.

A significant aspect of nonviolent non-compliance involves swaying public opinion so as to cause the oppressive party to suffer a deficit of legitimacy, consensus, ethical standing, and goodwill. A steady erosion of the legitimacy of the powerful party works to balance power so that conflict resolution may take place. It brings about a situation in which the other party is willing to come to the table. Public support, in the form of outrage against injustice or abuse of power, balances power and makes negotiation possible. One tends to think of such efforts on grand scales, but the same principles can be employed on a small scale, within a family, a business, or a community.

Pace e Bene, a nonviolence training organization, offers the following definition:[2] "Violence is any physical, emotional, verbal, institutional, structural, or spiritual behavior, attitude, policy, or condition that diminishes, dominates, or destroys ourselves or others."[3] Active nonviolence conveys the message: "I will not cooperate with your violence or injustice; I will resist it with every fiber of my being" while "On the other hand, I am open to you as a human being."[4] The nonviolent movement recognizes the need to engage in the oppositional embrace of conflict, while extending a hand that invites collaboration and mutual respect.

Gandhi, whose views were shaped in part by the teachings of Jesus, understood the need for spiritual transformation in nonviolent protest and conflict resolution: "What Gandhi called for and sometimes achieved was a struggle within each person's soul to take responsibility for the evil in which he or she was complicit, and having taken responsibility, to exercise self control, and begin to change."[5] Parallel to our discussion in the previous chapter, "He understood that in giving up our own responsibility for evil we also give up the possibility of changing it."[6] Gandhi understood nonviolence was not solely about protest, it was a process that redefined relationships – the conditions we hope to change must be addressed on both sides of the relationship, we must seek to heal the divine relationship between brothers.

In nonviolence or resistance movements we find mobilization intended to escalate conflict for the purpose of provoking the powerful party to collaborate in ending injustice. There is an effort to remedy the unwillingness of the powerful party to meet as a brother or sister. Gandhi advocated for attitudes found in the tradition of St. Francis. For example, "Soul force is … the word Gandhi used to describe the unitive power of love and truth that is at the root of all being and that can be unleashed to transform conflict and to create true peace, justice, and reconciliation."[7] Here we find a parallel between the mindset of a nonviolence movement leader and a mediator who uses a spiritually transformative style. However, there are important differences as well.

The primary difference between the nonviolent activist and the mediator concerns neutrality. The mediator maintains a neutral and impartial stance: he works with all parties equally to bring about reconciliation. A nonviolent activist advocates for one side and becomes a party to the conflict; they do not adopt a position of neutrality. Nonviolent protest and resistance helps the party lacking in power bring the more powerful party to the table to participate in a collaborative and principled effort to resolve differences and create mutual benefit. After the nonviolent movement has brought about a willingness to convene the mediator guides the parties to reconciliation.

While both efforts – nonviolent activism and mediation – are aimed at bringing about justice and peace, nonviolent activism advocates for one side in a conflict while mediation works equally with all sides from a neutral stance to help them find a solution.

Unlike a party who escalates conflict with the goal of dominating or destroying the other party (even if such escalation results in self-destruction), the wise nonviolent actor recognizes that, eventually, they will need to sit at the same table with the other party. They will continue to co-exist. The skilled and principled nonviolent activist uses techniques that lend themselves toward future reconciliation, eschewing tactics that create wounds that will make it difficult or impossible for parties to collaborate. In this sense, like a mediator, they take the broader view of the welfare of both parties. They strive to expand their view to encompass the other party with whom they dance in the oppositional embrace.

Nonviolence movements and organizations, however, face challenges when it comes to adhering to the *ethics of nonviolence*. A critical ingredient for success, it appears, is a charismatic spiritual leader who possesses the heart of a reconciler. Given that nonviolent activism advocates for one side against another, in the absence of charismatic spiritual leaders there is a risk the movement will be co-opted and compromised by political partisans who do not seek justice but rather personal gain and power.

Nonviolent movements can easily lose sight of nonviolent ideals and overlook solutions that benefit all parties involved. They may seek to swap positions with the previously powerful party and end up exercising their power unjustly, using *power over* rather than collaborative *power with*.[8] As long as the nonviolent activist maintains the original purpose and vision – to bring the other party to the table for a collaborative and mutually beneficial conflict resolution process – the use of nonviolent protest to balance power is a valuable option.

When the movement is co-opted by angry partisans who violate the "Principles of Nonviolence" as laid out by Dr. King[9] – turning from love to hate, turning away from friendship and understanding to demonize the other party, turning away from a focus on injustice to a focus on attacking others – the action no longer carries the moral weight of nonviolence principles. The effort becomes a simple escalation of conflict. When the nonviolence movement is seen as a mere ploy to grab coercive power the backlash can be extreme.

A factor that determines nonviolent protest success is perceived legitimacy of claims. When a nonviolent protester presents a claim with moral legitimacy they are viewed as a valid player by potential allies in the struggle. As an activist hopes to gain allies who will aid in the cause, when new recruits consider the actions they asked to perform are legitimate and just, they will lend support. Participating will raise their self-esteem.

However, when claims are specious, overtly partisan, lacking in equity for all stakeholders, and providing justice only to a special interest group, the effort repels potential supporters. The negative reaction may increase support for the opposition, who gains credibility and legitimacy when the activist lacks moral standing or legitimacy. This erosion of power is contagious. When nonviolent movements lose their moral foundation their decrease in legitimacy devalues the legitimacy of other nonviolent movements.

Nonviolent protest tactics become tainted when they are used by political partisans seeking coercive power. When this condition has arisen new methods of balancing power are needed.

When you face an imbalance of power that prevents resolution and the party across the table promotes an injustice, it pays to assess whether or not your cause has sufficient moral legitimacy to gain outside support. It pays to figure how you will insure your protest message conveys an acceptable truth. As with any tactic one might use to bring the other party to the table to collaborate, one must consider whether or not the tactic will induce the other party to come to the table or cause them to turn away, feeling insulted and disrespected. Does protest or non-compliance escalate the conflict in a positive manner or does it simply push hostilities to new heights?

In the future, as nonviolence movements take advantage of advances in the conflict resolution field, new techniques that do not rise to the level of protest or non-compliance will be adopted. These techniques will promote structured *learning conversations* during which parties and stakeholders will have an opportunity to share in educating and being educated on issues.

Learning conversations will be structured to include presentations of relevant factual issues while at the same time allowing participants to share the personal journey that led them to their current position and worldview. Facts will thus be set within the context of individual life experience rather than being sorted into polar opposite stances. Efforts will be made to expand the dialogue addressing contentious issues through formal, facilitated processes of shared personal narrative.

While there is a role for protest, resistance, and non-compliance in bringing a non-cooperative party to the table, contentious partisan conflict, in which each side demonizes the other, may actually diminish the effectiveness of such techniques, as the public increasingly turns away. This will create a need for more creative methods of addressing injustice and power imbalance.

In your assessment you may wish to consider unique approaches to opening or reopening a dialogue, not only with the other party but also with the larger group of stakeholders affected by the conflict. Make certain your position or cause carries sufficient moral weight and can be stated clearly and convincingly. Evaluate whether or not you are advocating against actual injustice or mounting a campaign to serve narrow interests or desire for coercive power. Engage in a comprehensive analysis of how all stakeholders will be affected by the outcome.

A special situation arises when we engage in nonviolent activism for causes other than our own – when we are recruited to an effort to remedy an injustice or an imbalance of power that offends the conscience. In such cases, we are not a direct party to a conflict but rather a recruit attracted by issues or causes. We become a stakeholder as a result of our empathy for a party embroiled in a conflict.

It is worth comparing the process of becoming involved in such a nonviolent movement with the process of being recruited as a mediator. As a mediator we are called upon to analyze and maintain awareness of our personal biases when we take on the job of facilitating resolution. If our biases are too extreme we recognize they inhibit neutrality; ethically, we have a duty to resign.

Assume we are asked to mediate the dissolution of a marriage and one of the issues with respect to the parenting plan is whether or not to continue treating a child's learning disorder with psychiatric drugs. One parent insists the treatment is critical to the welfare of the child, while the other parent is equally adamant that the treatment is harmful and must stop. If the mediator holds a strong personal position – for example, the position that administering psychiatric drugs to children is a heinous act – the mediator must resign or make his strong prejudice known to the parties so they can make the final decision regarding his continued involvement. If we can honestly set aside our biases or if we reveal our biases and allow the parties to decide whether or not those biases compromise impartiality, we may proceed with the parties' blessing.

As a nonviolent activist the ethical standard is lower. Nonetheless, it makes sense to thoroughly assess our biases and interests to make sure we are not inadvertently, unknowingly, or covertly promoting bias, rather than working for the good of all the parties. An example of an ethical violation would be a situation in which the party for whom we have been protesting and advocating reaches a settlement agreement with the opposition, but due to our biases and personal interests we block the agreement. We choose to continue the conflict in an attempt to satisfy our personal interests, perhaps our political aims, or our desire for coercive power, or our desire to punish the opposing party. When we take on the role of nonviolent activist we are not free from ethical obligations, though our obligations are not as rigorous as those of a mediator.

Stakeholder Consensus

When we hit an impasse we often look across the table and find fault with the other party, but often the cause of the impasse lies on our side of the table. Upsets and disagreements among our stakeholders sabotage our ability to reach a consensus that allows us to form an agreement with the other party. At this point, the mediator helps stakeholders explore techniques for reaching consensus.

In Gubbio the citizens no doubt had differing concerns. Those who lost loved ones suffered more deeply than others and carried a different set of concerns to the table. Francis might have been able to negotiate solely with the mayor and might have reached an agreement for the peaceful treatment of Brother Wolf. But there would be a risk that a citizen who lost a loved one would later sabotage the agreement by launching a surprise attack on Brother Wolf.

Francis most likely understood the liability he faced if he negotiated only with the mayor. He most likely realized that he needed to achieve a consensus and that he would have to handle all concerns and heal all wounds. He could not afford to overlook even a single resentful or hate-filled stakeholder whose emotional wound might lead to a resurgence of conflict.

We can also imagine that citizens who had not been personally harmed nonetheless would rally to support those who were harmed or lost loved ones. The citizens would not approve an agreement until their fellow citizens needs had been addressed and healing had begun. Francis, we imagine, made sure the entire group was consulted.

This same-side-of-the-table work may be time consuming, as differences among stakeholders may be significant. They need to explore differences in values, positions, interests, and needs. Such internal differences may have gone unnoticed previously and only when conflict with an outside entity surfaced did internal differences become evident. Hence, the mediator should not overlook checking for consensus among stakeholders.

Issues regarding organizational hierarchy may also need to be negotiated. The status of individuals, particularly those negotiating on behalf of the group, should be taken into account. Whether or not a person has the authority to negotiate and approve a settlement must be clarified – in many circumstances authority is tied directly to status within an organization. Internal conflict within the organization regarding approval authority can scuttle a negotiation and result in a considerable waste of time.

In addition, sending a negotiator who lacks approval authority is one sure way to alienate and anger the other party, sometimes making it impossible to resolve the conflict. The discussion regarding who shall have the authority to approve an agreement on behalf of others may expose existing disagreements within the organization.

Internal power imbalances may seed feelings of injustice and alienation among group members who then undermine the settlement agreement. It may be necessary to address power openly in order to resolve tension that could later undermine the effort. Likewise, it is important that stakeholders support management or the agreement may be unenforceable at the level of the rank and file. The other party, sensing a lack of support for leadership, may back away anticipating weak leadership will threaten the durability of the outcome.

In situations with multiple stakeholders problems can arise. A group member whose personal identity is contingent on aggressive or violent stances in response to the conflict can sabotage any possible agreement. For example, if Gubbio appointed a police force to protect the town from the wolf those chosen to man the force may have gained status that would be threatened by the impending reconciliation. If they feared a settlement would reduce or eliminate their power and status they might actively work against a resolution. A solution might require the mayor to devise a plan for the police to retain their status, even if it was an honorary status acknowledged in "annual recognition of valor" ceremonies.

While achieving consensus can be a problem, the opposite situation of *group think*, in which consensus is automatic and robotic, may stymie a creative negotiator who proposes changes needed to resolve a conflict. The rigidity of *group think* induces lemming-like behavior in which stakeholders would rather walk off a cliff than embrace changes needed to avert a clash with an opposing group. Faced with the need for internal change in order to resolve a conflict with an outside entity, the leaders of an organization previously subject to group think conformity may regret having established a conformist culture that now makes resolution impossible.

The most significant challenge standing in the way of gaining same-side-of-the-table consensus is the presence of a destructive third party working covertly to sabotage the trust, authority, or consensus needed to complete an agreement with an opposing party. You may have spent considerable effort designing and negotiating a creative plan that creates mutual benefit with the party across the table, only to have stakeholders on your side of the table block or sabotage the agreement as a result of their need to destroy.

In this case, the other side may (correctly) anticipate that stakeholders on your side of the table may commit future destructive acts and they may require assurances you are unable to provide, as you have not overcome destructive forces within your group, organization, or nation. While you have been focused on the enemy, locked in an oppositional embrace, you may have failed to address the hidden influence of the destructive third party in your own group. This is quite common.

In most, if not all, instances the negative hidden influence is at work creating destruction. The effects of the hidden influence can often be seen in the presence of extremist groups that make it impossible for leaders and peacemakers to achieve a consensus for reconciliation with other groups or nations. While it may appear that the root problem is the extremists in most cases the presence of extremists is a symptom of a destructive third party acting as a hidden negative influence.

In the course of mediating a conflict with an outside party you may uncover hidden negative influences on your side of the table and you may discover those influences precipitated the conflict in the first place. Previously, you may have been unaware of such destructive influences. The actual conflict you must resolve is with those at your side or at your back. Resolving conflict with the other party will need to be put on hold until you have handled internal sources of conflict.

In addition to consensus-building activities, there may be a need to collectively explore fundamental core values. This is not accomplished solely in an intellectual manner. Core values rest deeper in our hearts and therefore demand a more holistic approach. Thus we need processes that invite total participation.

The manner in which consensus is reached will vary and the degree healthy relationships exist will vary. Some groups are plagued with the hidden influence of destructive third parties while others run smoothly with policies that promote transparency and harmony. The common factor is the importance of consensus among stakeholders.

The Private Session

Transformative work often begins in private sessions with the mediator. In these sessions, a party grapples with emotion and personal change. This personal, heart-related work, contributes significantly to the final outcome. In these private sessions we redraft our personal narrative, and construct a new story of the future.

While the other side may not be privy to our inner struggle, they become aware of change when we subsequently interact in joint session. When a party returns to joint session after completing difficult work in the private session frequently the other party perceives a different person standing before them. Once they see the transformation they have empirical evidence that change is possible, which motivates them to move forward. When the other party is locked in a fixed position we tend to respond by resisting change. On the other hand, when the other party makes a visible change we are motivated to make a reciprocal change.

The private session with the mediator is the primary locus of initial changes. In private sessions we untangle the fixed oppositional positions one emotional strand at a time and thus bring about transformation. Once parties gain confidence in their ability to change and once they witness the other party's acceptance of change, they become increasingly willing to engage in mutual transformation during joint sessions, which eventually leads to reconciliation.

Other Causes for Impasse

The above discussion does not exhaust the possible reasons for impasse. As you assess your particular situation you may discover others that must be addressed.

A Franciscan View

Francis was not naïve when it came to the venomous influence destructive third parties wielded with weapons of slander, libel, and character assassination delivered with poison whispers and deftly aimed detraction. In the following passage, Bonaventure presents a powerful testament to Francis' views on this vital topic: "[Francis] abhorred like a snakebite the vice of detraction, as a foe to the source of piety and grace; and he firmly held it to be a devastating plague and an abomination to God's mercy because the detractor feeds on the blood of the souls which he kills with *the sword of his tongue* (Ps. 56:5)."[10]

Bonaventure continues: "Once when he heard a friar blacken the reputation of another, he turned to his vicar and said: 'Arise, arise, examine diligently and if you find that the friar accused is innocent, make an example of the accuser by correcting him severely.' Sometimes he decreed that a friar who had stripped another friar of his good name should be stripped of his habit, and that he should not be allowed to raise his eyes to God until he first did his best to restore what he had taken away. He used to say that the impiety of detractors is a much greater sin than that of robbers; for the law of Christ, which is fulfilled in the observance of piety, obliges us to desire the well being of the soul more than the body."[11]

Francis, in recognizing the cancerous influence of the detractor and in having the negative influence removed from the fraternal body, mirrors suggestions provided in this chapter. He did not allow the detractor to reenter until his pernicious behavior was terminated and the health of the host was restored. Francis understood that a fraternity, a marriage, a group, an organization, even a nation, cannot survive while the venom of the destructive third party's bite courses through its veins.

In Admonitions to the Order, which are guidelines intended to preserve the Brotherhood, Francis addresses the negative hidden influence of the detractor. Admonition 25 reads: "Blessed is the servant who would love and respect his brother as much when he is far away from him as when he is with him, and would not say anything behind his back that he would not charitably say in his presence."[12]

Robert Karris notes, "Francis is counseling: If you can't say it charitably to his face, don't say it at all."[13] Karris provides additional insight into the admonition with an excerpt from Francis' First Rule 11: "And let them slander no one. Let them not murmur, nor speak detraction against other, because it is written: '*Gossips* and *detractors* are *hateful to God*.' And let them be unassuming, showing all meekness to all people. Let them not judge. Let them not condemn."[14]

Reading this passage, I travel in my imagination through space and time to Umbria, the valley below Assisi where Francis traveled and preached. I wander into a shaded courtyard where a sign reads: Mediation. As I move toward a doorway that opens into the chamber where Francis meets with local farmers to facilitate the resolution of conflict, I look up to find the following words painted over the arch: *Gossips and Detractors Are Hateful to God*. Perhaps this is the most powerful statement we can direct toward the negative hidden influence of the destructive third party – the gossip and detractor.

In summing up Admonition 25, Karris echoes vital sections of this chapter: "The loose lips of gossip, slander, and detraction have sunk many a fraternity. And isn't it so self-righteously pleasant to talk about our deep fraternal love for all when the cantankerous brother who drives us up a wall is on vacation or away on an extended preaching assignment?"[15] As we debug the impasse that blocks our path to reconciliation, the negative hidden influence, the gossip, the slanderer, the character assassin, and the detractor deserve our strong attention.

When Francis met with the citizens of Gubbio I imagine he would have listened closely to determine whether or not any one of those present had a stake in fomenting fear and hatred toward Brother Wolf. I believe he would have neutralized those influences before pressing on toward reconciliation.

Scripture

Bold and arrogant, they are not afraid to revile glorious beings, whereas angels, despite their superior strength and power, do not bring a reviling judgment against them from the Lord. But these people, like irrational animals born by nature for capture and destruction, revile things that they do not understand, and in their destruction they will also be destroyed, suffering wrong as payment for wrongdoing. (2 Pt 2:11-13)

The lips of fools walk into a fight,
  and their mouths are asking for a beating.
The mouths of fools are their ruin;
  their lips are a deadly snare.
The words of a talebearer are like dainty morsels:
  they sink into one's inmost being. (Prv 18:6-8)

A slanderer reveals secrets;
  so have nothing to do with a babbler! (Prv 20:19)

There are six things the LORD hates,
  yes, seven are an abomination to him;
Haughty eyes, a lying tongue,
  hands that shed innocent blood,
A heart that plots wicked schemes,
  feet that are quick to run to evil,
The false witness who utters lies,
  and the one who sows discord among kindred. (Prv 6:16-19)

The beast was given a mouth uttering proud boasts and blasphemies, and it was given authority to act for forty-two months. It opened its mouth to utter blasphemies against God, blaspheming his name and his dwelling and those who dwell in heaven. (Rev 13:5-6)

CHAPTER NINETEEN

Closing

Finally, after many tears, they found compassion for Brother Wolf.

Francis asked the Mayor of Gubbio and Brother Wolf to declare a pact. The people would be safe from Brother Wolf. Brother Wolf would be safe from them. Everyone expressed joy that the shadow of fear had been lifted from their town.

The wife of the shepherd who was the first to fall to the wolf's hunger brought out food to feed Brother Wolf. She was crying in relief to have the burden of hate lifted from her spirit. More food was brought out and soon everyone was eating together.

Word spread to other towns and soon the people of Gubbio were proclaiming proudly that they had a special wolf, Brother Wolf.

He lived another two years like that until he died, cared for by the generous and forgiving town of Gubbio.

Mediation Principles

As the citizens of Gubbio find compassion for Brother Wolf, who had once been their enemy, a simple ritual gesture – a woman bringing food – completes the journey to reconciliation. At this stage, we acknowledge reconciliation with ceremony that may include a simple ritual such as sitting down together over dinner. Ritual acts symbolically close the door on the contentious past. Lessons learned find their final expression in acts that celebrate reconciliation and turn our attention to welcoming the emerging future.

If we rush to put the conflict behind us and allow reconciliation to pass as a mundane event we risk relegating the growth we experienced to a mere footnote in our life story. When we have transformed conflict and suffering into satisfaction, happiness, or wisdom, we complete the journey by embracing one another in a ceremony that recognizes our newly restored relationship.

In this chapter, we briefly explore how we acknowledge reconciliation through celebration and ritual ceremony. This includes drafting and formalizing documents, giving thanks for the contributions of others, engaging in ceremony that symbolically and artistically buries the past, celebrating and welcoming the future, creating shared moments of joyfulness, and making public announcements that notify stakeholders of the transition from conflict to reconciled relationship.

Celebration of Reconciliation

A ceremony or ritual may involve simple gestures performed with heightened importance and meaning. A handshake, hug, or the signing of documents may be mundane acts in ordinary time but in a ceremony celebrating resolution or reconciliation they are elevated to the level of unifying ritual. The ceremony may be elaborate and evolve into celebrations such as feasts or may simply involve breaking bread or sharing a toast.

It is worth noting there is a difference between the ceremony and ritual that may accompany reconciliation as part of conflict resolution and formal Catholic rites and sacraments, such as the sacrament of Baptism or the Eucharist, and the formal Sacrament of Reconciliation that involves formal confession. Instead, we refer to a less formal and sometimes improvised ceremony or ritual incorporated into the conflict resolution context.

That said, it is worth noting that in the *Taming the Wolf* approach, a spiritual transformation may take place and there may need for recognition of the Holy Spirit at work. Some individuals may wish to acknowledge the transformation by personal participation in a sacrament such as the Eucharist, but such formal observance of the Catholic sacraments should not be confused with our discussion of less formal proceedings not intended to take the place of sacraments or provide the same benefits. We are working on the assumption that although we may experience spiritual transformation, the process of conflict resolution most likely has taken place in a secular setting – except on those occasions when the process has addressed conflict within a parish or other religious setting.

Ceremonies that sometimes include artistic presentations, music, and dance mark the change and publicly acknowledge renewed relationship. The concluding ceremony may include elements of ritual as well as a celebration of accomplishment.[1] A public ceremony may be staged to acknowledge completion of the conflict resolution process before stakeholders and the public. A more private ceremony for the reconciled parties may take on a ritual quality as they embrace each other and the divine within, acknowledging inner and outer realities simultaneously.

Presenting a common reconciled face to each other and the public can demonstrate restored unity at both mundane and transcendent levels. The ceremony marks the end of the reconciliation process and the beginning of a shared future. Parties usher in a new reality with multiple overlapping levels of awareness, meaning, and significance. When we participate in ritual we may experience a metaphoric rebirth. Our transition from false self to divine self continues while we celebrate the transition in our social standing from combatants to brothers and sisters.

Through the power of symbolic acts our transformation seeps into the core of our identity. As we demonstrate and acknowledge who we have become, we are called on to integrate all ways of knowing – intellectual, symbolical, emotional, imaginative, spiritual, somatic – into a comprehensive mindful-ness of the transformed relationship. Given the significance of this endeavor we should allow adequate time and space for appropriate ritual to emerge. Michelle LeBaron notes, "Rituals should not be artificial impositions; they are most powerful when they arise organically from the group."[2]

Some reconciliation ceremonies have emerged organically and then be-came a common tradition within a specific culture, such as the tea ceremony in Japan. Finding or creating the appropriate ceremony to acknowledge the end of a conflict is a matter of creativity. We draw on the history of the spe-cific conflict and the nature of the relationship for ritual acts that provide appropriate recognition of the transformation. We may seek symbolic means that tap deeper ways of feeling. We discover "rituals provide containers for feelings, offering ways to acknowledge and share them even as losses, celebra-tions, or transitions are marked."[3]

We design activities that involve all the senses, knowing that "rituals draw on symbolic meanings, connecting feelings to various combinations of senses – smell, taste, sight, hearing, and touch – as transitions, resolutions, and pas-sages are marked. As people share metaphors and rituals, awareness of feelings and sensations is heightened and relationships are deepened."[4] Embracing all our senses delivers us into the realm of the artist.

In describing the work of peacemakers John Paul Lederach notes the par-allel between the artist and the peacemaker: "I have found that transforma-tion moments in conflict are many times those filled with a haiku-like quality that floods a particular process or space. We might call them moments of the aesthetic imagination, a place where suddenly, out of complexity and historic difficulty, the clarity of great insight makes an unexpected appearance in the form of an image or in a way of putting something that can only be described as artistic."[5]

The similarity between the insights experienced by artists and peacemak-ers recommends we consult artists when it comes time to design and choreo-graph reconciliation celebrations. Lederach describes a moving experience that took place at a conference in Ireland: "The song began and the dance troupe's grateful first steps brought hundreds in the audience to complete silence. The color slides of Belfast's troubled murals, children running from fire bombs, funeral processions, and parades riveted the eyes and captured the haunting feel of the music and lyrics juxtaposed against the ballet-like movements of these young women dancing together though from different sides of the violent divide. The whole of the Irish conflict was held in a public space, captured in a moment that lasted fewer than five minutes."[6]

He continues, "Without locating the specific documents I know that I cannot remember a single speech, proposal, or formal panel response. I do however remember, vividly, the image and feeling of those five minutes of combined music, lyrics, choreography, and photos. It created an echo in my head that has not gone away. It moved me."[7] Thus, when we seek to summon deep emotions and create an event that will sustain advances achieved in peacemaking, we may call on artists to help express that which transcends language.

While not all reconciliation celebrations require artistic production, all require symbolic acts that convey deeper meaning – acts that acknowledge the conflict we leave behind, engage the divine self we have transformed, and foster the I-Thou relationship we have postulated for the future. The more memorable the event the more invested in a peaceful future all parties will become.

Simplicity and honesty are key. "The artistic process rises to its highest level when it finds expression that is simple and honest. Elegance and beauty are often captured when complexity is reflected in the simplest of lines, curves, textures, melodies, or rhythms. Reconciliation that is framed as an intellectually complex process will too often create so much noise and distraction that the essence is missed. The key is to find the essence."[8] Modest but honest gestures appropriate for the circumstance may carry more power than elaborate fanfare lacking in fidelity.

Metaphorically the celebration forms the last section of the golden bridge over which parties travel to embrace one another. As we construct this section of the bridge ritual acts acknowledge the past and turn our attention toward the future. Walking across this last section of the bridge may unleash new and perhaps threatening emotions as we experience the purifying emotional catharsis.

While we seek to create or engage a ceremony or celebration that promotes catharsis the ritual must feel sufficiently safe that internal censors, which might inadvertently abort the process, will be circumvented. While it is true that "Catharsis works best through the physical expression of emotions such as laughter and crying"[9] it is incumbent on us to plan the event so as to maintain safety and hope.

In an earlier chapter, we compared our conflict resolution journey to the mythical hero's journey; we considered ourselves a character in our personal drama. This analogy is helpful once again as we bring to a close the lessons we have learned. In ritual we step out of ordinary time and, in the language of the mythical journey, we return from the other world (the realm of forgiveness and reconciliation) to the original or mundane world. The knowledge gained from our visit to the other world has the qualities of a special elixir, a special healing agent. In the symbolic acts of a ritual we demonstrate outwardly the inner lessons learned, which is a culmination of the hero's journey: "The old Self must be proven to be completely dead, and the new Self immune to temptations and addictions that trapped the old form."[10]

When we are transformed in conflict resolution we are renewed in a manner that lifts us up with a focus on that which is sacred in life. The reconciliation ceremony is designed with awareness that "... there is something of a transcendent nature that takes place in both the artistic endeavor and authentic reconciliation. This transcendent nature is the challenge of the moral imagination: the art and soul of making room for and building the creative act, the birthing of the unexpected."[11]

Satisfaction

When we embrace a reconciliation ritual we signal satisfaction – process satisfaction, psychological satisfaction, and substantive satisfaction – subjective measures of our pleasure. Reconciliation ceremonies or celebrations provide us with a method of giving a public face to inner satisfaction. We share our satisfaction and enjoy collaborative acts that signal agreement. We affix a stamp of approval on the outcome of the process, translating the I-Thou relationship into shared celebration. Ceremony and ritual at this point are not an afterthought but rather an integral part of the reconciliation process.

Formal Documents / Platforms for Change

A common ritual, particularly within the legal setting, involves signing documents that capture the new agreement. This may include promissory notes, contracts, parenting plans, peace accords, treaties, or other formal instruments that guide the future relationship. The documents may consist of a simple paragraph or can run hundreds of pages in length with varying degrees of formality and detail capturing the terms of the agreement.

Documents that capture the essence of the agreement provide both parties with comfort. While drafting a document may not rise to the aesthetic level of ceremony mentioned earlier, there is an art to capturing the intention of the parties accurately and precisely, and the language may be aesthetic. Parties typically rely on professionals, most often lawyers, to draft documents, but in some cases the parties will craft their own written agreement. When approached correctly, committing shared thoughts to symbols (words) that capture a relationship can be aesthetic and pleasing (though too often we consider it to be drudgery).

Formal agreements usually include descriptions of consequences that will arise in the event a party breaches the agreement. Enforcement provisions may be included: these are provisions that describe what will take place should a party fail to meet their obligations. For example, the written agreement may stipulate that if a party fails to adhere to a payment schedule the other party has the right to petition a court for a remedy, perhaps a judgment against the breaching party.

The contract may allow the party owed performance or remuneration to collect a greater amount as a penalty for the breach. There are many creative ways parties can include rewards and punishment to address broken promises. The process of addressing potential failures to comply can be surprisingly positive; it allows parties to jointly consider how they will approach future conflict in a controlled manner.

At the conclusion of a conflict resolution process, the parties are acutely aware of the wisdom of drafting provisions that describe how parties will handle future conflict. They may include clauses calling for a return to mediation to resolve future differences that arise with respect to implementation of the settlement agreement. These provisions prevent future conflict from spiraling out of control and become a framework for future collaboration.

A plan for resolving future conflict is a carefully designed response to the question, "How we will manage contentious differences in our relationship?" Whenever two people or two groups work together they encounter differences and experience conflict. The critical factor determining their future success and happiness is how well they plan to manage those differences.

When one considers conflict from a long-term perspective the goal is not to eliminate conflict but rather to plan to manage conflict. As we discover the interdependent nature of our co-existence and gain awareness of our unique differences, we understand the potential for conflict is a basic feature of life. We may imagine one way to eliminate conflict is to cease to be dependent on one another – but that solution guarantees the torture of isolation and loneliness. It would be a path to solitary confinement taken to an extreme. The other solution would be to eliminate all differences and erase uniqueness – but the resulting monotony would soon drive us mad.

Thus, the goal we seek is not elimination of conflict, but rather putting in place collaborative approaches to managing conflict such that both our interdependence and our differences provide us with opportunity to love one another as unique brothers and sisters. In terms of ritual, the aim is to learn to dance together with humility, grace, and skill. This desire can be reflected in the way we design our future through the agreements we draft.

Another purpose of a written agreement is to provide clarity that was missing in the past. Clarity prevents future conflict that otherwise might arise from miscommunication, misunderstanding, or misguided expectations. When making a commitment to abide by written provisions designed to guide the future relationship a party should take time to be certain their needs and expectations are clearly stated. Experiencing the conflict they have just resolved provides understanding of how a lack of thoroughness, clarity, and transparency created adverse effects, which should motivate them to employ greater diligence.

The conclusion of a conflict resolution process is a particularly good time to enter into a new contract, as our memory of navigating through troubles that came out of our failure to anticipate disagreements is fresh. Having overcome previous conflict we are more acutely aware of the need to clearly communicate intentions and expectations.

Some might consider formal written contracts tedious, unnecessary, or even offensive; however, working on guidelines for the relationship demonstrates respect for self and others. When we view the careful drafting of agreements as caring for the other party's concerns as well as our own, insuring those agreements are clear and comprehensive becomes more than a legalistic afterthought: drafting agreements becomes a purpose-driven act of respect.

Even when the focus is not reconciliation but rather getting the deal done, the formal written agreement has value with regard to insuring future compliance. When parties achieve reconciliation the agreement becomes even more important as it becomes a blueprint for managing their relationship in the days, months, and years to come. A mediator recognizes the value of formal agreements and facilitates the drafting of a memorandum of understanding that accurately captures the substance of the agreement. Capturing the agreement in a document reduces worry over possible misunderstanding or hazy memory.

A signing ceremony may serve as a symbolic event with a ritual aspect that endows the agreement with special meaning. The signing of the Declaration of Independence is an extreme example that illustrates the special significance that can accrue to signing an agreement. While creating and signing formal documents has value in most cases, if the task is not accomplished with creativity the result can be an agreement that is too rigid to withstand future challenges. Rigidly conceived agreements fail to incorporate the flexibility needed to manage future conflict. They may fail to provide for long-term peaceful existence.

John Paul Lederach, in *The Moral Imagination*, argues that "platforms for change" are needed to insure peaceful management of future conflict: "Social change needs dynamic adaptive platforms that respond to the nature of the environments where they must live. But processes that are adaptive without purpose create chaos without direction or ultimate shape. The challenge of social change is precisely this: How do we create smart flexible platforms, process-structures with purpose and the constant capacity for adaptation?"[12]

The platform incorporates social structures and institutional guidelines that make peaceful civic and personal relations possible even though conditions change over time. Lederach addresses large-scale conflicts that impact regions and nations but the concept can be applied at the level of individuals. When we consider how to structure and manage a relationship, whether in domestic relations, business relations, or political situations, it may pay to focus on creating a "platform for change" that serves us well into the future.

Rather than rely solely on standard legal agreements that may prove too rigid and inhibit our creative faculties, we may wish to step outside the box to design more dynamic solutions. Lederach's proposal calls for an act of moral imagination – a creative approach to organizing our personal and community relationships in a way that promotes peaceful co-existence and, in many cases, we may turn to our Faith to discover a foundation that gives birth to solutions for lasting peace.

Lessons Learned

As we consider a ceremony that will culminate in reconciliation we will want to incorporate the fruits of reflection. The conflict may have evoked insights that deserve to be highlighted in statements or presentations. We distill the elixir that returned us to health and share that elixir with the larger community.

For many the conflict resolution journey will have been primarily a spiritual journey. Conflict might have been a knock on the door announcing the need for spiritual growth; our faith may have been challenged. Our understanding of life may have been put on trial. We may have achieved satisfaction on the traditional vectors of process, psychology, and substance, while most of all learning to value spiritual transformation. When we consult our scorecard of earthly concerns we may not have logged a home run, but we may have found earthly concerns were mere shadow play compared to the value of spiritual formation. Perhaps the greatest lesson concerned the power of compassion and unconditional love to change lives.

A day of prayer led by spiritual advisers may provide an opportunity to recount spiritual lessons. Too often we sigh with relief and dash back to our busy daily routines without making the changes truly our own. In the long run, we gain more by deep understanding of the transformation we experienced. A moment spent validating our new status insures we do not stumble and fall into old ways. Some parties find this is an excellent moment to enter into a new covenant regarding future right action based on a moral code suggested or shaped by the conflict resolution experience.

Compassion & Unconditional Love

Compassion and unconditional love are the cornerstones of reconciliation. If parties are successful in mining such qualities, within a short time the conflict, which previously felt so real, begins to seem unreal and fabricated. It appears to have been a overwhelming veil of falsehoods. Once we part that veil life becomes as it should be – crisp, clear, and filled with light. We emerge from a debilitating fog. Whereas previously we came to accept conflict, discord, and struggle as real life, upon transformation we know life lived with unconditional love is most real. Issues, positions, and stances that precipitated conflict and violence seem foreign, fabricated, and insubstantial. We puzzle over how we could have become trapped in falsehoods.

Recalling our missteps, we now see them as dangers to be avoided, not fixed responses we are doomed to repeat. Unresolved conflict clouded our mind like a fever. We now strive to remain in the moment and guard against losing our innate loving presence; we vow to strengthen our awareness of the Holy Spirit at work within. We have glimpsed who we really are and now we refuse to allow life's pressures to squeeze the love from our hearts.

Conflict resolution may expose our flimsy facades and force us to discover the presence of the divine. The transformation we experience during conflict resolution allows inner discovery that is rare in most other circumstances. When we sit with enemies who have transgressed against us when we abandon our defenses and jettison our urge for revenge we are transformed. When we apologize and seek forgiveness our transformation reveals previously unimagined possibilities for renewal and resurrection.

Reconciliation magically restores our ability to change. We are no longer the person who entered the process. As a result, we may need time to wear the skin of this new person. We may feel ill-at-ease and in need of time to adjust to a new way of being and we may worry the change will not endure. Ceremony and ritual acknowledge and celebrate the change, and reinforce the transformation. Symbolic acts represent in a memorable path of transition from darkness to light, from strife to harmony, from stumbling with burdens to lightness of step, from fogginess to clarity, and from hatred to love.

The reconciliation ceremony may include publicly documenting our changes in a journal. On a larger scale, museums and memorials document major transformations in the collective life of a community or nation. We may wish to mimic their approach and create smaller memorials dedicated to personal reconciliation.

The prompts in the journal workbook can become an account of the transformation; an account that serves as a historical document. When future conflict arises, our responses, recorded in the journal workbook, can refresh our recollection regarding how we previously overcame barriers. Wisdom gained is stored in the responses; our entries serve as reminders to which we can return later when we become lost. We may create ongoing ritual that periodically restores our insights. We may return annually to the journal to celebrate the passage we navigated through difficult times.

Giving Thanks

Upon reconciliation there may be a need to express gratitude, and a special need to offer thanksgiving. In our ceremony we may acknowledge the reconciling hearts of those who fostered the peacemaking process and, in general, show recognition for work that is making the planet more peaceful. Too often media attention focuses on the dramatic and shocking effects of violent conflict rather than on the peacemakers who should be elevated to the status of cultural leaders.

When we celebrate reconciliation we create an opportunity to show gratitude. Humility nurtured during conflict resolution becomes thanks offered to those who contributed to our transformation.

Confidentiality versus Public Notice

In some instances, there are good reasons to maintain confidentiality. Confidentiality may have made a settlement possible. Without such protection a party may refuse to reconcile. In some cases, confession and apology, if broadcast beyond the immediate parties, brings unnecessary censure and embarrassment. Thus we must consider how we will balance the value of a public announcement with the value of confidentiality.

One component of forgiveness is a willingness to no longer speak of the other party's transgressions, which means in most cases mention of past transgressions should not be a part of a public announcement. When one party appears to desire the public embarrassment of the other party reconciliation has not truly taken place. On the other hand, a party's announcement of their own transgressions offered in an act of contrition with the purpose of bringing about deeper reconciliation may be valuable. If one party has been publicly discredited as a result of the conflict the other party's public accounting can restore the other party's Face and public standing.

In some situations, public notice serves both the parties and the community and allows stakeholders to achieve closure. Upon achieving reconciliation we can use shared celebration to alert stakeholders they should cease their hostility. In addition, engaging in a reconciliation ceremony may provide stakeholders with an experience of catharsis that dissipates hostility, thus averting a resurgence of conflict. As you design a ceremony and/or a celebration, assess the degree to which stakeholders or spectators are in need of a symbolic release of tension and hostility.

There may have been times when the community's desire for peace motivated parties to seek mediation in the first place, perhaps when the conflict threatened the community's well being. In these cases, although confidentiality may have been part of the process, a public announcement thanking the community for their encouragement is in order.

It should be noted that process confidentiality and post-settlement confidentiality differ. Public announcements delivered upon completion of the process can be crafted as shared statements of resolution and reconciliation. Parties may collaborate on joint statements and deliver a shared narrative that acknowledges the end of the conflict but omits private information.

In the absence of a joint statement, each party may agree to forego disclosing information the other party prefers remains confidential. The parties may negotiate into the settlement agreement a right to approve each other's public statements regarding the conflict and its resolution so the story presented to the public does not create confusion and misunderstanding. Though each party may decide how to address the press unilaterally, they may instead decide to present a unified public face and address the press or onlookers in a collaborative manner. The same concerns arise when the audience is extended family, employees of a business, or parents and employees in a school district.

How you address these groups and speak to their collective and individual sensibilities can be important. Onlookers who have previously taken sides may be inclined to continue the conflict unless they are provided with compelling reasons to accept the conflict is truly ended and they have no further role to play.

Thus, a reconciliation ceremony or celebration that involves the larger public should be tailored to preserve confidentiality while providing public notice and drawing all who have been affected by the conflict into harmony and understanding.

Public Announcements

The parties may ask the mediator to deliver a public announcement of reconciliation, as the mediator, skilled at reframing, may best communicate news of the settlement and renewed relationship. At other times, parties may rely upon public relations specialists, lawyers, or elders in the community to sponsor their public announcement by providing supportive statements that accompany the news.

In some instances, the mediator, a lawyer, or a public relations specialist may choreograph events to accurately communicate the importance of the settlement to the community. At such events, parties may ask for the support of the community in wishing them well as they move forward. A celebratory gathering may memorialize the passage from a state of conflict to a state of harmony. Public displays of collaboration and agreement between the parties also function as promises of future harmony to be fulfilled and further cement the parties' agreement with the pressure of public opinion.

Public Opinion

Public opinion may play a significant role. Conflicts and their resolution affect the local community and, in some cases, the global community. Public opinion and public pressure can play a significant role in motivating parties to convene mediation and to adhere to settlement agreements.

The Internet draws people closer in space and time. More and more people become aware they are stakeholders in the outcome of conflicts taking place in distant lands. A war between religious sects on the other side of the world determines the cost of fuel in our neighborhood. Being aware of the degree to which distant conflicts affect us, we tend to want more information on the causes at work. Who is being reasonable? Who is being unreasonable? Is social justice an issue? With such increased scrutiny it is more difficult for those who drive conflict to remain hidden, but at the same time those who wish to obscure their true intentions can use the expanding media as a propaganda tool to create misdirection and confusion.

In the future, the public will become increasingly sophisticated in the use of media and remaining informed regarding their role as a stakeholder. As they discern they have a stake in outcomes they will add their voices to the discussion. At times they may inadvertently promote additional conflict in their attempt to sway events. The contemporary peacemaker will want to be aware of how a conflict is perceived by the larger community of stakeholders, and will want to be aware of how their participation affects the outcome. Thus, when it comes to reconciliation ceremonies or celebrations, consideration should be given to the need to interface with distant stakeholders who access the conflict through the Internet or other electronic media.

As broader public scrutiny increases and the number of stakeholders expands the importance of public announcements and public events will grow significantly and the restoration of a positive and harmonious public image will become important to parties who reconcile. The greater the value that communities, religious and secular, place on peaceful resolution of conflict, the more important it will be to achieve public approval. New methods of engaging in large-scale public ceremony, augmented by electronic media, will be developed.

Faith Communities & Peacemaking

Religious communities can play a special role in spreading peacemaking and conflict resolution values, concepts, and practices. Most faith traditions value the role of confession, apology, forgiveness, and reconciliation. Members understand the reconciling heart. The extent to which religious leaders demonstrate and model reconciliation determines the extent to which the faith community adopts reconciliation as a core value.

In secular society the courts have been assigned the task of resolving civil conflict and have taken the lead in the formal dispute resolution movement. However, in the future, faith communities may drive cultural change when it comes to managing conflict and valuing reconciliation.

As members of faith-based groups gain increased proficiency in peacemaking they will become a force in muting the divisive role played by religious extremists. They will mobilize the faithful to play an active role in peacemaking and overshadow extremists' attempts to foment conflict. Men and women of faith may yet be the deciding factor when it comes to the continued survival of this planet.

At this point faith communities are learning to engage one another in respectful interfaith exchanges that honor core values of pluralism and inclusivity. A common ground that deserves heightened exploration concerns approaches to peacemaking or *the path to peace*. All faiths include teachings on peace and harmony making the time right for increased interreligious dialogue on peacemaking. Conferences that focus on shared values of peacemaking will be an important beginning to a new movement. If we concentrate on each faith bringing lessons of peacemaking from their tradition to a common effort we may see the true beginnings of global peace.

A Franciscan View

The life of Francis was rich with ritual, ceremony, and celebration. In addition to his love for the songs of the troubadours he enjoyed celebrating the sacraments of the Catholic faith. Celebration of the Eucharist held a special place in his heart. "Like the holy Apostle St. John who reclined his head against the Heart of our Lord at the First Eucharistic Banquet, Francis lived out his religious life in the same manner. The core of his consecration centered on the Eucharistic Christ whom he loved as his God and All."[13]

An event that deserves special note was Francis' conversion before the Cross of San Damiano. Susan Saint Sing imagines how we might experience kneeling before that Cross and allowing ourselves to be lifted beyond mundane space and time: "Spirit to spirit we feel the timeless caress of the Other. Ageless in it, we are never old, never alone, and have no need of power. Seamlessly we are enmeshed as our nature – made spirit – enters in. We have no need to linger in flesh. Our feet fly free to him whose feet are nailed above. The journey, no more than a few steps in height, though Everest-like in stature, we summit in him, through him and with him to the top of the world as we know it, only to find that we are prostrate on the floor."[14]

In her words we find a description of the journey we long to make as we overcome division and conflict and find ourselves spiritually transformed. If the rituals we employ to consummate our transformation are to possess Francis' touch, they are likely to borrow from his pivotal conversion moment at San Damiano.

Common gestures and actions of kindness also summon thoughts of Francis, for example, the greetings we use may echo his frequent greeting. "In all his preaching, he proclaimed peace, saying: *'May the Lord give you peace'* (Matt. 10:12; Luke 10:5) as the greeting to the people at the beginning of his sermon."[15] We may adopt his opening words as our own when we acknowledge resolution of our conflict and recognize the influence of the Holy Spirit in the outcome.

Francis was also no stranger to the power of the arts to lift our hearts and elevate our minds. The historical record informs us he admired the troubadours of his era. "The songs of the troubadours endlessly recount the desires, fears, and joys of the loving heart. This delicacy of feeling, this art of loving marked by veneration and tenderness – in a word, this 'courtesy' – found a deep echo in Francis' heart."[16] In "Canticle to the Creatures," we glimpse the manner in which he sought to praise all creation through song. Eloi Leclerc in *The Song of the Dawn*, which presents the canticle, remarks on the celebratory aspect of Francis' life, "... at the base of his capacity for wonder is the sensitivity of the artist and poet."[17]

Francis' canticle arises from his inner life just as our journey to reconciliation must arise from our inner life. "We cannot separate the wondered regard of Francis from his deep and interior life. Like the troubadours of his age, to whom he compared himself, he celebrated nature in terms of the love that fired his heart. His song of the world is intimately linked to his contemplation of Christ."[18] The canticle parallels rituals we seek, rituals that engage outward signs to release and summon that which we experience in our hearts.

The following passage from *The Song of the Dawn* echoes our hope that it is possible for symbols and language to speak of the magic of reconciliation: "Brother Sun, Sister Moon, Brother Wind, Sister Water, Brother Fire ... These images, which establish a direct kinship between man and the world, are meant to express reality in its wholeness and its unity. They erase all borders. They recover a plenitude of being that goes beyond any kind of split or rupture at the heart of being. They celebrate unity: the unity of man and nature, of spirit and life, of freedom and necessity. They sing of a return to the source of being, to the infancy of the world."[19] The canticle, like the ceremony and ritual we seek, relies on symbols to fire our spirit on its journey from the mundane to the profound. "If we admit this cryptic and symbolic dimension of the cosmic elements in their religious and poetic celebration, we begin to sense the profound meaning of the Canticle of Creatures."[20]

In ritual we seek to express the depths of our transformation, just as Francis poured out his heart in the canticle. "Under cover of a celebration of the world, Francis is dealing with himself, with his own depths. By dreaming of the 'precious' and 'fraternal' substance of things he fraternizes with the fascinating and redoubtable depths of the human soul."[21] In the same way we seek to express that which defies literal commentary, Francis uses metaphor and image to lift us to the realms of spiritual insight. "These great cosmic images – Brother Sun, Sister Moon, Brother Wind, Sister Water, Brother Fire, Sister our mother the Earth – all express a fraternal communion not only with natural realities but also with the intimate forces that work in the human soul."[22]

Francis did not write the canticle in his youth, when his legs were strong and his eyes were clear. Rather the song was composed later in life, during a period when he was "suffering intensely from his physical infirmities ...," when he was wracked with illness and declining eyesight.[23] "His canticle is the song of a person in whom night and its torments are transfigured into light."[24]

Leclerc frames the experience beautifully: "This ... profound experience, which here reaches the language, is an experience of reconciliation. This great serenity, which we should not forget, came at the end of a whole life, is the sign of an interior calm, a deep acceptance of self, a reconciliation between the highest part of man and the instinctive and affective forces that work obscurely within him. The primal forces of desire, those great life and death forces, have lost their troubling and menacing side here. Francis no longer had anything to fear from these wild forces. He did not destroy them; he tamed them, as he tamed the wolf of Gubbio. Isn't this wolf precisely the symbol of the agressivity that can destroy us but can also become a force of love?"[25]

When Leclerc writes of the canticle, "We are in the presence of a rather rare case of the spiritualization of life and the vivification of spirit,"[26] he might be writing about our aspiration for ritual that consummates reconciliation. The canticle poses questions appropriate for the culmination of reconciliation. "Doesn't fraternizing with all creatures mean opting for a vision of the world where conciliation is stronger than rupture? Isn't it opening oneself, beyond all separation and solitude to a universe of communion in a great breath of forgiveness and peace?... Such a spiritual experience touches the deepest part of the soul. It is always chaste and veiled. It is not known except through great symbols: in a celebration of the world where soul, fraternally united to all creatures, itself takes on the brilliant color of the sun."[27]

In looking to the Canticle for signs to guide creative ritual, we have looked outside the formal liturgy, but we should not forget that Francis, as noted previously, was inebriated with zeal for the Eucharist. "When Francis was ill, he would beg the clerics to celebrate Mass in his sickroom in order that he could receive the Lord. When this was impossible, Francis entered so deeply into prayer that it seemed he was present spiritually at a Mass, which he could not attend. Nothing could separate him from his Beloved Master."[28]

At the end of his life, Francis once again turned to the most celebrated and venerated sacrament of all. "He ... commemorated the Last Supper that Jesus celebrated with his disciples. This was one of Francis' last acts. He clearly indicated therein the meaning he wanted to give to his death: it was a communion and not a separation."[29]

Scripture

Then he poured water into a basin and began to wash the disciples' feet and dry them with the towel around his waist. He came to Simon Peter, who said to him, "Master, are you going to wash my feet?" Jesus answered and said to him, "What I am doing, you do not understand now, but you will understand later." (Jn 13:5-7)

Jesus said to them, "Come, have breakfast." And none of the disciples dared to ask him, "Who are you?" because they realized it was the Lord. Jesus came over and took the bread and gave it to them, and in like manner the fish. This was now the third time Jesus was revealed to his disciples after being raised from the dead. (Jn 21:12-14)

Now Jesus did many other signs in the presence of [his] disciples that are not written in this book. But these are written that you may [come to] believe that Jesus is the Messiah, the Son of God, and that through this belief you may have life in his name. (Jn 20:30-31)

Let us then pursue what leads to peace and to building up one another. (Rom 14:19)

CHAPTER TWENTY

Mission

IN PRECEDING CHAPTERS, I refer to the work of mediators but you may be wondering if the work outlined should be restricted to professionals. The obvious answer is that there should be no barriers to peacemaking. Making peace is our sacred duty, a mandate bestowed on us by the Prince of Peace, Jesus Christ. And the legacy of St. Francis, his devotion to Christ and peace, belongs to all.

At another level it makes sense to respect professional and social customs, and honor the boundaries used to distinguish and identify practitioners. The following discussion clarifies some of these concerns and considers the footprint of *Taming the Wolf* in the world of peacemaking and conflict resolution.

When *Taming the Wolf* was conceived its primary purpose was to serve as a guide for parties entangled in conflict who sought help through a conflict resolution process such as mediation. I had observed that most parties arrived at mediation unprepared; they were often disoriented and uncertain about their role as a party. They lacked materials that described the process in a thorough manner, materials that explained what was expected of them. Then and now, the primary purpose of *Taming the Wolf* is helping parties who find themselves entangled in conflict that is ruining their life, those who desire a road map to reconciliation. Ultimately, it is the parties themselves who become peacemakers – the professional mediator simply facilitates their peacemaking journey.

The second purpose, which came to view as I was writing, was addressing people's need to help others, a need that fills the hearts of so many. The conflict they wish to address does not involve them as a party, but rather as a stakeholder, as someone who suffers while watching others fail to find joy and contentment in life as a result of conflict. This group of concerned peace-makers ranges from the matriarch who wishes to heal a family to the lawyer or diplomat seeking to resolve high-profile conflict. The following briefly discusses how I see *Taming the Wolf* addressing those needs.

Taming the Wolf offers conflict resolution to professionals – mediators, lawyers, judges, pastoral counselors, and other advisers – a road map they can share with clients, a tool they can use to educate clients regarding the process they are about to undertake. When parties know how the process works the assistance provided by professionals becomes increasingly valuable, resulting in more satisfactory outcomes.

Secondarily, trained professionals may glean from the preceding pages the unique perspective of a Franciscan, which may enhance and compliment their current practice. The spiritually transformative style may suggest new approaches to old problems and provide concepts that can be employed to overcome impasses that proved challenging in the past.

Students training for a career in dispute resolution or peacemaking, whether through a law school or other venue, may find St. Francis to be the mentor they have been seeking. Perhaps there is no more valuable training than walking in the shoes of a party struggling with conflict. Using the journal workbook students can follow the path a party will take as they move through mediation. The student can use the journal workbook to track their progress through a conflict in which they are entangled, thereby preparing to understand the challenges and experience of the parties they are training to help.

But you might ask again, should conflict resolution be restricted to the professional mediator? It depends. At this time, there are no licensing requirements for mediators, though the debate over whether or not there should be is lively. There are those who lobby to restrict the work to attorneys; they argue that regulation of the profession should be assigned to Bar associations. Others argue the opposite view: that the beauty and success of mediation arise from its founding principles, which included creating diversity by encouraging practitioners from varied backgrounds to join the field. This approach provides parties with a wide selection of mediators who possess a range of skills for resolving a conflict.

Increased regulation by the legal community not only is unwarranted but will damage the profession by limiting practitioners to the views of the legal profession. However, this does not mean I do not see a need for mediators to understand and appreciate the law, especially when the dispute has reached the courts. In order to provide the best possible service to clients mediators need an appreciation of the lawyer's point of view and awareness of the challenges they face, as well as an understanding of how the courts function. If a mediator lacks familiarity with the basic parameters of the litigated case, they may not be able to fully serve their clients. At the same time, mediators need to maintain the flexibility and creativity that allow them to work outside the limitations of legalistic approaches to resolving conflicts.

There are also many mediators or conciliators who deliver conflict resolution services in venues other than the legal setting. They do not seek to address the litigated case. They may work within large organizations, such as universities, in the role of ombudspersons, or they may work in the human resources department of corporations, or within the healthcare system, or within the schools. They may function under another title in day-to-day affairs, then put on the hat of a mediator as they work directly with parties. They may spend as much time in conflict prevention as in conflict resolution, anticipating conflict before it escalates. These professionals may find *Taming the Wolf* offers an expanded view of how to approach conflict resolution and prevention. In many cases, they may view the *Taming* approach to educating and training a party in conflict resolution as a valuable conflict prevention tool – as the educated party becomes a peacemaker.

The term conciliator often overlaps with the term mediator, though at times it refers to delivery of specialized dispute resolution activities within government agencies, particularly those resolving disputes involving unions. Others use the term for mediation that eschews the evaluative approach that focuses solely on getting the deal done. They use conciliation to refer to facilitative or transformative approaches. The term is used in the context of Christian Conciliators who function as conflict coaches and mediators. Thus, those who wish to help others with these tools but who wish to avoid the legal setting may call themselves conciliators.

Yet others might label themselves reconcilers, noting their focus on reconciliation within the spiritual or religious context. This term is particularly useful in the context of *Taming the Wolf* and points to the desired goal – reconciliation. In this category we might find faith-based diplomats working to resolve interfaith conflict or we might find passionate individuals working for peace within a particular parish or religious community.

Peacemaker encompasses all of the above, though we may also use the term to identify those who strive to bring about reconciliation on the global stage. The term resonates with our thoughts of Francis, as peacemaker references a deeper commitment to bringing peace to all creatures. While other terms, such as mediator, reference what we do in the moments when we are engaged with the conflict resolution process, the term peacemaker speaks to our fundamental identity, to the spiritual mandate we have inherited. When we find ourselves becoming peacemakers in our hearts, when we live a spiritually transformative life, we live up to the legacy of Francis.

When conflict prevention and resolution become a way of life, rather than a response to crisis, we find ourselves coaching others in the introspective self-analysis found in the journal workbook. Those we touch are emboldened to become peacemakers and the solutions that previously eluded them become remarkably clear. If *Taming the Wolf* allows us to greet each day with the Face of Francis and to live life with deep appreciation of the indwelling Holy Spirit, if it allows us to recognize the presence of the divine in all creation, it has worked as intended.

In closing, I pray that you are able to go forth into the world with the Face of a Franciscan, bringing peace and joy and contentment wherever your earthly pilgrimage takes you.

ST. FRANCIS & THE WOLF OF GUBBIO

Legend adapted from Friar Rafael Brown, trans., *The Little Flowers of St. Francis* (New York, Doubleday, 1998).

INTRODUCTION

1   In many states, the law declares all work product (notes, photos, data, sketches) prepared for the purpose of mediation shall be confidential and exempt from discovery during trial. If you are involved in litigation, consult with your attorney regarding confidentiality provisions, as well as provisions regarding attorney-client privilege. If you are working with a mediator, consult with the mediator regarding the confidentiality of the material you enter into your journal. In some states, you may wish to add to your journal a note that says, "*This material was prepared expressly and solely for the purpose of mediation and/ or settlement conference. To the full extent provided by the law, the contents of this journal shall remain confidential and privileged.*"

CHAPTER ONE

1   Regis J. Armstrong, OFM Cap., Wayne J.A. Hellmann, OFM Conv., and William J. Short, OFM, eds., *The Prophet,* vol. 3 in *Francis of Assisi: Early Documents,* (New York: New City Press, 2001), 432.

2   Jean François Godet-Calogeras, "More Than A Legend: The Wolf of Gubbio," *The Cord* 52.6 (2002): 256.

3   Anonymous. "The Little Flowers of Saint Francis: A Translation and Re-editing of the Deeds of Saint Francis and His Companions by an Anonymous (After 1337)," in *The Prophet* (see n. 1), 3:601; Donald E.Demaray, *The Little Flowers of St. Francis: A Paraphrase* (New York: Alba House, 1992), 78.

4   Godet-Calogeras, "More Than A Legend," 260.

5   Leonardo Boff, *The Prayer of Saint Francis: A Message of Peace for the World Today*, trans. Phillip Berryman (New York: Orbis Books, 2001), 56.

6   Thomas of Celano, "The Life of Saint Francis (1228-1229)" in *The Saint,* vol. 1 in *Francis of Assisi: Early Documents,* eds. Regis J. Armstrong, OFM Cap., Wayne J.A. Hellmann, OFM

Conv., and William J. Short, OFM, (New York: New City Press, 1999), 171.

7   Armstrong, Hellmann, Short, *The Prophet,* 3:432 (see n. 1).

8   Bonaventure, *The Life of St. Francis,* trans. Ewert Cousins (New York: Paulist Press, 1978), 179.

9   Paul Sabatier, *The Road to Assisi: The Essential Biography of St. Francis,* ed. Jon M. Sweeney (Brewster, Massachusetts: Paraclete Press, 2003).

10 Boff, *The Prayer of Saint Francis,* 2.

11 Ibid., 6.

12 Ibid., viii.

13 Ibid., 34.

14 Ibid., 50.

15 Francis of Assisi. "Canticle of the Creatures (1225)," in *The Saint* (see n. 6), 1:113.

16 Regis J. Armstrong, OFM Cap., Wayne J.A. Hellmann, OFM Conv., and William J. Short, OFM, eds., *Francis of Assisi: Early Documents,* 3 vols. (New York: New City Press, 1999-2001).

17 Franciscan Federation, *The Rule and Life of the Brothers and Sisters of The Third Order Regular of St. Francis, Twenty-fifth Anniversary Booklet* (Washington, DC: Franciscan Federation, 2007).

CHAPTER TWO

1   For an excellent discussion of how to change the conversation see: Douglas Stone, Bruce Patton, and Sheila Heen, *Difficult Conversations: How to Discuss What Matters Most* (New York: Penguin Books, 1999).

2   Judge Alexander Williams III of the Los Angeles Superior Court would say to disputants arriving in his courtroom for settlement negotiations, "You can choose to fund the fight or fund the fix."

3   Thomas Jordan, "Glasl's Nine-Stage Model of Conflict Escalation," http://www.perspectus.se/tjordan/EscalatioJornmodel.html, 2000.

4   Deniable punishment is a covert harm done for which we can deny responsibility, for example, we can punish someone by tarnishing their relationship through covert gossip.

5   Jordan, "Glasl's Nine-Stage Model."

6   Ilia Delio, OSF, *Franciscan Prayer* (Cincinnati: St. Anthony Messenger Press, 2004), 82.

7   Ibid., 63.

8   Ibid., 111.

9   Ibid., 84.

10 Robert J. Karris, OFM, "Admonition Four," in *The Admonitions of St. Francis: Sources and Meanings* (St. Bonaventure, New York: The Franciscan Institute, St. Bonaventure University, 1999), 307.

11 Demaray, *The Little Flowers of St. Francis,* 46 (see ch. 1 n. 3).

12 Ibid., 46.

13 Ibid., 47.

14 Noel Muscat, OFM, "Ministerium Fratrum." *Franciscan Studies*. http://i-tau.com/frans-tudies/articles/

15 Ibid.

16 Helmut Rakowski, OFM Cap., "'Opus solidaritatis pax,' Peace is the fruit of solidarity: The spirituality of international economic solidarity in the Capuchin Order." Mission Articles: Articles in English, 2007. (Service of Documentation and Study on Global Mission (SEDOS), September 23, 2005). http://www.sedosmission.org/site/index.php?option=com_docman&task=doc_download&gid=657&Itemid=59&lang=en.

17 Ibid.

Chapter Three

1 The model can be found in Kenneth Thomas, "Conflict and Conflict Management," *Handbook of Industrial and Organization Psychology* (Chicago: Rand McNally, 1976).

2 Kenneth Thomas and Ralph Kilmann developed the "Thomas-Kilmann Conflict Mode Instrument" to identify typical responses to conflict. To access a self-scored test online, see the link at http://kilmann.com/conflict.html.

3 For an excellent introduction to principle-based, win-win, collaborative negotiation see: Roger Fisher and William Ury, *Getting to Yes* (New York: Penguin Books, 1981).

4 In the tit-for-tat strategy, if one party makes a competitive move, the other makes a competitive counter move; if one party makes a collaborative move, the other makes a collaborative move. It is a technique used to educate the opposing party.

5 Thomas and Kilmann describe conflict responses and provide questions to help you analyze which choices are appropriate for specific situations. http://kilmann.com/conflict.html.

6 The concept of an "I and Thou" relationship was inspired by philosopher Martin Buber. See Martin Buber, *I and Thou,* trans. Walter Kaufman (New York: Touchstone, 1970).

7 Delio, *Franciscan Prayer*, 137 (see ch. 2 n. 6).

8 Ian Morgan Cron, "St. Francis of Assisi: A Pre-Modern Mentor to the Postmodern Church," *Radical Grace* October–December 2008. (*Radical Grace* is a publication of The Center for Action and Contemplation.)

9 Within the mediation profession there is a growing trend toward studying mindfulness, the calm observation of our physical, emotional, mental, and spiritual states.

10 "Follow the Holy Spirit and his Holy manner of working" is a phrase found often in Franciscan literature, a phrase that might be taken as a mission statement.

Chapter Four

1 See J.P. Folger, M.S. Poole, and R.K. Stutman, *Working Through Conflict: Strategies for Relationships, Groups, and Organizations*, 5th ed. (Boston: Pearson, 2005), 52.

2 Ibid.

3 Ibid.

4   Stone, Patton, and Heen, *Difficult Conversations*, 106 (see ch. 2 n. 1).

5   Cron, "St. Francis of Assisi: A Pre-Modern Mentor," 8 (see ch. 3 n. 8).

6   For an informative discussion regarding the limits of the "fixed pie" view in negotiation and mediation see: Fisher and Ury, *Getting to Yes*, (see ch. 3 n. 3).

7   Stone, Patton, and Heen. *Difficult Conversations*, 83.

8   Ibid., 87.

9   Delio, *Franciscan Prayer*, 24, (see ch. 2 n. 6).

10 Bonaventure, *The Life of St. Francis* (see ch. 1 n. 8).

11 Delio, *Franciscan Prayer*, 113

CHAPTER FIVE

1   For a discussion of the challenges of "difficult conversations" see: Stone, Patton, and Heen, *Difficult Conversations* (see ch. 2 n. 1).

2   Arbitration resembles a trial but is usually shorter and less expensive as parties agree to limit time spent on pre-trial motions, discovery, presentation of evidence, and other procedural steps.

3   Discovery involves procuring information from the other party related to the litigation. It includes interrogatories, depositions, requests for admissions, and requests for production of documents or other evidence. Discovery can be time consuming and expensive.

4   The business community seeks efficient approaches to conflict resolution. For example, the CPR Institute for Dispute Resolution designs and implements agreements between corporations regarding the use of alternative dispute resolution processes. In the construction where real time dispute resolution is critical (as stopping construction and to wait for trial is cost prohibitive) Dispute Resolution Boards have emerged that offer timely hearings and findings.

5   In Small Claims venues litigants represent themselves in court.

6   "Self-help" may be the tool of the bully or someone with evil intentions. See chapter 18.

7   Jonathan D. Glater, "Study Finds Settling is Better Than Going to Trial," *New York Times*, August 8th, 2008.

8   Robert F. Cochran Jr., John M. DiPippa, and Martha M. Peters, *The Counselor at Law: A Collaborative Approach to Client Interviewing and Counseling* (New York: Lexis Publishing, 1999), 1.

9   Discuss mediation confidentiality and client-attorney privilege with your attorney with regards to notes you make in the journal.

10 Keith Warner, OFM, "Pilgrims and Strangers: The Evangelical Spirituality of Itinerancy of the Early Franciscan Friars," *Spirit and Life: A Journal of Contemporary Franciscanism* 10 (2000): 153.

11 Ibid. As quoted from: Michael Blastic, "The Conversation of Franciscans," in *The Cord* 46.2 (1996), 57.

12 Ibid., 164.

13 Ibid., 161.

14 Jim McIntosh, OFM, "Lessons of Gubbio," *Franciscan Reflections*, http://www.franciscan-sfo.org/FP/gubbio.htm (accessed March 24, 2009).

15 Delio, *Franciscan Prayer*, 23, (see ch. 2 n. 6).

16 Ibid., 38.

17 Ibid., 97.

18 Ibid., 109.

19 Ibid., 133.

CHAPTER SIX

1 As mediation is technically a voluntary process, it is counterintuitive for a judge to order or mandate mediation. Nonetheless, their strong recommendation that parties make a good faith attempt to resolve differences in mediation carries considerable weight. The "power of the bench" often is needed to move us past our resistance and get us to the table.

2 For a discussion of face variables see: Folger, Poole, and Stutman, *Working Through Conflict,* 147 (see ch. 4, n. 1).

3 For a discussion of "I messages" see: Stone, Patton, and Heen, *Difficult Conversations* (see ch. 2 n. 1).

4 Excerpted from an introduction to settlement conferences delivered by retired Judge Alexander Williams III.

5 For discussion of mediator styles see: Leonard L. Riskin, "Understanding Mediators' Orientations, Strategies, and Techniques: A Grid for the Perplexed," 1 HARV.NEQ.L.REV. 7.25 (1996).

6 The tendency of a party to reject offers the other party makes is called reactive devaluation. A mediator can express choices as hypothetical suggestions made by the mediator, lessening the tendency toward reactive devaluation.

7 The Friars of the Atonement at Graymoor have an established interfaith program. See http://www.geii.org.

8 Murray Bodo, OFM, *The Threefold Way of St. Francis* (New Jersey: Paulist Press, 2000).

9 Ibid., 8.

10 Richard Rohr, OFM, *Things Hidden: Scripture as Spirituality* (Cincinnati: St. Anthony Messenger Press, 2008), 42.

11 Ibid., 64.

12 Bodo, *The Threefold Way of St. Francis*, 4.

13 Ibid., 35.

14 Rohr, *Things Hidden*, 50.

15 Bodo, *The Threefold Way of St. Francis*, 8.

16 Ibid., 33.

CHAPTER SEVEN

1   The stages of mediation are not sharply delineated. They blend in a seamless manner. The use of stages is a conceptual tool that helps a mediator understand where he is in the process.

2   A mediation brief is a legal document drafted to inform the mediator of the facts of the case and applicable law. It provides a snapshot of the conflict, usually in legal terms. The mediation brief may address possible settlement scenarios.

3   Advances in technology may allow us to convene a joint session with the parties in separate locations. Video conferencing will allow for creative convening.

4   "Shuttle diplomacy" refers to peacemaking in which a mediator, diplomat, or emissary travels between two or more countries, carrying on negotiations in separate sessions. It may refer to a mediator helping parties in separate rooms.

5   Consult with your attorney regarding the litigation discovery phase.

6   A trial brief is "Counsel's written submission, usually just before trial, outlining the legal issues before the court and arguing one side's position." *Black's Law Dictionary* (St. Paul: West Group, 2001).

7   Mediation statutes include provisions that protect information revealed during mediation. Information revealed in mediation often may not be used in court. Legislatures recognize the importance of candid discussion in mediation, motivating them to draft confidentiality statutes. Confidentiality statutes vary in different venues, so it is important to consult with a lawyer.

8   A party may submit a confidential mediation brief intended only for the mediator. However, most mediators recommend briefs be shared between the parties.

9   John Paul Lederach, *The Moral Imagination: The Art and Soul of Building Peace* (New York: Oxford University Press, 2005).

10 Ibid., p 83.

11 See "Emotional Subjectivity" in Chapter 4 for additional discussion.

12 Vivian C. Sheer and Michael F. Weigold, "Managing Threats to Identity: The Accountability Triangle and Strategic Accounting," *Communication Research* 22.5 (October 1990), 596.

13 Ibid., 593.

14 Ibid.

15 Ibid., 595.

16 Ibid., 596.

17 Ibid., 605.

18 Ibid.

19 For more on the important subject of the hidden negative third-party influence see Chapters 11 and 18.

20 See Chapters 11 and 18.

21 Keith H. Basso, *Wisdom Sits in Places* (Albuquerque: University of New Mexico Press, 1996).

22 Brian Cox, *Faith-Based Reconciliation: A Moral Vision that Transforms People and*

Societies (Santa Barbara: Xlibris, 2007).

23 Eloi LeClerc, OFM, *The Song of the Dawn*, trans. Paul Schwartz and Paul LaChance (Chicago: Franciscan Herald Press, 1977); For the *Canticle of the Sun*, see Chapter 1.

24 LeClerc, *The Song of the Dawn*, 4.

25 Ibid.

26 Ibid.

27 Ibid., 5.

28 Ibid., 6-7

29 Ibid., 16.

30 Ibid., 17.

31 Ibid., 25.

32 Ibid., 24.

33 Ibid., 27.

34 Ibid., 36.

35 Ibid.

CHAPTER EIGHT

1 Immaculé Ilibagiza, *Left to Tell: Discovering God Amidst the Rwandan Holocaust* (Carlsbad, California: Hay House, Inc., 2006).

2 Laura Blumenfeld, *Revenge: A Story of Hope* (New York: Washington Square Press, 2003), 81.

3 Ibid.

4 Ibid.

5 Ibid.

6 Cox, *Faith-Based Reconciliation,* (see ch. 7 n. 22).

7 Chapter 16 addresses apology. Chapter 17 addresses forgiveness.

8 Paul Sabatier, *The Road to Assisi*, 7 (see ch. 1 n. 9).

9 Ibid.

10 Susan Saint Sing, *Francis and the San Damiano Cross: Meditations on Spiritual Transformation* (Cincinnati: St. Anthony Messenger Press, 2006), 17.

11 Ibid., 15.

12 Sabatier, *The Road to Assisi*, 34 (see ch. 1 n. 9).

13 Ibid., 36.

14 Ibid., 38.

15 Bernard Häring, *The Virtues of an Authentic Life: A Celebration of Spiritual Maturity*, trans. Peter Heinegg (Liguori, Missouri: Liguori, 1997), 87.

16 Demaray, *The Little Flowers of St. Francis*, 3 (see ch. 1 n. 3).

17 Sabatier, *The Road to Assisi,* 16.

18 Demaray, *The Little Flowers of St. Francis*, 20.

19 Ibid., 35.

20 Sing, *Francis and the San Damiano Cross*, 19.

CHAPTER NINE

1 For a description of "funneling" and other interview techniques see: Cochran, DiPippa, and Peters, *The Counselor at Law,* (see ch. 5 n. 8).
2 Delio, *Franciscan Prayer,* (see ch. 2 n. 6).
3 Ibid., 20.
4 Bonaventure, *The Soul's Journey into God*, trans. Ewert Cousins (New York: Paulist Press, 1978), 59.
5 Sing, *Francis and the San Damiano Cross*, 19 (see ch. 8 n. 10).
6 Lester Bach, OFM Cap., *Catch Me A Rainbow Too* (Kansas: Barbo-Carlson Enterprises, 1999), 308.
7 Ibid.
8 Bonaventure, *The Life of St. Francis*, 274 (see ch. 1 n. 8). Cousins cites II C 95,98, and Cf. VI 6-7, 234-235.
9 Delio, *Franciscan Prayer*, 20.
10 Sing, *Francis and the San Damiano Cross*, 40.

CHAPTER TEN

1 See Chapters 11 and 18.
2 See the works of Martin Buber for a description of the I-Thou relationship (ch.3 n.6).
3 Sabatier, *The Road to Assisi*, 42 (see ch. 1 n. 9).
4 Ibid. 50. (Quoting from the "Three Companions").
5 Karris, OFM, *The Admonitions of St. Francis*, 237 (ch. 2 n. 10).
6 Bach, *Catch Me A Rainbow Too,* 338 (see ch. 9 n. 6). (For the following story, Bach cites: cf "Mirror of Perfection" #101 <u>Omnibus of Sources</u>, 1237-1239).
7 Ibid.
8 Ibid., 339.
9 Ibid. 340
10 Ibid., 325.
11 Sabatier, *The Road to Assisi* 45.
12 Häring, *The Virtues of an Authentic Life*, 9.

CHAPTER ELEVEN

1 For a discussion of reshaping the stories we tell ourselves see: Sam Keen and Anne Valley-Fox, *Your Mythic Journey: Finding Meaning in Your Life Through Writing and Storytelling* (Los Angeles: Jeremy P. Archer, 1975 & 1989).
2 An exposition on the mythic archetypes that shape drama: Christopher Vogler, *The Writer's Journey*, 2nd ed. (Los Angeles: Michael Wiese Productions, 1998).
3 Judge Alexander Williams III (retired) provided litigants with a very informative introduction to the settlement process.

4 For a discussion of conversations that avoid triggering negative responses see: Stone, Patton, and Heen, *Difficult Conversations* (see ch. 2 n. 1).

5 Demaray, *The Little Flowers of St. Francis*, 79 (see ch. 1 n. 3).

6 Ibid., 97.

7 Ibid.

8 Ibid., 99.

9 Ibid.

10 Ibid., 85.

11 Ibid., 113.

12 Ibid., 114.

13 Ibid.

14 Ibid., 115.

15 Karris, *The Admonitions of St. Francis*, 226 (ch. 2 n. 10).

16 Ibid.

17 Ibid., 227.

18 Ibid.

19 Ibid.

20 Ibid., 228.

Chapter Twelve

1 The shift from positions to interests, the idea of going below the line is covered in the groundbreaking work of Fisher and Ury, *Getting to Yes* (ch. 3 n. 3).

2 Fisher and Ury, *Getting to Yes*.

3 Ibid., 18.

4 William Ury, *The Power of a Positive No: How to Say No and Still Get to Yes* (New York: Bantam Books, 2007), 5. See also William Ury, *Getting Past No: Negotiating Your Way from Confrontation to Cooperation* (New York: Bantam Books, 1991).

5 Fisher and Ury, *Getting to Yes*, 48.

6 Ibid., 49.

7 Abraham H. Maslow, *Motivation and Personality*, 2nd ed. (New York: Harper & Row, 1970).

8 John Corrigan, et al, *Readings in Judaism, Christianity, and Islam* (Upper Saddle River, New Jersey: Prentice-Hall, 1998).

9 For an excellent discussion of apology see: Aaron Lazare, *On Apology*. (Oxford: Oxford University Press, 2004).

10 Lewis B. Smedes, *Forgive and Forget: Healing the Hurts We Don't Deserve* (San Francisco: Harper Collins, 1984).

11 Abraham H. Maslow, *Toward a Psychology of Being* (New Jersey: John Wiley & Sons, 1968).

12 Cox, *Faith-Based Reconciliation*, (see ch. 7 n. 22). (See Chapter 4, "Demolishing Walls of Hostility, the Principle of Inclusion," 36).

13 Frank M. Rega, *St. Francis of Assisi and the Conversion of the Muslims* (Rockford, Illinois: TAN Books, 2007), 56.

14 Wendy A. Hoke, "St. Francis and the Sultan: Lessons for Today" *Catholic Universe Bulletin*, www.catholicuniversebulletin.org, 2009.

15 Rega, *St. Francis of Assisi and the Conversion of the Muslims*, 58.

16 Ibid., 59.

17 Ibid.

18 Ibid., 61.

19 Ibid., 60.

20 Cox, *Faith-Based Reconciliation*.

21 The Woodstock Institute for Negotiation is located in Woodstock, Vermont and can be reached at www.woodstockInstitute.com.

22 Demaray, *The Little Flowers of St. Francis* (see ch. 1 n. 3).

23 See "The Prayer of Saint Francis" at the beginning of this book.

24 Boff, *The Prayer of Saint Francis*, 54 (ch. 1 n. 5).

25 Bonaventure, *The Soul's Journey into God*, (see ch. 9 n. 4).

26 Ibid., 56.

27 Ibid., 111.

28 Ibid., 113.

29 James Finley, Merton's Palace of Nowhere (Notre Dame, Indiana: Ave Maria Press, 1978), 23.

Chapter Thirteen

1 BATNA is A Best Alternative to a Negotiated Agreement. See: Fisher and Ury, *Getting to Yes,* (ch. 3 n. 3).

2 Robert O'Donnell, "A Different Look at Power" (unpublished paper, Woodstock Institute for Negotiation, Woodstock, Vermont, 1987).

3 Ibid.

4 *Pace e Bene* at http://paceebene.org/

5 O'Donnell, "A Different Look at Power," 5.

6 Thomas of Celano, "The Life of St. Francis," 193 (ch. 1 n. 6).

7 O'Donnell, "A Different Look at Power," 6.

8 Ibid.

9 Ibid.

10 Finley, *Merton's Palace of Nowhere*, 131 (see ch. 12 n. 29).

11 Ibid., 22.

12 Ibid., 78.

13 Ibid.

14 Brian Cox, "Faith-Based Diplomacy and International Peacemaking," (lectures, Straus Institute for Dispute Resolution, Spring, 2006).

15 Thomas Merton, *Conjectures of a Guilty Bystander* (New York: Doubleday and Company,

1966), 142, quoted in Finley, *Merton's Palace of Nowhere*, 145.

16 James Finley, *Merton's Palace of Nowhere*, 40.

17 Ibid., 96.

18 Cox, "Faith-Based Diplomacy and International Peacemaking."

19 Ibid.

20 Delio, *Franciscan Prayer*, 27 (see ch. 2 n. 6).

21 Thomas of Celano, "The Life of Saint Francis (1228-1229)," 193.

22 "Earlier Rule (1209-1215)" in *The Saint*, 1:68 (see ch. 1 n. 6).

23 Karris, "Admonition 4" in *The Admonitions of St. Francis*, 72 (ch. 2 n. 10).

24 Karris, "Admonition 19" in *The Admonitions of St. Francis*, 194.

25 Bodo, *The Threefold Way of St. Francis*, 26 (see ch. 6 n. 8).

26 Boff, *The Prayer of St. Francis*, 51 (ch. 1 n. 5).

27 Earlier Rule (1209-1215), 72.

28 Sing, *Francis and the San Damiano Cross*, 68 (see ch. 8 n. 10).

29 Bonaventure, *The Life of St. Francis*, 200 (see ch. 1 n. 8).

30 Ibid., 274.

31 Ibid., 273.

32 Bernard of Clairvaux, *On Conversion*, Chapter 18, quoted in Karris, *The Admonitions of St. Francis*, 135.

33 Karris, "Admonition 27" in *The Admonitions of St. Francis*, 237.

Chapter Fourteen

1 O'Donnell, "A Different Look at Power" (see ch. 13 n. 2).

2 Ibid.

3 Ibid.

4 Ibid.

5 Robert B. Cialdini, *Influence: Science and Practice*, 4th ed. (Boston: Allyn and Bacon, 2001).

6 O'Donnell, "A Different Look at Power."

7 Ilia Delio, OSF, *The Humility of God: A Franciscan Perspective* (Cincinnati: St. Anthony Messenger Press, 2005), 166.

8 Ibid.

9 Ibid.

10 Ibid., 130.

11 For a discussion of a humble God who bends low to embrace humanity see: Delio, *The Humility of God*.

12 Michael H. Crosby, *The Paradox of Power* (New York: The Crossroad Publishing Company, 2008), 141.

13 Ibid.

14 Ibid., 140.

15 Thomas of Celano, "The Remembrance of the Desire of a Soul," 264 (ch. 1 n. 6).

16 Ibid.

17 Ibid.

18 Ibid.

19 Ibid., 265.

CHAPTER FIFTEEN

1 Lederach, *The Moral Imagination,* (see ch. 7 n. 9).

2 Ibid., 26.

3 Ibid., 27.

4 See: Cochran, DiPippa, and Peters, *The Counselor at Law,* (see ch. 5 n. 8).

5 Max H. Brazerman, "Negotiator Judgment: A Critical Look at the Rationality Assumption," 27 Am. Beh. Sci. 211 (1985): 211–24 in Charles B. Wiggins and L. Randolph Lowry, *Negotiation and Settlement Advocacy* (St. Paul, Minnesota: West Publishing, 1997).

6 Dean G. Pruitt and Kim Sung Hee, *Social Conflict: Escalation, Stalemate, and Settlement,* 3rd ed. (Boston: McGraw Hill, 2004), 157.

7 Ibid., 165.

8 Lederach, *The Moral Imagination,* 38.

9 Cochran, DiPippa, and Peters, *The Counselor at Law,* 126.

10 Max H. Brazerman, "Negotiator Judgment: A Critical Look at the Rationality Assumption," 27 Am. Beh. Sci. 211 (1985): 211–24 in Charles B. Wiggins and L. Randolph Lowry, *Negotiation and Settlement Advocacy* (St. Paul: West Publishing, 1997).

11 Ibid., 141.

12 Robert O'Donnell of the Woodstock Institute for Negotiation has developed a protocol that guides a party through "the dance." This is available at www.woodstockinstitute.com.

13 The previously cited protocol by O'Donnell can be used to help determine a reasonable zone (see n. 12).

14 James J. White, "Machiavelli and the Bar: Ethical Limitations on Lying in Negotiation," in Charles B. Wiggins and L. Randolph Lowry, *Negotiation and Settlement Advocacy: A Book of Readings* (St. Paul, Minnesota: West Publishing, 1997) 260–262.

15 Gary Lowenthal, "Truthful Bargaining by Lawyers," in Charles B. Wiggins and L. Randolph Lowry, *Negotiation and Settlement Advocacy: A Book of Readings* (St. Paul, Minnesota: West Publishing, 1997), 269–271.

16 David A. Lax and James K. Sebenius, "Three Ethical Issues in Negotiation," in Charles B. Wiggins and L. Randolph Lowry, *Negotiation and Settlement Advocacy: A Book of Readings* (St. Paul, Minnesota: West Publishing, 1997), 276–279.

17 Karris, *The Admonitions of St. Francis,* (ch. 2 n. 10).

18 Delio, *The Humility of God,* 111 (see ch. 14 n. 7).

19 Ibid., 112.

20 Ibid., 114.

21 Ibid., 116.

22 Ibid., 117.

23 Ibid., 119.

24 Ibid.

25 Murray Bodo, OFM, *Francis: The Journey and the Dream* (Cincinnati: St. Anthony Messenger Press, 1972), 57.

26 Ibid.

27 Sabatier, *The Road to Assisi*, 87 (see ch. 1 n. 9).

28 Delio, *The Humility of God*, 120 (see ch. 14 n. 7).

29 Bodo, *Francis: The Journey and the Dream*, 16.

30 Ibid., 59.

31 Ibid., 60.

32 Ibid., 22.

33 Ibid., 44.

34 Eloi LeClerc, OFM, *The Song of the Dawn*, 46 (see ch. 7 n. 23).

35 Office for Justice, Peace and the Integrity of Creation, "A Sensitive Heart," Section 2.3.2 of "Guidelines for the Animation of Justice, Peace and the Integrity of Creation," 2008.

36 Idem., "The option for the poor and justice," in Section 3.1.3.1 of "Guidlines" (see n. 35). Where referenced, GGCC is "General Constitutions of the Order of Friars Minor, Rome, 2004".

37 Idem., "JPIC in evangelization" in Section 3.2.1 of "Guidlines."

38 Bodo, *Francis: The Journey and the Dream*, 44.

39 Office for Justice, Peace and the Integrity of Creation, "JPIC in different areas of evangelization" in Section 3.2.1.1 of of "Guidelines."

CHAPTER SIXTEEN

1 For a comprehensive discussion of apology see: Lazare, *On Apology* (see ch. 12 n. 9).

2 Cox, *Faith-Based Reconciliation*, 78 (see ch. 7 n. 22).

3 Ibid.

4 Rohr, *Things Hidden*, (see ch. 6 n. 10). (See Chapter 4 "The Boxing Ring").

5 Ibid., 72. (Rohr notes morality can become counterfeit religion when Paul's observations in Romans 8:38-39 are overlooked.)

6 Franciscan Ethicist John Duns Scotus argues "the only act which is intrinsically good in all circumstances is the love of God" and "the only possible act intrinsically evil in all circumstances would be the hatred of God." He believes, "Since all acts other than the love of God are morally indifferent one must look to the circumstances in determining the act's morality." See Thomas A. Shannon, *The Ethical Theory of John Duns Scotus* (Quincy, Illinois: Franciscan Press, Quincy University, 1995), 126. (Now part of St. Bonaventure University).

7 Lazare, *On Apology*, 32.

8 See Luke 5:32 and 15:7; Mark 2:17.

9 Cox, *Faith-Based Reconciliation*, 77.

10 Lazare, *On Apology*, 163.

11 Confidentiality statutes vary from state to state, as well as at the federal level. Seek legal advice regarding the exact nature of the protections available in your specific situation.

12 Jonathan R. Cohen, "Advising Clients to Apologize," *Southern California Law Review* 72 (1999):1009.

13 Michael Henderson, *Forgiveness: Breaking the Chain of Hate* (Portland, Oregon: Arnica Publishing, 2001).

14 Cox, *Faith-Based Reconciliation*, 59.

15 Bodo, *Francis: The Journey and the Dream*, 10 (see ch. 15 n. 25).

16 Ibid., 67.

17 Ibid., 132.

18 Ibid., 104.

19 Rohr, *Things Hidden,* 38.

20 Ibid., 72.

21 Ibid., 76.

22 Ibid., 77.

23 Ibid., 81.

24 Bodo, *Francis: The Journey and the Dream*, 112.

25 Ibid., 101.

Chapter Seventeen

1 See: Lewis B. Smedes, *Forgive and Forget* (see ch. 12 n. 10).

2 Michael Henderson, *Forgiveness*, 127. (see ch. 16 n. 13) (Quoting Russian Irina Ratushinskaya.)

3 Smedes, *Forgive and Forget*, 133.

4 Ibid., 39.

5 Ibid.

6 Ken Cloke, *Mediating Dangerously: The Frontiers of Conflict Resolution* (San Francisco: Jossey-Bass, 2001), 87.

7 Henderson, *Forgiveness*, 112.

8 Cox, *Faith-Based Reconciliation*, 77 (see ch. 7 n. 22).

9 Smedes, *Forgive and Forget*, 79.

10 Ibid.

11 Rohr, *Things Hidden,* 37 (see ch. 6 n. 10).

12 Delio, *The Humility of God*, 166 (see ch. 14 n. 7).

13 Buber, *I and Thou,* (ch. 3 n. 6).

14 Delio, *The Humility of God*, 134.

15 Rohr, *Things Hidden*, 143.

16 Finley, *Merton's Palace of Nowhere*, 31 (see ch. 12 n. 29).

17 Ibid.,

18 Smedes, *Forgive and Forget*, 29.

19 Ibid., 49.
20 Ibid., 130.
21 Ibid., 24.
22 Rohr, *Things Hidden*, 133.
23 Henderson, *Forgiveness*, 98.
24 Smedes, *Forgive and Forget*, 72.
25 Ibid., 7.
26 Rohr, *Things Hidden*, 166.
27 Smedes, *Forgive and Forget*, 75.
28 Rohr, *Things Hidden*, 203.
29 Smedes, *Forgive and Forget*.
30 Ibid., 5.
31 Ibid., 22.
32 Ibid.
33 Ibid., 27.
34 Rohr, *Things Hidden*, 67.
35 Smedes, *Forgive and Forget*, 29.
36 Ibid., 37.
37 Rohr, *Things Hidden*, 135.
38 Ibid., 189.
39 Ibid., 152.
40 Cloke, *Mediating Dangerously*, 94.
41 Henderson, *Forgiveness*, 99 (see ch. 16 n. 13).
42 Ibid.
43 Cox, *Faith-Based Reconciliation*, 87.
44 Henderson, *Forgiveness*.
45 Ibid., 49.
46 Ibid.
47 Cox, *Faith-Based Reconciliation*, 88.
48 Phrase used frequently by Brian Cox, author of *Faith-Based Reconciliation*.
49 Smedes, *Forgive and Forget*, 136.
50 Lederach, *The Moral Imagination* (see ch. 7 n. 9).
51 Thomas of Celano, "The Life of St. Francis," 185 (see ch. 1 n. 6).
52 Ibid., 187.
53 Rohr, *Things Hidden*, 194.
54 Delio, *The Humility of God*, 112 (see ch. 14 n. 7).
55 Ibid., 160.
56 Ibid., 96.
57 Rohr, *Things Hidden*, 162.
58 Ibid., 151.
59 Delio, *The Humility of God*, 131 (see ch. 14 n. 7).

CHAPTER EIGHTEEN

1   See Karris, "Admonition 25," *The Admonitions of St. Francis*, 226 (see ch. 2 n. 10).
2   Laura Slattery, Ken Butigan, Veronica Pelicaric, and Ken Preston-Pile, *Engage: Exploring Nonviolent Living* (Oakland, California: Pace e Bene Press, 2005).
3   Ibid., 33.
4   Ibid., 57.
5   Ibid., 64.
6   Ibid.
7   Ibid., 72.
8   Ibid. See p. 115 for a discussion of "power over, power-from-within, and power with." Also see 122 for types of power "in the struggle against structural violence."
9   Ibid., 160.
10 Bonaventure, *The Life of St. Francis*, 253 (see ch. 1 n. 8).
11 Ibid.
12 Karris, OFM, *The Admonitions of St. Francis*, 226 (see ch. 2 n. 10).
13 Ibid., 228.
14 Ibid., 227.
15 Ibid., 228.

CHAPTER NINETEEN

1   For a discussion of the difference between ritual and ceremony see unpublished paper by Fr. Jim Clarke Ph.D: "Ritual: A Mythic Means of Transformation" .
2   For a discussion of the ways of knowing see: Michelle LeBaron, *Bridging Cultural Conflicts: A New Approach for a Changing World* (San Francisco: Jossey-Bass, 2003), 162.
3   Ibid., 278.
4   Ibid., 214.
5   Lederach, *The Moral Imagination*, 69 (see ch. 7 n. 9).
6   Ibid., 153.
7   Ibid.
8   Ibid., 160.
9   Vogler, *The Writer's Journey*, 211 (see ch. 11 n. 2).
10 Ibid., 217.
11 Lederach, *The Moral Imagination*, 161.
12 Ibid., 128.
13 Sisters of St. Francis of Perpetual Adoration, http://www.ssfpa.org/DesktopDefault.aspx?tabid=25.
14 Sing, *Francis and the San Damiano Cross*, 27 (see ch. 8 n. 10).
15 Bonaventure, *The Life of St. Francis*, 200 (see ch. 1 n. 8).
16 Ibid., 39.
17 LeClerc, *The Song of the Dawn*, 24 (see ch. 7 n. 23).

18   Ibid., 26.
19   Ibid., 27.
20   Ibid., 32.
21   Ibid., 33.
22   Ibid.
23   Francis of Assisi. "The Canticle of the Creatures (1225)", in *The Saint*, 1:113 (see ch. 1 n. 6).
24   Ibid., 39.
25   LeClerc, *The Song of the Dawn*, 36.
26   Ibid., 38.
27   Ibid., 49.
28   Sisters of St. Francis of Perpetual Adoration,
       http://www.ssfpa.org/DesktopDefault.aspx?tabid=25.
29   Ibid., 54.

CPSIA information can be obtained at www.ICGtesting.com
Printed in the USA
LVOW132108190212

269325LV00004B/3/P

9 780984 885305